University Planning and Architecture

The environment of a university – what we term a campus – is a place with special resonance. They have long been the setting for some of history's most exciting experiments in the design of the built environment. Christopher Wren at Cambridge, Thomas Jefferson at Virginia, Le Corbusier at Harvard, Louis Kahn at Yale and Norman Foster in Berlin: the calibre of practitioners who have worked for universities is astounding.

Pioneering architecture and innovative planning make for vivid assertions of academic excellence, while the physical estate of a university can shape the experiences and outlook of future generations to the benefit of architecture and the community at large. Yet as higher education continues to grow, it becomes increasingly challenging to perpetuate this rich tradition. This book is the definitive compendium of the prestigious sphere of campus design, profiling its abundant past and counselling for its future.

The book brings together two approaches, the historical and the strategic, to examine what constitutes a successful campus and how to apply these conclusions to real-life, modern-day contexts. It comprehensively documents the worldwide evolution of university design from the Middle Ages to the present day, uncovering the key developments which have shaken the world of campus planning. A series of case studies profiles universally-acclaimed campuses that, through their planning, architecture and landscaping, have made original, influential and striking contributions to the field. Drawing on these examples, the book then turns to a strategic investigation of the ingredients pivotal to successful campus design which are translated to create a 'good practice guide' for anyone interested in the creation or development of environments for higher education.

Jonathan Coulson and **Paul Roberts** are directors of Turnberry Consulting, a London-based development strategy consultancy created to assist landowners to develop real estate projects driven by quality and functionality. Both Coulson and Roberts have extensive experience working within the university sector, preparing and delivering development proposals and master-planning initiatives for institutions including the University of Oxford, the University of Hertfordshire, Coventry University and Cranfield University. **Isabelle Taylor** read for a BA in the History of Art at the University of Cambridge, followed by an MA in the History of Art at the Courtauld Institute of Art. She currently works at Turnberry Consulting as a researcher and writer.

University Planning and Architecture

The search for perfection

Jonathan Coulson, Paul Roberts and Isabelle Taylor

First published 2011
by Routledge
2 Park Square, Milton Park, Abingdon, Oxon OX14 4RN

Simultaneously published in the USA and Canada
by Routledge
270 Madison Avenue, New York, NY 10016, USA

Routledge is an imprint of the Taylor & Francis Group, an informa business

© 2011 Jonathan Coulson, Paul Roberts and Isabelle Taylor

Designed and typeset by Alex Lazarou
Printed in India by The Replika Press Pvt. Ltd., Sonepat, Haryana, India

All rights reserved. No part of this book may be reprinted or reproduced or utilised in any form or by any electronic, mechanical, or other means, now known or hereafter invented, including photocopying and recording, or in any information storage or retrieval system, without permission in writing from the publishers.

Every effort has been made to contact and acknowledge copyright owners, but the authors and publisher would be pleased to have any errors or omissions brought to their attention so that corrections may be published at a later printing.

British Library Cataloguing in Publication Data
A catalogue record for this book is available from the British Library

Library of Congress Cataloging in Publication Data
Coulson, Jonathan.
University planning and architecture: the search for perfection / Jonathan Coulson, Paul Roberts, and Isabelle Taylor.
    p. cm.
    Includes bibliographical references and index.
1. College buildings. 2. Campus planning. I. Roberts, Paul (Michael Paul), 1964– II. Taylor, Isabelle. III. Title. IV. Title: Search for perfection.
NA6600.C68 2011
727'.3–dc22

2010005915

ISBN13: 978-0-415-57110-4 (hbk)
ISBN13: 978-0-203-84635-3 (ebk)

Contents

Preface vi

Acknowledgements vii

CHAPTER ONE
University Planning and Architecture 1088–2010: A Chronology 1

CHAPTER TWO
Case Studies 39

Aarhus University 40

Columbia University 46

Free University Berlin 52

Harvard University 58

Moscow State University 66

Peking University 72

Princeton University 78

Qatar University 86

Rice University 92

Simon Fraser University 100

Stanford University 106

Temasek Polytechnic 114

Trinity College, Dublin 120

University of California at Berkeley 126

University of California at Los Angeles 134

University of Cambridge 140

University of Cape Town 148

University of Chicago 154

University of Colorado at Boulder 162

University of East Anglia 168

University of Illinois at Chicago 174

University of Oxford 180

University of Pennsylvania 188

University of Technology Petronas 194

University of Virginia 200

University of Western Australia 208

Uppsala University 214

Utrecht University 220

Yale University 226

CHAPTER THREE
Designing the Twenty-First-Century Campus 235

Notes 243

Bibliography 251

Index 257

Preface

> The college scene is impossible to think of without its setting of architecture. What student sensibility is there unresponsive to the beautiful nave where the daily chapel was held, the stately portico where the class would group itself to be photographed, the window of the study where Caesar was conned under sheltering eave and overlooking roofs and chimneys? And many an old grad has reflected that students may come and go, classes enter and graduate, but that venerable walls and carved chimney pieces, picturesque gables and vaulted archways endure forever. These remain his own because always present in his mind's eye and he prays that change and decay may never reach them.
> (C. Klauder and H. Wise[1])

The environment of a university – what we term a campus – is a place with special resonance. Aside from their functional necessity, buildings and landscapes form the heart and soul of these institutions. Higher education institutions are eager to give assurances of academic programmes of high standards of excellence, but it is crucial to remember that the campus too is part and parcel of the learning experience. Through its physical estate, a university can reinforce the high ideals of scholarship and institutional values to create a unique and defining sense of place.

The purpose of this book is to help institutional leaders, planners and designers to utilize the campus – one of the most valuable assets at any university's disposal – to its full potential. Through adroit planning choices, the entire environment can be shaped into an expression of institutional identity and ambitions. This book explores the rich history of university design in order to draw lessons that proffer scope for the modern-day campus.

It is structured into three parts: beginning with a chronological outline of the history of university planning and architecture, followed by a collection of case studies profiling individual campuses, and concluded by a good practice guide that consolidates the precepts of the earlier chapters into a practical edict for creating a successful campus master plan in a contemporary context. The case studies aim to provide an analysis of campuses across the world which have made an original, influential or particularly representative or arresting contribution to the milieu of university design from its medieval origins to the present day. The selection of case studies makes no claims to be a comprehensive survey of the genre but has carefully selected its examples against these overlapping and fluid categories: master plan; architecture; landscape; circulation; community; responsiveness to region and history; responsiveness to institutional mission and values; memorable places and innovation. Unavoidably, a number of worthy campuses have not been included within this list, not because they are not successful university environments but rather that the lessons they provide have been better illustrated elsewhere. For example, of the seven institutions bracketed under the banner 'New Universities' that were founded in the United Kingdom in the 1960s, only one, the University of East Anglia, has been featured as a case study. Each of the seven campuses provide illuminating insights into how the physical environment of universities was being re-imagined to accord with the new objectives and demands of higher education, but the University of East Anglia has been selected here as the most representative of this particular campus trend. The same method has been applied to select case-study examples from other university design trends or movements, such as Beaux-Arts planned campuses or the nineteenth-century European university.

Acknowledgements

The authors are indebted to the help of many people in the preparation of this book. Many universities provided invaluable assistance, and we extend thanks to Jan Ivar Mattsson and Lennart Ilke at Uppsala University, Palle Lykke of Aarhus University, Jim McConnell at the University of Glasgow, and Connor Wilson at UCL. Special thanks also go to Hans Antonsson and Gunnar Henricksson of Akademiska Hus, Jan Petersen, Olaf Lind, William Taylor and Julian Elliott.

We wish to thank Niall McLaughlin and Joanna Karatzas for preparing the plans that feature in each of the case studies. Our colleagues, Jenny Potts, Katharine Burgess, and Sarah Housley, provided much support, as did our editor at Routledge, Francesca Ford.

CHAPTER ONE

University Planning and Architecture 1088–2010: A Chronology

University design is a civic art form. This is a lofty claim, yet the following sweep through its rich history from its medieval beginnings to the landmark buildings of the present day, will serve to demonstrate how social, philosophical and cultural forces have come to mould academic design of each era. The university buildings and campuses encountered in this discussion are often not the clear and consistent realisations of their idealistic founders or designers, but are illuminating reflections of their cultural moment. From the medieval universities, whose proliferation and physical form was much shaped by the burgeoning of the city, to the colonial colleges of the fledgling United States, envisaged as expressions of the utopian social ideals of the American imagination, to the modernist visions of post-war institutions, products of the push to democratize higher education, university architecture is an architecture of ideology. This chapter will chronicle the history of campus architecture as a condensed narrative of the most energetic and innovative phases of university design over the last 900 years. This methodology omits many countries and institutions, focusing predominantly on the United Kingdom, continental Europe and the United States, the centres of the most stimulating achievements in this field.

EARLY BEGINNINGS

The medieval university was largely a European phenomenon, inaugurated by the University of Bologna, allegedly founded in 1088 (Figure 1.1).[1] Bologna, together with Paris and Oxford, form the triumvirate of European university prototypes, from which all universities descend. Medieval universities were essentially the products of the twelfth-century Renaissance, the rediscovery of classical learning that flourished in the 1100s. In centres of learning across Europe, renowned masters drew increasing numbers of students around them. Eager to safeguard and promote their mutual interests, they collected into scholastic guilds, akin to the guilds of merchants and artisans. Gradually these guilds were officially sanctioned by popes, prelates and princes, attracting an increasing number of students and thus evolving into the forerunners of the modern university. In Italy, the model of Bologna was copied at Modena,

1.1 Palazzo dell'Archiginnasio, the seat of the University of Bologna from 1563 to 1803
Photo: Ian Dagnall/Alamy

Date of foundation	University
1088	University of Bologna, Italy
1150	University of Paris, France
1167	University of Oxford, England
1209	University of Cambridge, England
1218	University of Salamanca, Spain
1222	University of Padua, Italy
1224	University of Naples Federico II, Italy
1240	University of Siena, Italy
1241	University of Valladolid, Spain
1290	University of Coimbra, Portugal
1303	University of Rome La Sapienza, Italy
1308	University of Perugia, Italy
1321	University of Florence, Italy
1343	University of Pisa, Italy
1348	Charles University of Prague, Czech Republic
1361	University of Pavia, Italy
1364	Cracow Academy, Poland
1365	University of Vienna, Austria
1385	Ruprecht Karls University of Heidelberg, Germany

Table 1.1: The oldest extant universities in the West

1.2 University of Salamanca
Photo: ©iStockphoto.com/*0597

Reggio nell'Emilia, Vicenza, Arezzo, Padua and Naples. Spain saw the founding of great schools at Salamanca, Valladolid, Palencia, and Seville. Universities in Cambridge, Coimbra, Prague, Cracow, Vienna, Heidelberg, Cologne, Louvain, Leipzeig, St Andrews, and others ensued in quick succession (Table 1.1). Over the course of two centuries, the university had established itself as the prime sponsor of learning within the major towns and cities.[2]

Over the period, universities took root in thriving cities supported by prosperous agricultural regions that allowed for relatively inexpensive living costs, gradually ingraining themselves within the urban centres and shaping the characters of their host cities. Yet despite this union, the university had no tangible presence within the city. Lectures took place in houses rented by the masters, while examinations and assemblies were typically held in churches and convents. The early medieval universities possessed no buildings; they were as yet an indistinct community of masters and students drawn from throughout Europe. The members of Paris's university, for example, largely originated from outside the Ile-de-France region and so as 'foreigners' the students and masters bore little fidelity to their host city, and, when scholarly privileges were called into question, they felt no compunction in moving to another centre. University migrations were a common phenomenon, and frequently the force which stimulated new universities, as evinced by the migration from Bologna to Vicenza in 1205 and Oxford to Cambridge in 1209. These episodes stimulated the acquisition of many of the earliest university buildings. Following the last major exodus of Bolognese professors to the University of Sienna in 1321, the municipality purposed to bind the university to the city by building a chapel exclusively for the city's scholars in 1322; it was the university's first edifice.[3]

As the Middle Ages progressed, as student populations increased and ceased to migrate, universities began to acquire property. In the fifteenth century, the University of Paris procured lecture halls, colleges, lodgings and churches on the left bank of the Seine, giving the university a distinctive presence in the area that became known as the Quartier Latin. In the same century, Salamanca erected a quadrangle to house teaching facilities, Las Escuelas (Figure 1.2) and the University of Orléans built its Salle des Thèses, the only secular medieval university building to survive in France. As the Italian Renaissance gathered pace, the universities of Italy also increasingly felt the desire for the prestige that accompanied owning purpose-built academic facilities. By 1530, the scholars of Padua were taught in the university building (Figure 1.3), and, spurred on

1.3 Palazzo del Bo, University of Padua
Photo: George Mattoscio

by rivalry, Bologna soon followed suit. The University of Bologna obtained permanent quarters in the Palazzo dell'Archiginnasio in the city centre in 1563. Entered through a magnificent portico, and sited around a courtyard, the complex housed seven lecture halls for law, six for arts and medicine, and two large halls. Over 6,000 heraldic shields, immortalizing the university's professors and students, and an incredible array of art work throughout the staircases, halls, teaching rooms and arches offer a glimpse of the rich history this building holds.[4]

The Palazzo dell'Archiginnasio typifies Spanish and Italian universities of the Renaissance in its four-sided courtyard format surrounded by arcaded cloisters and an impressive main façade. The model was transported to South America when its colonialists founded its first universities, the University of San Carlos in Guatemala (main building circa 1763) being one such example (Figure 1.4).

As the Renaissance progressed, universities old and new acquired befitting academic quarters, comprising lecture theatres, assembly rooms, chapels, libraries, and lodgings. These structures, often incredibly lavish, were physical manifestations of the omnipresence of the European university, a visible sign that the university had evolved from a loose association of scholars and masters into an

1.4 University of San Carlos
Photo: Mary Evans/Interfoto

1.5 Merton College, University of Oxford from David Loggan's *Oxonia Illustrata* (1675)
Photo: Mary Evans Picture Library

institution. The distinctive architecture and central urban locations of the late-medieval university indicate that its place in the life of the city was firmly established; the university towns became stamped with a personality of their own. The most iconic expression of this is, undoubtedly, the universities of Oxford and Cambridge.

The two universities of England distinguished themselves from their fellow institutions through their adherence to the collegiate system. The college first came into being, in fact, in twelfth-century Paris. Students as young as 14 were drawn from throughout Europe, and so halls or dormitories known as *hospita* catered for their housing needs. The Collège des Dix-huit was founded in 1180 by a wealthy English merchant, Jocius of London, to shelter 18 poor clerics while they attended lectures. Only a small amount of supervision took place in these foundations, usually by a master or cleric, and instruction remained external. A small number of residence colleges existed in Italy, but they failed to achieve the same popularity of those within Paris and England, probably because the supervision of scholars was not such a priority. Italian universities, unlike Paris, Oxford and Cambridge, did not enrol very young students. The colleges housed only a fraction of students, and, since Italian communes forbade teaching outside what they deemed the 'public university', teaching colleges did not evolve.[5]

It was only in England, at Oxford and Cambridge, that teaching colleges, comprising a body of scholars living under the teaching and guidance of masters of arts, gathered real momentum. Yet, the colleges were not present from the outset. In both centres, it was at first the norm for students to lodge with townspeople. Quickly, though, 'halls' or 'hostels' became popular, in which groups of students lived communally in a rented building presided over by a master. Beam Hall was one such establishment in Oxford; surviving intact in Merton Street, it illustrates their inherently domestic character that made little imprint on the architecture of the town. These transient establishments came and went; some 200 names have been recorded in Oxford. The colleges, however, achieved a permanent presence. With precise stipulations regarding discipline, study and the attendance of religious services, the colleges quickly assumed the residence functions of the halls, and in time took on teaching responsibilities. They differed from the early academic halls

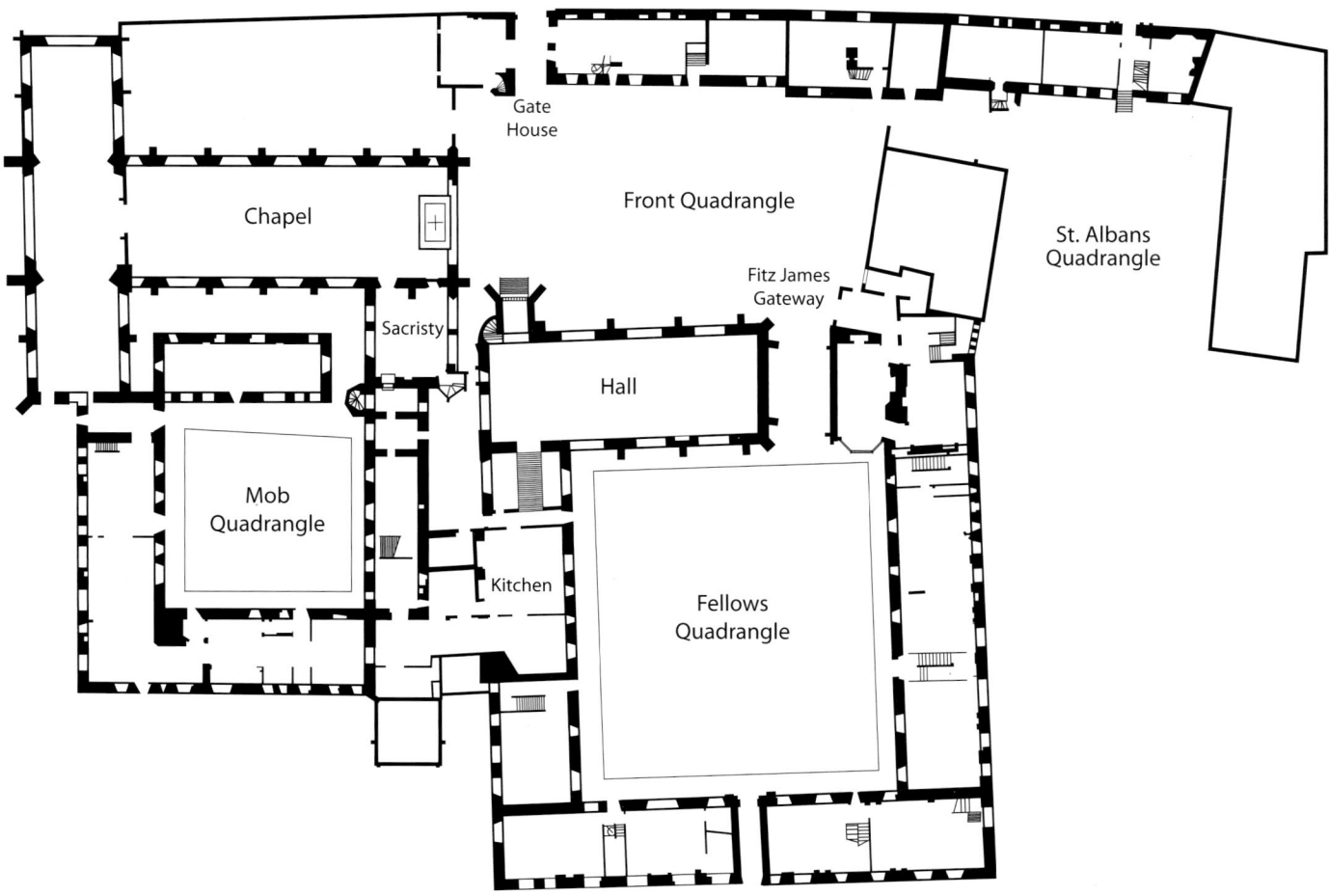

1.6 Plan of Merton College

in that the colleges received endowments of lands, rents and church revenues, and furthermore, wielded a tremendous architectural impact upon Oxford.[6]

The colleges erected the university's first impressive buildings. Their financial independence meant that the colleges could build liberally and lavishly. The longevity of their architecture stands as testimony to this patronage, which still dominates the identity of the two cities to the present day. The first colleges were founded in quick succession in the thirteenth century at Oxford: University College (1249), Balliol (1263) and Merton (1264), which possesses the earliest surviving collegiate buildings. When Merton was founded, no model existed as to the form an Oxford college should take. The buildings took shape in a piecemeal fashion from 1266, irregularly placed around a courtyard, reproducing an arrangement found in contemporary bishops' palaces and some nobles' houses. The first buildings to be constructed were the dining hall (much rebuilt 1872–1874) forming the south side of the quadrangle, the Warden's house on the opposite side, and a chapel on the third side, where work commenced in 1290. A rough, tawny-coloured limestone was employed throughout. A local material found in abundance, limestone remained the material of choice for collegiate and University buildings until the middle of the last century. Residential accommodation for fellows occurred with the construction of Mob Quad, to the south of the chapel, begun in 1287–1289. Consisting of four ranges of roughly equal length and height, this was Oxford's first collegiate quadrangle (Figures 1.5 and 1.6).[7]

The enclosed quadrangle, first seen in Merton, has proved the enduring language of collegiate architecture at Oxford and Cambridge to the present day, and indeed yielded considerable worldwide influence. The medieval universities of Scotland (St Andrews, founded 1413; Glasgow, founded 1451; and Aberdeen, founded 1495) appropriated much the same pattern. Reminiscent of monastic cloisters, it recalled the tradition of monastic learning that the universities inherited. Indeed, several colleges were actually founded in, or later took over, monastic structures, such as Jesus and Emmanuel at Cambridge. The enclosed courtyard format also served a defensive role, both keeping townsfolk out and keeping students in. Town–gown tensions were notorious, not only in England but

1.7 Sheldonian Theatre, University of Oxford
Photo: Bruce Ashford/Alamy

1.8 Wren Library, Trinity College, University of Cambridge
Photo: Architectural Press Archive/RIBA Library Photographs Collection

throughout European university towns, leading to fighting, pillage and even murder. That colleges could close themselves off from the outside, and thus exert heightened control over students, was one of their chief advantages over the academic halls.[8]

Initially developing gradually, piece by piece, the earlier colleges were often modest in appearance. But as more colleges were established and their status correspondingly grew, their founders soon became possessed of a competitiveness that led to increasingly impressive college buildings. As channels of patronage for the richest, most powerful men of the day, the colleges of Oxford and Cambridge contain some of the finest examples of Gothic architecture in England. Patronized by the leading political figures of public life, the prelates and monarchy, they epitomized the most fashionable trends pioneered by the most celebrated architects and exhibit a unity of design paralleled in few other places.

Indeed, the stylistic unity of the two universities remained conspicuous long after Gothic architecture had lost its cachet elsewhere in Europe. In the second half of the seventeenth century, however, Oxford and Cambridge underwent an architectural transformation, pioneered by the young trailblazer Christopher Wren. Recognized in the early 1660s as one of Europe's most distinguished scientific thinkers, he represented a new breed of architect in Oxbridge, with a theoretical as opposed to practical mastery of architecture. His first architectural commission came from his uncle, Bishop Matthew Wren, to erect a chapel at Pembroke College, Cambridge. The 1663 design introduced to the medieval town fully-fledged classicism. Cast in the form of a classical temple, this elegantly unassuming structure was the first example of pure classical architecture found in either Oxford or Cambridge. Contemporaneously, Wren embarked upon his first architectural enterprise at Oxford, the Sheldonian Theatre, completed in 1669 (Figure 1.7).

Wren's popularity amongst the Oxbridge colleges soared. At Cambridge, Emmanuel's chapel and Trinity's library (Figure 1.8) were erected to Wren's designs; at Oxford, he designed buildings for Trinity and Christ Church, and chapel screens for All Souls, St John's and Merton. Lauded as Oxbridge's conqueror of Gothic,[9] Wren can be thought of as the precursor of the star architects of the modern age, Eero Saarinen, Frank Gehry, Norman Foster amongst others, those critically acclaimed designers of headline-grabbing, prestige-generating structures hankered after by present-day university presidents and vice-chancellors. Wren's influence on the physical fabric of Oxford and Cambridge was unparalleled; through his works, the

Date of foundation	University
1636	Harvard College
1693	The College of William & Mary
1701	Yale College
1746	College of New Jersey (Princeton University)
1754	King's College (Columbia University)
1755	College of Philadelphia (University of Pennsylvania)
1765	College of Rhode Island (Brown University)
1766	Queen's College (Rutgers, The State University of New Jersey)
1769	Dartmouth College

Table 1.2: Colonial colleges and date of foundation

two universities became versed in an authentic classical vocabulary that formed the paradigm for nearly 200 years, propelled by the likes of Nicholas Hawksmoor, James Gibbs and James Wyatt. Wren inaugurated a new philosophy of collegiate architecture that rejected the medieval enclosed quadrangle in favour of openness, vistas with focal points, and hierarchical arrangements that characterized the Baroque style. College architecture had previously been dominated by ranges, uniform along their length with little or no central emphasis or axiality. A key development of Wren's Oxbridge designs were focal points positioned on strong axes. Directionality and central emphasis were introduced into the academic architectural vocabulary, an innovation that was to shape not only the English universities but also the thinking behind America's first colleges.

THE NEW WORLD: AMERICA'S FIRST COLLEGES

As Wren and his followers were transforming Oxford and Cambridge into new Romes, so the influx of English settlers to North America were busy creating their own new England on the opposite side of the Atlantic. The Puritan settlers conceived the colonies as a blank canvas, onto which they could project their ideal world, a pure world of the highest morals, in which every man strove to serve God and one another. Such ideals necessitated a society of capable rulers, learned clergy and cultured citizens; such a society, they realized, could only be achieved through education. Memories of Oxbridge remained vivid amongst the new settlers. By 1646, approximately 100 Cambridge men and a third as many Oxonians had settled in New England. Throughout seventeenth-century England, the value of education was widely promoted. In the early decades of the century, large numbers entered higher education in proportions not again known until the twentieth century. In 1636, a mere six years after the Massachusetts Bay was colonized, its General Court determined to found a college; the following year, Newtowne was decided upon as its location, a village six kilometres from Boston, soon renamed Cambridge after its high number of Cantabrigian inhabitants. Thus, the university institution made its first appearance in North America, and Harvard College was born. Eight further colonial colleges followed (Table 1.2).[10]

From the outset, the governing influence on these new degree-granting institutions was the English collegiate system, fully developed by the sixteenth century. Rejecting the pattern typical in continental Europe, in which universities assumed responsibilities only for teaching and paid little heed to students' social and housing arrangements, early American colleges were keen to pursue the English ideal of tightly regulated colleges encompassing living, social and academic pursuits. Harvard's Governing Board declared in 1671 that,

> It is well known…what advantage to Learning accrues by the multitude of persons cohabiting for scholasticall communion, whereby to acuate the minds of one another, and other waies to promote the ends of a Colledge-Society.[11]

However, from the start, American colleges distanced themselves from the monastic-like planning traditions of the medieval English foundations; it was not the notion of a cloistered setting that held the appeal for the colonial settlers, but rather the principle of a scholarly community moulded, even nourished, by the character of its surroundings.

To realize this, American institutions opted for distinctive spatial patterns. Beginning with Harvard, American schools rejected the enclosed quadrangle traditional in England. They favoured separate buildings sited in open landscape, approachable and accessible to the community. In 1642 Harvard saw the completion of a large, multi-purpose building, on a long, thin one-acre plot. It took the form of an E-shape plan, a plan apparently unknown in Oxbridge,

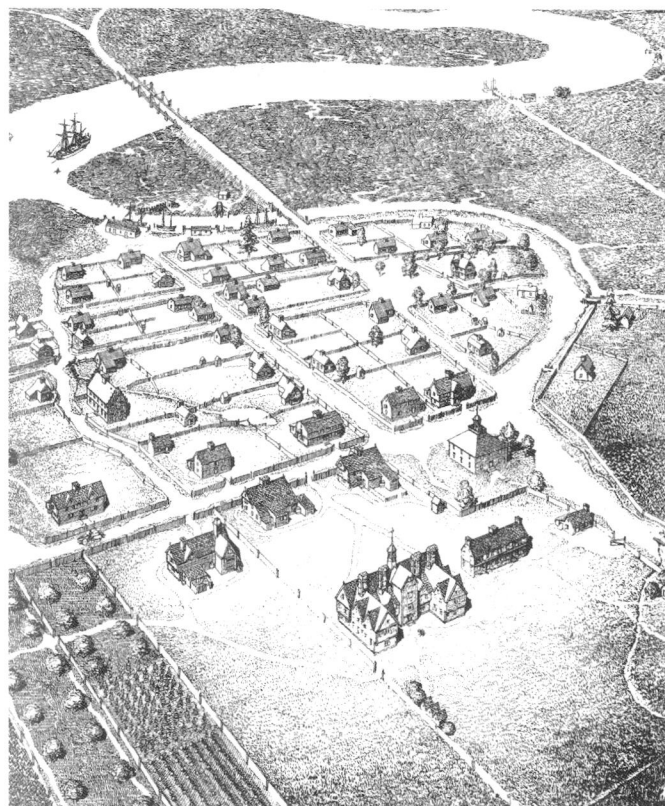

1.9 Conjectural view of Cambridge, Massachusetts, 1668, by H. Shurtleff. The foreground shows Harvard's four buildings: Old College is the largest building; to its right is Indian College. On the street front are the President's House and Goffe College
Photo: Harvard University Archives, HUV 2038

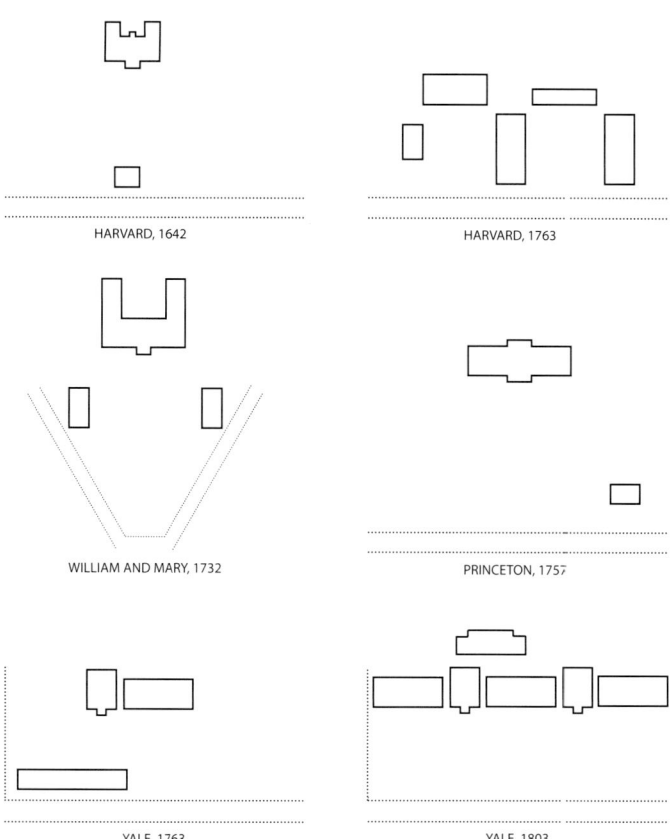

1.10 Early layouts of the colonial colleges
(Adapted from schematic plans, P. Turner, *Campus: An American Planning Tradition*, Cambridge, Mass: Architectural History Foundation, 1995, p. 19)

with short flanking wings and a central staircase tower projecting from the main block reminiscent of Elizabethan manor houses. Old College, as the building was later named, contained nearly all the college's activities under one roof, including a commodious hall, acting as lecture hall, dining room and communal living area, plus a kitchen, library and student rooms. Since lectures were, at this time, only a modest aspect of the curriculum, no additional classrooms were built. A central school-house of this type, frequently termed the Old Main and sheltering virtually all college functions, came to be a mainstay of American college architecture. Examples exist at the University of Colorado, Princeton University, Vassar College, and Swarthmore College. Harvard extended its premises in 1650 and 1655 with two further buildings neighbouring Old College, named Goffe College and Indian College. This layout of a series of separate structures set an enduring precedent for American colleges. It has been speculated that this type of spatial arrangement may have been conditioned by a variety of factors. Paul Turner proposed that the sense of boundless space may have engendered a comparably expansive layout, or that the use of wood as a building material suggested separate buildings to minimize fire risk. Ideologically, the new spatial layout may have been perceived by the Puritan colonialists as a means of establishing a distance from the catholic associations of the monastic-style linked complexes of England and from their impression of cloistered isolation. For the r colleges, the new settlers aspired to a cohesive relationship with the outside community, an ideology which would not be expressed by inward-turning buildings. Almost always, the American colonial college faced outwards to its community (Figure 1.9).[12]

Yet by no means did this spatial pattern always assume the same guise; the nine colonial colleges exhibit an impressive degree of experimentation in their planning and architecture (Figure 1.10). Virginia's first college, William and Mary, executed a plan in the 1720s in which a large building was neighboured symmetrically by two smaller structures, in an arrangement reminiscent of the sixteenth-century villas of Palladio. Its domestic character may have been a response to the college's educational ambitions, for it espoused a pragmatic syllabus, more attuned to the community than the traditional New England college. It was a layout often adopted in the early nineteenth century, at Ohio University (Figure 1.11) and Antioch College for example. An alternative organisation was laid out at Princeton, where the single academic building, Nassau Hall (Figure 1.12), was set back imposingly from the road behind a large green, a precedent repeated at Brown (1770) and Dartmouth (1784–1791) (Figure 1.13). Yale's early buildings, beginning with the long and narrow edifice erected in 1717, took on the form of an elongated façade to the town's Green (Figure 1.14), creating a

1.11 Cutler Hall, Ohio University
Photo: Ohio University Communications and Marketing

linear plan later reworked at institutions including Dartmouth, Brown, Amherst, Bowdoin and Wesleyan. These diverse plans demonstrate the colonialists' immediate recognition that their distinct social and educational ideology necessitated a revised approach to campus planning distinguished clearly from their English roots.[13]

The most pervasive manifestation of the connection between campus planning and the social and pedagogical idealism of the young nation was that of the University of Virginia. Its foundation in 1819 represented the culmination of a campaign begun by the country's third president, Thomas Jefferson, when Governor of Virginia in the late eighteenth century, to reform public education by creating a series of free schools. The campus that resulted is frequently hailed as the United States' most celebrated. Not only did it introduce refined neo-classical design to the American university, but it emphasized physical environment as a pivotal feature of educational vision.

Designed by Jefferson himself, the layout was simple: a wide, tree-lined central space flanked by a series of ten pavilions, each housing an individual subject, opening at one end to a stunning prospect

1.12 Nassau Hall, Princeton University
Photo: Library of Congress, Prints & Photographs Division, HABS NJ,11-PRINT,4B-1

1.13 Dartmouth Hall, Dartmouth College
Photo: Courtesy of Dartmouth College Library

over the Virginian plantations, and terminating at the other with the functional and symbolic axis of the campus, the Rotunda Library (Figures 1.15, 1.16). Each pavilion served as a professor's house and classroom, connected at the rear with colonnades onto which student residences opened. The central lawn was envisioned as a space for recreation, campus gossip and scholarly exchange, while the colonnaded pavilions provided numerous front doors, and thus numerous opportunities for social encounters. In its spatial arrangement, Jefferson's University of Virginia stands as one of the most decisive moments in the history of campus design. Its impact was felt as far away as twentieth-century China, for at Tsinghua University in Beijing a grand focal point is provided in the form of a copy of Jefferson's Rotunda, built in 1917.[14]

The concept of a spacious, open green surrounded by a succession of structures serving both as professors' residences and classrooms, was unparalleled in campus planning. Jefferson advocated to the trustees that the model institution should be 'an academical village.' This phrase has enjoyed immense currency as the paragon in campus values, and encapsulates Jefferson's ambitions for the institution. The

1.14 Old Brick Row, Yale University
Photo: Yale University

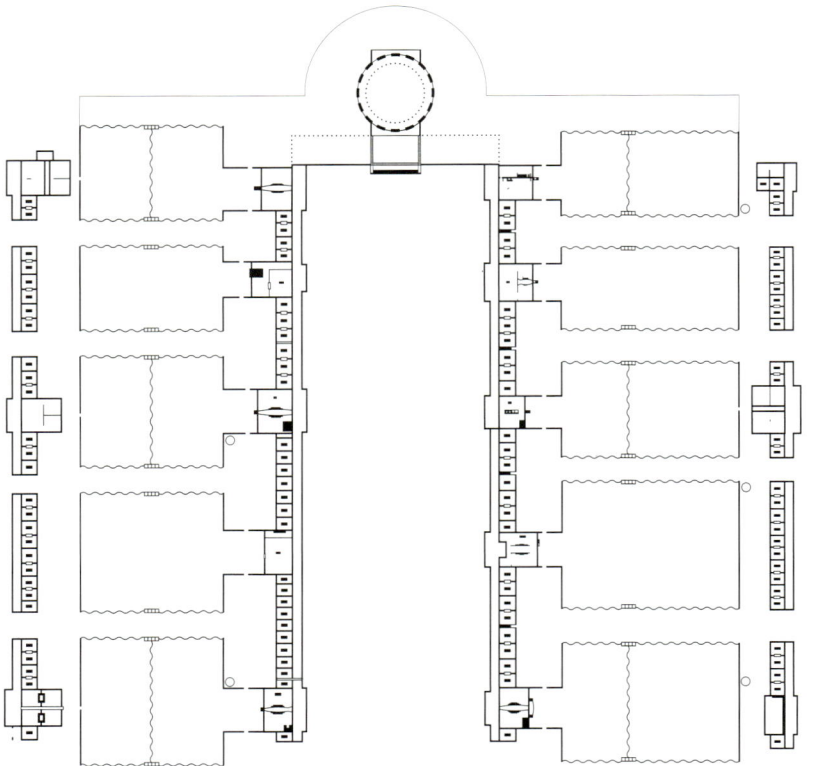

1.15 University of Virginia, based on Jefferson's 1822 plan

1.16 The Lawn, University of Virginia
Photo: Jane Haley/UVA Public Affairs

effect is one of an intimate, scholastic household. When himself a student, Jefferson had thrived on the personal relationships with his tutors, a practice he contrived in later life as a teacher himself. He valued teaching based upon close personal contact. The proximity of the living and classroom space of the lecturers and the students made physical this ideal.

NINETEENTH-CENTURY AMERICA: PICTURESQUE NATURE

As the nineteenth century progressed, the design of college campuses and buildings became increasingly ambitious, displaying far greater sophistication and a more profound unity of conception than preceding ages. American campus planning underwent a series of transformational phases in this period, namely those of picturesque nature, the Beaux-Arts movement and the Gothic Revival.

Nature was the first of these themes to find expression in the nineteenth-century college. It was a long-held conviction, maintained particularly by the early Puritan colleges, that institutions should be located in the countryside away from the pernicious influences of the city; in the nineteenth century this concern was joined by more aesthetic considerations. Recognized both for its beauty and uplifting potency, nature became one of the most compelling considerations in the location and planning of American colleges. Locations overlooking seas or lakes, or those perched on elevated hilltops were increasingly sought-after amongst new schools, achieving an unparalleled relationship with the natural environment. This affinity with the landscape was unheard of amongst the European universities, and one of the signal features which distinguished the American campus from its European peers.[15]

The natural environment was popularly held as beneficial to students' wellbeing and moral character. In 1878, commentator Charles Thwing asserted, 'if Yale were located at Williamstown, Harvard at Hanover, and Columbia at Ithaca, the moral character of their students would be elevated in as great degree as the natural scenery…would be increased in beauty.' The edifying capacity of landscape was a central motivation to one of the most prominent

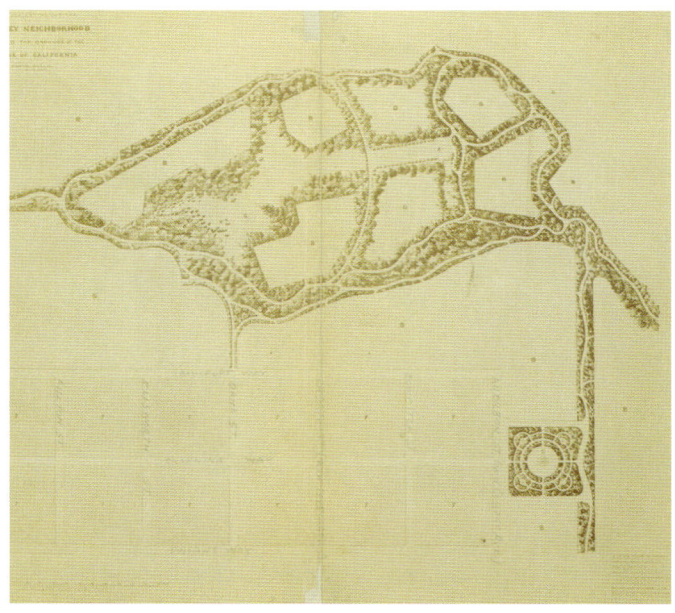

1.17 Plan for the College of California by Frederick Law Olmsted, 1866
Photo: Courtesy of The Bancroft Library, University of California, Berkeley

figures in nineteenth-century campus development, Frederick Law Olmsted. Amidst the fast-paced industrialization and urbanization of America, Olmsted believed in nature as an antidote to city life and employed its remedial powers in his designs for parks and campuses. He envisaged a new campus ideal, an irregular and picturesque layout of buildings and walkways that followed the contour of the land. His designs (never executed) for the College of California's new site, soon named Berkeley, for instance, placed the school in a park-like setting, permeated with meandering roads (Figure 1.17). Convinced of the impact of physical setting upon behaviour, Olmsted championed the location and design of the campus as a key ingredient of the civilizing mission of higher education. In his recommendations for the Massachusetts Agricultural College he argued,

> You must embrace in your ground-plan arrangements for something more than oral instruction and practical demonstration in the science of agriculture…You must include arrangements designed to favourably affect the habits and inclinations of your students, and to qualify them for a wise and beneficent exercise of the rights and duties of citizens and of householders.

The college was to be a 'model rural neighbourhood', of relatively small buildings scattered along a main road and around a village green. Olmsted's plans for Massachusetts were, however, summarily rejected by the college trustees. His subsequent article, 'How Not to Establish an Agricultural College', though, caught the attention of other institutions across the country and, ultimately, his tenets on the benefits of uniting community and nature became widely known amongst educators, resulting in a plethora of campuses built as clusters of structures informally set within park-like grounds.[16]

1.18 Iowa State University
Photo: Courtesy of Iowa State University

His influence stretched across the country, including the University of Vermont, Smith College, Stanford University, Washington University in St Louis, Gallaudet College, and the agricultural colleges of Iowa (Figure 1.18), Kansas and Michigan. Often termed the first landscape architect, he established the importance of landscape as a component of campus design. His philosophy of place would be a central influence on American campus design far into the next century.

NINETEENTH-CENTURY AMERICA: THE BEAUX-ARTS MOVEMENT

Quickly, however, a new paradigm for campus design gained ground – the Beaux-Arts model. While Olmsted structured his campuses around the natural environment to harness its healthy, civilizing potential, Beaux-Arts planning rejected nature and instead evolved as an urban pattern. The Beaux-Arts approach to planning was based on the 'City Beautiful' movement, a movement originating in the 1893 World's Columbian Exposition in Chicago. The most consummate, impressive case of Beaux-Arts planning to be produced in the United States, the Exposition had a resounding impact upon both city and campus design. The approach prescribed formal axes on a grand scale lined with monumental buildings, which complemented the ethos of the modern American university. The closing years of the nineteenth century witnessed the formation of the modern American university. The number of academic courses mushroomed, as did extra-curricular activities and student numbers; commensurably the organization of the American university became ever more complex. Many universities began to consider themselves as cities. Bywords such as 'City of Learning' and 'Collegiate City' came into common usage, and, indeed, came to shape the built form of the institutions.[17]

The new thinking in campus planning was strongly influenced by Jefferson's design for the University of Virginia. The pattern of a longitudinal axis dominated at one end by a strong focal point and flanked by subsidiary buildings found expression time and again at the hands of Beaux-Arts practitioners, who applied secondary axes and auxiliary buildings to the plan. The first outstanding illustration of this approach was Columbia University in New York, designed by Charles McKim in 1894 (Figure 1.19). Grand structures lined an axial network of streets and public spaces, culminating in a *cour d'honneur*, which led up to the central building, the library (Figure 1.20). Unlike the traditional American college, the new university required a greater number of teaching buildings, laboratories, libraries, and gymnasium amongst others, and the integration of these facilities within a unified campus became a chief preoccupation of university planners. Columbia, through its application of the Beaux-Arts system, achieved a unity and organizational clarity that provided an influential solution to this problem.

The Beaux-Arts method was adopted by universities across the United States, including the University of California at Berkeley, Rice University, Emory University, the Southern Methodist University, the University of Delaware, the University of Rochester, the University of Southern California and the University of Maryland (Figure 1.21). When the University of Havana moved to a new site in the opening years of the twentieth century, it too embraced a Beaux-Arts layout, creating a grand, neo-classical complex that dominates its urban expanse. Particularly striking is the prime vista leading to the Rectory, culminating in a monumental flight of stairs and double

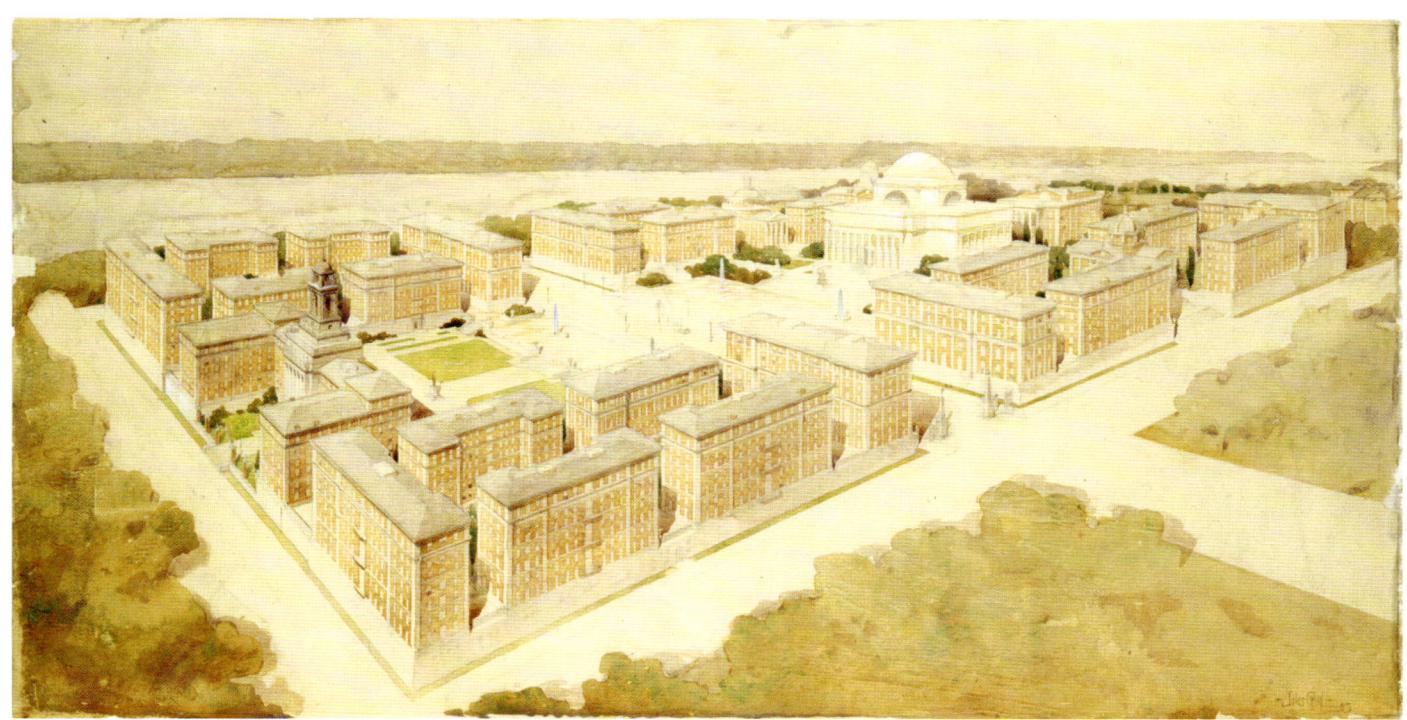

1.19 Columbia University, McKim Mead and White's bird's eye view of projected campus built to full density
Photo: Collection of the New York Historical Society

1.20 Low Library, Columbia University
Photo: ©iStockphoto.com/Peter Spiro

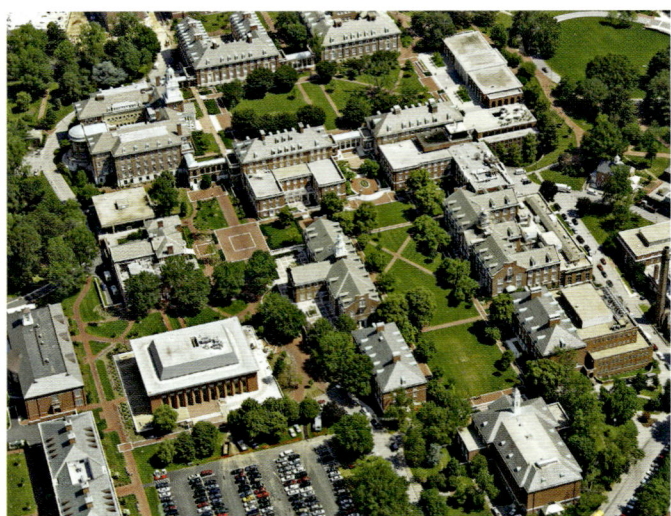

porch of Corinthian columns (Figure 1.22). American architect Henry Killam Murphy transported Beaux-Arts planning as far as China in the 1920s, designing for Yenching University a campus governed by two perpendicular axes yet integrating traditional Chinese landscaping traditions and architecture. Although each applied the Beaux-Arts axial formula, campuses were shaped in accordance with the individual topographies, structure and ideology of the schools. The classical vocabulary was most widely adopted, but theoretically any architectural style could be assumed. Colonial architecture, for example, was employed on occasions to signal venerability, traditional American values, or to harmonize with extant buildings on campus, as was the case with Johns Hopkins University (Figure 1.23). Henry Hornbostel at Emory University appropriated an Italian Renaissance style as an expression of its geographical setting, the architect perceiving a similarity in flora and terrain between northern Italy and Atlanta. The movement endowed America with campuses of vastly different appearances, yet united by bold plans of organizational clarity that imbued higher education with a grand civic expression befitting its stature in an urbanizing society.[18]

NINETEENTH-CENTURY EUROPE

The European university had not been altered by any significant development in the design of its physical fabric since the Renaissance, but in the second half of the nineteenth century, European universities were the subjects of a building boom. The century saw a tremendous expansion in education as new social, economic and intellectual forces gained momentum. New trade had augmented national wealth and prompted a rise in the numbers and influence of the middle-class, which in turn encouraged the progress of higher education. At the beginning of the century, most universities in Europe were quartered in archaic premises. In Paris, the teachers and students of the faculties of sciences and theology were forced to lodge in the dingy rooms of the 'Old Sorbonne', built in the mid-seventeenth century. Vienna's medieval university occupied yet older buildings, dating to the early sixteenth century. It was common practice for universities to take over edifices designed for other purposes, including convents, private residences and mansions. Aix-en-Provence's law faculty was sited in a fifteenth-century hospice, and numerous Italian universities taught in Renaissance palaces, often in disrepair and unfit for purpose. These

CLOCKWISE FROM LEFT

1.21 University of Maryland
Photo: © John T. Consoli/University of Maryland

1.22 University of Havana
Photo: ©iStockphoto.com/Amanda Lewis

1.23 Johns Hopkins University
Photo: J. Brough Schamp

historic buildings were the frequent recipients of criticism from their unhappy inhabitants. In France, the reports of general inspectors made for particularly vitriolic reading, while the first ministerial statistics in 1868 concluded most faculties conducted teaching and research in inadequate, detrimental conditions. In the nineteenth century, university premises were restored or constructed at breakneck speed across the continent. Paris gained palatial settings for the ancient Sorbonne and the new École des Beaux-Arts; the Swedish universities of Lund and Uppsala underwent rebuilding projects in the 1880s; and the German states went to great lengths to ensure their universities possessed impressive buildings, including those at Halle, Heidelberg, Göttingen, Leipzig, Munich and Karlsruhe.[19]

Although the nineteenth-century American campus housed an eclectic mix of historical styles, it was nineteenth-century Europe that explored to the maximum the associative power of historical style in giving form and meaning to educational institutions. The nineteenth-century explosion of university construction was not merely a utilitarian or perfunctory business. The grandiose buildings that resulted were highly potent, highly expressive structures communicative of the socio-political climate, of modern conceptions of education and of a youthful spirit of exuberance. In 1889, the Danish literary critic, Georg Morris Cohen Brander, wrote of Uppsala University's new main building that 'the whole is suited to propose to youth a spirit of progress. Everything here says to the young: Grow and go higher and become a professor!'[20] The new university structures were not corralled behind walls as the medieval colleges of Oxbridge, or isolated amidst rolling countryside like many of the American colonial colleges, but rather were large, imposing city-centre structures, loaded with symbolic capital. Huge single structures typified the new university buildings. The synergy of the university and city brought with it significant cultural advantages, though it restricted the ability to minister to specific academic functions. Invariably, all university functions were housed within a single, dominating building, except residences which continental institutions did not provide. Gottfried Semper's neo-classical edifice for the Swiss Federal Institute of Technology in Zurich (completed 1864), the University of Graz's new main building (opened 1895) (Figure 1.24), and Helgo Zettervall's Renaissance palazzo for Lund University (completed 1882) (Figure 1.25) exemplify this trend. Academic construction was set against a background of social, economic and political tumult, which exerted a tangible influence upon the architectural experiments of the nineteenth century. The outcome was a collection of assertive buildings that sought to define learning in the modern age.

In an increasingly secular society, the new university buildings were the cathedrals or temples of learning. This is exhibited no more manifestly than in the Greek temple-inspired embodiment of London's newly founded university college. London's first university was established by a group of social reformers in a bid to create an enlightened alternative to the traditionalist and churchly Oxbridge colleges. Today known as University College London, in 1826, architect, classical scholar and archaeologist, William Wilkins was selected to design its building. A star in the ascendant, Wilkins had made his name through his neo-Grecian creations for Downing College, Cambridge (designed 1805) and the East India Company College (1809), riding on a crest of popularity for the Greek Revival. Lofty classical models were employed by the architect at University College London, openly declaring the foundling college's grand aspirations and the cultural acclaim for Antiquity. With little heed to functional requirements, lecture halls, common rooms and corridors were condensed into a single harmonious unit of neo-classical symmetry. Charged with overtones of Athenian openness, purity, wisdom and independence, the architecture bespoke of the establishment's institutional opposition to the ecclesiastical, esoteric and privileged Oxford and Cambridge, embodied in its Gothic physique (Figure 1.26).

Consolidating as it did, the ideal of the classical curriculum and its nobility, the Greek Revival was embraced by universities. Johann Carl Ludwig Engel's classically-inspired University of Helsinki stands symbolically beside the Cathedral and Senate, the triumvirate dominating the city's Senate Square. Designed in 1833, the university was one of a series of major public and private buildings designed by Engels as part of an extensive development of the city after becoming a Russian duchy in 1809. Thus it stands as a physical symbol of new nationhood. Likewise, the grand new university complex in Berlin, the Humboldt, pronounced national recovery after gruelling defeats at the hands of Napoleon, while Ghent University's founding in 1817 was symbolic of the United Netherlands and then of the new Belgium.

Neither was Paris lacking in grandiose new schemes. Its academic district, the Latin Quarter, evoked the resonant capacity of architecture

1.24 University of Graz
Photo: University of Graz

1.25 Lund University
Photo: Mikael Risedal

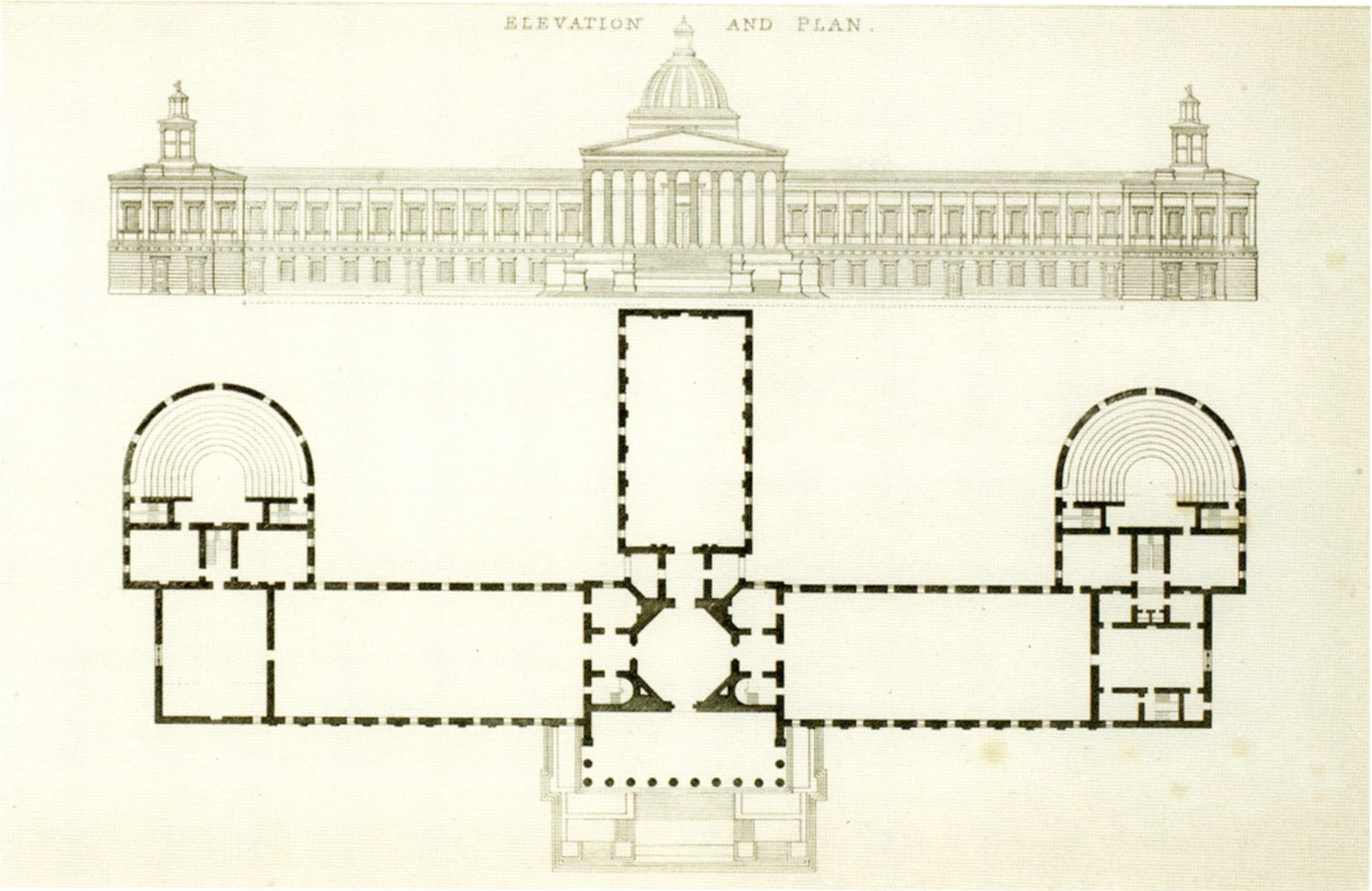

1.26 University College London, elevation and plan
Photo: UCL Special Collections

to symbolize the doctrines of higher education. The neo-classical fabric of the Collège de France was expanded in the 1830s by architect Paul Letarouilly. Letarouilly spent many years in Rome, where he became steeped in the communicative, propagandizing potential of architecture. Contemporaneously, architect Felix Duban was creating a complex of buildings to house the École des Beaux-Arts. He sought to create a building which evoked a summary of France's architectural history, germane for a school of art and architecture.

Such stylistic plurality was evident in much nineteenth-century European architecture, none more so than the development of Vienna's Ringstrasse. This splendid new site became the home of a grand series of public buildings in the second half of the century, the physical embodiment of the revived city. Alongside the Grecian Parliament and the Gothic City Hall, stood the university (completed 1884), a Renaissance palace of learning designed by architect Heinrich von Ferstel. Ferstel had studied the university palazzi of Bologna, Padua, Genoa and Rome, and his design epitomizes the forms of Renaissance Italy combined with a Baroque monumentality. The building, together with the adjacent town halls and parliament, was conceived as a striking monument to the growing power of the Austro-Hungarian Empire and Vienna as its capital.

In its Renaissance guise, Vienna University was commensurate with many of its peers. The nineteenth-century academic architectural

1.27 University of Liverpool
Photo: University of Liverpool

vernacular was monumental and symmetrical, and dominated by neo-classical Renaissance styles. The trend spread throughout Europe, except for the new academic institutions of England, the so-called Redbricks. First coined by a professor at the University of Liverpool (under the pseudonym Bruce Truscot in his text, *Redbrick University*,

1.28 University of Manchester
Photo: Courtesy of the University of Manchester

1.29 University of Sydney
Photo: Eric Sierins

published 1943), the expression was inspired by the red brick and terracotta Victoria Building at the University of Liverpool (1892) (Figure 1.27). It was one of six new civic institutions in England's most populous cities, the hubs of the industrial revolution, Birmingham, Bristol, Leeds, Liverpool, Manchester and Sheffield. These universities sought to open up education with a marked departure from the grandeur and social privilege of Oxford and Cambridge. Non-collegiate, aimed at local students, and often financed by wealthy industrialists, these universities grew up contemporaneously with their host cities, becoming entwined within the urban fabric and often undistinguishable from public buildings that accompanied the Victorian surge of the middle classes.

Manchester University is an archetypal example of the pattern these civic institutions followed. Beginning life as Owens College in 1851 under the will of John Owens, a prosperous merchant, and reorganized on several subsequent occasions, it enjoyed a burst of expansion until the outbreak of the First World War. Much of this building was conducted under Alfred Waterhouse. From 1869, he designed the university's initial neo-Gothic buildings that make up Waterhouse Quadrangle (Figure 1.28). Ministering to home-based students, the designs did not include residential quarters, but large rooms and science laboratories. Although a quadrangle format, the composition thus digressed from the collegiate Oxbridge model, while stylistically it was radically different from its continental compeers.[21] Waterhouse Quadrangle illustrates the passion for Gothic that swept England at the height of the Victorian age. Gothic architecture, associated with the social and cultural ideals of the Middle Ages, was seen as a means of remaking the modern world and thus was seen as appropriate for the civic universities. At Manchester, Waterhouse designed a series of buildings embracing this style in its plethora of buttresses, gables and a dramatic tower. His architecture did much to characterize High Victorian collegiate building; he went on to design the initial buildings for the universities of Liverpool and Leeds, as well as Girton College, Cambridge.[22]

THE GOTHIC REVIVAL

The Gothic Revival was of British genesis but its characteristics were variously adopted elsewhere. It made its appearance at the Australian universities of Melbourne, Sydney (Figure 1.29) and Adelaide (Figure 1.30), in New Zealand at Otago, and in Canada at McGill, Toronto and McMaster. Neo-Gothicism made its way even to South Korea, in the Main Building of Bo-Sung Special University complete with crenellated tower and pointed windows. But it was championed most thoroughly in America, and it was the college campus that supplied the most consummate evidence of the style there. Although preceded by a scattering of Gothic academic buildings, the first wave of Gothic Revival swept over America in the 1830s. The architectural style was allied to the planning principles of both picturesque nature and Beaux-Arts, producing in the United States a complexity of campus design unsurpassed anywhere else in the world. In 1838, the style made its first appearance at Harvard (Figure 1.31). Gore Hall, a library, was modelled roughly on King's College Chapel in

1.30 University of Adelaide
Photo: Michael Mullan

Cambridge, but although its architectural details were Gothic in style, its relationship with its neighbouring buildings was far from medieval. Typical of nineteenth-century neo-Gothic collegiate architecture in the United States, Gore Hall maintained the traditional 'open' quality of American plans, consisting of unconnected units implanted within a large, essentially open space.[23]

By the middle of the century, Gothic Revival structures were becoming an increasingly common sight on college campuses. At the heart of its old campus, Yale erected a King's College Chapel-inspired library, now Dwight Chapel, in 1842, designed by Henry Austin. The Gothic Revival was perceived increasingly as more than an architectural fashion, and to college presidents, it became a highly potent tool; to a still relatively young nation, it proffered the immediate appearance of age and venerability, qualities fiercely coveted amongst the American colleges. From the mid to late nineteenth century, the desire to invest university architecture with historic connotations and the impression of

1.31 Gore Hall in Harvard Yard, Harvard University
Photo: Library of Congress, Prints and Photographs Division PAN 6a06249

1.32 Pembroke Hall, Bryn Mawr College
Photo: Bryn Mawr College

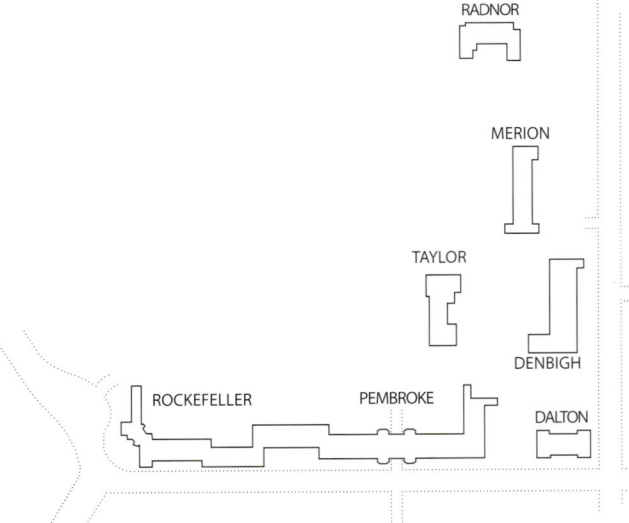

1.33 Detail of plan of Bryn Mawr College, circa 1905. Cope and Stewardson were responsible for Radnor Hall, Denbigh Hall, Pembroke Hall and Rockefeller Hall

permanence and nobility became more pronounced. In 1896, Princeton President Woodrow Wilson declared, by 'building our new buildings in the Tudor Gothic Style we seem to have added to Princeton the age of Oxford and Cambridge.'[24] After a fire razed its original buildings in 1857, Bethany College in West Virginia employed the architectural firm of Walter and Wilson, who set out a long, meandering Gothic range that immediately suggested having been built over time. An instant heritage was thus created, compensating for its lost buildings. Although any historic style could, in theory, serve this purpose, it was Gothic that was popularly conceived as the most appropriate. In the 1880s, Harvard's president, Abbot Lawrence Lowell, bemoaned the college's Colonial Georgian structures, complaining,

> We have none, or next to none, of those coigns of vantage for the tendrils of memory or affection. Not any of our older buildings is venerable, or will ever become so. Time refuses to console them. They look as if they meant business and nothing more.[25]

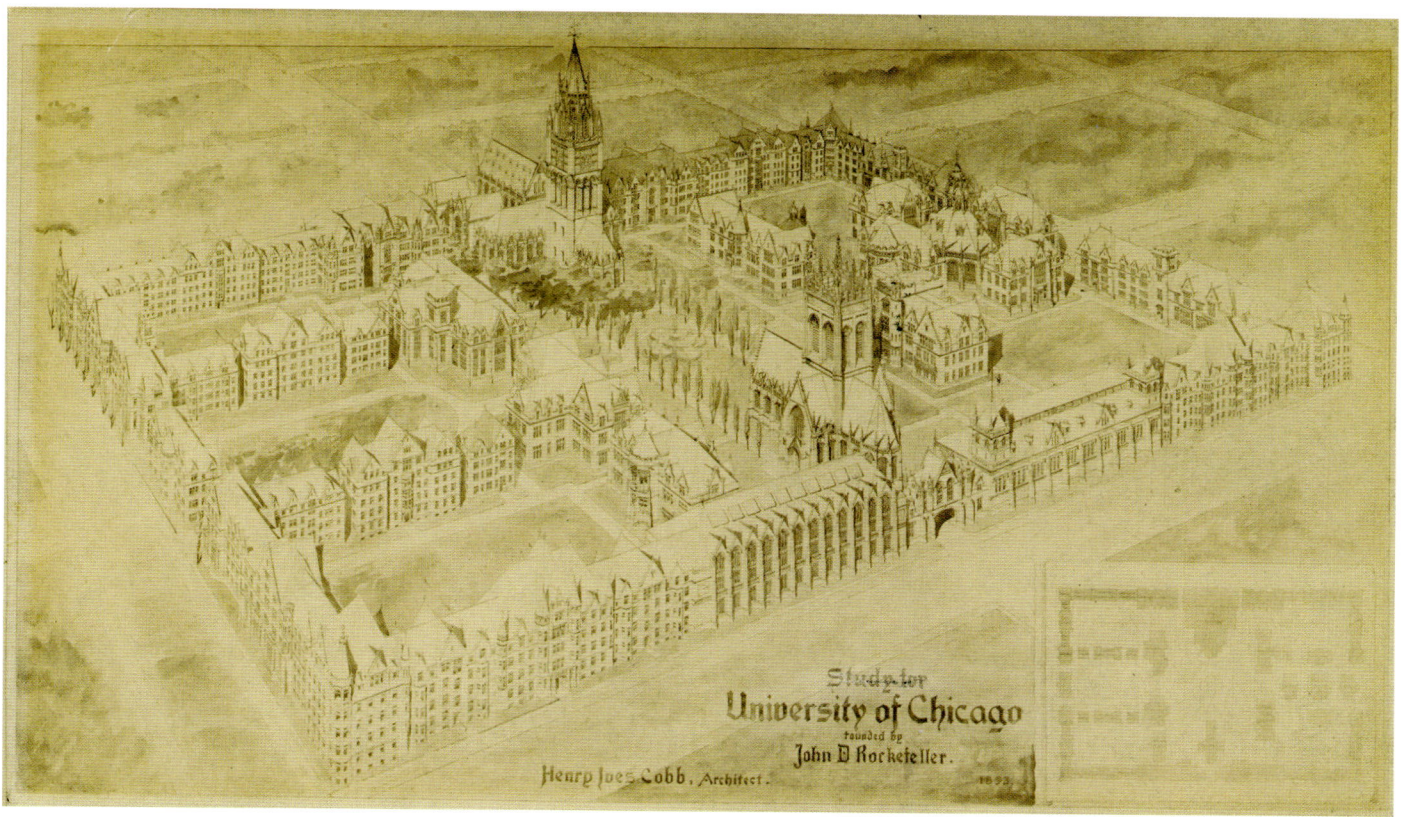

1.34 University of Chicago campus plan, 1893
Photo: Special Collections Research Center, University of Chicago Library

The original buildings of the colonial colleges, despite their age, were felt to be inadequate symbols of venerability because of their plainness. It was medieval architecture alone that was perceived to hold the key to evoking memory. In 1910, after Princeton had begun its period of 'Gothicization', Andrew West, dean of the Graduate School, sketched the campus as

> quadrangles shadowing sunny lawns, towers and gateways opening into quiet retreats, ivy-grown walls looking on sheltered gardens…these are the places where the affections linger and where memories cling like the ivies themselves, and these are the answers in architecture and scenic setting to the immemorial longings of Academic generations.[26]

In the 1880s a new phase in Gothic Revival college architecture was inaugurated, Collegiate Gothic. It was based upon the late-medieval architecture of the Oxbridge colleges. In 1886 Bryn Mawr College employed two young Philadelphia architects, Walter Cope and John Stewardson. Influenced by a trip to Oxford and Cambridge, the architects set about capturing the picturesque qualities of Tudor Gothic Oxbridge on Pennsylvania soil. The college asserts that its Cope and Stewardson-designed Radnor Building, dating to 1887, was the country's first essay in Collegiate Gothic.[27] The towered, crenellated silhouette of Pembroke Hall, 1894 (Figure 1.32), and Rockefeller Hall, 1897, formed a long, winding border to the southern edge of the campus, marked by two towered entrance gateways. Using a meandering linear series of structures to define a boundary was unprecedented in American university planning (Figure 1.33). At the University of Pennsylvania, the pair further challenged American notions of campus planning by housing new residences within an enclosed quadrangle. Running counter to the traditional American ethos of openness to the community, the quadrangle marked a symbolic border between the outside world and the privileged life of academia, revealing the growing introspection of education.[28]

The graceful scale, the refined detailing and the iconic skyline of spires and towers of Collegiate Gothic held the imagination for the next 40 years. The careers of its practitioners flourished, most notably Charles Klauder, James Gamble Rogers and Ralph Adams Cram. Klauder scattered Princeton, Wellesley College, the University of Pittsburgh and Cornell University with his own brand of monastic-like building, while it is to Rogers that Yale owes its Collegiate Gothic façade (Figure 1.35).

The vogue for Collegiate Gothic was propelled by ideological motivations. At the turn of the twentieth century, educators progressively despaired of the growing complexity of the country's large universities, and turned increasingly to a resurgence of traditional collegiate values. They called for a heightened sense of community, propelled by intimate relationships between students and teachers. And for this, they turned to England. To regain a sense of fellowship between scholars and their professors, Harvard and Princeton both imitated Oxbridge's tutorial system. In 1928 Harvard introduced the

1.35 Harkness Tower, Yale University
Photo: Michael Marsland/Yale University

'house' system and, two years later, Yale the 'college' system, in which undergraduates were divided into colleges or houses, where they resided, dined and received some lessons.

This educational philosophy instigated not only changes to teaching practices, but also led to a review of the ideal campus. The enclosed quadrangle of the medieval colleges of Oxford and Cambridge sprang to the fore as the superlative physical manifestation of the new ideals. Enclosed courtyards, quadrangles, and loggias, evocative of Oxbridge's cloistered spaces, appeared across the country as American colleges entered a new mood of introspection and elitism. From 1924–1938, Harvard erected a succession of seven narrow dormitories around its historic central campus, the Yard, creating a structural and metaphorical barrier from the bustling city surrounding it indicative of its new drive towards clubby collegiality.[29]

One of the keenest advocates for the use of the medieval quadrangle was Ralph Adams Cram. A fervent champion of the moral capacities of architecture, Cram pictured Collegiate Gothic as a counter to materialism, the erosion of traditional values, and all else that was amiss in modern society. Cram put his theories into practice on several campuses, most notably at Princeton. His 1906 Princeton master plan featured a series of quadrangular, or near quadrangular, halls built in the Gothic idiom. Cram wrote,

> Certain psychological principles were laid down at once… First of all, a university was conceived as a place where the community life and spirit were supreme, …a citadel of learning and culture, …containing within itself all necessary influences towards the making of character, repelling all those that work against the same: a walled city against materialism and all its works.[30]

Cram's remark that a university should be 'half college and half monastery' epitomizes the mettle of American collegiate planning in the opening decades of the twentieth century. Campus plans embraced the antiquated vocabulary of English medieval architecture and the ordered, enclosed format of the quadrangle. In Europe, similarly, historicism dominated the vast, single-structure units that housed universities. Yet, across the world, the discourse of university architecture and planning was soon to be shaken by the advent of war.

THE POST-WAR REVOLUTION

In the years after the Second World War, higher education was rocked by a period of change. Student enrolments soared during this time. While it has been estimated that Germany, France and Britain had a combined university population of at most 150,000 at any one time preceding the war, within decades the numbers pursuing a university degree had reached millions. In America, the G.I. Bill of 1944 resulted in a wholly unexpected volume of new students, often non-traditional applicants, flooding into higher education. Across Europe and the United States, university enrolments surged again in the 1960s as the 'baby boom' generation came of age. The nature of universities evolved, as faculties diversified and degree courses multiplied. There arose a consciousness that it was the duty of the modern nation to broaden and strengthen education, attended by a growing dissatisfaction with the elitism that accompanied traditional university education. Inevitably, the enlargement of higher education

1.36 Illinois Institute of Technology
Photo: Architectural Press Archive/RIBA Library Photographs Collection

occasioned a corresponding surge in university building, while the changing patterns of university education meant many of the time-worn aspects of campus design became outmoded. America, the United Kingdom and Germany were the countries in which these changes had the most tangible effects.[31]

For America, this was amongst the most vibrant periods of university development. Many institutions became, in their scale and complexity, mini-cities. Le Corbusier observed 'the American university is a world in itself'. Urban issues, such as movement and circulation, came to the fore in typical universities, dictating revised attitudes to university architecture and planning. Modernism rose to prominence, characterized by angular, unfussy forms and a rational approach to organisation, only to be supplanted again by a revival in traditionalism and historic architecture. The post-war period was thus one of heady development for university building, set off by an equally heady time for modern architecture.

The term modern architecture refers not simply to all buildings of the modern age, but more specifically to an architecture conscious of its own modernity and striving for change. In the years leading up to the Second World War, the International Style defined the architecture of the modern era. The style can be viewed as a byword for a cubist mode of architecture with its crisp, muted forms, robust use of concrete, steel and glass, and regularity, it was the realization of the new era of social and technological confidence.[32] In the 1930s, the International Style, and other modern movements, gained a firm footing in worldwide architecture, yet their use at colleges and universities was startlingly seldom and enveloped in controversy. The impassioned traditionalism of higher education institutions, the same traditionalism that half a century earlier had led American campuses to turn to medieval Oxbridge, fiercely suppressed the advent of contemporary design. Only a handful of modern collegiate designs had emerged by the late 1930s in America, including Ludwig Mies van der Rohe's Illinois Institute of Technology (Figure 1.36), Frank Lloyd Wright's Florida Southern College (Figure 1.37) and The Architects Collaborative's design for Black Mountain College in North Carolina (Figure 1.38). A bitter polemic of style was conducted through the architectural press, yet amidst this the larger issues of university planning were usually forgotten in the debates. Hence, as Paul Turner highlights, in the widely-publicized critiques of Illinois Institute of Technology, designed 1938–1940, Mies van der Rohe

1.37 Florida Southern College
Photo: Florida Southern College

1.38 Model of design for Black Mountain College
Photo: Harvard Art Museum, Busch-Reisinger Museum, Gift of Ise Gropius, BRGA.87.8. ©DACS 2009

was applauded for his uncompromising evocation of modernism while the plan is, in many respects, surprisingly conventional. The buildings are aligned on a symmetrical and axial plan to create a central quadrangle and secondary collection of structures, an arrangement reminiscent of Beaux-Arts organization.[33]

Progressively, though, the modern idiom gained an increasing hold on university architecture. Illinois Institute of Technology signalled a new direction of campus architecture in the United States, and this momentum was continued by Walter Gropius at Harvard. Gropius's Graduate Centre, completed 1950, consisted of eight plain rectangular blocks grouped around an informally connected series of courtyards. This was a Modernist form, reflective of practical considerations such as permitting maximum light and air. The dormitory blocks are intricately connected by bridges and covered pathways. The Graduate Centre proclaimed an architectural manifesto for the post-war age: institutional heritage and context should not impinge upon campus design, unless in an abstracted manner. The distinct identity and sense of continuity that was so prized on pre-war campuses was renounced. Yet the Graduate Centre still reflected the same socio-educational values of the previous century. Gropius was keen to stress the 'philosophical concept of communal living, of cooperative activity and of interchange of ideas', and pronounced that 'living in this kind of a group of buildings, a young man may unconsciously absorb ideas and principles that would seem abstract and remote in the classroom, but which translated into concrete, glass, light and air assume a convincing reality'.[34]

Gropius was just one of many eminent modernist architects working in America in the twentieth century. The list includes Mies van der Rohe, Josep Luis Sert, I. M. Pei, Minoru Yamasaki and Paul Rudolph. Many of their American efforts were driven towards universities and colleges, and they stand as some of the earliest landmark buildings, omens of the infatuation with iconic building that would come to dominate campus development later in the century. Alvar Aalto, for instance, was commissioned to design the Baker House dormitory at Massachusetts Institute of Technology (completed 1949); Le Corbusier's only building on America soil was Harvard's Carpenter Centre for the Visual Arts; Yale Art Centre, completed in 1954, was designed by Louis Kahn. These diverse interpretations of modern design were conceived as objects of art in themselves. They looked markedly different from each other, and paid little heed to neighbouring buildings. These landmark structures represent not only the triumph of the Modernist style, but, moreover, a new approach to planning that took hold on American campuses. Traditionally, campuses were shaped by a master plan, with specified formal, stylistic prescriptions guiding the placement and general appearance of buildings. With the ascendancy of modernism, architects moved away from this tradition. Growth, they argued, could not be catered for within rigid frameworks, and the conventional master plan was progressively renounced in favour of more fluid and informal approaches to planning. New structures assumed individual forms and varying positions in response to the 'here and now'. Spatial composition and visual coherence lost their value.[35]

Colleges seized upon this convenient concept. As the need for more teaching and living accommodation became pressing, institutions across America constructed new structures, often sizeable and unconventional, upon their open spaces. With this new approach, Yale embarked on a new phase of growth in the 1950s under President A. Whitney Griswold. Griswold's enthusiasm for modern architecture was reflected in the commissioning of several landmark structures from distinguished modernist architects. Kahn's Art Gallery, Saarinen's Hockey Rink and Morse and Stiles colleges, Gordon Bunshaft's Beinecke Rare Book Library, Paul Rudolph's Art and Architecture Building and Philip Johnson's Kline Science Centre all led to the creation of an 'architectural laboratory' of styles. The visual unity of the campus was not a motivating concern, each architect being given a free hand. 'Buildings, like people', Griswold reasoned, 'ought to be different from one another.'[36]

This approach has conditioned the campus of the Massachusetts Institute of Technology (MIT) since the Second World War. In the 1940s development began on the West Campus, opposite William Bosworth's neo-classical, Beaux-Arts main complex. Since

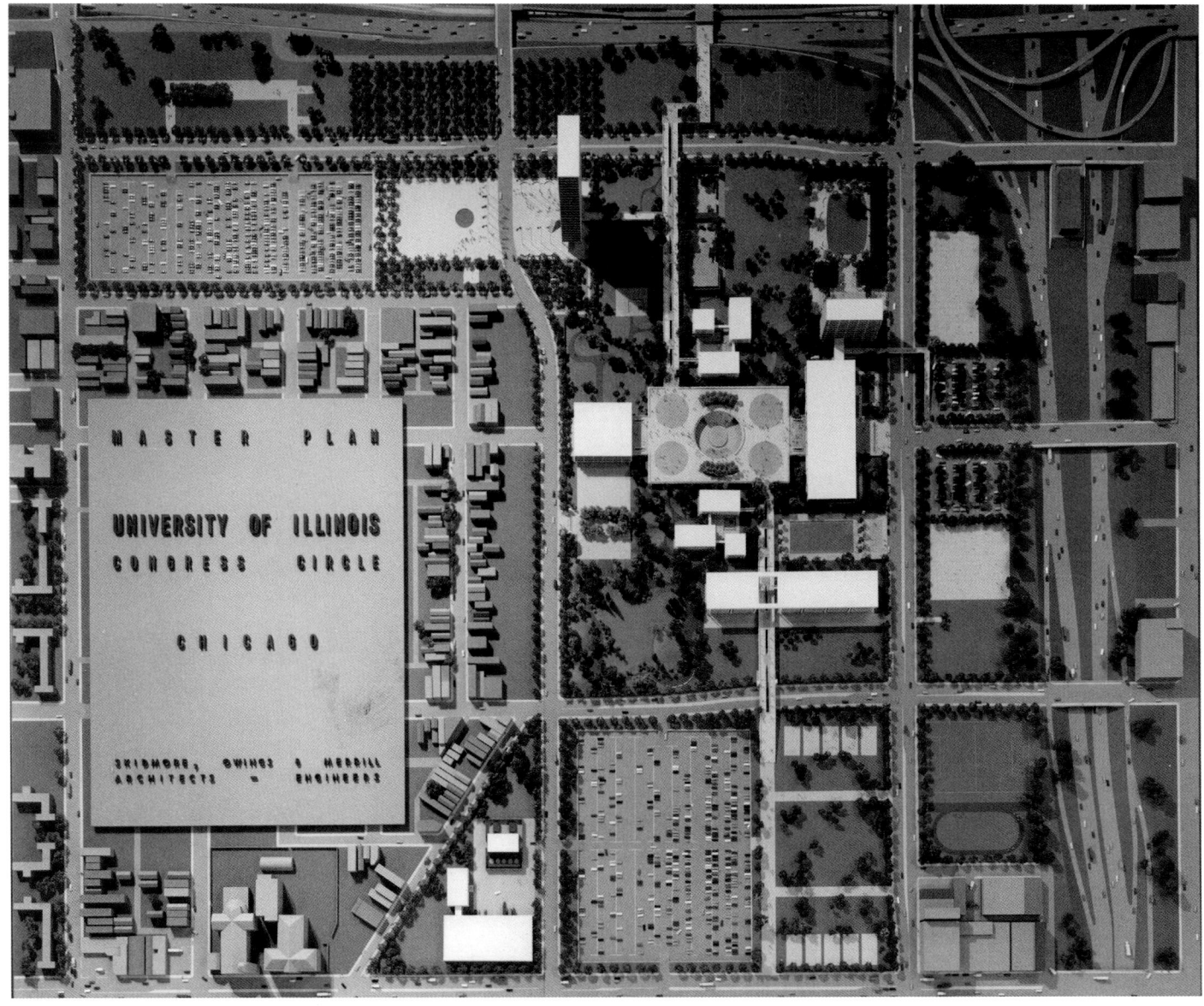

1.39 University of Illinois at Chicago master plan
Photo: University of Illinois at Chicago Archives and Photo Services

that time, the site has continually evolved as an experimental ground of distinctive individual edifices. Eero Saarinen was one of the first architects to leave his imprint upon the campus, in his daring 1950s commissions of a chapel and auditorium. Saarinen's buildings are indicative of MIT's planning approach. The institution classifies this as real-time planning, a strategy that engenders imaginative yet sensitive responses to emerging needs and the cultural moment. The campus has been, however, prey to the pitfalls of forsaking a comprehensive master plan. William Mitchell, Professor of Architecture and Media Arts and Sciences at MIT, observes, MIT building has too frequently degenerated into 'narrowly framed, opportunistic projects that don't contribute to the formation of a larger social and architectural whole'.[37]

New approaches to campus design continued to evolve in the United States. An increasingly influential component was circulation, both pedestrian and vehicular, as ambitiously demonstrated at the Chicago Circle campus of the University of Illinois by architect Walter Netsch (Figure 1.39). Netsch's design featured elevated pedestrian walkways forming an additional layer of traffic above the ground and connecting the outer-lying car parks to the campus core. The core was a network of buildings of different heights, shapes and relationships to one another. Rather than dividing the campus by faculty, Netsch's grand innovation was to organize it instead by functions. All administrative offices were located in a high-rise tower, with classrooms in another building, laboratories in another, and so forth. This system, Netsch argued, was the remedy to the feelings of isolation experienced on a commuter campus. In forcing both professors and students to walk between classrooms, laboratories, and libraries, opportunity for social contact between members of the university would be generated. On its opening in 1965, the

1.40 Kresge College, University of California, Santa Cruz
Photo: Alan Nyri

campus was pronounced as the prototype of twentieth-century America's urban university.

Similar concerns increasingly reverberated through the world of campus planning. At the Indian Institute of Technology in Kanpur, constructed 1959–1966, architect Achyut Kanvinde connected buildings with a system of two-tier pedestrian walkways while vehicular circulation was confined to the campus perimeter to protect the coherence of the campus centre. The plaza and sunken garden at its core reflected Kanvinde's conscious efforts to stimulate cross-disciplinary interaction.

Chicago Circle and the Indian Institute of Technology attest to the importance placed upon fostering community within post-war campuses, particularly in America. In 1957, the State of Californian voted to create three new branches of the state university. The three new campuses at Santa Cruz, San Diego and Irvine were purposed to grow to multi-university proportions of around 27,000 students each. Yet Clark Kerr, president of the state university system, was determined to mitigate the dangers of size by nurturing an atmosphere of collegiate intimacy. 'The big campus,' Kerr reflected,

lacks the inestimable virtue which the small liberal arts college counted as its hallmark: the emphasis on the individual which small classes, a residential environment and a strong sense of relationship to others and the campus can and do give. Each of the university's new campuses is an experiment in combining the advantages of the large and the small.[38]

The most complete, most sophisticated realization of Kerr's educational axiom were the plans for the Santa Cruz campus (1961). Santa Cruz represented a new phenomenon in campus planning, that of the 'whole cloth' campus. Rather than emerging in piecemeal fashion, demand required that large proportions had to be constructed at once. This sudden appearance of almost entire new campuses characterized by unity and totality was a post-war development that transformed the guise of higher education in the United States, United Kingdom and Germany. Santa Cruz's objective was that of a bucolic college idyll, with students and their professors living and studying communally, reminiscent of Jefferson's academical village. Activities were concentrated in a series of colleges, where students were to live, dine and receive some teaching. One of its constituent

1.41 University of Sussex
Photo: Keith Paulin

colleges, Kresge, was amongst the most renowned campus designs of the decade (Figure 1.40). The idea that the college should be a community was translated into a physical setting by architects William Turnbull and Charles W. Moore, by interpreting the school as a compact Italian hill town. Dormitories, classrooms, and dining halls, opened out onto a snaking street, cultivating the desired sense of intimacy, while plazas created communal spaces for socializing.[39]

Kresge College represents the peak of the alignment of educational reform with the new social and architectural momentum of 1960s California. This phenomenon was not isolated to America alone though. In post-war Britain, changes in educational thinking gradually came to surface in the closeted world of higher education, and developing a fitting architectural image for this new thinking came to be one of the chief priorities of late 1950s and 1960s modernism.

While the university system of America was both extensive and convoluted, the English system was small and firmly hierarchical, headed by Oxford and Cambridge, and followed by 'the rest'. After the foundation of Oxford and Cambridge in the twelfth and thirteenth centuries, no new universities were chartered in England until University College London in 1826 followed by the wave of Redbricks later in the century. In post-war Britain, however, change was in the air. The 1960s saw the development of the third generation of English university institutions, the New Universities. The decade saw the greatest growth in the history of university education in Britain. The number of universities doubled from 22 to 46, and the student population rose from 108,000 in 1960 to 228,000 in 1970. The term New University was applied to the universities of Sussex (1961), York (1963), East Anglia (1963), Lancaster (1964), Essex (1964/5), Warwick (1965) and Kent (1965). Their foundations necessitated a construction surge which has been likened to the great period of cathedral building in the twelfth century.[40]

University building served a leading role in the advancement of British architecture in these years. Built on greenfield sites, free from the constraints of urban surroundings, the New Universities demanded a different approach to conventional British university design. They generated a spirit of adventure amongst educationalists and architectural circles alike, attracting the interest of the country's leading architects. As instances of 'whole cloth' campuses, they presented architects with unparalleled opportunities to experiment with advanced theories of planning and design, driven by a search for

1.42 Ruhr University at Bochum
Photo: Ruhr-Universität Bochum, Press and PR Office

the best solution to realize the new priorities of higher education. At Sussex, Basil Spence used the principle of the court as its underpinning feature (Figure 1.41). He idealized the 'interlocking courtyards' and the 'colonnades where friends can walk and talk' of Oxford and Cambridge; nurturing a sense of community was a priority for him from the outset. He contended that the 'undergraduate is still an adolescent' who seeks 'confidence and protection from buildings'. The concept that the university should be the ideal community in microcosm was as relevant in post-war Britain as it was across the Atlantic. At the University of East Anglia, the search for the ideal community afforded a different response. Denys Lasdun, appointed in 1962 as planner and architect of the greenfield campus, conceived the solution to be a large central complex consisting of long, irregular, single teaching blocks, or 'Teaching Wall', housing almost all teaching and research functions. It was a dramatic departure from the twentieth-century pattern of individual units planted across the campus. From its spine of teaching accommodation budded wings of stepped residences connected to the Teaching Wall via walkway platforms. The residence blocks, or Ziggurats, borrow the Oxbridge device of a staircase surrounded on each floor by a set of rooms, with communal kitchen at the centre. In so doing, Lasdun and Vice Chancellor Frank Thistlethwaite sought to create small 'communities'. Lasdun's aim was a group of university buildings which would grow organically, harmonizing 'buildings and landscape…in a total vision…visually as well as functionally'.[41]

The same themes evinced in the formation of the New University campuses were also evinced, albeit to a lesser degree, in Germany. The historic universities of continental Europe had for centuries been characterized by their concentrated presence in central urban spaces as a single large and imposing building. Residences were not provided. By the mid-twentieth century, these institutions may have possessed a large, purpose-built centrepiece building but their activities were typically scattered across an assortment of separate sites. They lacked the campus or collegiate environment of the Anglo-American institutions, and their institutional presence was derived more from the scholars and teachers than from their physicality. Yet, in post-war Germany some select examples brought university architecture dramatically to the fore.

After the wane of the German universities under the Nationalist Socialist German Workers' Party in the 1930s, 1945 marked a period of renewal in higher education. Initially, rebuilding was compelled by quantity rather than quality. At many universities, modern campuses for the sciences were built in town outskirts, as in Tübingen and Heidelberg, proffering improved facilities and comfort but uninspiring

1.43 Morse and Stiles Colleges, Yale University
Photo: Michael Marsland/Yale University

design. In the late 1960s, a rather grim standardization evolved, and the stacked block, roughly 120 metres (400ft) long and 12 or so storeys tall, came to dominate. Between 1970 and 1971, 91 of these were erected. Their 'frightening monotony' was quickly lamented in the architectural journals.[42]

Several high-profile new universities, however, countered this stagnation. One such example was the Ruhr University at Bochum (Figure 1.42). Hentrich Petschnigg and Partner of Düsseldorf completed plans in 1963, and building commenced early in the following year. The 'whole-cloth' campus derived its plan from the same concerns witnessed in the United Kingdom and United States, namely those of community, totality and harnessing nature to promote well-being. It was placed on a substantial site of over 1,330 acres, on the edge of the picturesque Ruhr valley. This scenic backdrop was, founders asserted, a means of offsetting the downtrodden image of the industrial region. Like Lasdun at East Anglia, planners resolved to cluster the main buildings in a relatively high density area leaving the remaining land open. The design consisted of 13 almost indistinguishable 12-storey towers, set in two parallel rows enclosing the central communal buildings. Containing the library, arts centre, administrative offices and the *Auditorium Maximum*, surrounded by the agora, the central area was intended as 'the market place where the meeting of *magistrorum et scolarum* can take place'. Bochum was conceived as the ideal German campus. It possessed a totality of conception and a textbook application of educational philosophy. Yet, Bochum deviated from the Anglo-American model in its decision to locate the residences and many of the recreational facilities away from the campus proper. A compact town complex, today known as the 'Unicenter', was built immediately north of the campus to house shops, a market and cafes. This choice ultimately affected how the campus was used, to a deleterious end. The highlight of the campus, the central forum, was sadly underused. The university came under severe criticism. Berlin's architectural journal, the *Bauwelt*, castigated its colossal size and monotony as damaging to wellbeing. Greeted with little but criticism, it has largely been forgotten by architectural histories.[43]

To shift the scene to contemporary America, fashions in campus planning were again in transition. Although by the 1960s Modernism had prevailed in the battle of architectural style on the American campus, a handful of architects began to look with interest at the traditions of university planning. The forerunner of these was Eero Saarinen, in his design for Morse and Stiles Colleges at Yale (1960–1962) (Figure 1.43). The two undergraduate colleges were organized on an irregular layout that produced a series of semi-courts of rough

1.44 Lewis Thomas Laboratory, Princeton University
Photo: Venturi, Scott Brown and Associates, Inc

1.45 Williams College
Photo: Courtesy of the Williams College Museum of Art/Michael Lavin Flower

stone and concrete walls. Sets of 12 individually-shaped rooms were arranged around staircases, emulating the Oxbridge model. There is nothing explicitly medieval in style about these buildings, yet it is clear that Saarinen took inspiration from the university's Gothic past. Yale president, A. Whitney Griswold, later reminisced,

> I urged Eero to go to Oxford and look at the walls, particularly the rubble ones. In my imagination they had a quality that was close to that of surrounding Yale buildings, such as the gym… He felt that he could produce an atmosphere akin to that of the existing colleges using the elements of the building itself – courts, walls, towers, rather than the superficial decoration.[44]

Saarinen's prominent commission brought the neo-traditional approach to general attention, raising a storm of polemic amidst architectural circles. One critic wrote that its picturesqueness 'disgusted me'.[45] Yet despite Morse and Stiles' extensive condemnation, Saarinen's application of historical tradition gradually pervaded academic architecture. Institutions across the country discovered a reawakened desire to harmonize new building with old. Attributes of earlier buildings were applied to new projects. At Stanford University, all new construction was unified by the red-tile roofs of the original quadrangles. The original Collegiate Gothic buildings of Washington University in St Louis were echoed in the silhouette of a new complex, designed in 1966.[46] Thus universities entered another phase of development, one conditioned foremost by aesthetics and a revival of the American campus tradition. For the rest of the century, and indeed into the present, the chronology of worldwide university design was defined not by innovations in planning but by fashions in architecture.

POST-MODERNISM AND THE STARCHITECTS

By the 1980s, fashion had turned to the past and historicist roots were firmly embraced within the architectural genre. The restoration of open space, human scale and order once again became concerns of campus architects and planners, and, as the focus of attention remained on historicism, historical stylistic forms were applied to new structures. This idiom was known as postmodernism. The term was applied to a wide spectrum of architecture whose designers rejected the unforgiving starkness and absence of contextual resonance

1.46 Simmons Hall, MIT
Photo: B.O'Kane/Alamy

that had come to characterize modern architecture by the 1970s. More specifically, the label designated a creative manipulation of motifs and references from the past into contemporary architectural vocabulary.

The architect Robert Venturi is often heralded as one of the most influential proponents of postmodernism, both within the university sector and the design world at large. Venturi, Scott Brown & Associates' 1993 design for Princeton's George LaVie Schultz Laboratory is a homage to the Collegiate Gothic that characterizes much of the campus (Figure 1.44). The window glass is divided into panes, evocative of leaded mullions. The single, dominating limestone column that is cut into the façade at the doorway recalls the tradition of ceremonial entrances. Amongst the innovators of postmodernism, Venturi was joined by Charles Moore. His predilection for whimsy is well displayed in the 1983 extension to the Williams College Museum of Art building. The extension is noted for its 'Ironic' columns, Ionic columns in which the capital is detached from the cylinder by a foot of empty space, thus in fact providing no structural support to the cantilevered offices that they appear to carry (Figure 1.45).[47]

Postmodernism dominated campus design for nearly two decades. The 'free-for-all' of the post-war years was tempered by plans that proposed rational organization of space and human-scale buildings. The movement was exemplified by Michael Dennis's plan and architectural designs for Carnegie Mellon University (1987). Organizing elements were applied on the northern half of the campus, including an east–west pedestrian street and two quadrangles, giving definition to a loosely arranged area of the site.[48]

The rise of post-modern architecture engendered the appearance of the star architect and the iconic building. Wren's Sheldonian Theatre at Oxford, Lloyd Wright's Florida Southern College and Saarinen's Kresge Auditorium and Chapel at MIT have all become icons, but were not originally conceived or immediately recognized to function as such. Yet with the proliferation of the mass media, buildings have become celebrities in themselves. Following the opening of Frank Gehry's Guggenheim Museum in Bilbao in 1997, iconic architecture has swept all before it. The building mesmerized audiences, immediately vaulted the city to prominence and revived its economic fortunes. Consequently, iconic architecture has since been equated with successful branding. Universities have not been immune to the captivating potential of world-famous signature architecture; indeed, the prime trend in campus development in the past two decades is that of the iconic building. Curves, jagged contours, blobs, bulges, hi-tech materials and vivid colours

1.47 Stata Centre, MIT
Photo: Jorge Salcedo

1.48 Arizona State University
Photo: Courtesy SkySong, the ASU Scottsdale Innovation Centre/Michael Norton

materialized on campuses as higher education institutions the world across entered into an arms race to erect the idols of the architecture world.

MIT is an exaggerated exemplar of this trend, having inaugurated a billion-dollar building programme in the 1990s to transform its campus into an architectural showpiece by hiring a series of adventurously innovative architects. Steven Holl's Simmons Hall opened in 2002 (Figure 1.46). A radical experiment in dormitory form, the building employs the metaphor of a sponge that interplays with an anodized aluminium grid of windows. Frank Gehry's laboratory complex, the Stata Center, opened two years later to a sensational reception (Figure 1.47). The eccentric building appears as though it may collapse at any moment as walls stagger and collide at angles and curves, while materials change from brick to steel to brushed aluminium to bright paint to corrugated metal. Norman Foster is another architect active on university campuses whose name is synonymous with landmark buildings. Characterized by straightforward plans, exposed structural frames and crisp mixtures of glass and metal, Foster's structures appear at the Free University Berlin, University of Cambridge, Imperial College London, Stanford University, University of Toronto and University of Technology Petronas.

The landmark building has become associated with a cachet that appeals to the modern university leader. The iconic landmark has the potential to not only generate headlines but, if successful, to incite awe and reverence. Whether Rem Koolhaas's Educatorium at Utrecht University (1997) or Pei Cobb Freed & Partners' SkySong at Arizona State University (in progress) (Figure 1.48) will achieve the same reverence as the Sheldonian Theatre or Nassau Hall, only time will tell. Yet, as headline-grabbing buildings, they court publicity and brand their universities as cutting-edge institutions; as competition for the best students becomes increasingly fierce, this holds much appeal to educationalists. New and less academically renowned universities often turn to contemporary architecture to place themselves on the map, such as the library at the University of the Sunshine Coast, which was founded in 1994 in Queensland, Australia.

Iconic architecture and its celebrity practitioners are, however, currently the victims of something of a backlash.[49] The 'sugar-rush' appetite for icons has come under criticism for its commercialism, while the buildings themselves are often bemoaned as vacuous, impractical and perniciously expensive. In such a climate, it will be interesting to see if this trend continues or if a revival of traditional campus design methods supersedes it.

1.49 University of Oxford skyline
Photo: Photolibrary Ltd

SUMMATION

Over the course of nearly a millennium, university design has rendered form and meaning to the built environment of higher education. Each era has had their own unique interpretation of this task, and today the result is a rich tapestry of architecture, landscape, ambiance and identity. A study of the chronology of university development provides a series of defining moments as institutions have responded to changes in teaching, research, social ideologies and mobility, and fashions. The inauguration of the quadrangle, enclosed on four sides by ranges of buildings, that was first seen at Oxford and quickly assumed at Cambridge, was the first of these pivotal episodes. It spurred a torrent of imitations and mutations the world over from its initial conception to the present day. The second episode was that of the creation of the colonial colleges, which rejected the cloistered English colleges for open arrangements that would exert a tremendous impact upon the American campus tradition. The nineteenth century witnessed a succession of important developments in the appearance and plan of the university. European higher education flourished as vast, monolithic buildings were constructed in a profusion of historical styles. Architects appropriated the language of different countries and past ages, to imbue their new structures with symbolic resonance. In America, in the early years of the century, Thomas Jefferson pioneered a momentous design, advocating an axial arrangement of structures that embodied his academic philosophy. In the mid-century, Frederick Law Olmsted introduced to the American campus a new approach predicated upon loose groupings of buildings in park-like settings. The last years of the century saw the rise of the Beaux-Arts movement, which countered the picturesque informality of Olmsted's philosophy with axial plans dominated by focal points, followed by the rise of the Gothic Revival. The latter saw an adoption of the Oxbridge typology of a medieval vocabulary, followed by its spatial patterns of cloistered quadrangles, colleges and introspection.

The next development was the advent of Modernism in the mid-twentieth century, which pioneered new stylistic idioms and the rejection of the master plan. From the 1960s, the field of campus design was transformed by the preponderance of the 'whole-cloth' campuses which afforded greater totality of vision than had been previously possible. Finally, from the 1970s onwards, the overall trend in university development elicited a preoccupation not with experimental planning, but with experimental architectural styles, resulting first in postmodernism and then the iconic building. This chapter has limited its focus to campuses in the countries of origin of these trends, yet these episodes in planning and architecture have been adopted and translated the world across.

Changing fashions are undoubtedly a comprehensive factor in this evolution of university design. As Ludwig Mies van der Rohe declared in the 1920s, 'building art is the spatially apprehended will of the epoch'. Yet, through this trajectory of development, the same themes and concerns reoccur time and again. Notions of community, totality and the ameliorating potential of nature have been potent forces as educationalists and architects sought out the best solutions to meet the demands of higher education. Moreover, universities have consistently harnessed the expressive capacity of architecture as an outward symbol. 'Education,' Martin Pearce suggests, 'is an invisible substance; architecture allows it to become material.'[50] The tenet that academic philosophy can be conveyed through built form is central, and, as this brief survey illustrates, this can manifest itself in multifarious guises. The search for aesthetically inspiring yet practical surroundings for higher education has afforded a wealth of magnificent buildings and, on occasions, extraordinary opportunities for experimentation as visionary practitioners have been drawn to the field of university design by the atmosphere of innovation fostered by academic idealism. Given the freedom to explore new technologies and only the boundaries of the imagination to restrain, the future of campus design is one to behold with anticipation and expectation.

CHAPTER TWO
Case Studies

2.1 Plan, Aarhus University

Aarhus University
Aarhus, Denmark

Aarhus University is unique within the canon of university design. Its alliance with a single architectural firm, C. F. Møller, sustained through nearly eight decades, has produced a campus overwhelming in the homogeneity of its architecture and planning. Its ensemble of lecture theatres, classrooms, laboratories, offices and libraries is compellingly pulled together by the dogged application of a single architectonic vision, creating a village of simple, rectangular yellow brick buildings capped with yellow tile roofs within a parkland setting (Figure 2.2). Founded in 1928, Aarhus University was intended from the outset to be different from Denmark's only other university, Copenhagen. The University of Copenhagen was representative of the historic universities of continental Europe. Non-residential,

2.2 Aerial view, Aarhus University
Photo: Jan Kofod Winther

2.3 Textured brickwork, Aarhus University
Photo: Poul Ib Henriksen

its premises were scattered throughout the city. In contrast, Aarhus University sought to define itself by offering teaching, social life and accommodation upon one site; in other words, by developing upon the Anglo-American campus model. In 1929, Aarhus City Council donated a 27-acre site to the university, and a competition was launched to plan the campus and design its first buildings.

The competition was won in 1931 by the triumvirate of architects C. F. Møller, Kay Fisker and Povl Stegmann alongside landscape architect C. Th. Sørensen. Their proposal fused modernist planning with a park-like setting. Displaying enormous sensitivity to the natural beauty of the rolling terrain, their plan shied away from any traditional institutional monumentality in favour of a dispersed layout of independent buildings determined in height and area by their function. The design evinced the popularity of the Bauhaus School, and was particularly influenced by a school in Bernau near Berlin recently completed by Hannes Meyer, director of the Bauhaus School. The school's buildings sensitively interacted with its undulating site through horizontal and vertical displacements, a method which was to be important at Aarhus. The Bauhaus aesthetic heavily informed Møller, Fisker and Stegmann's 1931 design. Cubistic blocks with flat copper roofs, horizontal window strips and smooth white façades characterized its buildings. The buildings as realized, however, were somewhat different.[1]

The university was almost entirely dependent on private donations, which had a profound effect upon the physical form the campus was to assume. A gift of yellow bricks from a local manufacturer induced a change from the concrete, copper-roof Bauhaus style utilized in the competition entry to a language of yellow brick and yellow tile buildings. The first building, housing the chemistry and physics institutes, was completed in 1933. Simple, almost austere in external appearance, it utilized the donated yellow brick for its walls and had a saddle roof pitched at 30 degrees clad with yellow tiles. The strained economy of the 1930s is palpable in its form, yet its fabric is by no means meagre. Its modest, unornamented profile reflects the development of a Danish functionalist style, which the campus came to epitomize. Its modernist leaning is manifested in its angularity – almost severity – while its simplicity and brick construction reveal empathy for Danish building and form. The first building was followed by residence halls (six were built up to 1947) and five professors' houses (razed 1970) identical to it in their materials, colouring and clean uninterrupted profiles.[2]

The style of these buildings was greeted with cynicism by some members of the University Union, familiar only with the ideals of classicism, and when plans began to be formulated for a main building in 1937 the Building Committee demanded greater monumentality. By this time, the Møller-Fisker-Stegmann partnership had formally dissolved and Møller undertook its design alone. The Main Building, as completed in 1946, was indeed infused with a subtle grandeur. Its simple yellow brick and yellow tile fabric was embellished by brick patterning which texturized the building's gables that projected northwards to form the university's principal entrance (Figure 2.3). The free-standing arcade which linked them provided a romantic gesture. Wave-length patterning of yellow tiles covered the floor and ceiling of the Vandrehallen inside. Such features invested the Main Building with a levity that contrasted with the austerity of the first building. The most handsome, eye-catching element of the building is the main hall, the Aula. A vast, theatrical space reminiscent of Danish ecclesiastical architecture in its shape, its southern façade is one large glass expanse stretching right up to the gable (Figure 2.4). This was a bold use of glass at the time, and it offered a magnificent vista across the rolling grounds. Its dramatic image was immediately adopted as the visual symbol of the university. From the retaining wall of the building curves a mini, open-air amphitheatre whose steps meld into the natural slope of the land.

The fluid integration of architecture and landscape is fundamental to the design of Aarhus's campus. As soon as construction commenced on the first building, the landscaping began, led by Sørenson. Sørenson's vision was one of a tree-clad park populated by oaks alone. He planted individual acorns across the site, which have matured into a magnificent tree canopy and created a simple yet affecting setting for the institution. His monomania for acorns was not necessarily popular at the time, but it provided a fitting counterpart

2.4 Aula and amphitheatre, Aarhus University
Photo: Torben Ekserod

to the homogeneity of the architectural palette and moreover had symbolic, practical and economic advantages. Oaks were safe to grow near buildings, and, in the straitened years of the Depression, planting acorns was a prudent option. Furthermore, the promise encapsulated within the acorns to flourish into mighty oaks seems analogous with the ambitions held for the university itself. Sørenson's sole digression from oak was the climbing ivy that ascends the walls of many of the buildings. A distinctive feature of the campus, the ivy softens the angularity of the structures and its vivid show of green, red or brown leaves changing in rhythm with the seasons enlivens the yellow walls.

The ivy is testament to the marriage between artifice and nature that was engineered from the campus's earliest days. The buildings, perfectly attuned to their topography, appear to grow organically from the ground. The result is, as Møller christened it, a 'park university'. The university is set in rolling moraine, bisected along its north–south length by a brook dammed into two artificial lakes. The plan preserved this ravine, pushing buildings to the campus edge and creating a pastoral hollow at its centre. The buildings were orientated perpendicularly either north–south or east–west, organized loosely in clearings in linear groups of varying heights, lengths and breadths. This variance allowed for a degree of individuality for each separate institute within the unbending formula of yellow brick, yellow tile and identical roof profile.[3]

In the 1960s, Denmark's growing prosperity led to a corresponding growth in higher education, a phenomenon which was reflected in Aarhus's building activities. The decade saw the erection of an administration complex (1964) and library (1963) at the northern periphery of the park, both adopting the planning and stylistic format that had characterized the campus for the past three decades. The area of the campus expanded in stages as additional land abutting the park was purchased. Vacated military barracks were acquired and razed in the 1960s, extending the estate westwards. The science buildings that were erected upon the site evidenced the effect of increasing pressure for space upon the physical environment. Whilst adhering to the architectonic blueprint, the complex was organized so densely that its interior has been likened to a labyrinth and the vision of a 'park campus' was lost.[4]

Predominantly, however, the university's expansion has not compromised Møller's original concept. Quality of design and

2.5 View towards Aula, Aarhus University
Photo: Torben Ekserod

craftsmanship has largely been upheld to high standards, a feat that has proved achievable because of the restraint and cost-efficiency of the original vision. Despite the changing tides of architectural fashions over its 80-year history, the buildings form a unified entity with only minor modifications in building style. Vital to this has been the retention of the C. F. Møller practice, from the 1930s to the present day. The development guidelines that were prepared by the practice for the campus in 1988 outlined its future in broadly identical terms to those used by Møller half a century earlier. Buildings, it counselled, should 'grow directly out of the ground', and take the form of staggered blocks with gables. Functions requiring large spaces, such as lecture theatres, should be accommodated in one-storey blocks laid out perpendicular to taller buildings. Exteriors should remain clean in their profile, devoid of extraneous detail such as cornices or architraves. Yellow brick and tile remained the material of choice. Comparison between the 1946 Main Building and the park's most recent addition, a 2001 auditorium complex, reveals the degree to which Møller's concept has been upheld. Yellow bricks and tiles characterize its exterior. On its northern façade, one gable wall is pierced by a great wall of glass, in perfect dialogue with the south face of the Aula across the parkland (Figure 2.5).

Employing the architectural language of the oldest buildings for contemporary ones could have anachronistic results. But this has not been the case at Aarhus. The simplicity of organization and design, the nuances of regional and national traditions and the subjugation of the built environment to the natural has lent a timelessness to the campus. The rigid formality of the built environment has invested Aarhus with an exceptionally strong design identity, but it has its drawbacks. The plan offers no room for change. Thus the blocks of the auditorium complex adopted the long rectangular shape of other campus buildings despite the format being impractical in terms of acoustics.[5]

Young climbing ivy has begun to take root on the auditoria's exterior in the pattern of many of the university's older buildings, which will in time strengthen the interaction between the structure and its landscape. Both C. F. Møller's 1988 guidelines and 2001 master plan for the campus valued the importance of retaining the original landscape programme. The 'banalization' of the grounds with flower beds was cautioned against, for example, so that the campus retains its oak-park atmosphere. A key ingredient to this is that the campus has not yielded to the motorcar. Small car parks are scattered around the periphery, but cyclists and pedestrians have priority. Departments are connected by undulating pathways which weave through the park to take best advantage of vistas of buildings and nature. Used by university members and the public alike, the park constitutes a key green space of the city at large. Its public nature is made clear by the absence of fences or walls defining its boundary. Wayfinding on the campus is, however, problematic. The uniformity of the buildings hinders orientation, while there are few maps to alleviate this. Each building is, though, clearly labelled with white lettering, a feature of the original buildings enforced by recent preservation frameworks.

To preserve the parkland quality of the campus, it is unlikely any further standalone buildings will be erected there. Instead the university is catering for its growth by expanding its premises outside the park, both on land immediately adjacent and on satellite campuses. Between 1979 and 2001, the university increased its footprint by 75 per cent. Neighbouring former military barracks have housed the Aesthetics Department since 1998, and in 2000 the Theology Department moved into an orthopaedic hospital building, built in the 1940s, next to the administration building. From 1999 humanities were relocated into a new sub-campus, called the Nobel Park, opposite the park, which combines university and private commerce buildings (Figure 2.6). Although the opus of the C. F. Møller practice, the Nobel Park contrasts with the piquant identity of the yellow village in the main park. The height of the buildings and their compact layout evidences an urban density at variance with the park campus. Notwithstanding its 'park' appellation, tarmac and cars have replaced the sylvan aesthetic of its parent campus. It likewise employs a different architectonic aesthetic. Instead of yellow, pitched-roofed buildings, those at the Nobel Park are cuboid, red brick, flat-roofed structures linked by glass stairwells. While the main campus employs strict angularity and consistent materials, it avoids insipidity through its commune with nature and variety in height and distribution of blocks. At the Nobel Park, there is no such divergence, resulting in an insentience contrasting with the older site.[6]

The main campus possesses an individualism which is difficult to replicate. Its understated yet noble architecture and rigid yet organic homogeneity have created a unique campus that is laudable for its consideration to landscape and Danish traditions and the diligence with which its original master plan has been heeded.

2.6 Nobel Park, Aarhus University
Photo: Søren Kjeldgaard/AU-photo

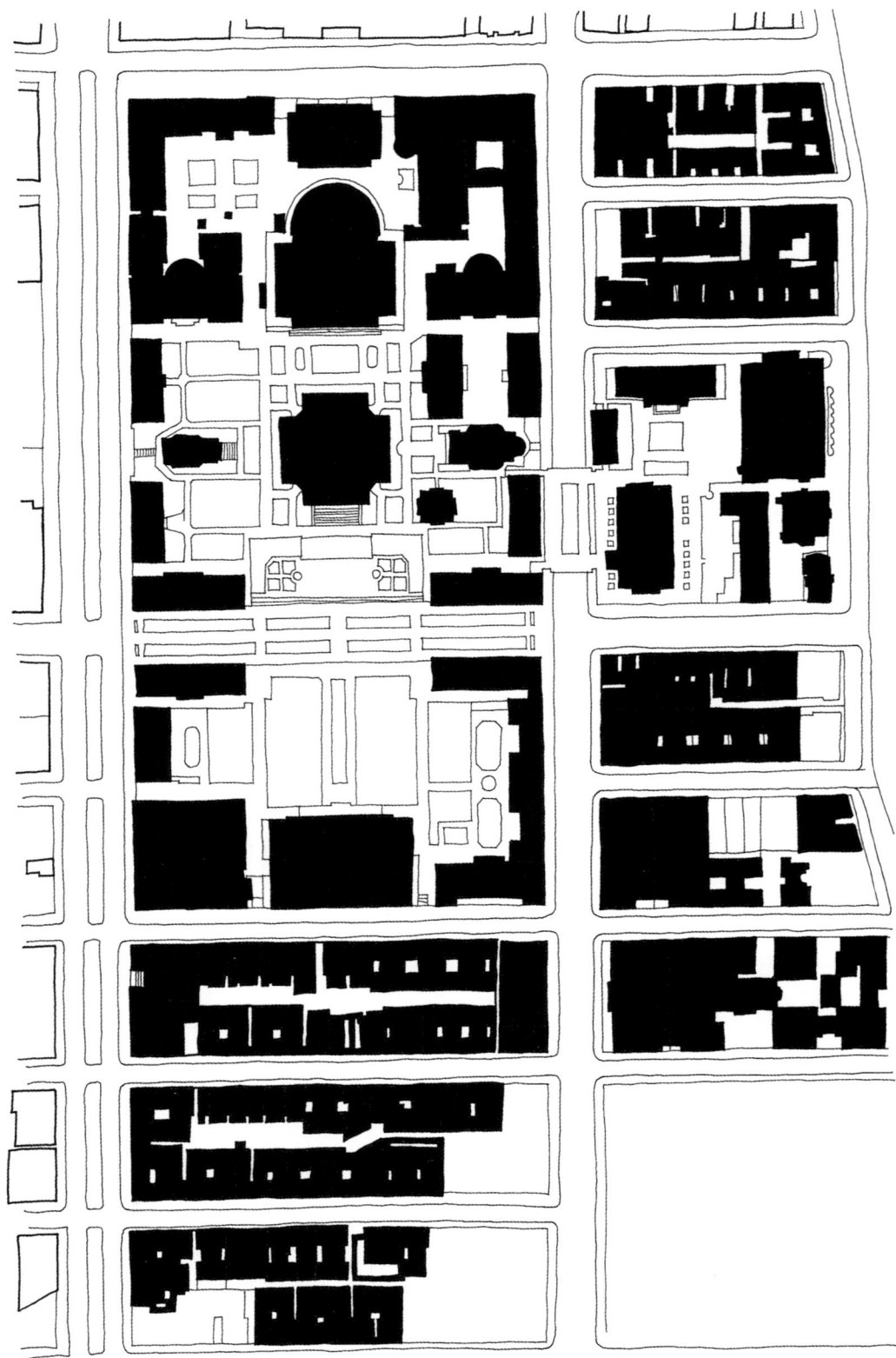

2.7 Plan, Columbia University

Columbia University
New York, USA

Beginning with a schoolhouse on what is now lower Broadway in Manhattan, Columbia University has occupied a string of locations in New York City since its foundation in 1754. After outgrowing the Midtown location to which it relocated in 1857, the university purchased its present site in Morningside Heights in 1892. Today the central campus covers 32 acres, divided broadly into three areas: the Upper Quadrangle, from 116th to 120th Streets; the South Quadrangle, extending south from 116th to 114th Streets; and the East Campus, bounded by Amsterdam Avenue, Morningside Drive and 116th and 117th Streets. When it was acquired the 17-acre plot was a wide rectangle sited in urbanizing open country from 116th to 120th Streets, today it is in all respects an urban campus integrated with the structure of the city. Although more spacious than its earlier locations, the property was considerably smaller than many other colleges, necessitating a compact, adroit use of space. Furthermore, the area was one of uneven topography, and the new campus was set on a rocky plateau that fell steeply five metres at 119th Street. Despite these demands, the college's trustees, led by President Seth Low, had ambitious plans for the site. It was intended to establish Columbia as an influential educational presence, as well as ensure that it was not surpassed in grandeur by its rival New York University, whose new complex was then being planned.

Architect Charles McKim was appointed in 1893 to shape Columbia's new campus. His firm was increasingly being viewed as the leading protagonist of the rising Beaux-Arts movement. The movement's principles of axial organization, grand scales, and formal civic spaces, tallied with the university's high pretensions, and in 1894 McKim delivered Columbia with an impressive Beaux-Arts scheme, formal yet adventurous, that deftly responded to the demands of the site (Figure 1.19). Its hilly topography prompted a plan of an elevated campus set upon two separate platforms. Principal academic buildings were to be placed on the higher south terrace and orientated to the south towards central Manhattan, to provide maximum sun exposure. The buildings were grouped around a series of intimate courts, creating a complex enclosed on three sides and open to the south through a large entrance piazza, from which rose a flight of granite steps to the crescendo of the composition, the monumental Low Library (1897) (Figure 1.20). The building is the campus's most dominant feature. Assuming a Greek cross

2.8 Earl Hall, Columbia University

ground plan and capped by a low dome, it was raised above the rest of the campus upon a tall base. An august portico of ten fluted Ionic columns marked its entrance. Numerous illustrious sources have been proposed for its design, such as the Pantheon, Baths of Caracalla, the Rotunda at the University of Virginia, the Library of Congress, and the Administration Building at the Chicago World's

2.9 Havemeyer Hall, Columbia University

Fair of 1893. To cultivate associations with these distinguished, well-known monuments would have summoned specifically the qualities of intellectual ancestry, civic-mindedness and high-thinking that the institution desired to communicate. The Low Library formed the centre of an east–west axis, accommodating St Paul's Chapel and Earl Hall (assembly hall) (Figure 2.8), and a corresponding south–north axis, leading north from the plaza to the (never-realized) University Hall. The 15 buildings that were planned to surround the library were envisioned as a harmonious grouping organized around an architectural hierarchy. The secondary structures – Chapel, Earl Hall and University Hall – were all given individualized treatments with the former two designed with colonnades stretching across their façade to co-ordinate with the façade of the Low Library. Anchoring the south-east and south-west corners of the site, Dodge and Kent Halls were the two most conspicuous teaching buildings. Their siting meant they were visible from the flanking north–south public roads and, when viewed from 116th Street to the south, they appeared to flank the library. To reflect this important position, Dodge and Kent Halls were distinguished by a two-storey colonnade on their 116th Street façades to create the illusion from the south that the library's parade of columns extended the width of the campus. The remainder of the teaching buildings – Fayerweather, Havemeyer (Figure 2.9), Schermerhorn, Mathematics, Lewisohn and Philosophy Halls – were less detailed buildings, although their exterior, street-facing elevations had high granite bases that enforced the effect of an enclosed complex (Figure 2.10).[7]

To McKim, the university's urban disposition suggested itself naturally to 'pure Classic forms…embodying the principles of the early Renaissance masters'; to the trustees, what mattered was that the style was functional and tractable enough to adapt to various building types; one that many architects were proficient in to allow for the development of the campus over time; and, most crucially, one that appealed 'most strongly to the taste and judgment of the educated public' whilst being 'appropriate to the municipal character of the situation'. Unequivocally, the classical language of architecture was deemed the most becoming choice to meet the demands and aspirations of the new campus and in succeeding years McKim, Mead & White designed for it a range of buildings dressed in the robes

2.10 Columbia University

of Antiquity and the Italian Renaissance. Surrounding the Greek temple-like library, classrooms are housed in red brick buildings with white limestone trim and Renaissance-inspired rectilinear massing, symmetry, quoins, pediments, and rustication. McKim's monumental ensemble of buildings not only epitomized the classical fashion of the day, but its broad historical and contemporary associations were designed to carry an image of Columbia as cultivated, progressive and publicly-minded.[8]

McKim's Columbia was one of the first successful manifestations of Beaux-Arts campus planning, creating a bold vision for what an urban American college ought to look like. The use of axes and unique architectural style has shaped Upper Quadrangle, yet the plan was never wholly completed. The 1894 plan intended the vertical axis to be terminated by a stately neo-classical student centre, University Hall, but its erection was stalled until the site was filled by the unpopular Uris Hall in the 1960s. In his plan, McKim incorporated small, intimate courtyards surrounded by classroom buildings, but only one such courtyard was ever realized, the St Paul's Chapel – Avery – Schermerhorn – Fayerweather quad. Its counterparts remained unrealized, as, largely due to budgetary constraints, the three structures needed to enclose them were never built. Over the years, the vacant spaces intended as courts have come to be treasured as rare open space within the metropolis.

In 1903 the university purchased a nine-acre site south of Upper Quadrangle, referred to variously as South Field, South Lawn or South Quadrangle. The university again turned to McKim to prepare its master plan. The plot was envisaged as a physical extension of the original campus, replicating its planning and architectural modes and organized around two quadrangles. The plan was never completed as such, and it exists today as a wide green lawn framed by buildings aligned along the street boundary. Building began along the eastern perimeter with Hartley and Livingstone (now Wallach) Halls (1905), the university's first dormitories. These continued the red brick and limestone Renaissance-hybrid aesthetic of Upper Campus. They were joined on South Field by Hamilton Hall (1907) and Journalism Hall (1913), and later in 1934 by the vast Butler Library (Figure 2.11). The Low Library's interior quickly proved impracticable, and by the 1920s its cramped conditions had become unworkable. James Gamble

2.11 Butler Library, Columbia University

Rogers designed its replacement in 1931. Located directly opposite its predecessor across a lawned forecourt, the enormous Butler Library continued the campus's brick and limestone vocabulary in a Classical Revival design. Its long colonnaded façade, terminating in unfortunately dumpy brick pavilions, is largely held to lack the grace and authority of the Low Library.[9]

After the completion of Butler Library, the driving vision of a unified, inspiring environment faded, and the 1950s and 1960s saw the erection of utilitarian buildings stylistically incongruent to their setting, heedless of the impact of their scale and shapes and insipid in design. To many, Mudd Hall (1961) on the north-east corner of Upper Campus singularly symbolized this deterioration. Voorhees, Walter, Smith & Smith designed it as an ascetic, plain box that made no concessions to the buildings around it. On the east campus, which had been purchased from 1910–1914, Harrison and Abramavitz designed the new Law School (1961). Again starkly alienated from the red brick and limestone classicism of the earlier buildings, the Law School has an exterior of vertical glass panels divided by vertical concrete louvers. A barren concrete bridge linked it to the Upper Campus but this proved an inhospitable trajectory, windswept in winter and torrid in summer. By the time of the construction of Uris Hall (1964), condemnation of Columbia's building activity was rampant. Uris was an unadorned, limestone behemoth and its design aroused a storm of controversy, with students picketing outside the building site. Students Harry Parnass and Alan Lapidus criticized,

It ignores the masterplan drawn up for the campus in the Eighteen Nineties by McKim, Mead and White, which prescribed a low building for that site. It will 'crush' the Low Memorial Library by towering over it....The building should have some image relating to the students. This building looks no different from a post office or a branch office of an insurance company.[10]

In the 1970s, the university endeavoured to absolve its earlier imprudence by commissioning more distinguished designers to produce more accomplished buildings, beginning with the Sherman Fairchild Centre (1977) by Mitchell/Giurgola Associates. It was on a cramped, but visually important site at the north-east of Upper Campus. It terminated a main walkway along the east side of Low Library. Referring to the campus's brick and limestone vocabulary, the building's metal frame is clad with red quarry tile panels. It was immediately acclaimed in the press. Critic Suzanne Stephens noted 'the classical-style architecture nearby is referred to through proportions of the screen wall panels and the rhythmic progression of open and closed panels'. Bernard Tschumi's 1999 addition to South Campus, Lerner Hall, similarly aspired to a modern resonance with its historic setting, yet it provoked controversy from the outset. Designed as a reimagining of McKim's 1903 master plan, it is spatially divided into a glass-walled atrium to the north, flanked by white stone and red brick wings on the street wall. The brick and stone components attempted an affinity with the residential halls proposed in the 1903 plan, while the atrium was claimed to be a glass-enclosed parallel of the courtyard that would have existed between them. The vast glass wall reveals a series of escalating ramps intended to mimic the steps of the Low Library as a social gathering place, yet they have never fully functioned as such and instead are held to simply slow inter-level movement.[11]

It is not unfair to say that Columbia has had a chequered planning history. Columbia has suffered inimical relations with its local neighbourhood in post-war years due to its vehement policy of buying all available real estate in the vicinity, which led to accusations of forced eviction and gentrification. Uproar peaked in 1968 over the long-running saga of the university's attempts to build a gymnasium in nearby Morningside Park, when protests erupted over claims of segregation and expropriation of public land and forced the project to be abandoned. The 2003 announcement to erect a new satellite campus in West Harlem to relieve the university's lack of space has fostered similar objections over displacement and disruption in the local community.

However, despite these denouements, the Morningside Heights campus of Columbia University is an irrevocably impressive ensemble. Its built environment is severely disadvantaged by its size; Yale and Princeton have three times the space per student that Columbia has. Nevertheless, McKim's master plan guided (at least until the Second World War) development to ensure that a campus of power, elegance, order and beauty has been carved upon the limited plot. These qualities converge in the undoubted climax of the Beaux-Arts masterwork, the Low Library. Set on the highest point of the terrain, the eye is irresistibly drawn to the impressive structure. No less impressive is its approach. From the spacious plaza set before it, a climatic progression of steps rises to the library, interrupted by terraces adorned with enormous urns and bronze lamp standards. The effect is overwhelmingly theatrical and inspiring. These steps, since the campus's earliest days, have proven themselves as the social hub of the university. 'Meet me on the library steps' quickly became an undergraduate byword. Although its original function has long since been discharged, the Low Library and its entrée have come to symbolize the university as a whole. This has been crucial to developing a recognizable brand, a vital ingredient in cultivating its place in the hearts and minds of students, alumni and visitors.[12]

Low Plaza is a uniquely attractive, and hence social, space. Most of its surface is decoratively paved with red brick and Istrian marble, harmonizing with the materials of the surrounding buildings, and abutted by panels of lawn. Columbia has, however, a tendency of being rather lackadaisical in its approach to landscaping. No landscape plan was commissioned until 1905, when the Olmsted Brothers were commissioned to advise on the landscape's improvement. Funding for the plan's implementation was unforthcoming, and the campus's open spaces remained somewhat ad hoc in their composition. The university has made efforts in recent decades, though, to harmonize and enhance its environment. In the 1980s, additional planting and benches were provided for on campus and in the surrounding vicinity. The bridge between the Law School and Upper Quadrangle, known as Revson Plaza, was landscaped to render it a more hospitable route with the addition of a grassed central canal and sculptures by renowned twentieth-century sculptors, such as Henry Moore, Jacques Lipschitz and David Bakalar. One of the most revolutionary changes to the landscape came in 1953, when 116th Street between Broadway and Amsterdam Avenue was pedestrianized and transformed into a landscaped promenade. The decision united South and Upper Quadrangles, plus created a much more tranquil, expansive setting for the college.

Despite several unwise post-war development choices, the physical setting possesses an enviable harmony. The consistent palette of red brick and limestone and stately Renaissance architectural idiom has proved flexible and enduring. It distinguishes the institution from the surrounding beige-brick apartment blocks, while also proving adaptable to higher education's changing needs. The extensions to Pupin Physics Laboratories and Schermerhorn Hall, for example, assumed a plainer yet architecturally consonant style to the older buildings. The paving of campus too employs a consistent palette of materials and colours. Its red and white palette harmonizes with the buildings and unifies the campus into one entity, so that despite its cramped Manhattan setting Columbia University possesses a unique and clear collegiate persona.

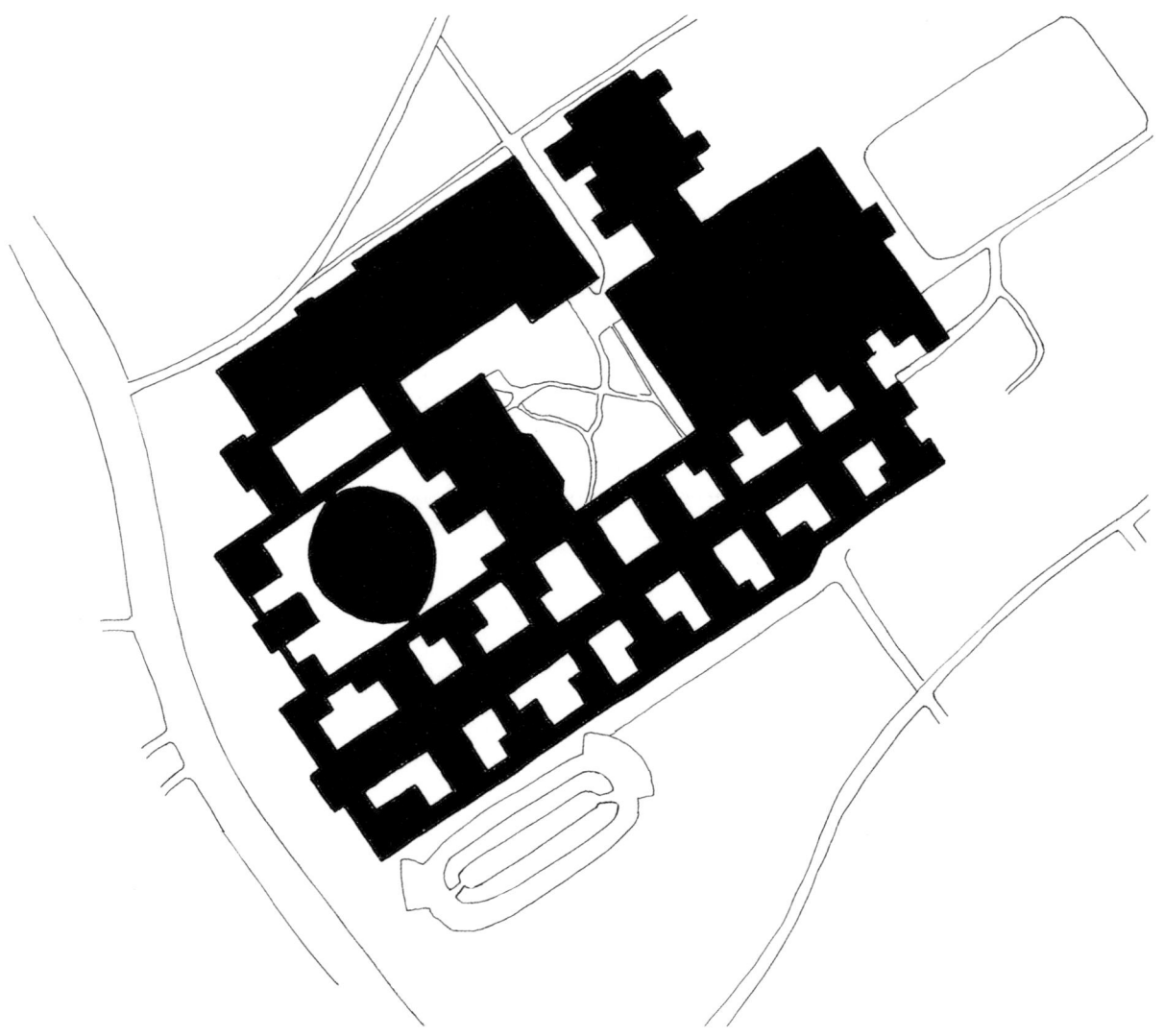

2.12 Plan, Free University Berlin

Free University Berlin
Berlin, Germany

The regime of the National Socialists had a devastating impact upon higher education in Germany. From 1933 to 1945 large numbers of lecturers were dismissed, all ideas of academic freedom were forgotten and by 1939 the system had shrunk to almost half its size. The end of the Second World War marked the beginning of a lengthy period of rehabilitation in the German university system, impelled by the restoration of intellectual liberty. Symptomatic of this was the founding of the Free University Berlin in 1948. It was established in the suburb of Dahlem, in the American sector of Berlin, predominantly as a result of American efforts and funding. Its creation was a reaction to the repression and political manipulation of the renowned Humboldt University in the Soviet-controlled East Berlin. Thus from the outset, the university was envisaged as a pioneering departure for German higher education. It was intended as a model for democratic higher education in Germany, free from the bridle of fascism or communism. This pioneering spirit not only manifested itself in the name of the new university, but in its physical form as well.[13]

The university was initially accommodated in the scattered private villas of leafy Dahlem and in the institute buildings of the former Kaiser Wilhelm Society. Rapid growth in student numbers meant that new buildings were quickly planned, including the Henry Ford Building. Completed in 1954, this structure was designed by Berlin architects Franz Heinrich Sobotka and Gustav Müller to house teaching rooms and an auditorium. Inspired by the maxim 'democracy as client', the architects sought to saturate the building with light, symbolic of freedom and openness. The length of its façade is a glass wall

2.13 Rostlaube, Free University Berlin
Photo: Reinhard Görner/Freie Universität Berlin

2.14 Silberlaube, Free University Berlin
Photo: Reinhard Görner/Freie Universität Berlin

punctuated by white pillars, creating an impression of lightness despite the building's large footprint.

The most significant element of the Free University Berlin's campus in terms of the remit of this study is the so-called Rost- und Silberlaube complex (Figures 2.13 and 2.14). This monolithic structure is what makes the university interesting as a campus study. In 1963 the university launched an international competition to design a new campus for its philological institute on the Orchard Site in Dahlem. The brief made clear demands as to growth and fostering inter-disciplinary relations. It stipulated that the humanities and mathematical-natural science facilities needed to be capable of eventual expansion by 20 and 60 per cent respectively, and that the building should include spaces which encouraged dynamic exchange between members of different faculties. The competition was won by Parisian firm Candilis Josic Woods, and partner Shadrach Woods assumed responsibility for the project.[14]

The resultant complex is a vast, continuous mono-structure comprising two sections – the Rostlaube and Silberlaube – designed around the principles of growth and communication (Figure 2.15). Wood's winning entry was a low-rise rectangle, essentially two storeys plus basement, structured around a web of internal pedestrian streets.

These were the primary sites for community interaction. The main streets gave the building a clear pattern around which space was assigned as 'built' or 'non-built' areas organized in terms of zones: activity, study and rest. The activity zones with the heaviest usage, such as lecture halls, seminar rooms and cafeterias, were sited along the main pedestrian streets at ground floor level. Interval spaces along side streets and on the upper storey were allotted to research, specialized teaching and individual interchange. Rest zones took the form of courtyards and roof terraces distributed throughout the rectilinear grid. These took up 50 per cent of the floor space, and offered the complex a chance to breathe. A vivid colour scheme was applied to walls and floors for orientation purposes.[15]

The architects sought a complex that fully exploited every opportunity to encourage contact amongst its inhabitants. Departments were not separated into different buildings, thus the psychological and physical barriers that traditionally divided disciplines were not enforced by architectural ones or the creation of individual departmental identities. Rigid hierarchies were exchanged for pluralism and tolerance expressive of the spirit of artistic and social revolution of the time. The University of Illinois at Chicago may have served as a type of model for Woods. Although the Chicago campus housed

2.15 Aerial view, Free University Berlin
Photo: Bavaria Luftbild/Freie Universität Berlin

each function, whether classrooms, laboratories, or offices in its own separate structure, Woods praised its intermingling of faculties and flexibility of its physical plant. Flexibility was key to Woods's conception of the modern university. As growth and change were inherent in the nature of the institution, Woods envisaged spaces that could be dismantled or created within the fixed grid of internal streets. Externally, the façades were fabricated from Cor-Ten-clad steel panels in set sizes, which could be moved and replaced as the building grew. Inside, demountable and moveable partitions similarly permitted changes in organization.[16]

Woods's campus was a striking departure from archetypal German examples. Germany had not responded to the campus model developed in the Unites States and United Kingdom. Typically, its universities were city-based, multi-site institutions scattered around the city landscape. In its suburban, densely organized site, the Free University was more akin to the campus model. Yet the Free University did not aspire towards the Anglo-American tradition of a marked institutional presence. A crucial difference between the Anglo-American and German traditions is the latter's lack of a specific institutional identity. The academic function of the German university was not identified by any particular architectural style or specificity and thus it merged into the urban fabric. In many ways the Free University belonged to this tradition. Woods gave his complex no central focus, no entrance façade and even no central entrance. No one elevation is given precedence over another. The megastructure sits discretely in its surroundings. Despite its vast footprint, it makes no grand architectural gestures and is essentially restricted to two storeys in height to harmonize with Dahlem's villas. Woods emphasized that the building was an instrument, not a monument.[17]

A myriad of influences seemingly affected this unusual design. Le Corbusier's *Five Points Towards a New Architecture* can be detected in the Free University's flat roof gardens (point two) and the free planning of the ground floor (point three), while its structure was based upon his Modulor, a proportional system tailored to human scales based on irregular grid intervals. The complex's internal circulation and courtyards are reminiscent of the bazaar streets and riads of Morocco, where Georges Candilis and Shadrach Woods met and worked for four years. The Free University's design may also have been related to 1950s architectural avant-gardism. The era bred an interest in the concept of the ideal city in a rapidly fluctuating world, in which the strict boundaries between house and city were dissolved and flexible large-scale structures played a key role.

2.16 Philological Library, Free University Berlin
Photo: Nigel Young/Foster + Partners

In this sense, the Free University itself was conceived as an ideal city. With decentralized faculties dispersed throughout the adaptable, single structure intended to promote free social interaction, Woods's vision was informed by the aspirations of the ideal modern city rather than the pattern of German academia. However, this vision proved in reality unattainable. Its form, in practice, engendered detachment rather than integration, which in time brought forth vandalism, notably graffiti.[18]

The Orchard Site has suffered radical reversals in its popularity. The praise lavished upon the design's originality and innovation upon its publication in 1963 soon turned to vilification after the erection of the first section (1973). Its Cor-Ten façade proved a failure. The material was intended to take on a rusty patina – a quality which gave rise to its Rostlaube nickname – which would act as a protective coat. In the Free University's case, however, the protective surface failed to form and the steel corroded in numerous places. The building's flexibility was also heavily derided. Like many of the buildings of the period designed to respond to changing usage patterns, such as the Nakagin Capsule Tower in Tokyo, the potential to transform the Free University's ground plan was not exploited. Another of the plan's unique features not fully exploited was its outdoor spaces. Envisaged as leisure areas, the courtyards and terraces were thoughtfully designed. The surfaces were covered with grass or gravel and planted with trees grouped together in various ways, so that each environment was unique. Nevertheless, the university community failed to fully engage with the spaces and they sunk into neglect.[19]

Recent years, however, have seen a reawakened interest in the Orchard Site's physical plant, from architectural historians, critics and the university itself. In 1997 the university inaugurated a complete reappraisal of the complex. Both the Rostlaube and Silberlaube urgently needed renovation. Both buildings contained asbestos, their flat roofs leaked and the Cor-Ten steel had rusted; furthermore, the complex lacked a clear layout. Norman Foster & Partners was appointed to direct its overhaul. Completed in 2004, the restoration project returned the structure to full glory and made its fresh planning approach appreciable once again. Effort was made to minimize the scale of alterations and keep the original fabric where practicable. The original colour scheme, incorporating red, yellow, green, blue and purple, that was employed as a way-finding device was restored and once again enlivens walls and floors. The degraded Cor-Ten was replaced by bronze panels, which differ little in appearance from the original modules. Where change was embraced was in the structure's organization. Foster himself exhaustively examined the building's network of streets, outdoor spaces, and 'zones', resulting in a modernization of the university's dated special concept to render the building more functional for academic life. The original building's shortcoming was the confusion created by the lack of demarcation between individual institutes, which led to first-year students wandering corridors in search of their seminar rooms. The circulation system was oft criticized for its complexity, augmented by arcane street signage. Foster's concept was predicated upon the intention of uniting the nine separate departments. Each institute was allotted its own visibly separate area, and each gave up its individual library to be replaced by a large, central library. In 2003 Foster's new library opened (Figure 2.16). It was inserted into six of the original courtyards, united by the removal of linking sections of the existing building. The hemispherical new library, dubbed the Berlin Brain, joins to Woods's complex at two points, maintaining the original objective of cross-connectivity. Importantly, the central location of the building within the complex means that the institutes and the library are in close proximity. The whole building consists of a single, enormous, light-filled room. Like the Rostlaube, the Brain is restricted in height yet its hemispherical shape has allowed an increase in accommodation equal to over half the complex's footprint.[20]

The Free University's Orchard Site has its flaws, yet from its opening it offered a completely new formula for the spatial organization of a university as a network of opportunities for communication, reflecting the zeitgeist of flexibility, innovation and democracy. The internal streets should not be viewed as mere corridors; they fulfil their purpose of encouraging informal exchange amongst the university's community. The building's experiments with connectivity and circulation render the campus a unique, interesting specimen of the 1960s spirit of innovation that resulted in a revolutionary era in campus design. With Woods's design made more practicable for modern usage by Foster & Partners' reappraisal and the dramatic addition of the Philological Library, the relevance of this building is affirmed.

2.17 Plan, Harvard University

Harvard University
Cambridge, USA

On 28 October 1636, the Great and General Court of Massachusetts Bay convened a meeting. Amongst the afternoon's busy agenda was an epochal act – the endowment of £400 towards the construction of 'a schoale or colledge'. The founding of a college only six years after the colonization of Massachusetts Bay was a bold feat. Yet the colony leaders were unwavering in their belief that for the experiment to prosper, the New World needed a leadership of educated men. The College opened in 1638 upon a one acre plot of land in Newtowne, a village six kilometres from Boston (quickly renamed Cambridge in recognition of the English university of which many of the Colony's leaders were alumni). This plot has grown over the centuries to form the heart of the university today, Old Harvard Yard. In the Old Yard, Harvard has developed a setting captivating for its sense of place, indelibly tied to the essence and reputation of the university.

How the Yard has achieved this rare quality is a chronicle of seemingly haphazard decisions. Harvard Hall I, the college's first

2.18 Burgis view (1726), showing (from left) Harvard Hall II, Stoughton Hall, and Massachusetts Hall, Harvard University
Photo: Harvard University Archives, HUV 2126.2

2.19 Memorial Hall, Harvard University
Photo: Erik Patton

purpose built structure, was the largest hitherto built in the English colonies. The ground plan took the form of an E-shape, an unusual shape for an academic building, not seen at Oxbridge and possibly derived from Elizabeth manor houses. The building contained almost all college functions: a hall (for lectures, recitations, and college functions), a kitchen, buttery, library and student rooms. From the outset the college adopted the English residential system. Despite the additional costs incurred, the trustees held a firm conviction in the advantages of an intimate community where scholars studied, slept, dined and worshiped together. The same tenet will be encountered throughout the history of American higher education. Harvard's spatial arrangements also proved influential. Rejecting the linked ranges of the Oxbridge colleges, Harvard's next stage of development was the creation of a number of separate structures. By 1655 Harvard consisted of four buildings: Harvard Hall I, Indian College (demolished 1697), the president's house, and Goffe College (demolished 1670s). Harvard Hall I and the Indian College were set well behind the latter two structures, which were positioned close to the street front (Figure 1.9). The buildings were located on the boundary of the College's narrow land, with little consideration of visual unity. This spatial layout may have stemmed from a practical consideration to minimize fire risk amongst the wooden structures, or perhaps from a wish to realize in physical form one of Harvard's founding ideologies, that it was purposed to serve its community and thus should be open and accessible to it.[21]

The arrangement of the Yard was transformed, though, with a new programme of rebuilding beginning in the 1670s. Following its deterioration, Harvard Hall I was replaced in 1671–1677. Significantly, it did not face the west towards the street-front, but south. It was positioned as the north range of a three-sided courtyard, which was to be completed by a new president's house (1680) on the south and Old Stoughton College (1698, razed 1781) on the east, marking the inception of a more formal approach to planning. In 1718, the president's house was replaced by a more substantial dormitory, Massachusetts Hall, today's Harvard's oldest surviving building. Architecturally, it demonstrated greater sophistication than Harvard's earlier buildings, possessing a simple, early Georgian dignity. The form of its roof and twin panelled chimneys of the gable ends proffered a model that succeeding generations of Harvard architects would turn to (for instance, Kirkland House, 1913). Harvard, Stoughton and Massachusetts Halls formed an overall pattern constituting a small, well-defined, three-sided courtyard – a concept that can be traced to Emmanuel College, Cambridge (Figure 2.18). Both centres of Puritanism, Emmanuel and Harvard shared notable links, not least that Harvard's Board of Overseers was formed overwhelmingly by Emmanuel alumni.[22]

The three-sided courtyard was to hold an influential position in the American college tradition, appearing again at Harvard in the eighteenth century as another open quadrangle was created. To form a three-sided courtyard with Harvard Hall II, two buildings were erected to the north: Holden Chapel (1744) and Hollis Hall (1763). The tiny Holden Chapel was undoubtedly Harvard's richest building to date. Possessing paired pilasters, a full wooden entablature, and a carved tympanum, it is a simple yet classically elegant structure. Hollis Hall, built as a dormitory to cater for increased enrolment, was four storeys high, with a central section capped by a pediment. In appearance, it was highly similar to the recently-built Nassau Hall at Princeton.[23] The chapel was, interestingly, entered not from the courtyard, but from the west – the street façade. The area of both the courtyards remained exposed to the west, orientated in the direction of the Cambridge Commons. The planning was palpably shaped by a desire to cultivate interaction with Cambridge. The open courtyard format of the Yard reflected the medieval ideal of a scholastic community living and studying together, yet Harvard considered itself a part of society, and thus the separate structures that constituted the Yard were orientated outward rather than inward. It was a trend that clearly distinguished it from its English predecessors and it endured until the late nineteenth century.

In 1764, fire destroyed Harvard Hall II. Its replacement, the current Harvard Hall, was a consciously eloquent expression of the school's rising stature. In High Georgian style, the centre of the main façade and the end elevations were pedimented. A cupola rising above the central pavilion signalled the building's presence on the skyline. Although architecturally neither avant-garde nor monumental, the early buildings of Harvard demonstrate the understated grandeur and totality that can be achieved by conforming to one building material and style, in this case red brick and Georgian.

2.20 Memorial Church, Harvard University
Photo: Photolibrary Ltd

In the first half of the nineteenth century building continued, to apparently little programme. Various building materials and styles were adopted, yet two structures of this period have come to establish the perimeters of the Old Yard: Holworthy and University Halls. Holworthy (1811) formed the northern boundary of the Yard, while University (1813) determined its scale. Designed by Charles Bulfinch, the later building evidences the Federal Style in its low pitched roof, symmetrical façade and cornice with dentils. In its granite surface adorned with Ionic pilasters, it provided a vivid contrast to its plain, red brick predecessors. The building inaugurated the development of an academic precinct in front of University Hall that transferred the focus of the institution away from the public realm towards a more intimate hub.[24]

The most prolific phase of building at Harvard yet occurred with the election of Charles Eliot as president (1869–1909). During his term, 35 substantial new structures or reworkings came to fruition (compared with 34 in the school's previous 233 year history). Despite this, Eliot was no architectural devotee. His concern was purely for functional, well-constructed buildings, an attitude that offered to benefactors of the college and their architects considerable leeway in presenting aesthetic preferences. The buildings of this era were a veritable medley of architectural styles. The Old Yard was further delineated by Thayer Hall, built in 1869 in a heavy Italianate style; by Weld Hall, of Northern Renaissance design dating to 1870; and Matthews Hall, a neo-Gothic structure built in 1871. Sever Hall was built to accommodate classrooms in 1880, sited in the eastern third of the yard parallel to University Hall. Designed by H. H. Richardson, it presents a classically Richardsonian combination of lavishness and monumentality, yet seeks an affiliation with the historic buildings of the Old Yard. Like them, it employs red brick and its eastern doorway is a type of High Georgian entrance that would be at home in the Old Yard.

Under Eliot, Harvard also greatly extended its presence north of the Yard, in an area which came to be known as the North Yard. An impressive number of buildings were constructed in a menagerie of architectural styles scattered across the North Yard. Memorial Hall (Figure 2.19), designed in the 1870s by the firm of Ware and Van Brunt, is a Ruskinian-Gothic building, awe-inspiring in its scale and imaginative silhouette; Hemenway Gymnasium, by the firm Peabody and Stern, was completed in 1878 as a novel mixture of Renaissance, Queen Anne and Gothic forms; Austin Hall, designed by H. H. Richardson in 1881, is a neo-Romanesque structure in pink granite and sandstone; Langdell Hall (by Shepley, Rutan and Coolidge, 1906) with its imperial porticoes, white limestone façade and classical detailing was alien in spirit to all its neighbours. Not only did architectural style enjoy free rein in this period, neither was a definitive plan for development adopted, a circumstance that was bemoaned. The president's son, Charles Eliot, rued that 'permitting donors of buildings and gates to choose their sites is fatal to general effect.' Architect Charles McKim later cautioned that 'some plan is woefully needed at Harvard'.[25]

Such recommendations came to fruition under President Lowell (1909–1933). An enthusiast for architecture, Lowell displayed tremendous concern for the proper planning and control of the physical growth of the institution and during his tenure much of Harvard assumed the physical character it is known for today. The construction of the huge Widener Library (1914) immediately to the east of Old Yard, and its companion piece opposite, Memorial Church (1932) (Figure 2.20), defined a new quadrangular space, the Tercentenary Quadrangle, where the commencement exercises are held. The most important manifestation of the Lowell administration's policy of land use and acquisition was the development of a new campus of freshman dormitories, near the Charles River – the South Yard. The Georgian Revival was selected as the university's official architectural idiom, along with the adoption of a single architectural firm, Shepley, Rutan and Coolidge. It was a far more formal and consistent approach than had ever been enacted before at Harvard, and it engendered a new and harmonious brand of Harvard architecture throughout the enlarged campus.

Shepley, Rutan and Coolidge's 1910 master plan provided a series of freshman dormitories, which later became the foundation of the House system. The introduction of the House System in 1919 saw the remodelling of these dormitories and fresh construction in the South Yard to create seven houses (since expanded to ten) in which undergraduates resided, dined and took some instruction, modelled on Oxbridge's colleges. Like the English medieval colleges, the houses assumed the form of linked structures grouped around enclosed or nearly enclosed courts. In their

2.21 Harvard University
Photo: ©iStockphoto.com/Daniel Loiselle

inward-turning, sequestered nature, these structures represent a striking departure from the traditional model of separate collegiate buildings gregarious to their community. Yet in physical terms, the houses perfectly project the spirit of colonial Harvard. Forming a stately border to the Charles River, the buildings alluded to the eighteenth-century architecture of the Harvard Yard. At each individual house, ornamentation subtly differed thus imbuing each academic community with its individual identity. McKinlock Hall, for example, copied the entrance of eighteenth-century Hollis Hall, whilst the ornate scrollwork on Dunster House's gables was inspired by that on Holden Chapel. The new desire for collegiate intimacy also wielded an impact upon the character of the Yard. In the 1920s and 1930s, seven narrow halls were slotted along its boundary (Figure 2.21). Screening out the noise of the ever-growing Cambridge, the halls formed a physical barrier between the university and host city that reflected Harvard's new interpretation of the educational ideal. With Lowell's additions, the character of Harvard Yard was fixed, to be preserved until the present day despite the momentous changes that would shake the history of Harvard's architecture in succeeding years.[26]

Like other campuses across the world, with the aftermath of the Second World War came a significant transformation in the architecture and planning of Harvard University. The neo-Georgian forms that had come to dominate the college were abandoned in favour of the International Style. This distinctive new flavour had much to do with the appointment to the faculty of the Graduate School of Design in 1937 of the modernist Walter Gropius. In 1949, Gropius received his first commission from the university to design a Graduate Centre. It was amongst the first pure examples of the International Style in the country, characterized by a continuous vocabulary of stark linearity, strip windows and rectangular, modular forms. Gropius was the first of a string of internationally renowned architects that the university was to employ in succeeding years. New building materials, styles, and scales were introduced into the Harvard topography and the placement of buildings became more a matter of pragmatism as land became scarce. Buildings of the period included the Undergraduate Sciences Centre. Designed by the firm of Josep Luis Sert in 1970, the lines and massings of the centre served to integrate the new structure to its North Yard setting. The eastern façade echoed the building line of immediate neighbour, the Gordon McKay Laboratory, while the southern façade responded to a newly-created mall next to it. This new green space was the result of the construction of a large vehicular underpass on Cambridge Street in 1966–1968, which created a pedestrian mall between the North Yard and Harvard Yard, a vast improvement in terms of both safety and aesthetics. So as not to overwhelm and destroy this green space, the Science Centre took the form of a stepped elevation rising from the mall from a single storey to a six-storey spine at its northern elevation.[27]

Despite radically new forms, modern Harvard architecture has admirably sought to establish relationships with its predecessors. The spirit of Harvard's historic architecture remains as dynamic in the South Yard's newest dormitories, a graduate housing complex designed by Kyu Sung Woo, completed 2008. The modest yet elegant design is a harmonious continuum of the River Houses. It has a river façade of brick, and a western low-rise elevation clad in wood in deference to neighbouring wooden frame, three-storey houses, while the layout reproduces the much-used Harvard motif of an open courtyard.

A pattern emerges within the chronology of Harvard's development, that architects have accommodated their designs to educational requirements and objectives, but also to the campus's earlier buildings, those structures distinguished by their dignity and venerability. These are the qualities with which the campus resonates, and it is much to do with Harvard's largely avoiding attempts at 'heroic' architecture. The critic Montgomery Schuyler astutely commented in 1909 of Harvard's architecture, 'there is not in it, on the part of each succeeding builder, that itch to signalize his work by difference from that of his predecessors which is responsible for the chaotic miscellany of so many campuses. The characteristic is rather of deference than of difference.'[28] What makes the campus a successful unit is that it has eschewed the 'grand statement' in favour of a regard for its surroundings. An eclectic cross-section of colonial, Georgian, neo-classical, Gothic Revival, modernist and post-modernist buildings comprise the Harvard campus, yet the college is for the most part characterized by an enviable harmony. Building to a human-scale contributes much to this visual success. The majority of buildings are kept low, usually two- to five-storeys, and, in the case of the Yard and South Yard, are arranged to form courts. Such unity has not engendered monotony, for the skyline is punctuated by lively vertical elements – towers, spires, cupolas, engaging roof forms – that demarcate the buildings of special import within the bustling urban topography. Indeed, since its earliest years, Harvard has been involved in a complex dialogue with the city of Cambridge. It has contended with the constant challenge to create and preserve its green space as the university expanded and the urban mass encroached. Its open spaces, though, are what make the campus. The buildings frame the courtyards, quadrangles, and other open spaces that have come to form the archetypal image of the campus, which, for centuries, has nurtured an ever-strengthening affection for the university in those that pass through its gates.

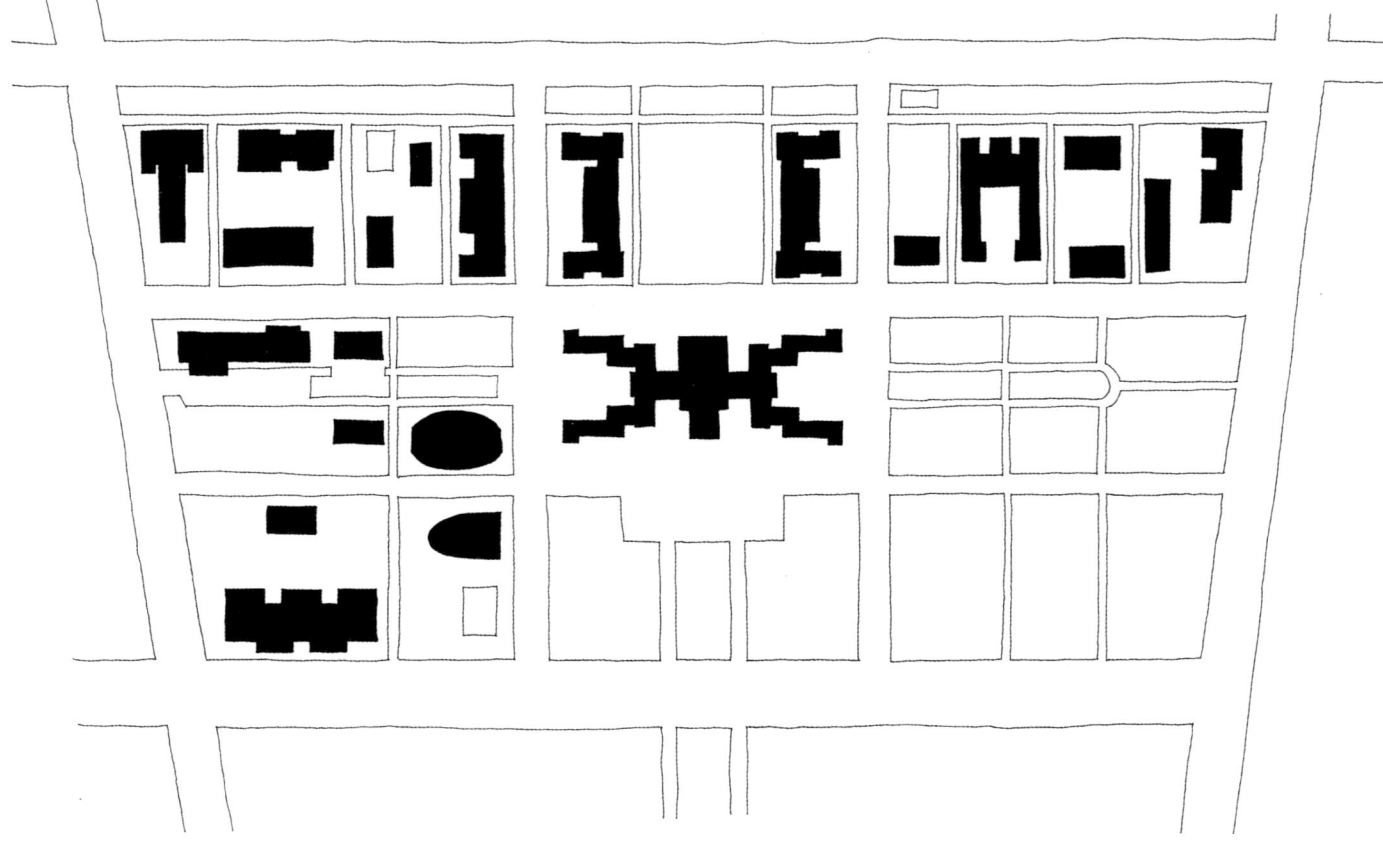
2.22 Plan, Moscow State University

Moscow State University
Moscow, Russia

Out of the ashes of the destruction wreaked by the Second World War, in the late 1940s and 1950s the Soviet Union inaugurated a new phase of monumental building. Cities such as Stalingrad, Smolensk, Minsk, and Kiev were rebuilt almost from afresh, while Moscow became the centre of a new histrionic style of building, characterized by 'Stalinist Gothic' skyscrapers. Moscow was transformed by a parade of showpiece complexes under the 'Master Plan for the Reconstruction of the City of Moscow'. On 13 January 1947 a resolution was passed by the Council of Ministers of the USSR to erect a series of eight high-rise buildings (only seven were realized) across Moscow, an agenda actively promoted by Stalin. The resolution envisaged

> a series of high rise buildings which should be, in terms of size, technology and architecture, a new form of construction… The proportions and skylines of these buildings must be original in composition, both architecturally and artistically. They should be linked to the historical development of Moscow.[29]

One of these towers was destined as the new home of the Moscow State University (founded 1755), replacing the neo-classical building it had occupied since the late eighteenth century. The university and the other six complexes, known collectively as the Seven Sisters, displayed what is termed as Stalinist Architecture, an idiom that combined striking monumentalism with patriotic and traditional decorative motifs. There was little correlation between their physical form and their function. Despite housing a range of occupations, including government offices, hotels and apartments, the buildings shared a common aesthetic, which melded sixteenth- and seventeenth-century Muscovite architectural motifs, the classicism of the unbuilt Palace of the Soviets, and elements of early-twentieth-century Manhattan skyscrapers, such as the Woolworth Building. It was a bombastic architecture, whose grandiosity was further heightened by the carefully chosen sitings of the towers. In accordance with current Soviet town planning theories, the buildings were diffused at key points around the city, forming a 'necklace' encircling the city's heart. By creating vertical reference points, these landmark buildings radically transformed Moscow's skyline, investing it with a unique identity.[30]

2.23 Moscow State University
Photo: © FlyFishka – Fotolia

2.24 Moscow State University
Photo: Julija Sapic

The skyscraper built to house Moscow State University is visible across the city (Figure 2.23). Its site is the highest point of the Vorobievy Hills overlooking the River Moskva, and its placement created a new vista from the Kremlin along the river. It signalled the primary direction of the city's development, to the south-west of the centre, and stood as the chief reference point when approaching the city from several main entry roads. The elevated plateau, moreover, provided a rare opportunity for experimentation in the field of university planning.[31]

In terms of planning and architecture, Moscow State University was wildly different to other educational institutions designed at that time. A comparison with contemporaneous examples such as Black Mountain College, Illinois Institute of Technology, and Harvard's Graduate Centre reveal the degree of the institution's individuality that is intimately bound to the socio-historical context of Stalinist Russia. Rather than a scattering of individual buildings, the university was conceived as a single, huge structure. Built from 1949–1953 under the architects Lev Rudnev, Pavel Abrosimov, and Alexander Khryakov, the enormous complex consisted principally of three component parts: the main building rising to 26 storeys, flanked by a pair of 18-storey tall wings. The whole is governed by absolute symmetry. The main section is a stepped pyramidal construction, surmounted by an opulent spired tower. Containing auditoria, libraries, lecture rooms, laboratories, lounges, cafeterias and service rooms, it originally housed all academic functions. The two adjoining wings provided accommodation for students, supplemented by a further stepped extension of 12 storeys for staff housing flanking each wing. The scale of the ensemble is nothing short of breathtaking. Its width is imposingly colossal, a scale upheld by the grand entrances approached by wide staircases and tall rusticated base. The unrelieved, regulated pattern of tall, narrow windows enforces the impression of soaring, upward motion, recalling New York's skyscrapers. The façades are enlivened by its undulating plane of projections and recessions, pillar-like lanterns and statues upon plinths. The main elevation is accented at its centre point by a classicizing motif of a ten-column wide portico, supported by an Ionic colonnade. The grandiose entry leads down to a rectangular pool with fountains, and equally symmetrical yet beautiful landscaped gardens.[32]

The visual impact of its external appearance was the chief priority of the campus's design. Function was of far less import to Stalinist urbanism than form, and accordingly many planning decisions for the university building were dictated by the all-embracing totality that characterized urban development of the era. Although undoubtedly this uncompromising approach reaped rewards in terms of its imposing presence and the panoptic absoluteness of its aesthetic, subjugating the functioning of the university to an umbrella concept has had negative effects. The complex is wasteful of inside space, producing vast tracks of corridors that hinder internal communications. The sum of the 67 lift shafts, for example, is over six kilometres, while the cumulative length of the corridors is 33 kilometres. Charles Jencks has referred to the building as a 'battery-hatch palace' of students in regards to its planning. Similarly profligate is the building's decoration. Despite the fact that the country lost approximately 30 per cent of its national wealth during the Second World War, the luxury of the interior space is arresting. Walls, floors and ceilings enjoyed lavish treatments. The steel structure was clad with brick then adorned with a profusion of classical ornamentation; walls were encrusted with friezes, murals and reliefs of Russian heraldry, images of celebrated scientists, inscriptions and ornamental motifs. Sculptures were placed at high, impossible to see from ground level. The opulence is awe-inspiring (Figure 2.24).[33]

The university's design is emblematic of the peak of Stalinist architecture, and enormously revealing as to how architecture was exploited to express the ideology of the Soviet state. The construction of the university building and its sister ensembles in Moscow consumed staggering sums of money at a time when the country was lying in ruins. Grand façades were prioritized above the undeniable needs of the overcrowded population; function, design and material were subordinated to symbolic mission, glorifying Muscovite culture and its centrality within the Communist world, and, fundamentally, the authority of Stalin's dictatorship. The overwhelming size of the university complex is a compelling demonstration of the power of the state. At the time of construction, it was the tallest building in the world outside of New York, rising to 240 metres. Its spire alone is 57 metres tall, while the star and wheat motif at its apex weighs 12 tons and is nine metres in diameter. Ultimately, the university building was a means via which the state communicated with the masses, championing its supremacy. Looming monumentally over the city, it symbolized the pervasive presence of the regime.

MOSCOW STATE UNIVERSITY

2.25 Library, Moscow State University
Photo: ©iStockphoto.com/Evgeny Dontsov

Contemporary commentators extolled the building. 'The rich plasticity of the volumes and the skylines of the University complex, and the symphonic nature of the whole, are instructive and brilliant examples of innovatory Russian town planning,' wrote one critic in 1953. Its reconciliation of function and form was commended by contemporaries.[34]

Although this quality is questionable today, the university complex should be recognized for its success in terms of placemaking. Rarely can a single building dominate a metropolis as Moscow State University does. To Russians, the skyscraper is as much an emblem of the city as is the Empire State Building of New York. Its prodigious size and grandeur imbue the institution with an unforgettable identity. This placemaking capacity is the signal achievement of the complex. Although its original message of the authority of Communist totalitarianism is today deplored, the complex demonstrated to the maximum the expressive potential of architecture. Today its symbolic potential can be appreciated as a representation of the prestige and magnitude of education.

Since the completion of Rudnev's complex in 1953, the university has expanded into buildings immediately surrounding the tower.

2.26 Moscow State University
Photo: ©iStockphoto.com/Evgeny Dontsov

The Departments of Biology and Soil Science are located in a C-shaped structure, characterized by a restrained Socialist classicism with the same repetitive organization of windows. The new library, opened in 2005, shares a similar aesthetic (Figure 2.25). Reviving the classical realist idiom of the main complex, it is an angular mass, with tall base and vertical bands of windows. The entrance is a colonnade of four pilasters imposed upon a façade of glass. The Faculties of Journalism, Psychology and the Institute of Asian and African Studies now occupy the Palladian-style building that housed the university from the late eighteenth century until 1953. Built by Matvei Kazakov from 1782 to 1793, and rebuilt after the Fire of Moscow in 1812 by Domenico Giliardi, the university was transferred to this neo-classical building by Catherine the Great.

Akin to Rudnev's design, these buildings are architecturally assertive, imparting a sense of the prestige and might of the Moscow State University. The complex is an indulgent piece of statement architecture, but one noteworthy for its encapsulation of the propagandist aims of the institution and the political regime. The university's muscular silhouette creates a presence on Moscow's skyline not easily forgotten (Figure 2.26).

2.27 Plan, Peking University

Peking University
Beijing, China

Peking University was founded in 1898 in central Beijing, where it remained until 1952 when, cramped for space, the university relocated to its present site in the Haidian district of north-west Beijing, termed the university district in reference to its dense cluster of higher education institutions. The university appropriated the grounds and buildings of Yenching University, a Christian college that had been founded earlier in the century but was closed following the establishment of the People's Republic of China in 1949. The Yenching site had an illustrious heritage. In the eighteenth century, Emperor Ch'ien Lung's Minister of State, Ho Shen, developed the land into a country estate, known as Shu Ch'un Yuan, or the Garden of Modest Gaiety. After the emperor's death, Ho Shen was executed and his estate was transformed into a series of parks, palaces, gardens and residences by the Manchu Emperors. By the time Yenching University acquired the site in 1920, it had lapsed into a state of neglect, yet with its panorama of man-made hills, grottoes, islands and lakes, it still possessed the essence of a

2.28 Classroom building, Peking University
Photo: Tao/Robert Harding

beautiful, imperial setting. This setting Yenching was to fully exploit in the construction of its new campus, between 1921–1926.

The man who assumed responsibility for its design was an American architect, Henry Killam Murphy. He executed a number of important commissions in early twentieth-century China, personally favouring educational buildings and campus plans designed in a Chinese style. In referencing Chinese models, Murphy believed that his campuses bridged the gulf between the religious and educational values of the West and those of the Far East, thus better integrating the Anglo-Christian Yenching into its backdrop. The plan he devised for the campus was a Beaux-Arts inspired composition predicated upon an arrangement of perpendicular axes and three-sided quadrangles, traditional to Chinese design.[35]

The chairman of the Grounds and Buildings Committee, Dr Galt, later recalled how the planning process was begun:

The first task was the location of an axial line which should serve as a base for the arrangement of symmetrical courts and quads. On the occasion of Murphy's first visit to the site with this purpose in mind, he stood upon one of the artificial hills on the site looking westward toward the mountains. His gaze fell upon the highest of the Jade Fountain pagodas and he exclaimed, 'There is the point we are looking for.' The line of our main axis shall be directed to the pagoda on the Jade Fountain hill.[36]

In Beaux-Arts fashion, Murphy provided a grand entrance to the campus though the brightly painted West Gate, guarded by two attendant stone lions, which revealed a lawned quadrangle approached by a small stone bridge. The three-sided Main Quadrangle was dominated by the eastern building, Bashford Hall (now the Office of the President), which was flanked to its right and left by McBrier Hall (now the Building of Foreign Languages) and a science building (Northern Chemistry Building). To the south of this grouping, was set out the Science Quadrangle, and to its north was a further quadrangle, framed by McBrier Hall to the south and Ninde Hall to the east with the remaining sides left open for future expansion. To the north of this court, four large dormitories arranged in pairs bordered a landscape of private parkland with its crowning point of a large lake known as Weiming Lake. At the south west of campus, Murphy grouped the Women's College. The symmetrical, axial plan of the buildings has resulted in a lucid campus linked by a network of paths, in which the pedestrian, not the car, has supremacy.[37]

In stylistic terms, the design embraced 'the splendid heritage of Chinese Architecture…in an adaption [sic] of the native style, as exemplified in the beautiful buildings within the "Forbidden City"'.[38] The university's newly appointed first president, John Leighton Stuart, fully concurred with Murphy's reflections on the use of the Chinese architectural mode for its symbolic and aesthetic currency. 'We had determined from the outset to use an adaptation of Chinese architecture for the academic buildings', he recounted:

Graceful curves and gorgeous colouring were designed for the exteriors while the main structures were to be constructed throughout of reinforced concrete and equipped with modern lighting, heating and plumbing. Thus the buildings were in themselves symbolic of our educational purpose in preserving all that was most valuable in China's cultural heritage.[39]

The campus buildings largely assumed a palatial guise, resplendent in their colour, ornament and general luxury. In vernacular tradition, the buildings were rectangular in plan with robust pillars and beams carrying overhanging roofs of hipped or hip and gable types, decorated with carved creatures suspended from the ridges. Dark red pilasters stood out against the white walls upon granite pedestals, while the whole was treated to vivid paint work in sumptuous colours (Figure 2.28).

The most striking architectural element of the composition was the Boya Tower. Rising to a height of 40 metres, the tower was located on the banks of the lake. In fact a water tower, Murphy cloaked the utilitarian structure with a pagoda-like exterior. The pagoda was, he espoused 'the most purely symbolic of Chinese buildings and the most distinctive man-made feature of the Chinese landscape'. Modelled on the octagonal Ming Dynasty structure at Tung-chou, east of Beijing, the tower immediately invested the campus with a historic presence and a visual landmark, emblematic of the institution. Murphy similarly applied a Chinese veneer to the original library building. Adopting local traditions, it was designed as a rectangular

2.29 Luce Pavilion, Peking University
Photo: Jonathan O'Donnell

building with columns supporting a tiled roof. Yet fusing Western methods, the columns are embedded into plastered walls that divide the interior spaces in a Western way and Chinese grillwork shades western-style windows. Whereas in traditional Chinese structures, interior spaces flow into exterior ones, Murphy's plastered walls firmly separate the inside and out.[40]

Murphy's Beaux-Arts approach to planning continued to hold sway, when, in 1984, the university decided to expand the campus in response to rising student numbers and growing academic programmes. Consequently, the campus saw the construction of new facilities for the Geophysics Department, Law Department, Guanghua School of Management, Centre for the Study of Chinese Archaeology and a new university library. All were predicated upon the traditional Chinese aesthetic of the original buildings, yet reflective of their modern context in their simpler, more sober exteriors and contemporary construction methods.

The Arthur M. Sackler Museum of Art and Archaeology was sited so as to form the third side of the quadrangle to the north of the Main Quadrangle. Completed in 1993 to designs by Prentice & Chan, Ohlhausen, it complemented the Ming Dynasty style of the surrounding buildings in its architecture and its siting around a central courtyard. The new university library (1998) provided a spacious eastern addition to the 1970s existing library. Designed by Guan Zhaoye, it evinces a thoughtful response to the surrounding landscape and structures. It was sited on an open green space near the south bank of the lake, adjoining the eastern side of the old library. Two classroom buildings were demolished to make way for a green lawn opening out from the library steps. The lawn has achieved popular status on campus as a venue for studying, student activities and socializing. The building incorporates many of the features of the historic buildings, such as an overhanging tiled roof supported by tou-kung brackets. The Guanghua School of Management (1997), to the south-east of the library, espoused a similar creed. Designed by the Beijing Institute of Architectural Design, it harmonizes well with the campus environment. Conforming to the architectural idiom, the building's four dark grey sloped roofs with coloured glazed tiles are

2.30 Front Quadrangle, Peking University
Photo: J G Wang

2.31 Peking University
Photo: Gary Larson

supported upon grey and white exterior walls. The complex is set around a courtyard, surrounded by buildings on three sides. Internal and external courts provide spaces for interaction.[41]

Predominantly, therefore, Peking's campus has grown in holistic fashion, with its modern approaches to layout, architectural styles, and landscape remaining attuned to those of the 1920s. Notably, its buildings have consistently responded to the campus's garden setting, integrating functional units into the surrounding landscape. The campus espouses Chinese landscaping traditions sensitive to the natural topography. The informal landscape is stunningly beautiful. Around the lake, foot paths meander between trees and pools, while at its centre, a graceful octagonal structure with scarlet pillars, the Luce Pavilion, sits upon an island reached by an arched bridge (Figure 2.29). Interspersed within this setting is a wealth of notable Chinese relics. Many objects previously housed in the YuanMingYuan – a large complex of palaces and gardens to the north-west of Beijing's old city walls destroyed in the nineteenth century – found their way to the campus, including the two towering marble columns carved with entwined dragons that stand on the lawn before the Office of the President Building (Figure 2.30). Believed to date to 1742, they used to stand in YuanMingYuan's Ancestral Temple. The two stone unicorns standing guard outside the office building also have a YuanMingYuan origin.[42]

Such treasures vitally enrich the campus, cultivating a compelling sense of place and ancestry that distinguishes Peking within the collection of universities in the Haidian district. Creating a memorable sense of place is a feat at which the university has excelled. The luxurious west gates, with their vivid red doors and pillars and dazzlingly coloured cornices superintended by two marble lions, provide an eye-catching entryway and immediately demarcate the university's grounds. Its institutional identity is further underscored by the harmonious treatment of landscape and architecture, with its palette of evergreens, willows, cherry blossoms, and overhanging tiled roofs sloping gracefully down to deep-red columns. The result is an accessible and edifying academic environment.

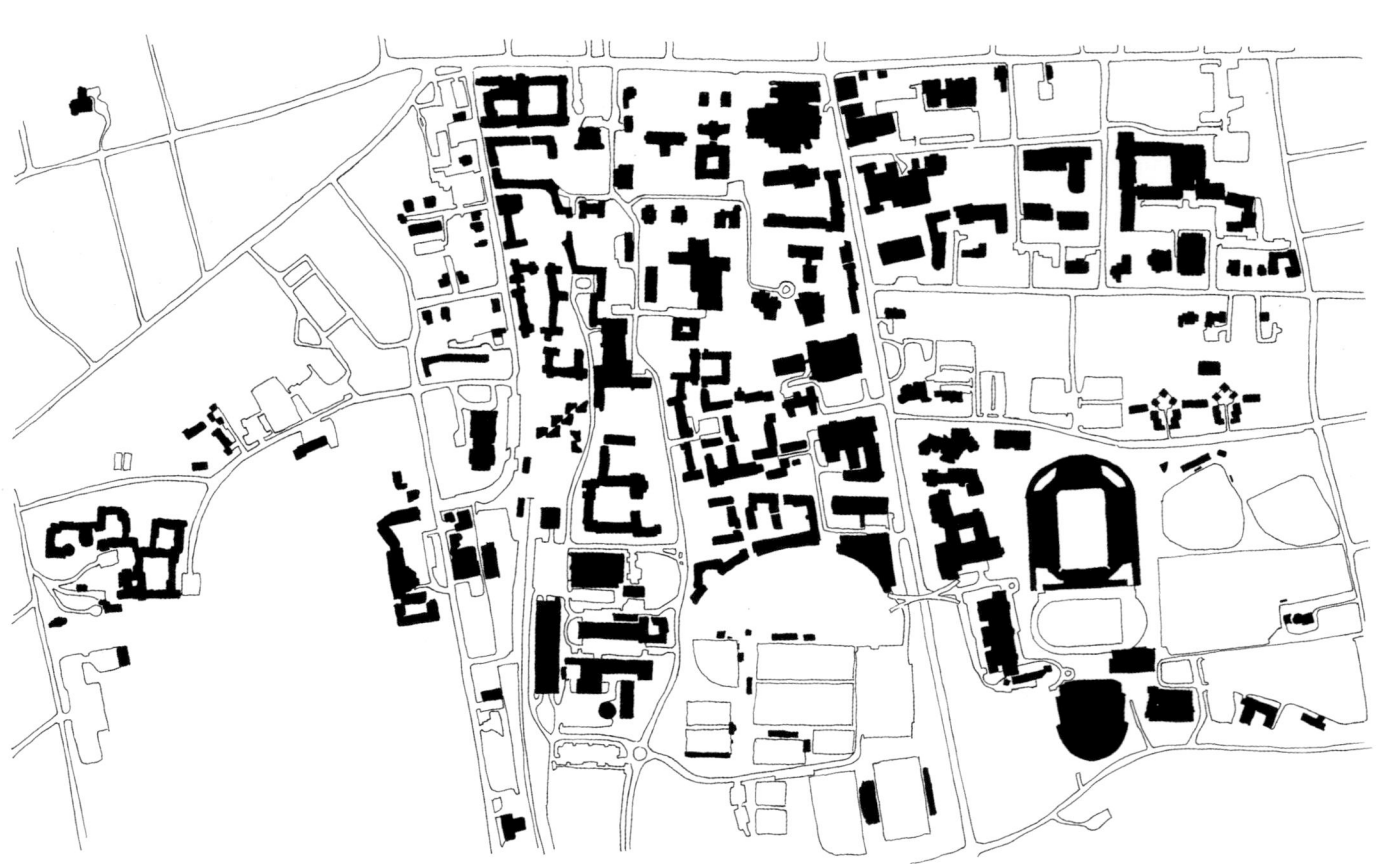

2.32 Plan, Princeton University

Princeton University
Princeton, USA

In 1753 the trustees of the College of New Jersey – the name by which Princeton University was known for its first 150 years – reached a portentous decision to relocate the young institution. Founded in Elizabeth in 1746, then located in Newark, Prince-Town became the college's permanent home in 1756, chosen for its seclusion 'from the various temptations attending a promiscuous converse with the world, that theatre of folly and dissipation'.

Upon a four-acre plot, the college took root. Its layout tangibly differed from the organization of its colonial predecessors, resulting in a distinctive physical environment. Its first building was Nassau Hall, erected in 1756 (Figure 1.12). An enormous, single structure, Nassau Hall contained the whole community. All 150 students and professors ate and boarded, recited their lessons and prayers, and congregated for assemblies within its walls. An impressive, pedimented building,

2.33 Alexander Hall, Princeton University
Photo: Éamonn Ó Muirí

it was built in the fashionable Georgian style. Its honey-coloured local stone has since been used time and again on campus, visually harmonizing its many buildings. Unlike the three-sided courtyards of Harvard or the enclosed quadrangles of the ancient English colleges, Nassau Hall was not planned to have flanking buildings. The apparent efficiency and rationality of housing all activities under one roof soon established it as a model for the perfect collegiate building. In the later eighteenth and early nineteenth centuries, its form was imitated at Harvard (Hollis Hall, 1762), Brown (University Hall, 1770), Dartmouth (Dartmouth Hall, 1784–1791), South Carolina (Rutledge Hall, 1803), and Rutgers (Old Queen's College, 1809). Nassau Hall was set deep into its plot back from the public street, creating a spacious 'village green' setting in its foreground. Symbolically distanced from the town and yet still open to the world, this arrangement proved both a defining characteristic of the college's early spatial composition and influential upon American campus development at large. It prompted the first use of the Latin word *campus*, meaning field, a term which has since come to embody the distinctive physical character of the American university.[43]

In March 1802, Nassau Hall was ravaged by fire and the trustees turned to English architect, Benjamin Henry Latrobe, to rebuild it. Latrobe's contribution to Princeton did not end there, however, and he was placed at the helm of an ambitious building project. Latrobe designed two twinned structures at the north-east and north-west corners of Nassau Hall. Stanhope Hall (1803) is the only one of these buildings to survive (its pair was razed in the 1870s). These two buildings marked Princeton's evolution toward a symmetrical and neo-classical plan, a transition that was expedited by the arrival of amateur architect, Joseph Henry, at the college. In 1836, inspired by Latrobe's example of organization, Henry provided the first written master plan for the university's future development. Its growth was to be guided by the neo-classical tenets of balance, symmetry, clarity and simplicity, values that informed the siting of the subsequent buildings, Whig and Clio Halls. Built in 1838 to designs by Charles Steadman, Whig and Clio Halls bring Athens to New Jersey. The two Greek temples were built facing the south façade of Nassau Hall to define the southern perimeter of campus. They were positioned symmetrically behind Nassau Hall, so that each could be seen from the street and terminated parallel walks that skirted the sides of Nassau. Their siting strengthened the classical order of the grounds. (In the 1890s, they were rebuilt closer together to permit an expanded sight line southwards from the street.)[44]

Soon, however, the neo-classical vogue came to be displaced. Romantic landscaping ideas of the Victorian landscape architects Andrew Downing and Frederick Law Olmsted supplanted the axial formality of early-nineteenth-century planning and Princeton's symmetrical outlines were blurred by a new enthusiasm for the spontaneous picturesque. This change was driven by Princeton's eleventh president, James McCosh (1811–1894). Arriving at the college in 1868, McCosh transformed the campus into an English country estate, characterized by oblique lines and meandering walkways that revealed surprises at every turn. During his 20-year term, the campus was for the first time enlarged beyond the confines of the Nassau Hall precinct. Witherspoon Hall was built in 1877 to the south-west of Nassau Hall on an elevated site overlooking the train station. With its west side facing the railway line, the five-storey building was designed to be the public face of the increasingly self-assured college to those approaching by rail. Chancellor Green Library (now Chancellor Green Hall) was another of McCosh's projects. Built in 1873 to designs by William A. Potter, its siting represented the first significant rupture of Latrobe and Henry's symmetrical vision for the Nassau quadrangle. Latrobe's Philosophical Hall (pair to Stanhope) was demolished to afford the library a prominent position. Facing outwards toward the street, Chancellor Green Library reveals an important characteristic of McCosh's campus; it signalled Princeton's reorientation to the public realm. Potter was also responsible for Alexander Hall, a great assembly hall built directly west of Nassau Hall in 1892 (Figure 2.33). Like the library, it faced directly to the street. Although subsequent changes have made it less easy to appreciate today, Alexander Hall, together with Nassau Hall, the library, Dickinson Hall (destroyed by fire in 1920) and the John C. Green School of Science (destroyed by fire in 1928) formed a streetscape looking out towards the wider world. With its residential halls hidden beyond to the south, the college was effectively planned with two personas: one private and the other public.[45]

Alexander Hall's robust, Romanesque aesthetic also marked a turning point in the campus's history. Despite its early popularity, the building was soon subject to ridicule and it was one of the last

2.34 Blair Hall, Princeton University
Photo: Ellen Isaacs/Alamy

not to espouse the Collegiate Gothic idiom that came to dominate the campus. The style was a defining characteristic of the campus regeneration that was inaugurated in 1896, the year the College of New Jersey proclaimed itself Princeton University. Princeton acquired a heightened self-confidence, and embarked upon a momentous course of growth and construction that shaped much of what we know as Princeton today.

Its grounds were transformed into a collegiate ideal of seclusion and exclusivity, informed by the cloistered quadrangles of the English colleges. Upon visiting Cambridge in 1899, Princeton's president, Woodrow Wilson wrote, 'I bring away from it a very keen sense of what we lack in our democratic college, where no one has privacy or claims to have his own thoughts'.[46] The campus recoiled from the outside world, turning in upon itself to provide a Utopia of academia free from the diverting traffic of modern life. The appearance of the FitzRandolph Gate on the street facing Nassau Hall was a telling symptom of the growing division between college and community. Inspired by the secluded courts, the beauty and ostensive spirituality of Oxbridge, the university trustees mandated that the Collegiate Gothic style alone was to be used for all future construction, and they engaged the services of architectural firm Cope & Stewardson to begin the process with the building of a series of dormitories. After achieving widespread recognition for their meandering Collegiate Gothic buildings for Bryn Mawr College and the University of Pennsylvania, the pair was perceived as the natural choice to actualize Princeton's ambitious new vision. Their first commission was Blair Hall in 1896 (Figure 2.34). A snaking dormitory building on the south-western boundary of campus, it created a fortress-like stone screen enclosing the college from the railway line. Approached from below by a steep flight of stairs, Blair Hall proffered entrance to the college through a richly vaulted archway piercing a massive, turreted tower. Although its purpose as a gateway has been weakened by the removal of the train station to the south, the building still carries a powerful resonance. One of Princeton's chief landmarks, Blair Arch is a symbolic portal between the world outside and the elite world of higher purpose within. The quixotic passion for Collegiate Gothic was no mere aesthetic trend, but represented an intellectual and moral retreat from the squalid realities of industrializing America.

In 1906 the role of supervising architect was created to co-ordinate Princeton's transformation into an orderly Gothic and quadrangular setting. Ralph Adams Cram undertook this responsibility, and set about preparing a master plan for the university's future development. Cram sought to liberate Princeton from what he described as its 'pleasure park' appearance, a random coalition of buildings of varied styles and little cohesion which resulted from donors' freedom to dictate location and style, to be replaced by a homogenous university, unified both in its architecture and layout. Following the lead of Cope and Stewardson, Cram's plan recommended ranges of buildings that served as boundaries along the campus edge. Buildings were planned to create a delicate network of partially enclosed quadrangles, organized around a framework of axes and vistas. He wrote of his plan that it conceived the university as 'a citadel of learning and culture…a walled city against materialism and all its works'.[47] The success of his plan comes from the interplay between enclosed spaces and openings from which unexpected vistas extend. The design, he wrote,

> Should not reveal itself at once and from any spot, but gradually, through narrowed and intensified vistas, the unforeseen opening out of unanticipated paths and quadrangles, the surprise of retirement, the revelation of the unexpected.[48]

More than any other individual, it was Cram who shaped Princeton's environment. As supervising architect, he oversaw the construction of approximately 25 buildings, designing four of them himself. The Graduate School was one such commission. Built in 1913 and distanced 1.6 kilometres south-west of campus, it is a highly developed academic complex structured around an irregular, picturesque arrangement of quadrangles that cultivate an aura of scholarly erudition. Its masterly siting upon a hill marked by the profile of Cleveland Tower, inspired one twentieth-century art historian to describe it as 'the finest example of Collegiate Gothic architecture in America'.

The architectural firm Day & Klauder also assumed the Collegiate Gothic baton, producing a series of masterful, inventive interpretations of the style. The firm was responsible for the dormitory grouping at the north-west corner of campus envisaged in Cram's 1907 master plan, Holder and Hamilton Halls (1910). The complex assumed the form of two enclosed courts, anchored by the elegant silhouette of a 43-metre tall tower which echoed that of Canterbury Cathedral. Alive to the rich language of Gothic, the ensemble revels in its rhythm of gables, rectilinear tracery and pointed archways, extending even to the inclusion of a monastic cloister.[49]

Gothic reigned dominant until the mid-twentieth century, but in the second half of the century, Princeton cautiously began to experiment with modernism. The focus for this was the development of the eastern precinct, which housed the athletic facilities, eating clubs and science facilities. Robertson Hall (1965) stands in a conspicuous location as a western gateway to the precinct (Figure 2.35). Designed by Minoru Yamasaki, it is an elegant yet curious edifice that blends the strikingly modern with echoes of Antiquity. Intentionally reminiscent of a Greek temple, the building is wrapped by a ribbon of slender, tapering, concrete columns that march in locked step around its perimeter. Brilliantly white in sunlight, at night light luminously spills out from its soaring vertical expanses of plate glass. Further to the east, the massive Engineering complex terminates the boundary of the precinct. The Engineering Quadrangle (1962) and the adjoining Von Neumann Engineering Research Laboratory (1979) are ranked amongst the least successful elements of Princeton's environment. Incongruous to Princeton's campus, this is a soberingly utilitarian series of buildings. Although at its heart lays a surprisingly attractive, landscaped garden, even this glimmer of cheer is illogically hidden within the esoteric distribution of buildings. The Engineering Quadrangle illustrates the problematic nature of this precinct. No overall plan guided its growth and buildings rarely have any accord with their neighbours, the result being an inharmonious scattering of structures with no unifying focus.[50]

The second half of the twentieth century also saw an expansion of the south campus. Contemporaneous to the Engineering Quadrangle, the Architecture School was built in 1963. Its rectilinear forms, sparse ornamentation, flat roofs and regular patterning of windows mark it out as a product of its time, but its design is far more compelling than that of the Engineering Quadrangle, and is integrated into its surroundings. Volumes are broken up into human-scale spaces; it utilized the red brick and limestone trim vocabulary of its neighbours; and incorporates a string-course in deference to its neighbour, 1879 Hall. Post-modernism was introduced onto south campus with the Thomas Molecular Laboratory (1986) and the George LaVie Schultz Laboratory (1993) by Venturi, Scott Brown Associates (Figure 1.44). The long, rectangular forms of the buildings are relieved by interplay of colour and patterns in brick and limestone, alluding to the brick and limestone façades that populate this area of campus, such as

2.35 Robertson Hall, Princeton University
Photo: Janice Hazeldine/Alamy

Guyot Hall (1909). The entrance façade of the Thomas Molecular Laboratory whispers of Princeton's Gothic Revival heritage, with its ogee-like arch drawing focus to its main door. Similarly, the windows of the Schultz Laboratory are divided into panes, reminiscent of the leaded mullions of this tradition. Venturi's buildings thus enter into the spirit of the campus, responding to its neo-Gothic architectural legacy yet not descending into parody.[51]

As these modern science facilities illustrate, the Collegiate Gothic is an essential ingredient of the campus's persona, indistinguishable from the identity of the college itself. Much aided by generous endowments, Princeton has attracted designers with innate grasps of the expressive qualities of Collegiate Gothic. President Wilson addressed alumni in 1902:

> We have added a thousand years to the history of Princeton by merely putting those lines in our buildings which point every man's imagination to the historic traditions of learning in the English-speaking race.[52]

Princeton was one of countless American universities of the period to enlist Collegiate Gothic as a device to invest their settings with venerability and permanence by championing the medieval ancestry of their educational ideals. Blair Arch, Holder Tower, and Cleveland Tower have all become entrenched as landmarks of a campus steeped in tradition. The university's crenellated towers, elegant oriels and characterful grotesques are indelibly imprinted in the minds of its students, professors, alumni and visitors as 'being Princeton'. The historical decision in 1896 to remodel the campus marked the beginning of an aesthetic and ideological commitment to the style still important to the modern university, as the recent Whitman College (2007) demonstrates (Figure 2.36). This sprawling residential complex on south campus utilized not only the Gothic vocabulary, but also traditional load-bering masonry construction. Designed by classicist Demetri Porphyrios, ranges of buildings are arranged to evoke the irregular walled towns of the Middle Ages, guarded on its western side by a tree-planted moat. A bridge leads through an arched gateway into the large open courtyard. The variety and intricacy of Whitman's massing and scale, combined with the extravagantly high quality of build, leave the visitor with the sense that Whitman's walls will last, and be enjoyed, for centuries to come. The issue of how its campus architecture should represent its values and identity has been well prioritized at Princeton. The university has predominantly followed a policy that cultivates a spirit of its permanence, heritage and gravity.

2.36 Whitman Hall, Princeton University
Photo: Janice Hazeldine/Alamy

The campus does not rely on any one extraordinary individual building for this spirit; its charm arises from the surprises of its vistas or the contrasts between open space and enclosure that are products of the planning approaches taken in its 250 year history. Amongst its buildings, a network of large and small open spaces interweaves. Humanized in scale, they provide edifying environments for relaxing, studying or merely passing through en route to other destinations. The importance of landscape has long been recognized by the university. Harold Shapiro, president from 1988 to 2001, acknowledged,

> One of the university's most valuable resources is the beauty of the campus landscape. The landscape is similar to a work of art in the powerful responses to beauty it is capable of eliciting from us, and the pleasure it gives us.[53]

Historically, the psychological heart of the campus is Canon Green, the open expanse between Nassau Hall and Clio and Whig Halls, but carefully planned and maintained landscapes are dotted throughout the grounds. McCosh Walk, for instance, is a pedestrian path creating an east–west axis across central campus to the Engineering Quadrangle, shaded by a colonnade of soaring elms and beeches. The college courtyards, Scudder Plaza before Robertson Hall, and McCosh Court beside the University Chapel provide places of tranquillity and calm.

The precinct around the Chapel was designed by Beatrix Jones Farrand, and no discussion of Princeton's campus could go without mention of the landscape gardener whose work is as defining a part of Princeton's environment as is Collegiate Gothic. From 1912, Farrand spent 30 years shaping the campus, and established the rules which continue to guide landscape design at Princeton. She instituted systematic guidelines for its landscaping to provide uninterrupted views and circulation and to emphasize the architectural lines of buildings, through climbing plants and creepers. Farrand cleared shrubs and low branching conifers that hindered movement and views; chose plants that bloomed in spring or autumn to coincide with the school's calendar; and used creepers and wall plants within quadrangles to keep them uncluttered. Whitman College's espaliered hydrangeas and climbing Boston ivy continues patterns established by Farrand. This perpetuation of landscaping traditions positively contributes to the unity of campus.[54]

The thoughtful planning and stewardship of Princeton's physical environment has produced one of America's most impressive scholastic settings. This setting is the product of the campus's gradual evolution, shaped by a series of distinct chapters of growth and several master plans. Since its earliest incarnation as a large single structure set in open green land which pioneered the use of the word *campus*, Princeton has been a trailblazer in campus organization. From its geometric and symmetrical neo-classicism of the 1830s, to the informality of the picturesque nature phase of the 1870s, to the distinctive silhouettes and quadrangular planning of Collegiate Gothic, and the appearance of modernism and post-modernism in the second half of the twentieth century, Princeton's campus epitomizes many of the collegiate planning trends of the last 250 years. It has succeeded in uniting these by utilizing the constant themes of human-scale building and enclosed landscapes. An intimate network of outdoor spaces framed by richly decorated architecture, Princeton has carefully carved for itself an identity that powerfully proclaims its values, history and ambitions.

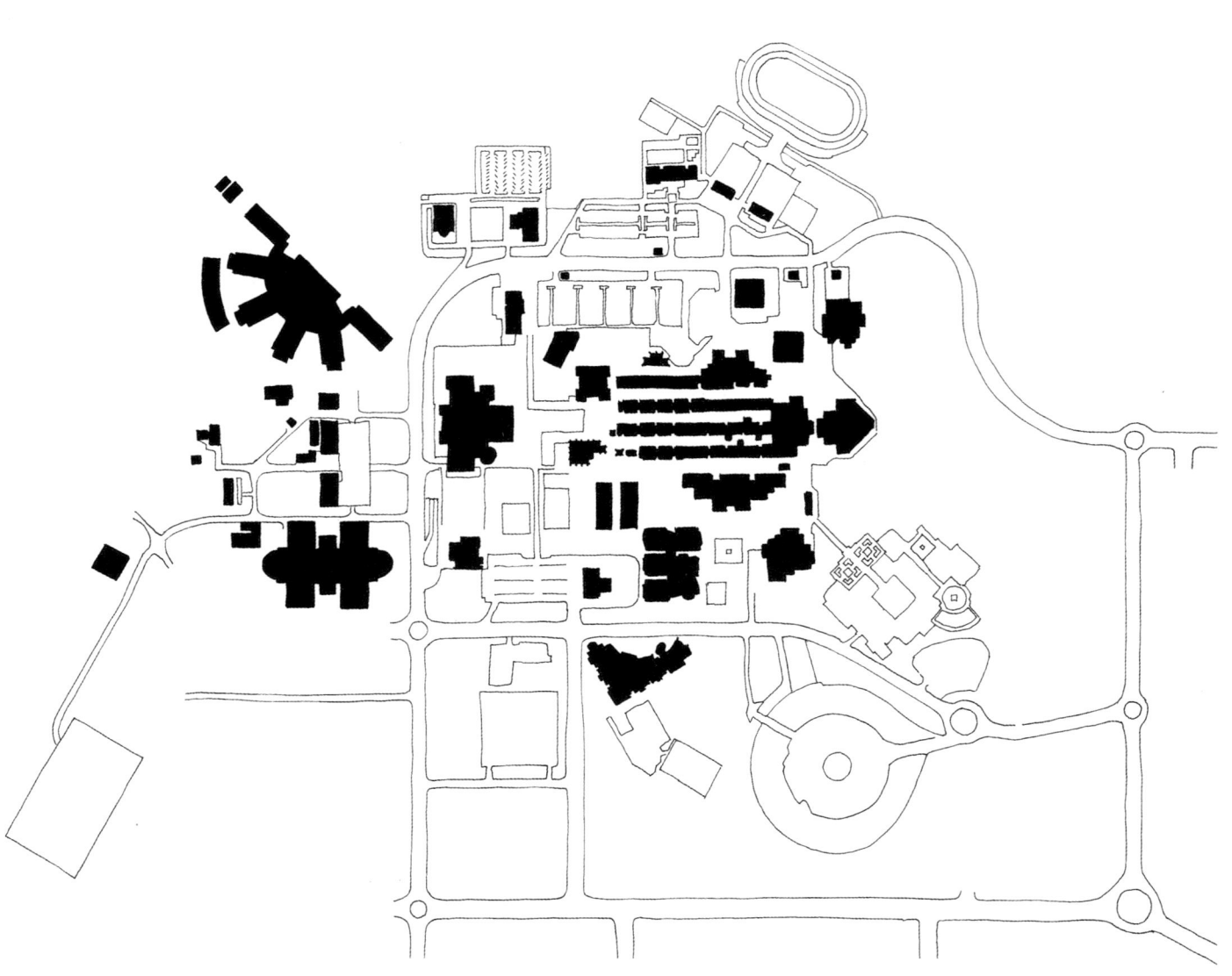

2.37 Plan, Qatar University

Qatar University
Doha, Qatar

With the tremendous wealth generated by the oil industry in the Arab States in the second half of the twentieth century, came an equally striking impact upon the lives of those in the Gulf nations. The technology and industry of the modern West permeated through the culture. Yet certainly from the last quarter of the century, architecture was a vehicle for exploring methods of integrating modern technologies with the old traditions of building that reflected the lifestyles and mores of the ancient culture. Inspiration has been sought from ancient decorative motifs or symbolic historic buildings and re-imagined to meet present conditions. These efforts towards a renewed cultural identity have often been directed towards the building of educational institutions, a trend of which the University of Qatar is a paramount example. Founded in 1973, the university is a 'whole-cloth' campus designed by architect, Kamal El Kafrawi. The campus embodies an Islamic presence, yet caters for the technological and administrative needs of the contemporary university.[55]

This result has much to do with the approach of the architect. He initially made a lengthy, careful study of the traditional ways of life in Qatar, and its older buildings, uncovering a palpable influence of Bedouin traditions:

> Architecture is a tangible expression of a civilisation, the product of the intellectual, social, economic and political activity of a whole people; construction technology is simply the tool with which to give form to this expression. One has therefore closely to analyse the environment of villages, towns and cities in the Arab world, to determine the effects of Western contemporary Architecture. Since the technology has been applied without the philosophy which underlies it, the modern buildings are foreign to the area, which shows how far Arab architecture has lost direction, and the profound effect this has on the individual and his environment.[56]

It was not until two years later that his design began to take shape, and when it did it bore the fruits of his study. From the outset, El Kafrawi dismissed the use of Western building forms as obstructive to the creation of an Islamic community. However, he also recognized the irrationality of ignoring modern technology by

2.38 Qatar University
Photo: QU students and employees

2.39 Engineering courtyard, Qatar University
Photo: QU students and employees

designing and building in a purely traditional way, without change or improvement. Instead, El Kafrawi reasoned that European and American technologies should be used within the university to enhance the building forms traditional to the Islamic culture, thus enjoying the material advantages of twentieth-century progress whilst rooting the institution to its native civilization and constructing an identity reflective of a bond with the Qatari people. The architect sought to borrow from Western technology as much as was necessary and from Arabic architecture as much as was practicable.[57]

Building began in 1980, with the first phase entering completion in 1985. The university was located away from Doha's commercial district to create a dramatic setting that exploited the natural topography (Figure 2.38). Situated on an elevated site, the graded incline, descending towards the lowlands and with views across the sea, proffers an impressive panorama. The campus is structured around a ring road, within which are housed the academic buildings with sports and ancillary facilities on the outside. The two colleges for men and women are located at the north and south ends of the campus, with a mosque, auditorium, library, cultural centre and so forth, in between. As a 'whole-cloth' campus, the buildings form an ensemble of visual unity in terms of material, colour and form. The low-lying academic buildings are laid out upon two geometric forms, an octagon 8.4 metres in width and a square of 3.5 metres in width. The two forms are connected to form a modular grid pattern repeated across the campus. These modular shapes represent a fresh take on old Islamic geometric patterns, yet contemporary technologies were profited by in the use of precast concrete as the primary construction mode.

Circulation on the campus is provided not by the western system of corridors and enclosed stairways, but rather by a strategy honed to Qatar's individual circumstances. This involves a series of internal and partly covered courtyards for horizontal movement, and open stairs in those courtyards for vertical movement (Figure 2.39). Although less cost-effective in terms of built space, this system reflects the country's hot climate and was envisioned to promote social interaction by the frequent use of the courtyards.[58]

2.40 Library, Qatar University
Photo: QU students and employees

Similarly, climatic conditions are addressed in the university's approach to controlling and harnessing natural light. The light levels appropriate for visual and psychological comfort were established through scientific research, and these were achieved throughout the campus through various traditional solutions that have been applied for centuries. Cubic structures were constructed on the roofs of the modular built units, creating Towers of Light that provide filtered aerial lighting into the rooms below (Figure 2.40). Overhead lighting reflects the light to create subdued indoor illumination. Square lobbies adjoin the octagonal units, and act as indirect light sources for the octagonal lecture rooms. Finally, carved timber screens, known as Mashrabiya, are found throughout the campus. Mashrabiya is the name of a distinctive type of wood carving particular to the Arab East and developed in ancient architecture, which was used mainly to allow cool breezes to enter homes in the heat of summer. Placed on vertical windows in Qatar University, they diffuse light entering the buildings thus reducing bright glare. Furthermore, as decorative forms in themselves, they provide an aesthetic dimension to the campus. All these elements control and manipulate light intensity, while intensifying bonds with the past.[59]

Past and present were further connected through El Kafrawi's approach to ventilation. Millennia ago, it was discovered that at higher elevations the air is cooler than at lower levels, and to profit from this the wind-tower was invented. The Tower of Winds is the historic form of natural ventilation used throughout the Gulf region, and through his study of the Doha locality El Kafrawi noted the few surviving wind-tower houses and modernized the principle for his purpose. The wind-tower structures crown the University buildings, dispensing natural ventilation to lecture rooms and residences to support mechanical ventilation and air conditioning. The striking outline they create on the skyline, furthermore, has become one of the most notable features on campus. They divest the buildings with a distinct form and meaning, with the additional dimension of cultural identity.[60]

Natural temperature control is further provided by a series of low-tech, time-honoured solutions. External walls are comparably

2.41 Qatar University
Photo: QU students and employees

thick, ranging from 0.6 to 1.5 metres to provide insulation. Employing octagonal built units reduces the length of time the sun shines on any one side, thus moderating heat absorption. The complex geometric forms also produce greater shading for outside areas and courtyards. The garden courtyards themselves were planted to cool air near buildings, for air around water and vegetation is naturally cooler. Serving multiple functions, these courtyards range from open to partially screened, and are enlivened by fountains and flora. They function to soften the geometry of the built environment and provide pleasant, varied settings for casual meetings and activities (Figure 2.41).[61]

The octagonal built form reflects El Kafrawi's concern to cater for change. The eight-sided format of the lecture rooms allows for a surprising degree of flexibility in teaching methods. The lecturer can stand in the middle of the room, establishing proximity with all members of the class, or he can adopt a traditional location at one extreme of the room facing the whole audience. The layout as a whole anticipates future expansion as the fledgling university develops, for the octagonal plan can be extended in any direction without external constraint on sources of ventilation or light.[62]

The campus is not without its faults, however. A 2008 assessment of the campus revealed weaknesses in its circulation system. The site is confusing, and many users have difficulties navigating the site. When asked how easy it was to find their way around the campus, 70 per cent of respondents replied that it was difficult. The explanations cited included, 'bad signage system', 'corridors and buildings all look alike', or 'difficult to distinguish between different colleges'.[63] In their repetitive modular format, the exteriors of the buildings give little intimation of their interior function, which has disorientating and disconcerting repercussions.

Yet despite its flaws, the campus represented an important innovation in the formation of a modern Arab architecture. The design identifies with the contemporary world, yet creates a subtle, traditional environment reflective of the university's cultural aspirations. Referencing and reinterpreting traditional building forms, it establishes continuance with Arabic culture that strengthens the psychological bond with the national character, establishing a sense of continuity in the modern university. It is rooted to its locale through quotations of Islamic architectural forms and its sensitivity to climate and topography, and in so being establishes a distinct identity that stands it apart from its peers. It is at once both deferential to the Arab culture and a unique landmark upon the Doha skyline.

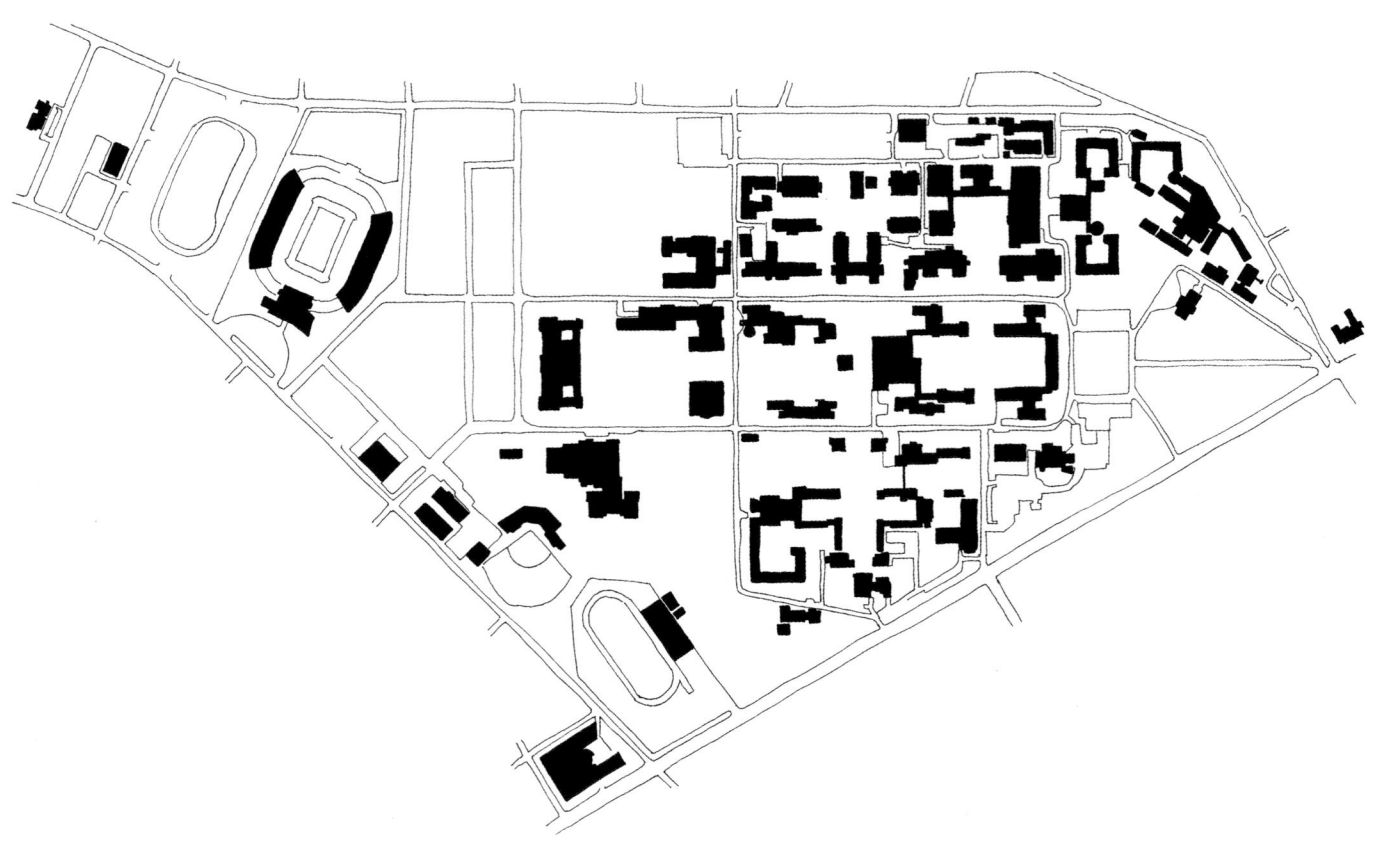

2.42 Plan, Rice University

Rice University
Houston, USA

> We wanted something that was beautiful, if we could make it so, Southern in its spirit, and with some quality of continuity with the historic and cultural past. Manifestly the only thing to do was to invent something approaching a new style.
> (Ralph Adams Cram[64])

On the flat coastal plains of Texas, Rice University is an oasis of Arcadian parkland, a Mediterranean fantasy within the industrial metropolis of Houston. Opening the doors for the first time in 1912, the Rice Institute, as it was known until 1960, immediately captured the country's imagination, and has continued to do so ever since. What distinguishes Rice as special is its construction of a unique identity and history almost instantaneously from a blank and prosaic canvas.

The foundling institute was shaped greatly by the determination and vision of its first president, Edgar Odell Lovett. In 1909 he engaged the Boston architectural firm, Cram, Goodhue and Ferguson, to prepare a master plan for the new university's site, a flat, bare expanse of 277 acres. The 1910 General Plan was a lucid, dynamic and Beaux-Arts inspired vision, with groups of buildings arranged around open and closed courtyards, organized hierarchically along major and minor axes (Figure 2.43). The major axis ran 1.2 kilometres west to east through the centre of campus, bisecting a vast Academic Court, and terminating in the Persian Gardens (never executed). Structures were clustered according to function – residential, academic, and athletic – then grouped by subject discipline (humanities, engineering and sciences) in quadrangles along the main axis and parallel east–west axes. The long, thin rectangular forms that Cram, Goodhue and Ferguson's buildings were to take both suited the hot, humid climate,

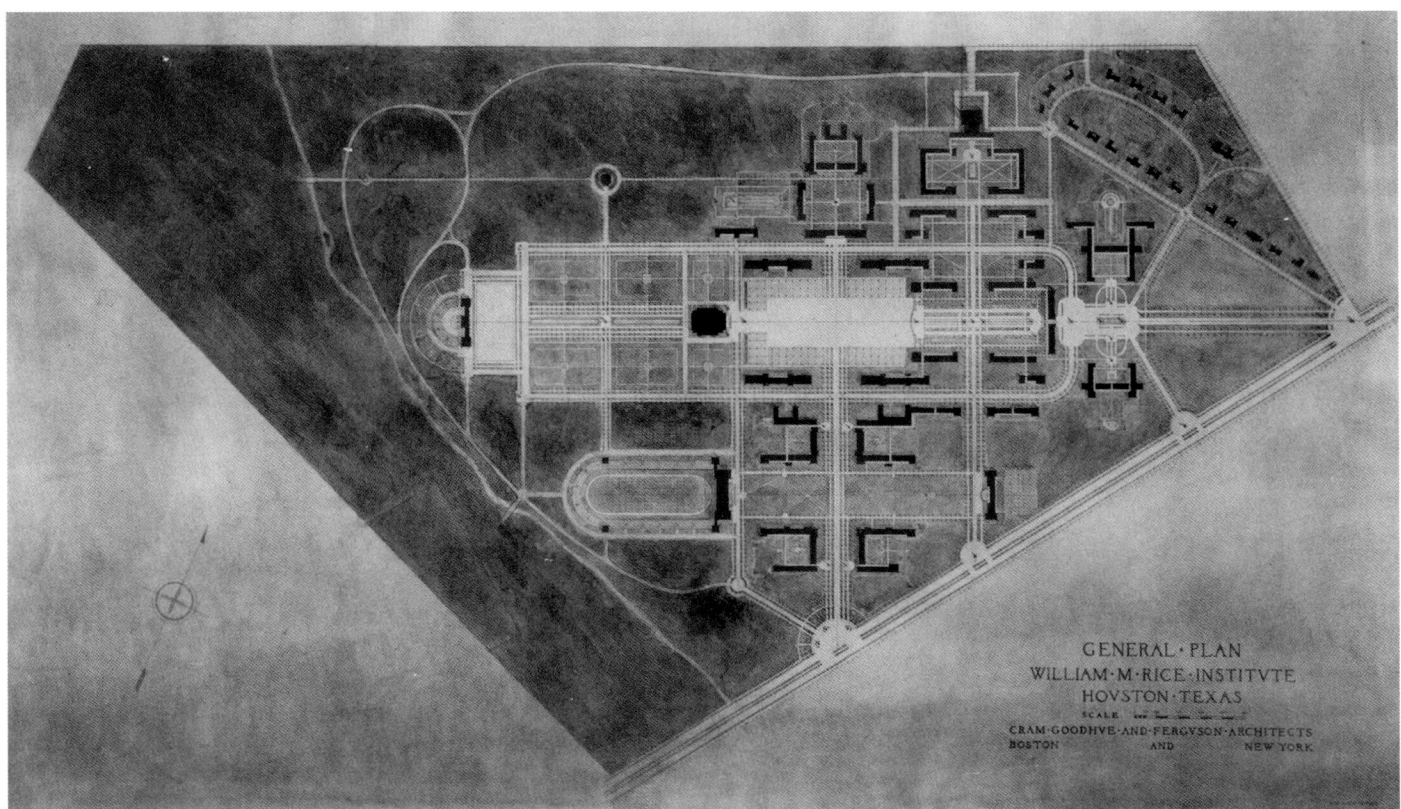

2.43 General Plan, 1910, Rice University
Photo: Woodson Research Centre, Rice University

and underlined the axial organization. Of especial significance to the spatial organization were the trees and hedgerows that the General Plan prescribed to direct vision and movement. The privet hedges and live oak trees created green *allées* that transformed the immeasurable tract of coastal plain into gardens regulated by rhythm, direction and hierarchy. As the university aged and its tree-canopy matured, these verdant *allées* created compelling, complex spaces.

This inspiring sequential experience began at Entrance One, marking the presence of the university on Main Boulevard. Consisting of an arced screen wall and gate piers, Entrance One (1912) signalled a transition into the bucolic world of academia. From this gateway proceeded a carefully structured ceremonial procession leading up to the Academic Quad. The General Plan advised that a line of southern magnolia trees followed by double rows of oak trees line this approach, channelling movement and vista to the centrepiece building of Academic Court, Lovett Hall (1912) (Figure 2.44).[65]

Designed by chief architect, Ralph Adams Cram, Lovett Hall was the institute's first building. Cram recalled that the commission presented him with 'no possible *point d'appui*,…no historical or stylistic precedent, and no ideas imposed by the President or Trustees,' impelling him to invent a stylistic idiom that would be appropriate for the Texan school. Motivated by Houston's Mediterranean-like climate, Cram devised an architectural language welding elements from 'Southern France and Italy, Dalmatia, the Peloponnesus, Byzantium, Anatolia, Syria, Sicily, Spain…knit together as well as possible in a unity…'[66] Lovett Hall is the most pronounced illustration of Rice's exotic neo-Byzantine, Islamic-influenced architecture. It features Hellenistic and Justinian-inspired carvings, hints of the Hagia Sophia and round Byzantine arches (Figure 2.45). Like Cram's other campus buildings, the structure is a horizontally elongated rectangular building, thin in section to enhance ventilation in the humid climate, arranged symmetrically around an archway entrance. As distinctive as its architecture were the colours of Lovett's materials: rose-hued brick, red granite, white marble, and polychromed marble. The distinctive architecture gave to Rice an identity. The newborn institute lacked both history and traditions, and it was this that Cram managed to contrive.[67]

Sharing Lovett Hall's aesthetic were Cram's other designs, the Mechanical Laboratory and Power House (1912), which provided the northern boundary of the Engineering Quad to the north of the Academic Court on a secondary east–west axis, and the Physics Building (Herztein Hall, 1914). The latter sits at right angles to Lovett Hall, on the northern perimeter of the Academic Court. Cram also designed three residential buildings, South Hall (now Will Rice College, 1912), East Hall (now Baker College, 1915) and West Hall (now Hanszen College, 1916), that formed the basis of the university's present residential college system at the southern portion of campus, grouped into four quadrangles on a secondary east–west axis. The dormitory group shared the round-arched windows and arcades of the academic buildings, with overhanging hipped red-tiled roofs, projecting wooden window bays, and iron balcony railings that impart overtones of Spanish Mission.[68]

With the Second World War came a new president and an overhaul of the board of trustees, a change which was reflected in an altered approach to campus planning and a revitalized building campaign. Between 1946 and 1950, the university doubled its total number of structures, adding M. D. Anderson Hall, Abercrombie Engineering Laboratory, Fondren Library, a president's house, Weiss College, Rice Stadium, Rice Gymnasium and Autry Court. Although embedded within conservative practice, these buildings signalled a rejection of Cram's General Plan, led by local architectural firm Staub & Rather. The most dramatic evidence of this is the siting of the Fondren Library across the main axis, blocking the transition from the Academic Court to the Great Square to the west. The destructive impact of this decision in terms of loss of space and vista is irrefutable, yet the vision that Cram had forged was so vivid and tenacious that the overarching scheme proved resilient to these alterations.[69]

Further injury was inflicted upon Cram's vision in the 1950s, with the construction of the Rice Memorial Centre in 1958. Positioned in alignment with Anderson Hall rather than set back as the master plan dictated, the structure was built in one of the groves of oak trees that defined the boundary of the Great Square, compounding the loss of spatial integrity of this space initiated by the Fondren Library. Yet architect Harvin C. Moore's design for the building does demonstrate an assertive use of materials and detailing. Llano granite courses, striped brick and limestone walls, and lobbies floored with polished travertine succeed in translating the substantiality of Cram's original buildings to the modern student centre. The cloister, a later addition to the complex built in 1969 to designs by White, Klatt &

2.44 Lovett Hall, Rice University
Photo: Tiffany McElweenie

2.45 Lovett Hall (detail), Rice University
Photo: Sabrina Thach

Porcher, is a highly gratifying space. Surrounding a courtyard of low plant beds and live oaks and lavishly paved with brick and marble, it is a perfectly proportioned, well-designed area that ranks amongst Rice's most successful outdoor spaces.[70]

From the late 1970s, a new design agenda came to the fore at Rice. A fresh generation of trustees came to recognize architecture's capacity for expressing the university's mission and philosophy, as well as the headline-grabbing potential of leading architects. Activating this trend was the extension to Anderson Hall (1981), by world-renowned practitioner James Stirling. Stirling embraced the idyllic quadrangles of Cram's vision, proffering a restrained design that reflected not only the original palette of brick and stone but also the General Plan's aesthetic expression and planning approach. The result was an L-shaped addition to the original School of Architecture that created an open courtyard. Materials harmonized with the old, and eaves and cornice lines were maintained; only the asymmetrically placed circular window of the west end and the two conical metal and glass skylights suggest its modern provenance.[71]

With this precedent, the university's ambitious architectural patronage was continued with Herring Hall by César Pelli & Associates. Completed in 1984, this post-modernist structure effectively blurred the boundary between past and present. The building is located in a prominent position along the main axis, forming the southern boundary of the Great Square in a position where the General Plan had allocated a structure. Organized as a long, thin, U-shape building, its central feature is a courtyard which Pelli aligned with the courtyard of the Rice Memorial Centre opposite, while its entrances similarly align with the principal axes of the Memorial Centre and the Earth Sciences complex. Thus, Pelli demonstrated the continuing applicability of the original organizing principles by reconditioning those buildings that had veered from Cram's concept back into the fabric of the General Plan. In terms of stylistic expression, Pelli adapted the visual grammar of Rice's architectural inheritance to a modern context. Herring Hall employs St Joseph's brick which had been used by Cram; its south-facing street façade echoes the composition of the square ground-floor windows and horizontality of the Abercrombie Engineering Laboratory. Yet Pelli's design is very much in tune with a modernist ethos. Unlike Cram's richly carved neo-Byzantine structures built from load-bearing masonry, Pelli sheathed red brick and glass over a steel skeleton, its underlying construction cloaked but not disguised. The loggia, for example, provides glimpses of this frame for, while its columns present a brick façade to the exterior, they are steel on the interior face. Different coloured bricks are utilized on the long and end walls, while non-load bearing walls are distinguished by a lively diaper pattern. Articulating the building's construction and organization in this way reveals Pelli's modernist agenda.[72]

The arrival of Stirling and Pelli on campus altered the direction of Rice's campus. Their two buildings offered models as to how the contemporary university could embrace the architectural legacy of Cram. They integrated modern architecture within its historic setting, by restoring the spatial order of the General Plan while acknowledging the altered conditions between the 1910s and 1980s through modern building techniques.

The success of Stirling and Pelli ensured the continuity of the practice of hiring high-profile architects during the 1990s. This decade witnessed a sustained construction boom on campus, marked especially by the westward expansion of the campus beyond the Great Square, where Cram had intended extensive Persian Gardens. Alice Pratt Brown Hall (1991) marked the new western termination of the extended main axis. Designed by Ricardo Bofill and the Taller de Arquitectura, the huge, low building, presented an imposing aspect. Its eastern façade, which faced a newly-created plaza, stretched 142 metres across, dominated by a repetitive syncopation of giant concrete columns and narrow windows. Except for the use of St Joseph's brick, Brown Hall displayed no concern to establish contextual references with Rice's architectural identity. Since this site was devoid of a mature tree covering, the hall makes for a conspicuous, isolated structure. It is related only on its eastern side toward Jamail Plaza, installed by Sasaki Associates in 1998. A dark brick and granite paved square, it represented a new type of exterior space on the Rice campus. Edged by four garden parterres, the plaza centres around a low, domed fountain. To the south of the plaza is James A. Baker III Hall (1997). A bulky, red brick and white trim building, it is strongly inspired by Cram's designs, with a hint of Islamic detail that alludes to the siting of the intended Persian Gardens, in the shape of its first-floor windows for example.

2.46 Rice University
Photo: Bruce Sogoloff

Architects Hammond, Beeby & Babka have accented the triple entrance portal with masonry detailing and recessed round arched windows. In 1993, John Outram Associates designed an addition to the Engineering Quadrangle, Duncan Hall (1996). Adjacent to Cram's Physics Building and Lovett Hall, it is an eccentric, colourful building that perpetuated Rice's tradition of creating decorative motifs using brickwork.

2005 saw the inauguration of a new master plan, devised by Michael Graves and Associates to provide for 50 years of campus growth. The plan counselled for future development on the south-west portion of the campus, along a north–south axis extending south from Jamail Plaza. Supplementing the plan, the university has pursued further construction. Amongst the most recent is the Brochstein Pavilion (2008). Designed by Thomas Phifer and Partners, the structure is a 550-square metre glass box housing a café and lounge to the west of the Fondren Library. The project was designed as an informal space for students and faculty to reintroduce vitality back into the centre of campus, which has been diluted by the residential colleges at the campus's boundaries, and to transform the unstructured, neglected Great Court into a centre of activity. The building is roofed by a white steel and aluminium trellis that overhangs the structure to cover and shade the surrounding terrace. In the overhanging roof and porches the architect consciously acknowledged its architectural context. Wide double doors span its perimeter, connecting the interior with the terrace and opening it to the landscape. Landscape was a key factor in shaping the design. New concrete walks, rows of live oaks, planting beds and long, black concrete pools were inserted into the courtyard, encouraging the activity within the centre to spill out into the gardens.

As Brochstein Pavilion's siting on Cram's grand east–west axis demonstrates, the spatial organization of Cram's vision has on occasions been sorely infringed. Blocking the impressive vista of the Academic Quad with the Fondren Library is the most glaring example of this. The original plan was tremendous in its scope, and it was never fully executed. Yet, in spite of this and the inescapable workings of time, Rice is distinguished for the steadfastness with which the essence of Cram's concept has been preserved. This has much to do with the strength, lucidity and coherence of the General Plan, structured around a central axis with supplementary axes. Architecture and landscape architecture have been conceived in harmony to reinforce and define the main spaces, the streets, the quadrangles, the courtyards and plazas that establish Rice's sense of place. The arched walkways and porches featuring in Rice's oldest architecture to its most recent are integral to Rice's physical identity (Figure 2.46). The construction of a distinctive aesthetic at Rice, combining an inventive fusion of medieval Byzantine and Moorish elements, gave the new campus an immediate institutional legacy. The buildings impressed with their authority, strength and richness. And the perpetuation of Rice's original integration of architecture, planning and landscape design within its current construction programmes enables the campus to remain as emotionally compelling as ever.

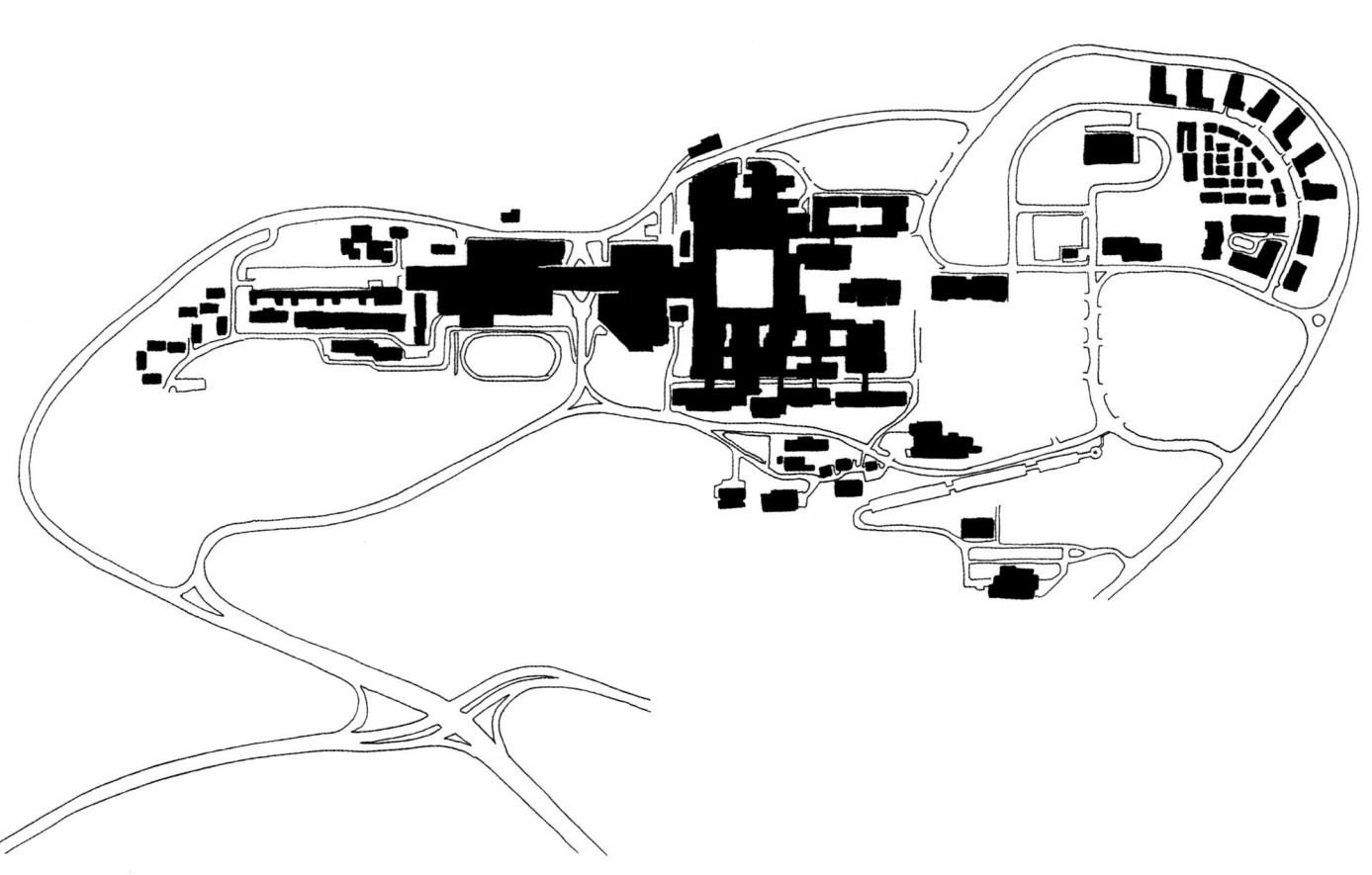

2.47 Plan, Simon Fraser University

Simon Fraser University
Burnaby, Canada

Located 10 kilometres from central Vancouver on a secluded hill top, the buildings of Simon Fraser University at Burnaby nestle into its summit, stepping naturally down the graded terrain. They appear such an integral, organic part of the landscape that it is hardly believable that its core campus was built in only a handful of years in the mid-1960s. In 1962 predictions were made that more student places would be needed in the Vancouver area for the 1965 intake, and in early 1963 it was decided to found a new institution, Simon Fraser University. With phenomenal pace, a 1,200 acre site was donated by the town of Burnaby and an architectural competition open to local practitioners was launched by the middle of that year. Construction began a few months later and by autumn 1965, the new campus received its first intake of 2,500 students (Figure 2.48).[73]

From the outset, the import of the physical fabric of the university was realized. Despite looming time pressures to have the campus

2.48 Aerial view, Simon Fraser University
Photo: Waite Air Photos

2.49 Academic Quadrangle, Simon Fraser University
Photo: Clara Lo

in working order for the start of the academic year of 1965, newly appointed chancellor Gordon Shrum considered its design and planning a vital priority: 'We have a general artistic responsibility to the whole public to create buildings that set a high standard of beauty and efficiency.' For Shrum, creating an attractive, edifying environment was requisite to any university. 'Architecture determines the nature, the inner philosophy of a university', he wrote.[74] Under Shrum, impressive architecture was to be the delineating factor that proclaimed the ambitions and ideologies of higher education in modern Canada, and in this lofty goal he found a like mind in the 1963 competition winner, Arthur Erickson.

Erickson, together with Geoffrey Massey, received the commission to prepare the master plan for the site. Their plan, the first phase of which was completed in 1965, represented a sweeping rethinking of the traditional North American campus. They sought an atmosphere of learning predicated upon a move away from hierarchy and formality, towards an integration of disciplines and a focus on informal exchange. This they achieved through an innovative organization of space, divided by use (academic, social, recreational and residential) rather than by department. The typically dispersed university campus was compressed into a single building taking the form of a linear spine to which all buildings would be linked. Almost all teaching rooms and faculty offices were housed in the huge Academic Quadrangle, with lecture theatres and laboratories on the adjacent, terraced hillside. The Quadrangle in turn leads via a grand series of steps to the heart of Erickson's design, the covered mall. This wide rectangular expanse serves as a ceremonial plaza and social space, flanked by the library, theatre, student centre, and coffee shop. Given the intemperate climate, it is covered by an enormous glazed roof, while the entire complex of service, recreational and academic spaces is unified by uninterrupted covered walkways that stretch a kilometre from end to end. The design concept, eulogized Erickson, fostered interdisciplinary relationships and the sharing of knowledge through proximity and common spaces, while the social character of the university was embodied in its walkway system. It represented a careful fusion of academic philosophy and design.[75]

The competition judges were keenly impressed by the design's capacity for expansion. Building began at the centre of campus densely clustered, and grew outwards as required. This strategy provided the campus with an impression of completeness at early stages of its construction, while preparing the ground for future growth. This provision for growth has stood the campus well in its future development, and is a vital consideration for campus planners.

Containing the campus in this manner enabled more of the surrounding landscape to be left undisturbed. Perched on Burnaby Mountain's summit and surrounded by pine forest, this setting is one of the chief assets of the campus. Consideration of the setting was a key influence on the form its architecture was to assume. Rejecting high-rise buildings as adventitious for a hilltop location, Erickson built close to the contours of the land. Responding to the topography, terraces are cut into the hillside, gracefully ascending and descending with the ridge of the site so that it melts into the natural terrain. Providing a fluent progression from the wooded slopes to the built environment was of great importance to the architect. Extending the linear spine of buildings along the mountain's east–west ridge afforded buildings views to the north and south, and aligned them with one of Vancouver's signal landmarks, the First Narrows (Lions Gate) Bridge. The Academic Quadrangle in particular offers spectacular vistas; by raising it upon concrete pilotis, Erickson has dissolved the boundaries between this central teaching facility and the distant landscape, creating a monumental space (Figure 2.49). Comparisons with a Greek acropolis or medieval monastery perched upon a mountain have frequently been cited; Erickson himself has mentioned several dramatic hilltop cities when discussing Simon Fraser, including the Zapotec centre of Monte Albán near Oaxaxa in southern Mexico, the acropolis of the Greek city of Pergamum in Turkey, and the abandoned Mughal city of Fatehpur Sikri in India.[76]

The basic plan is predicated upon a long series of large squares with repetitive elements, in which massive horizontal beams supported

2.50 Mall, Simon Fraser University
Photo: Susan Gittins

by piers serve to organize the mass and control views across the landscape. Erickson revels in a Brutalist vocabulary, above all in the abundance of concrete. 'Unfinished concrete cleaned by sandblasting or bushhammering is the basic structural and finishing material,… becomes as noble as any limestone', wrote Erickson.[77] Simon Fraser was built using reinforced concrete with large spans and cantilevered floors reflecting the late-modernist conviction that buildings should be honest to construction and severe in decoration. This expanse of exposed concrete was complemented by a brace of modern construction methods. The glazed roof of the central mall was a notable engineering feat, composed of deep girders and steel tie-rods (Figure 2.50).[78]

Erickson's design catapulted him to international recognition. Simon Fraser was published in journals the world across as the new paradigm for the current expansion of higher education, and its designer went on to enjoy a degree of fame unparalleled by a Canadian architect.

In the decades since the completion of the first phase of the masterplan, the university has continually expanded outwards. The 1970s saw the construction of the administration building (Strand Hall), the classroom complex (Robert C. Brown Hall), the top two floors of the library, and the student centre; the Applied Sciences Building, Education Building, Diamond University Centre, McTaggart-Cowan Hall and Halpern Centre date from the 1980s; and in the 1990s was built the Maggie Benston Centre, Hamilton Hall, East Theatre Annex, and the West Mall Complex.

In the 1990s, Erickson's practice was commissioned to produce an updated master plan for the site. The plan defined that ongoing development should maintain the high density layout and the system of continuous sheltered pedestrian circulation. Foremost in this plan was the construction of the West Mall Complex, in 1996. Continuing the main building spine to the west and the interdisciplinary spirit that originally informed Erickson's design, it is an enclosed 18,000 square-metre building housing several academic faculties, lecture theatres, classrooms, and laboratories, split into three zones. These zones are the mall zone, containing laboratories, classrooms, lecture theatres and social spaces shared by the whole academic community; the departmental zone, housing the various faculties; and the atrium, which divides the mall and departmental spaces. Fully connected with the existing spine building, the new complex is integrated with existing circulation paths to the gymnasium to the north, library to the east and student housing to the west. Like the original 1960s buildings, the structure steps down the site with integral courtyards, maintaining the university's tradition of evocative views whilst providing ample natural light for interiors.

The West Mall perpetuates Simon Fraser's vocabulary of exposed concrete exteriors and robust massings. This aesthetic, though, has not been without its detractors in the years since the campus's opening. Its appearance is frequently affected by the weather, as a member of the History Department, Charles Hamilton, has commented. Hamilton observed that on fine summer days the university was nothing short of breathtaking, but in the midst of dismal winter could feel like a prison. Erickson's buildings were also notorious for construction flaws. As early as 1969, a university overhaul identified 200 leaks that needed attention. Earlier that year, the mall had to be sectioned off following glass roof panels breaking following a particularly heavy snowfall. These failings were ascribed to hasty construction along with cost-cutting, not to poor design. Erickson has criticized the recent building of two residential complexes, The Towers at the west end and UniverCity at the east, for digressing from the master plan. He advised that development should maintain a low, horizontal profile along the mountain top, and he condemned the placement of UniverCity on a higher elevation than the Academic Quadrangle.[79]

UniverCity is a huge construction project designed to redress the lack of a residential community atop Burnaby Mountain (Figure 2.51). The mega-structural residences envisaged by Erickson remained unrealized due to financial constraints, and Simon Fraser grew up as a predominantly commuter campus devoid of evening and weekend activity. With construction commencing in 2001, UniverCity extended Erickson's campus with a mixed-use community of shops, residences, a school and social amenities. The enterprise demonstrates an increasing phenomenon instituted in late-twentieth-century North America in which universities moved into the realm of town planning to address perceived shortcomings in their local community by constructing new buildings in nearby neighbourhoods or on vacant land. The linear spine of the academic core was stretched eastwards to form the High Street along which high-density development is

2.51 UniverCity
Photo: SFU Community Trust

structured. While the Main Mall is punctuated by the Academic Quadrangle in Erickson's complex, so at UniverCity the High Street is interrupted by the Town Square, a public space envisaged as the heart of the collegiate town. Although the verticality of the condominium towers prompted censure from Erickson, UniverCity has espoused a commitment to an architectural style congruous to the original campus.[80]

The visual impact of the architecture of Erickson's campus is stirring. It exemplifies the advantages that can come from a 'whole-cloth' campus, both in terms of aesthetic harmony and in the melding of academic intentions and layout. Abandoning the traditional segregation of departments, the layout necessitates an interdisciplinary use of space and thus greater interdisciplinary engagement. The central mall forms the hub of this desired social interaction. A dramatic and dynamic space, it has been discussed in terms of an intellectual agora or marketplace. Philip Johnson, one of the most influential American architects of the twentieth century, described the mall as 'the best central device for a campus that I know of.'[81] Flanked by the library, a thoroughfare for students on their way to lectures and classes, and lined with benches for informal meetings or moments of pause, the mall evidences how architecture can create an atmosphere of community. In fact, its spatial organization was perceived to be so conducive to student interaction that it was held responsible for the campus unrest in the late 1960s. If the mall is the social hub, then the visual hub is the Academic Quadrangle. The enclosed space, a beautifully landscaped lawn interspersed with a pool and planting, provides a memorable space that captures the imagination. The elevation of the classroom and office accommodation upon concrete piers allows for breathtaking vistas across the horizon. One of the signal achievements of the campus's design is its utilization of this natural asset. Careful consideration was applied to achieving the best views across the landscape and to integrating the concrete complex with its surroundings, rooting the university to its site and providing an attractive draw to students, parents and academics alike.

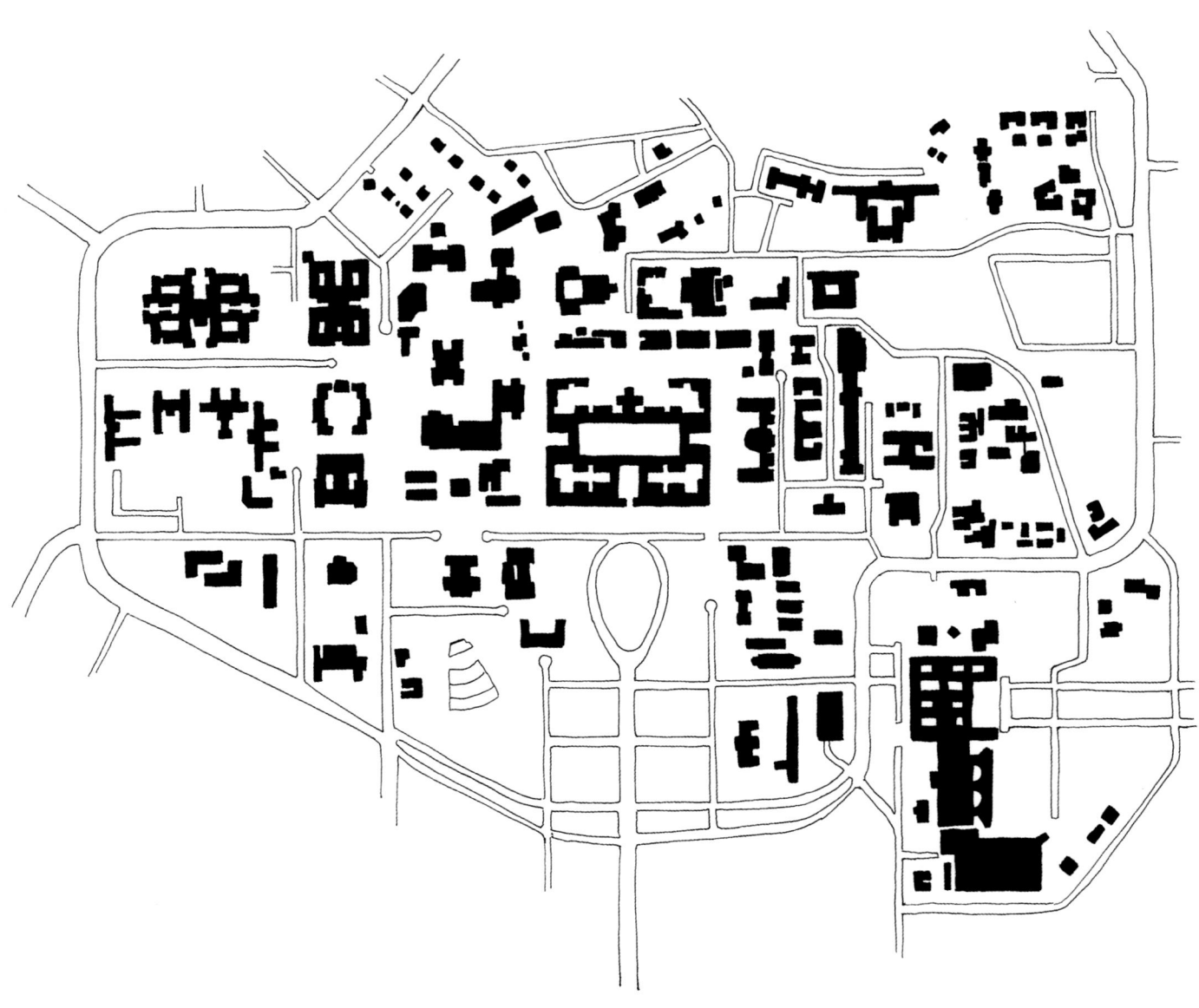

2.52 Plan, Stanford University

Stanford University
Palo Alto, USA

> The student has no need for luxury. Plain living has ever gone with high thinking. But grace and fitness have an educative power too often forgotten in this utilitarian age. These long corridors with their stately pillars, these circles of waving palms, will have their part in the students' training as surely as the chemical laboratory or the seminary room. Each stone in the quadrangle shall teach its lesson of grace and of genuineness.
>   (President David Starr Jordan,
>   Opening Day Address, 1 October 1891)

Stanford University, probably more than any other American college, was moulded by personal motive. Leland Stanford was one of the country's wealthiest citizens when in 1884 his only child, Leland Jr, was fatally struck with typhoid. Within weeks, the broken-hearted parents had determined to commemorate their son by founding a university on their Californian estate in Palo Alto, south of San Francisco. Resolved that the commemoration of their son's memory demanded nothing less than magnificence, Leland and Jane Stanford envisaged a monumental campus laid out with imposing vistas of the surrounding valley and foothills. To realize this, in 1886 they

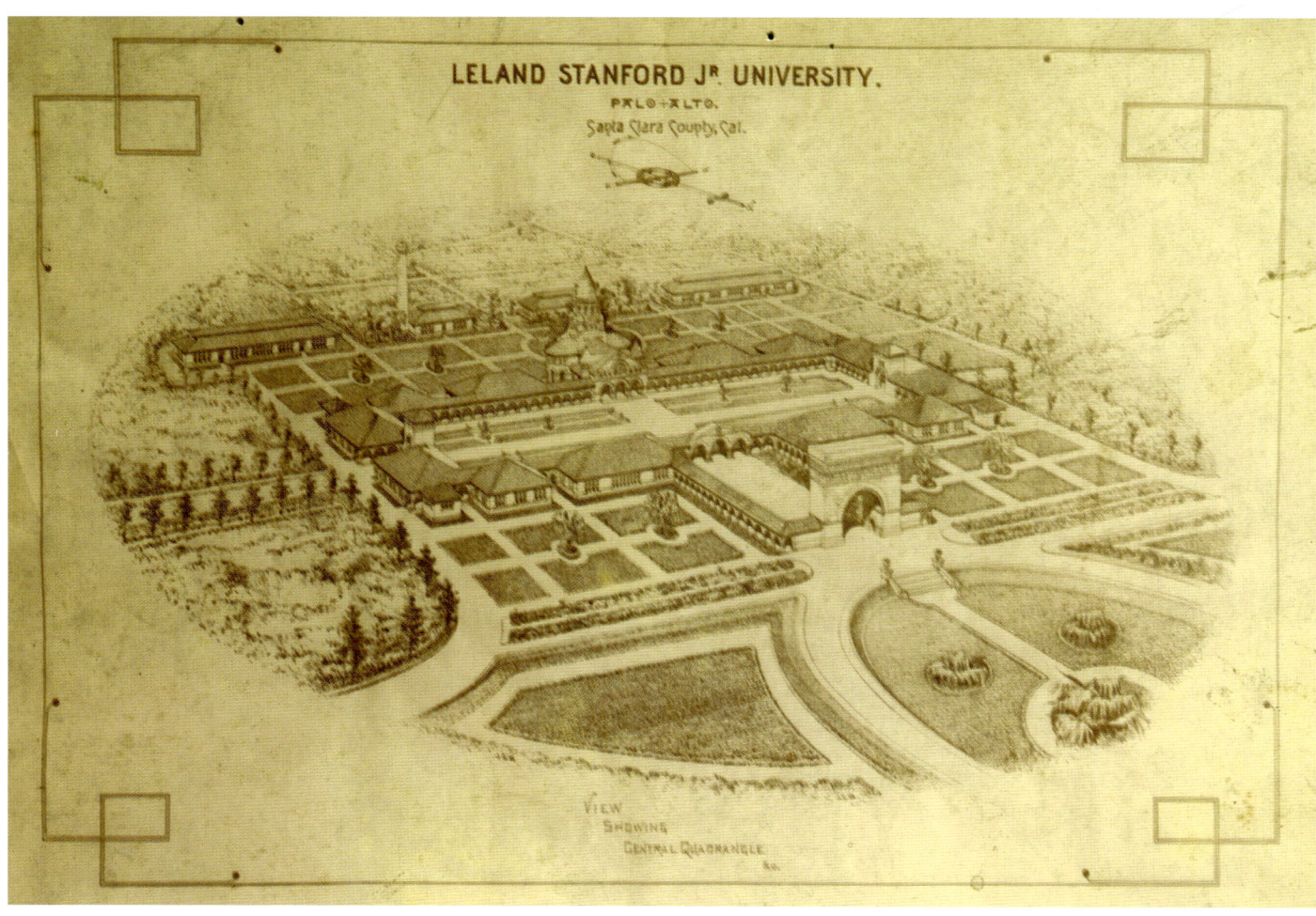

2.53 Master plan 1888, Stanford University
Photo: Courtesy Stanford University Archives

2.54 Stanford University
Photo: Christophe Testi

employed two of the country's most renowned campus design firms, those of landscape architect Frederick Law Olmsted, and Shepley, Rutan and Coolidge, led by Charles Coolidge.

The resulting master plan of 1888 was innovative in several approaches (Figure 2.53). It demonstrated a scale of ambition and gravity unparalleled in American campus design. Distinguished by its formality and unity, the master plan proposed a long approach lined with palm trees establishing a north–south axis leading to a sequence of contained quadrangles. This *allée* punctuated the north side of a large rectangle of low buildings, named the Outer Quad, which surrounded a continuous courtyard of one-storey buildings, known as the Inner Quad (Figure 2.54). Across this was laid a secondary east–west axis, which was to be extended by subsequent courtyards built as the university grew. The axial monumentality, organizational clarity and totality of conception of the plan have led to suggestions of a possible proto-influence on the City Beautiful movement, which burgeoned following the 1893 Columbian World Exposition in Chicago.

The plan distinguished itself from the American collegiate tradition in its rejection of an open arrangement of isolated buildings in favour of enclosed courtyards bordered by low, arcaded classroom buildings. To Olmsted, this format of linked yet autonomous departments enforced a philosophy of different disciplines united by a shared pedagogic ideal. The sequence of quadrangles was linked by a system of arcades, the use of which forms another remarkable aspect of the 1888 design. Arcades or colonnades were not novel in terms of American campus design, but their use at Stanford is singular. They not only function practically to protect from the weather and guide circulation, but moreover unify the entire fabric of the university. This aspect of the design was amongst the only features that held unanimous support amongst Leland Stanford, Olmsted and Coolidge.[82]

Stanford University's campus was the product of a by no means easy collaboration between these three figures. Builder of a transcontinental railroad, governor of California and United States Senator, Leland Stanford was familiar with controlling large-scale enterprises, and from the outset he assumed an active role in the planning of his university, frequently asserting himself over Coolidge and Olmsted. His dominating presence accounts for the significant differences between Olmsted's previous 'picturesque' campus projects and Stanford. Rejecting Olmsted's initial proposals for an informal arrangement of buildings nestled in the foothills of the 8,000 acre estate, Stanford insisted upon a formal composition on a flat site more conducive to the Stanfords' memorializing motives. His

2.55 Memorial Church, Stanford University
Photo: Jim Feliciano

intervention was the cause of much anxiety for Olmsted, particularly in the matter of ensuring the campus would be appropriate to its Californian setting. In July 1886, he complained, 'I find Governor Stanford bent on giving his university New England scenery, New England trees and turf, to be obtained only by lavish use of water.' However, Olmsted prevailed over his employer and instead of lawning the quadrangles, they were paved with stone blocks and planted with palms, fitting for the dry climate.[83]

Olmsted was also determined that the university's architecture must reflect its region: 'If we are to look for types of buildings and arrangements suitable to the climate of California it will rather be in those founded by the wiser men of Syria, Greece, Italy and Spain.' Indeed, Coolidge's designs for Stanford bear a Mediterranean taint. The architecture is characterized by short columns with carved capitals, low round arches, heavy stone walls, and one-storey buildings roofed with red tiles, reminiscent of Spanish architecture. Coolidge was responsible for the central hub of Stanford's campus, beginning with the Inner Quad (1887–1891). Undoubtedly the essence of the university, this space stands today much as it did in 1891 when the university first opened. Rough-faced sandstone arcaded buildings capped with red-tile roofs surround eight islands of Mediterranean plantings in a paved surface. Memorial Church on the south range of the quadrangle terminates the north–south Palm Drive axis. Designed in 1887, the entrance front is embellished with a plethora of elaborate Romanesque-style foliate carving and dense mosaic decoration (Figure 2.55).

From the moment the university first opened its doors in 1891, these buildings and spaces were received with popular acclaim. Yet as is so often the case, the original conception was never completed. Enough was carried out so that the spirit of the master plan remains, but from 1893 campus development veered from the 1888 vision. In 1893 Leland Stanford died and control over the project was passed to his wife until her death in 1905. Jane Stanford demonstrated a bold readiness to repudiate from the engineering and architectural principles set out by her husband and his designers. The planned linear expansion of quadrangles was unrealized, and instead she constructed a series of four structures along Palm Drive. These included a museum (1894), chemistry building (1902), library (1906) and gymnasium (1906), all built in a neo-classical style in striking contrast to the Mediterranean-Romanesque aesthetic of the Main Quad. Furthermore, Jane Stanford rescinded her husband's instructions to reinforce the new outer buildings. This was to have grievous

2.56 Green Library, Stanford University
Photo: ©iStockphoto.com/mcswin

consequences when, in 1906, the area was hit by an earthquake. The destruction at Stanford was enormous, but it was largely confined to those buildings built under the control of Mrs Stanford that had not been reinforced.[84]

The earthquake initiated a change in the approach to construction and planning at Stanford. The memorializing agenda of the design was abandoned now both the Stanfords had died, while the intrusion of buildings along Palm Drive was also discontinued. The period from the earthquake recovery to the Second World War was a relatively consistent one in terms of campus planning. The San Francisco firm of Bakewell and Brown were appointed consultant architects to the university, and were responsible for most of the new buildings. They attempted to order the university's development by retaining the quadrangle as the principle for expansion, but in many ways their adherence to the original master plan was ostensible. Plans were laid for a new library quad, east of the Inner Quad along its cross axis. Instead of the open, interconnected courts proposed by Olmsted to harmonize with the indefinite addition of quadrangles along this axis, Bakewell and Brown truncated this axis by positioning the Green Library directly upon it, revising the organization of buildings and circulation. Likewise, the Physics 'Tank' (built 1957, demolished 1996), the Durand Building (1969) and the Mitchell Earth Sciences Building (1970) intercepted open vistas along three of the original six axes. In each instance, what was considered at the time as the boundary of the academic buildings was later outgrown.

In terms of style, though, the work of Bakewell and Brown followed that of the original buildings. The most distinctive aspects of Coolidge's structures – the arcades, sandstone-coloured walls (although sandstone was replaced by concrete), red-tile roofs, and building scale – continued as the unifying stylistic language. Although arguably lacking the architectural superiority of the original quadrangles, their buildings were compatible with the monumentality desired by the Stanfords. The Green Library, built by Bakewell and Brown in 1919, is a commandingly large, five-storey building (Figure 2.56). It utilizes a stylistic mixture of Mediterranean, Gothic and Mission elements, including figural carving, robust buttresses, an arcade running along its façade, round arched windows, and red tile roofs. Its vast, three-portal entrance front is reminiscent of the great medieval cathedrals. The Thomas Welton Stanford Art Gallery (1917) also sported a medieval aesthetic. The concrete building is clad with a rough-faced sandstone veneer and roofed with red tiles and has a round-arched entrance. To the east of the gallery, the horizontal rhythm of the campus was interrupted in 1941 by the construction of the Hoover Tower. Rising nearly 90 metres, it established the only vertical accent of the campus. Said to be modelled after the campaniles of cathedrals in Salamanca and Mexico City, the tower is a smooth, white square shaft pierced by a row of round-headed arched windows, rising to a polygonal drum and red tile roof. A synthesis of uncompromising modern design with historicizing elements, the iconic tower makes for a conceptually and stylistically singular presence on campus.[85]

Post-1945, Stanford's approach to planning and construction rapidly altered. Alike other campuses across America, it was assailed by modernism. Eldridge T. Spencer, appointed director of the newly created university planning office, renounced the campus's established ingredients, such as quadrangles, red tile roofs and arches, in favour of forthrightly contemporary structures, perceived as appropriate for modern life. Long, one- or two-storey, flat-roofed blocks with large expanses of glass came to predominate. Whereas earlier buildings had camouflaged their steel and concrete construction, under Spencer Stanford adopted a vigorous, mighty concrete aesthetic. Stern Hall (1948, Spencer & Ambrose) drew from the modernist teachings of Gropius, Mies van der Rohe, and Le Corbusier. A severely rectilinear design with flat roofs and concrete walls, it was likened to vapid industrial units by contemporaries. The dormitory was organized as low, horizontal blocks bordering courts, yet despite this concession to earlier campus architecture, Stern Hall elicited a flood of complaints. In response, a university policy was instigated that necessitated new buildings to visually connect with the older quad buildings, through the use of red tile roofs and sandstone-colour walls for instance. Thus despite differences in sizes, shapes and construction, central campus buildings from the 1960s to the 1980s shared a loosely similar aesthetic. Architect John Carl Warnecke was a key campus figure at this time, and one who successfully blended traditional references with contemporary design. He was responsible for the Meyer Memorial Library, completed 1966. Its red tile roofs and columns relate to the Main Quad, yet the building retains a distinctly modern appearance through its thin, elongated piers, vertical strip windows and precast concrete vaults.[86]

2.57 Aerial view, Stanford University
Photo: Nancy Nehring/Photographer's Choice/Getty Images

As the university approached its one hundredth anniversary in 1991, thought was given to its future. In the 1990s the university embarked upon a phase of restoration and revitalization at Stanford, marked by a revived interest in Stanford's built and landscape heritage. The paving of the Inner Quad was renewed, while its buildings have been preserved through seismic upgrading. A subsidiary east–west axis laid out by Olmsted along the northern edge of the Main Quad was reinstated by the pedestrianizing of Serra Street to create Serra Mall. Campus expansion centred just west of the Main Quad, which formed the hub of the Science and Engineering schools. The opportunistic siting which had characterized development in the precinct in the post-war decades invited the production of a new master plan informed by the prescripts of the original plan. The resulting Near West Campus plan organized new structures around a clear east–west axis on a quadrangle outline. With the demolition of the Physics Tank, an unimpeded palm-lined view was reinstated from the Main Quad through to the Science and Engineering Quad. The plan gained impetus with a donation from Bill Hewlett and David Packard in 1994. Bordering the courtyard space, the new Sequoia Hall, Moore Materials Research Building and the Packard Electrical Engineering Building share a similar language of arcades, deeply recessed windows, clay tile roofs, stucco walls with granite-clad bases and copper eaves. The Hewlett Teaching Centre and Packard Electrical Engineering Building frame an entrance to the quadrangle on its north range in dramatically modern fashion through their metal and glass vocabulary. The landscape enclosed by these buildings is divided into four lawns bordered by Italian stone pines, directing circulation paths. Steel and stone freestanding arcades frame this space, in a contemporary allusion to the Main Quad arches. Anchoring the south-west corner, the Jerry Yang and Akiko Yamazaki Environment and Energy Building proclaims Stanford's awareness of the importance of energy efficiency. Opened in 2008, the centre abounds with green innovations. It has been projected to use approximately 50 per cent less energy and 90 per cent less water than other buildings. Recycled redwood is used for trellises, skylights fill its four atriums with natural light, solar panelling provides energy, and rainwater is recycled. Its cream stone walls and clay roof tiles evoke the architectural themes of the Main Quad.

The Near West Campus master plan is a typical example of sector planning, which manages large-scale expansion in the manner of a new campus. The plan grouped a variety of academic fields together to promote interdisciplinary communication. This principle is exemplified in the Clark Centre for Biosciences and Engineering

(2003). An enormous building positioned between the central science and engineering buildings and the medical complex, it was designed as a 'social magnet' for the university, drawing students, academics and researchers from multiple fields together. The work of Foster & Partners, it is arranged as three curving, glass-encased wings orientated inwards towards a striking central courtyard overlooked by balconies. This device is intended to promote pedestrian movement (as well as curiosity) through the building, plus display the centre's high activity level. The red-rust painted steel and limestone exterior is an acknowledgement of Stanford's red-tile, stone façade vernacular. Reflecting the 'green' agenda the outdoor balconies shade the building from the sun, reducing the air conditioned volume by approximately 15 per cent.[87]

From its original buildings to its most recent, Stanford's design legacy is a powerful one. The perpetuation of a specific architectural vocabulary – arcades, red tile roofs, and buff-coloured walls – reconcile newer generations of construction as 'of Stanford'. The arcades in particular are trademarks of the university. They offer shelter from the rains and shade from the blazing sun; establish orderly circulation patterns between classrooms and buildings; act as informal meeting and resting spots throughout campus, enhancing community presence; and also function as a cohesive element, visually linking and unifying buildings of varying sizes, shapes and proportions. Buildings are only one facet of Stanford's design identity, however; landscape and the treatment of space have proved equally vital components. Cultivated flower gardens, urban plazas, formal lawns, drought-tolerant Californian landscapes and unmown meadows contribute to a dynamic landscape mosaic that nourishes the eye and the mind. Native plants, such as the Californian poppy and the coast live oak feature predominantly, strengthening the campus's affiliation with its Californian setting. Open lands buffer the campus, including the Arboretum flanking Palm Drive. A quiet, unmanicured refuge leading to the academic core, the Arboretum has been the subject of a number of improvement projects. An Oak Revegetation programme, for instance, was initiated in 1992. The 1989 Landscape Design Guidelines noted,

> Preserving [the] landscape character is important not only for environmental reasons, but also for the University's intellectual future: the 'Stanford ambiance' is often cited by both students and faculty as a reason for choosing Stanford as a significant factor in their satisfaction with the experience here.

The juxtaposition of the undeveloped Arboretum with the geometry of the ceremonial Palm Drive enhances the dramatic impact of the space.

Palm Drive is evidence of how Stanford's sophisticated planning has utilized the power of sequence to create a monumental experience (Figure 2.57). Its double row of palms focuses attention on the destination ahead, first glimpsed as the face of Memorial Church framed by the foothills. Upon reaching the Oval, the view dilates to reveal the entire façade of the Main Quad. The drama of the sequence emphatically cements its place in the visitor's memory and ranks amongst the most laudable features of Stanford's master plan. The priority given to sequence of movement across the campus, reflected in its arcades, pathways and axes, connects the spaces together into a unified whole and facilitates passage across campus. Outside the central core, this logical totality has been in places lost, notably in the Library Quad. Yet its rigour was such that the grandeur, rationality and beauty envisaged in the original plan continue to be in evidence at Stanford. The strength and clarity of the 1888 concept has delivered a lasting framework relevant and practicable to the present day, grounded in its grand scale, response to location, and unique sense of place.

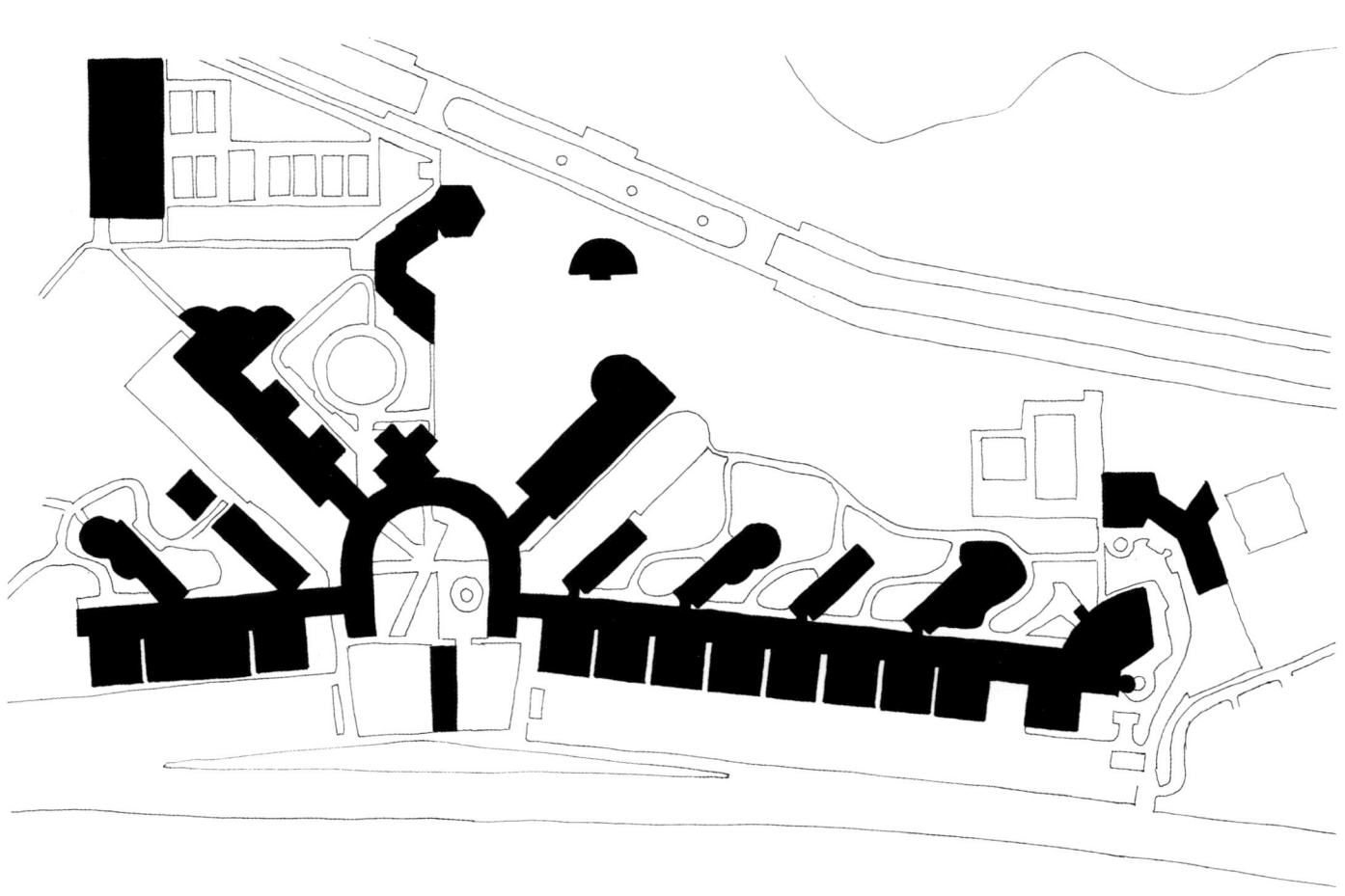

2.58 Plan, Temasek Polytechnic

Temasek Polytechnic
Singapore

The tiny city-state of Singapore in south-east Asia owes much of its success to its system of exemplary education. Temasek Polytechnic is one of five polytechnics in Singapore's higher education programme, founded with the aim of educating the contingent of managers, technologists and designers necessary to support Singapore's competitive edge in the twenty-first century. Built from 1991 to 1995, the campus of Temasek Polytechnic was the last work of celebrated master James Stirling. The commission was awarded to James Stirling Michael Wilford & Associates and built several kilometres east of Singapore City. Responsible for the master plan and most of the buildings, the practice sought to create a landmark out of the polytechnic. The 75 acre campus for 11,500 students and 1,500 staff was built in a single undertaking, an impressive feat that created an instant academic community.

The non-residential community is structured upon a highly controlled layout with a clear focus. This focus is a huge, six-storey horseshoe-shaped administration building pierced by an enormous square window that proffers vistas across the campus to the south (Figure 2.59). The building wraps itself around a raised entrance plaza facing the urban centre of Tampines New Town, and under which is submerged an auditorium and multi-purpose theatre available for public use. An elevated covered footbridge carries pedestrians

2.59 Entrance, Temasek Polytechnic
Photo: Temasek Polytechnic

TEMASEK POLYTECHNIC

2.60 Temasek Polytechnic
Photo: Temasek Polytechnic

from the plaza across a dual carriageway to public transport links. From the horseshoe building extends four wings, radiating from its core like the spokes of a bicycle wheel into the campus's park. Each wing houses one of the institution's four schools: engineering, business, design and applied science. The wings are governed by a clear organizing principle: their plans begin with an entrance in the curve of the administration building, from which extend pedestrian concourses covered by the upper levels of teaching accommodation, ending in a student cafeteria overlooking the parkland. Priority is given to ease of movement within the wings; external staircases sheltered by overhangs optimize vertical circulation, while the most heavily used facilities, such as lecture theatres, are located on or below concourse level to reduce vertical movement. The elongated spines of the engineering and applied science blocks form the northern façade to the campus. On the north side, a series of short wings project from their length, housing laboratories stacked over lecture halls. On their southern lengths, further annexes jut out at an angle of 45 degrees to form laboratory towers. Provision for growth is considered, for each wing is capable of being lengthened outwards without compromising its integral character.

The social and administrative nucleus of the design is the raised plaza at its centre. Open and accessible to the urban centre to its north, the space betokens an open and accessible relationship with its local community. Its periphery is enclosed by an arcaded promenade lined with banks, shops, and galleries as well as the school entrances, establishing it as a hub of activity rather than a mere thoroughfare. The arcade recalls the traditional south-east Asian five foot way, a pedestrian walkway indented into the front of the ground floor of a building and sheltered from rain and shine by the overhanging upper storeys. On the opposite façade of the horseshoe building, locking into its southern exterior is the eccentrically-shaped library tower. The highest building on campus, its silhouette rises above the administration block (Figure 2.60). Its distinctive profile signals the polytechnic's presence on the Singapore skyline and denotes the importance of book-based learning to its scholastic mission.[88]

From the outset, Temasek embraced within its mission a desire to foster individuality within an encompassing community. Although part of an integrated design, each school has a different environment, one that best reflects its particular demands. The business wing is composed largely of lecture theatres and seminar rooms, while applied science has extensive laboratories as well as lecture theatres. The design school has the most distinctive environment; its Kasbah of craft workshops to the east and large, double-height studios to the west provide Temasek's most impressive teaching spaces.

The design was informed by a desire to create not a mere utilitarian environment, but one conducive to nourishing intelligent, rounded students. One means of so doing is by encouraging social interaction. The concourses that carry pedestrian traffic along the length of the school wings were intended as channels for casual interaction. Sheltered by upper floors yet open at the sides to allow cooling breezes to circulate, they offer a hospitable environment to favour this. Speaking in 1991, Temasek's then-principal Dr N. Varaprasad lauded the importance of the design's capacity to let 'staff and students from the different schools interact and exchange ideas'.[89]

2.61 Temasek Polytechnic
Photo: Temasek Polytechnic

To ensure no one department is isolated from another and to foster the desired interdisciplinary communication, a pedestrian network weaves its way around campus that connects all facilities within a five minute walk from the centre.[90]

Equally important in its quest for an edifying environment, is the design's exploration of the stimulating potential of landscape.

2.62 Interior colour, Temasek Polytechnic
Photo: Temasek Polytechnic

Its picturesque panorama to the south across the Bedok Reservoir and beyond to rolling, green parkland is capitalized on by the angling of the radiating wings to maximize views. A rich visual experience is achieved by the changing vista from the approach to the central plaza. The view through the great window of the arced administration building gradually transforms from sky to reveal the green idyllic setting as one climbs the approach ramp. Within the bounds of campus, a number of different landscape environments have been forged. Fanning out to the south from the great window, is a triangular formal garden composed of systematically ordered trees upon a verdant lawn criss-crossed by footpaths (Figure 2.60). The canteens of the school wings spill out under large canopies into the campus grounds. Enclosed within the horseshoe building the plaza provides another variety of landscape, characterized by ornamental flowerbeds and fishponds, evergreens and potted palms (Figure 2.61). A diverse landscape experience sets the tone for a stimulating environment.

The planning and design also make concessions to Singapore's climate to create a more congenial environment rooted to the temperament of its locale. Building orientation, position and scale are all reflective of this consideration. Lecture theatres shade the design studios, while at the engineering school offices shield the laboratories from the heat of the sun. Buildings are kept shallow to facilitate the flow of air, while the laboratories of applied science are angled so as to channel breezes from the reservoir inside. The window of the administration block likewise permits the cooling wind coming off the reservoir to pass across the central forum. Moreover, to accommodate the fierce tropical storms and torrid sunshine of Singapore's climate, the dispersed parts of campus can all be accessed upon the protection of covered walkways. Covered concourses give access to the schools, a covered bridge shields students entering the campus from the nearby bus stop, and the shops and facilities in the plaza are sheltered by an arcaded promenade. Pedestrian routes are additionally generally located on the northern, shadier side of the buildings.[91]

Numbering as one of the design's most memorable, place-making features is an apparently aesthetic whim: colour. Temasek is aglow with a vivid array of colours animating its simple architectural forms. While the complex is jacketed in a pale lilac colour, tantalizing snatches of bright orange, red, yellow, purple-brown and blue are glimpsed as one traverses the carefully orchestrated network of paths. Each school has its own distinctive colour ceiling, the horseshoe building has orange window reveals, whole walls are painted block colours and stout painted columns form a rhythmic march of colour along the concourses (Figure 2.62). In what could otherwise have been monotonous, grey circulation arteries, these painted columns and flamboyant painted walls revel in a daring yet successful joy of colour to imbue these spaces with personality and pageant. The use of bright colour on buildings is, furthermore, a Singapore tradition.[92]

The indulgence in colour is evidence of a conscious revolt against an insensate monolith machine-for-learning in favour of a cultivating, unifying academic environment. Balancing the curricular and extra-curricular, or the 'academic with the humanistic' as James Stirling reflected, the design values the importance of the students' recreational needs in its sensitive response to climate, landscape and layout. 'Whether it's Oxford or Cornell University, all educational buildings should aid in the efficient process of teaching and learning and yet allow students to enjoy campus life,' explained Stirling when Temasek's master plan was unveiled.[93] The polytechnic's plan lays emphasis on establishing an animated and hospitable setting, for example, in exploitation of vistas and in encouraging activity to flow outside, and in its easily comprehensible layout. It utilizes traditional devices to deliver a comfortable environment, such as the twenty-first-century interpretation of the five foot way and the covered network of connecting paths.

The design also does much to establish an identity for the ingénue institution. The curving dynamism of the horseshoe against the angular hulk of the library, the eye-catching drama of the 'great window', and the riotous parade of the coloured pilotis all ensure the complex cuts a dramatic figure that imbues it with memorable presence. Yet subtler, quieter devices also contribute to the presence of the place, such as the design school's internal bridges or the tranquillity of the fish ponds. The European architects, James Stirling Michael Wilford & Associates, have realized an urbane network of particular places that is distinctly Singaporean.

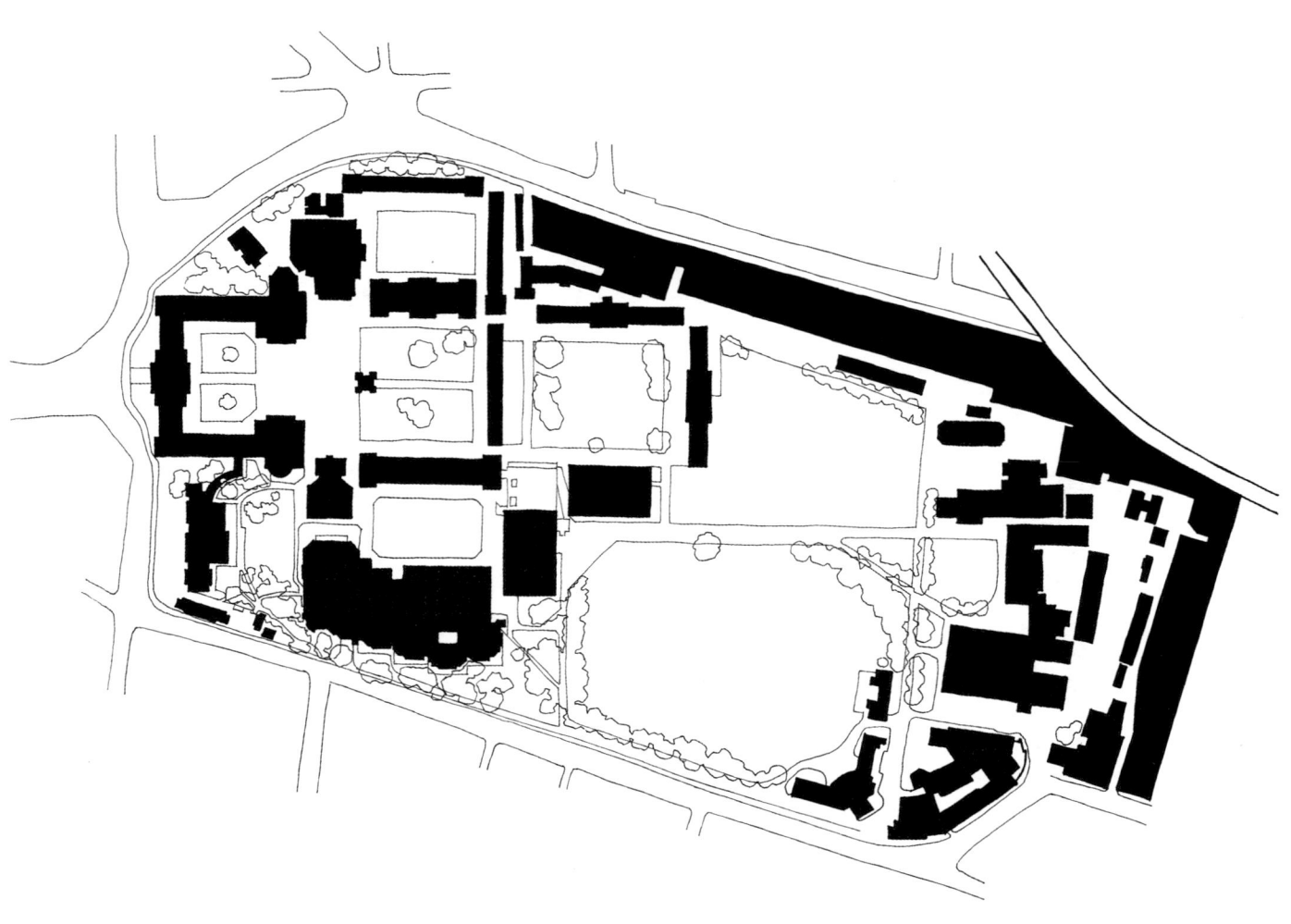

2.63 Plan, Trinity College, Dublin

Trinity College, Dublin
Dublin, Republic of Ireland

At the heart of Dublin's city centre, the imperious West Front of Trinity College, Dublin presides over College Green, the three-sided square from which the college's campus derives its name. The façade's arched entranceway gives forth to Front (or Parliament) Square, a fine Georgian set piece bounded by a paired theatre and chapel. The mid-nineteenth-century Campanile at its eastern end demarcates the transition to Library Square, beyond which the campus extends to the north, east and south in a network of further squares and playing fields, with science buildings forming the eastern boundary. While its architecture dates back to circa 1700, development of the College Green site extends as far as 1166 when it housed the medieval Priory of All Hallows. Fifty-four years after the monastery's dissolution in 1538, the Dublin Corporation surrendered the site for the establishment of a college. The foundation stone of the new college was laid in 1592 and when the first students matriculated two years later the university consisted of a red brick quadrangle which formed the nucleus of the grounds until the eighteenth century and established the precedent of courtyard organization which has proved to be the basic planning principle at Trinity College, Dublin.

With the eighteenth century came an extensive building campaign. Library Square was planned in the late 1690s to accommodate the growing student body and took shape in the early 1700s with the erection of three brick residential ranges. The eastern range – the Rubrics – is the only one of these to survive today (Figure 2.64). The square was bounded to the south by the library, built 1712–1724. Designed by Thomas Burgh, the imperious building was basically a long, double-height chamber raised upon an arcade, echoing Wren's library at Trinity College, Cambridge. Although the Old Library functions today in effect as a museum, its grand Georgian façade continues to dominate the campus. Library Square was closed circa 1725 by a west range. Upon the razing of this block in 1839, the vista from Library Square to the Front Gate which is experienced today was opened. In the 1750s work commenced on the Front Square as it is known today. Completed in 1759, the monumental West Front was built to designs by Theodore Jacobsen, architect of the Foundling Hospital in London (Figure 2.65). Ninety metres long and 17 metres tall, the palazzo-like structure presents a suitably impressive façade to the city and an apt parallel to the Bank of Ireland on the opposite side of College Green. The Square was completed

2.64 Rubrics, Trinity College, Dublin
Photo: Trinity College, Dublin

2.65 West Front, Trinity College, Dublin
Photo: Trinity College, Dublin

in the 1790s with the erection of an examination hall, known as the Theatre, and a chapel to designs by William Chambers, architect of London's Somerset House. The classical structures have matching temple-like façades.[94]

Although no over-arching master plan was constituted, the nineteenth century saw the planning and construction of many individual sectors of campus which created the Trinity College recognizable to the modern visitor. The kitchen garden north of Library Square had been designated in 1774 for new residential accommodation, but development of the site was not fully effected until circa 1817 with the completion of the square dubbed Botany Bay. The utilitarian plain ranges do not compete in visual grandeur with the earlier squares; they have in fact been dubbed 'gloomy, prison-like'. However, the setting was substantially enhanced in 1955 with the construction of three tennis courts and surrounding planting.[95]

With the demolition of the west range of Library Square in 1839, the question arose of how to utilize the vacant space. Despite extravagant proposals by the college's architect Frederick Darley for a museum and lecture rooms on the site, it was decided that the grand spatial effect of the unified Library and Front Squares should be retained. The courts were visually linked by the erection in 1854 of Charles Lanyon's Campanile (Figure 2.66). Its classically proportioned arched silhouette greets visitors passing through the West Front's gate, and is established as the college's architectural emblem. In 1853 an alternative site for a museum was selected to the east of Library Square, between College Park and New Square. Its Ruskinian Gothic exterior represented a tremendous deviation from the college's earlier neo-classical architecture. Bringing Venetian palazzo romance to Dublin, the eclectic, richly decorated exterior featured over 180 differently carved capitals. With the new museum filling the south side of New Square, the principal squares of the western campus

2.66 Campanile, Trinity College, Dublin
Photo: Trinity College, Dublin

UNIVERSITY OF CALIFORNIA AT BERKELEY

2.70 Sather Gate, UC Berkeley
Photo: David Sanger Photography/Alamy

plan the College of California's new campus. As would become a characteristic of his campus designs, Olmsted imagined an irregular, picturesque and informal park-like setting that was on axis with the Golden Gate Bridge. This axial arrangement bespoke of more than merely wanting to capitalize on impressive scenery; it carried a symbolic resonance. California was, in many ways, perceived as the new promised land. Following the gold rush beginning in 1848, the state was envisioned as a new economic power, and simultaneously as a pastoral idyll. These prophecies came to be symbolized by the Golden Gate and so in aligning the university with this structure, Olmsted was aligning it with the special destiny of California itself. Although Olmsted's plan was never executed, in lining the campus with the Gate he set a precedent which his successors were to follow.

Olmsted's designs were supplanted by a new plan by architects David Farquharson and Henry Kenitzer, commissioned in 1868 when the College was transformed into the University of California. Their design included a sweeping arc lined with buildings in the then-popular French Empire style. South Hall is the sole building from this scheme to survive. Built in 1873, it is the oldest building at Berkeley. Its façade is of brick and granite, decorated on the north and south sides with cast-iron reliefs depicting fruits and grains native to California, with a mansard roof animated with dormers and chimneys. The campus opened in the same year with only 100 students. Enrolment, however, rapidly grew. During the 1890s student numbers had risen to 2,500, making new buildings an imperative. Furthermore, there emerged a general dissatisfaction with the aesthetics of the campus at this time. One student rued in 1892 that 'none of the buildings here compare in beauty with the Leland Stanford University'. The growing sense of promise that seemed to radiate from California nurtured the conviction that the state's university should too embody this promise in its physical setting. With this mindset, the Regents launched an international competition for a comprehensive campus master plan in 1897, financed by Phoebe Apperson Hearst. The competition was grand and ambitious in scale, and, moreover, came to be highly influential in American campus planning in its emphasis on the potential of architectural design. Hearst articulated that,

I have only one wish in this matter – that the plans adopted should be worthy of the great university whose material home they are to provide for…and that they should redound to the glory of the state whose culture and civilisation are to be nursed and developed at the university.[100]

From the outset, this vision was strongly shaped by the classical architectural idiom and the Beaux-Arts movement.[101]

The competition coincided with the burgeoning of the Beaux-Arts and City Beautiful movements, much popularized by the 1893 World's Columbian Exposition in Chicago. The fair dazzled North America with an ideal vision for public buildings and their surroundings, and presented Berkeley with a new language to express the unique destiny of California and its educational republic. Out of approximately 100 entrants, the 11 competition finalists were all École des Beaux-Arts trained. The winning entry, by Frenchman Emile Bénard was an urban plan based on grids of boulevards and squares. Yet soon after he was announced as winner in 1900, problems began to emerge. Speaking little English and unwilling to come to Berkeley to supervise the plan, Bénard was replaced by John Galen Howard. During his tenure as campus architect from 1902–1924, Howard produced several revised plans and designed numerous buildings in the Beaux-Arts tradition.[102]

The Berkeley campus is still to a large extent underpinned by Howard's master plan. His vision was informed by two principles. Firstly, he adhered to Beaux-Arts planning. Secondly, he utilized the metaphorical capacity of the built environment – both in its organization and architecture – to capture the zeitgeist of the young state and the ambitions of the university that represented it. The plan was based upon a system of axes hinged upon a major east–west axis aligned with the Golden Gate Bridge, creating a campus of classical and monumental organization. The Beaux-Arts composition was enlivened by an interweaving of minor and major thoroughfares, some orientated north to south and others east to west. Some axes were open-ended and others were closed; some were perpendicular and others sinewing to the contours of the land. Within the scheme, alike disciplines were clustered together. Agricultural and natural sciences occupied the west of the central *allée*, the humanities the centre, and engineering and physical sciences the east, and all were

2.71 Sather Tower, UC Berkeley
Photo: Andrew Rittenburg

linked by a common architectural guise. Howard designed buildings of varying sizes united by a consistent use of white Raymond granite, red tile roofs and classical details. The campus appeared united by a collective image, and its classical character carried connotations of Athenian wisdom signifying the scholastic and cultural aspirations of the university and California at large. The large Agricultural Complex, occupying a prominent position on the main axis at its western end, demonstrates how architectural detail was used in ideological fashion. Hilgard Hall (1917) is one of its three constituent buildings. Its west façade is dominated by an imposing, giant Tuscan colonnade with Renaissance-style sgraffito friezes of fruit, flowers, farm animals, native plants, baskets and cornucopias overflowing with the products of the land ornamenting the entablature and window spandrels. The message is that of the fecundity of Berkeley and California in both an agrarian and an intellectual sense.[103]

Across campus, a hierarchy of structures was created through scale and detail. With its imposing proportions, fine ornamentation and central placement on the principal axis, the library was established at the apex of this ranking (Figure 2.69). Its site, wrote Howard, 'has been more seriously considered, perhaps, than any other single question relating to the plan, unless it be the main axis'. Located on the southern boundary at the midpoint of the main *allée*, the Doe Memorial Library projects further forward than most of its neighbours emphasizing its importance within the plan, a concept reinforced by its impressive façade. Robust and massive, the Raymond granite façade carries a symmetrical progression of engaged Corinthian columns raised aloft on a tall basement, and framing large windows. Symbols of Athenian wisdom decorate this façade. Athena presided over the main entrance as a bronze bust, while her serpents coiled themselves amongst books and acanthus leaves on the columns' capitals.[104]

In 1908 construction began on the formal entrance to the campus – Sather Gate and Bridge (Figure 2.70). The gate terminated the south point of a secondary north–south axis. In organizational terms it reinforced the campus's axial structure while ideologically, it embodied the pedagogic ideals and ambitions of the university. Howard's design for Sather Gate consists of four masonry piers clad in granite, each bearing a glass globe. Ornate bronze grills and an arch span the space between the piers, creating a welcoming transparency apt for a state university. The university insignia occupies the centre of the arch. Inside the gate, a concrete bridge, lined with classical balustrades, spans Strawberry Creek to lead into the heart of the campus. The gate no longer marks the ingress to the campus proper, for in the 1940s the university purchased the block of Telegraph Avenue to the south that now houses the Student Union and Sproul Hall. Nevertheless, it has maintained its status as a focal point for political demonstrators or religious preachers.[105]

Howard's master plan gained its visual peak in 1914 with the completion of Sather Tower, the campus's most prominent and unifying landmark (Figure 2.71). 'It will be the most salient feature,' wrote Howard, 'dominating the composition in the same way that a cathedral tower dominates and unifies the vast and varied fabric.' Positioned at the intersection of two secondary north–south and east–west axes, its lofty presence reinforced the Beaux-Arts layout. Stylistically, the Sather Tower was modelled on the campanile of Piazza San Marco in Venice. Formed of a Raymond granite shaft soaring 94 metres from a balustraded podium and approached on three sides by expansive steps, the tower is deserved of the epithet 'a lighthouse of learning'. At the corners of the upper zone are four plinths carrying pyramidal obelisks topped with flaming bronze urns. The whole culminates in a spire terminating in a spiked bronze lantern. These bronze flames and spire symbolize Berkeley's pursuit of the light of truth, serving, Howard explained, to 'point the University's way upward…unifying its ideals and punctuating its message'. To the west of the tower extends Campanile Way, an important secondary east–west axis that provides a core pedestrian spine within the campus's classical heart. Providing views to the east of the Sather Tower and views to the west of the Golden Gate Bridge, the route proffers a visual connection between these two icons of the university's mission and philosophy. The axis was enforced by the placement of Wheeler Hall in 1917, opposite to the Doe Memorial Library (Figure 2.72).[106]

The campus core as designed by Howard remains as one of the most extensive and comprehensive Beaux-Arts schemes to be erected in the United States. Enjoying a free creative reign on campus, his vision shaped Berkeley. However, with a change in university personnel in the 1920s, Howard's decisions were increasingly challenged. Relations between the administration and Howard deteriorated critically to such an extent that in 1924 he was dismissed. Howard's

2.72 Wheeler Hall, UC Berkeley
Photo: Stefan Didak

Beaux-Arts vision was largely respected by his successors and new buildings harmonized with the old. The succeeding supervising architects George W. Kelham (1927–1938) and Arthur Brown Jr (1938–1948) held fast to Howard's master plan, designing buildings in a pared-down classicism, such as McLaughlin Hall (1931), Sproul Hall (1941) and the Bancroft Library Annex (1949).

In 1948, however, the role of supervising architect was replaced by the Office of Architects and Engineers, and the development of the campus began to proceed along very different lines. The university entered into the greatest period of expansion in its history. Enclosed by the city and the foothills, the campus's lack of building land prompted the university to adopt a policy of building tall, infill structures. Central campus buildings erected during the 1950s to 1970s generally adopted one of two approaches. The first involved the continuation of the neo-classical architectural idiom espoused by the early structures, albeit simplified and plainer. Mulford Hall, Lewis Hall, and Donner Laboratory illustrate this type, often sharing a vocabulary of symmetrical façades, hipped red tile roofs and minimal ornament. Contrastingly, the second approach departed from the established stylistic language. A variety of alien architectural styles invaded the campus, such as Alumni House in the International Style and Wurster Hall in the Brutalist mode. Buildings grew taller: the six-storey Earth Sciences Building (now McCone Hall, 1961), seven-storey Latimer Hall (1963) and ten-storey Evans Hall (1971). These structures frequently possessed flat roofs, plain concrete or stucco façades, huge expanses of physically and visually similar spaces, and proportions that eclipsed their predecessors. Moreover, these buildings broke away from the master plan, and their siting was governed by opportunism. This ad hoc approach has since been attacked for its deleterious effect on campus vistas and natural landscapes. In several cases these Modernist buildings were sited in prized outdoor areas, interrupting the axes and formal spaces of the earlier master plans. Evans Hall, for instance, has been widely condemned. It obstructs the east–west central *allée* from the Hearst Mining Circle to the Golden Gate Bridge. Moffit Library (1970) similarly blocked this axis, pivotal to the original conception of the Beaux-Arts campus. Following campus demonstrations in 1964, Frank McShane entitled an article 'The Horrors of Berkeley, or Did Architecture Make Students Riot' (*Art News*, September 1965). In his article, 'A Campus that went Astray', Allen Temko lamented 'the devastation of the once magnificent campus of the University of California in Berkeley' (*San Francisco Chronicle*, 24 April 1978).[107]

As a complex urban environment, the campus has necessarily been the subject of continual growth and change as it responds to the evolving demands of higher education. The difficulties in preserving the distinctive quality installed by older buildings and landscapes while reacting to expanding student bodies, programmes and modern technologies has been a continual concern. Yet Berkeley has succeeded largely in retaining those place-making characteristics which are essential ingredients to campus identity.

Undoubtedly, the setting contributes to its sense of place. Howard was sensitive to the power of nature and synthesized the college with the natural landscape, creating a campus prized for its natural beauty. The meandering Strawberry Creek with its tree-lined edges encircles the campus core like a green necklace. Green spaces, both formal and informal, offer places for recreation and repose, including the Grinell Natural Area, Eucalyptus Grove, Memorial Glade and Faculty Glade. Vistas glimpsed to the western frontier proffer splendid views to San Francisco Bay and the Golden Gate Bridge, evoking the spirit of optimism in which the university was founded.

The university has grown vastly in proportion since Howard prepared his 1899 master plan, yet the spirit which informed it is still very much alive. Howard's classical core is the defining essence of Berkeley's built environment. It is shaped by an orderly and intelligible Beaux-Arts layout, punctuated by landmarks such as Sather Gate and Sather Tower which stand as tangible symbols of the institution. Howard left a legacy of visual harmony linked by shared materials, colours and textures (white granite or concrete walls, bronze or wood trim, red tile roofs) and classical motifs. This unity is enlivened by an interplay of shapes, sizes and placings as well as the interplay of major and minor axes. In its organization and classical references, the campus has been a lucid embodiment of the Californian ethos and the ambitions of the university. The result is a campus of strong self-identity.

2.73 Plan, UCLA

University of California at Los Angeles
Los Angeles, USA

Of the nine constituent schools of the University of California, the Los Angeles outpost (UCLA) has the highest student total (39,650) and the most industrious building programme ($1.7 billion deployed between 1986 and 2005) despite its 419 acre campus being amongst the smallest in the system. Currently consisting of over 170 buildings, the campus has grown to large proportions in a relatively short time-span (Figure 2.74).

Founded in 1919, its downtown LA location quickly proved inadequate for the burgeoning institution and in 1925 the Westwood site, chosen for its accessible yet picturesque setting on rolling terrain overlooking the ocean, was purchased for UCLA's new campus. David Allison was appointed Executive Architect, to work alongside George Kelham, the supervising architect from Berkeley. Kelham devised a grand Beaux-Arts scheme, arranged around a principal east–west axis. The uneven site was accommodated in a series of dramatic terraces and steps graduated down the western face of the hill. Four large buildings, which were to become UCLA's signature buildings – Royce Hall, Powell Library, Chemistry and Physics – were grouped along the main axis. Royce Hall, the campus's first building, established the precedent for the Lombardian Romanesque style which held sway at UCLA until the Second World War (Figure 2.75). Historical revivalism was then rife in America, and the Romanesque enjoyed particular

2.74 Aerial view, UCLA
Photo: UCLA Capital Projects

2.75 Royce Hall, UCLA
Photo: Eugene Buchko

popularity amongst Californian educational institutions. Northern Italy seemed an appropriate reference for the campus because of the similarities in climate and landscape. Regent Edward Dickson, UCLA's co-founder, believed the school should have a distinct physical character expressive of its individual situation.[108]

Royce Hall was designed by Allison. Strikingly modelled upon San Ambrogio in Milan, it has a two-storey arcaded and vaulted loggia between paired irregular towers. As at San Ambrogio, coloured bricks and tiles enliven various sections of Royce's wall surface. Its open arcaded cloisters intimate the original intention to connect it with flanking buildings. Facing Royce, Kelham designed the Powell Library (1930). A brick and terracotta façade and red tile roof was sheathed over a steel and concrete frame to create a stately Romanesque structure with octagonal dome. San Ambrosio and San Sepolcro provided specific Northern Italian models. Paired with Royce and Powell were the Chemistry (now Haines Hall) and Physics (now Humanities) buildings, creating a space known as Dickson Plaza (Figure 2.76). The plaza between these four structures and the steps and terraces leading westward down the sloping terrain reflect the architects' original vision to create an Italian hilltop town upon Beaux-Arts axial foundations. To the south of this group, Kelham designed Moore Hall (1930) in the same Romanesque vein. Terracotta and brickwork patterns embellish the entrance façade, from which projects a gabled portico with octagonal columns. To the west, the U-shaped outline creates a landscaped court. Together with the University Residence (1930) and the Men's and Women's Gymnasiums (1932), Royce, Powell, Chemistry, Physics and Moore formed the original campus buildings. United by a commonality of material, scale and the Romanesque, these buildings form a distinctive, integrated campus nucleus.[109]

Landscaping was devised to complement the Lombardy theme. Impressively spacious, Dickson Plaza is a brick and buff stone paved court with terracotta balustrades. From it descends a red brick staircase named Janss Steps, which extends down the stepped elevation to the western campus (Figure 2.77). With the erection of Franz Hall in 1940, the Lombard theme was first extended to southern campus. Franz was planned as the cornerstone of a southern science complex, today called the Court of Sciences. The three-storey structure

2.76 Dickson Plaza, UCLA
Photo: Alan Nyri

employs an economized Romanesque idiom, complete with tile roof and tower.

The post-war years saw significant departures in the planning of the campus. Allison's revision of Kelham's plan included the consequential decision to locate the Medical School on the south portion of the Westwood site, rather than off-site as Berkeley had done. This necessitated a dense arrangement of high-rise structures upon south campus. From 1946, the gully to the east of Dickson Plaza was filled in to provide extra building space upon which was constructed Dodd Hall (1948), Perloff Hall (1952) and Schoenberg Music Building (1955) surrounding a large paved expanse, Dickson Court. With these, central campus was completed. Dodd Hall marked an important turning point in campus development. Its round arches, square tower and decorative brickwork patterns marked the last of UCLA's Lombard Romanesque buildings. Upon the appointment of Welton Becket as supervising architect in 1948, the Romanesque style was discontinued. Its high construction costs were unachievable in the post-war economy, while its historicism seemed at odds with the philosophy and requirements of modern life. UCLA's governors pressed for a plainer style consistent with the red brick and stone of the original fabric, and succeeding years saw campus expansion employ various architectural styles.

In the 1950s, UCLA's rapid growth spurt was clothed in a transitional architecture, compromising between the Romanesque and modern. Engineering I was constructed in 1950 on the western edge of campus by the firm Allison and Rible. Constructed of red brick and concrete, the concrete was painted a buff colour to concede to the Romanesque. Perloff Hall occupied a prominent site, bounding the newly formed Dickson Court to the north. Keen to maintain architectural unity with the neighbouring Dickson Plaza buildings, architect Paul Robinson Hunter clad the concrete building with red brick and tile roofing, yet its clean, angular lines and absence of decoration signal its contemporary genesis.

Kelham's campus plan envisaged a student population of 5,000. Yet in 1960 the University of California's president Clark Kerr instituted a new master plan for all the system's campuses, which ordained for UCLA a new enrolment total of 27,500. This tremendous growth necessitated tremendous planning consequences for UCLA. Not least was the parking problem. Little space had originally been allotted to parking, yet the new master plan compelled space for 20,000 vehicles. Becket planned a series of multi-level car parks throughout the campus filtering off a new ring road, aimed to minimize inner-campus traffic. Becket also focused upon organization of land use. The campus was subdivided into three sectors: north campus, including graduate studies, arts and social sciences; central campus, combining education, English, architecture, law, and music; and south campus, housing engineering, mathematics, sciences and medicine. The north campus was developed in the 1960s. Not only were any concessions to the Romanesque abandoned in favour of individual, modern design, but the Beaux-Arts principles of symmetry and clarity were replaced by an informal, capricious approach. The exigency to provide space for UCLA's rapid expansion seems physically manifest in the tall profiles and loose planning of its buildings. North campus buildings were planned with minimum footprints to maximize space for landscaped open areas, rendering upward growth inescapable. Bunche Hall (1964) symbolizes this trend. Looming over north campus, Bunche is UCLA's tallest structure at 11 storeys. Architect Maynard Lyndon elevated it two storeys from ground level so as not to obstruct pedestrian circulation. Its appearance is wholly alien to the familiar red brick and limestone of central campus, and its protruding square windows earned it the nickname of the 'Waffle'. Undoubtedly it has proved UCLA's most controversial and disliked structure.[110]

Since the mid-1980s, the campus has undergone comprehensive remodelling. A running joke prevails at the Los Angeles branch of the University of California system that UCLA is actually an acronym of 'Under Construction in Los Angeles'. In 1984, the campus occupied 350 acres; by 2005 it had grown to 528. The campus continues to be an incessant hive of building activity. Recent building has increasingly utilized star power. I. M. Pei has designed the replacement hospital, Raphael Viñoly the CNSI building, and Cesar Pelli a new research complex. Despite these heavyweight names, though, recent construction has been judicious in its sensitivity to UCLA's architectural heritage. The contextual materials of red brick and limestone are consistently employed, creating a distinctive 'UCLA feel'. Harry Cobb's Anderson School of Management (1995) reinterprets the traditions of Dickson Plaza in its strong horizontal lines and red brick and beige colouring, and thus extends the UCLA identity to its peripheral site on north campus. Connection to central campus is enforced by the axial path that extends north from the base of Janss Steps to a paved plaza at the centre of the complex. Its pathways use the same type of geometric paving of brick inlays and buff-coloured concrete seen in Dickson Plaza and Court, a device which enhances continuity across campus. Pelli's Biomedical Research Building and Orthopaedic Hospital Research Centre (2007) similarly gives itself over to red brick and cast stone, evoking traditional references within a contemporary silhouette. Its curving elevations echo the sweeping path of the periphery road, and curl around the existing life sciences building. A new pathway forms a strong link between the eastern campus entrance opposite and the Court of Sciences. Richard Meier's Broad Centre (2006) has a highly contemporary exterior finish of concrete, steel, glass and teak, yet seeks integration with the old campus by incorporating bricks into its paving and courtyards.

Yet notwithstanding this incessant construction, UCLA sustains an exceptional commitment to cultivating its open spaces, which is its signal achievement. Roughly a third of the total site is open space. Throughout campus lie pockets of green or plazas creating an outdoor environment that consistently receives praise. Open space preserves include Dickson Plaza, the Murphy Sculpture Garden and Meyerhoff Park, the large sloping lawn flanking Janss Steps in central campus. The Sculpture Garden fills the heart of north campus. One of the most celebrated parts of campus, over 70 sculptures are displayed within a five-acre park landscaped with stone walls, lawns, sitting areas and well-conceived planting. Formal paved plazas on campus include the Court of Sciences, the Inverted Fountain before Franz Hall, and the Powell Library courtyard, a newly developed area designed for quiet reading between the south wings of the building. Many of UCLA's buildings have U-shape plans, investing the campus with enclosed, intimate spaces, such as the courtyards of Moore and Rolfe Halls, which hold hallowed places in campus memory. South campus is, however, underprivileged in the space given over to landscape. The entrance gateway designed in 1991 by Hodgetts & Fung Design Associates, therefore, significantly contributed to the environment. It consisted of a new entry extending northwards from the southernmost tip of campus with a pavilion, pool and soft and hard landscaping. The red and beige paving that is carried through from the entrance into south campus brings UCLA's base iconography into this precinct.[111]

The red brick and buff patterning of the network of pedestrian ways visually binds the campus together. The campus has strong pedestrian axes, which inform its circulation patterns. The axis from Janss Steps to Dickson Court, the original east–west alignment, is the most prominent amongst these. Bruin Walk forms another important east–west channel, providing a pivotal link between central campus and the north-western residential area, while the pathway alongside the Biomedical Science Research Building is an important pedestrian link between a campus entrance and the Court of Sciences. Unlike some urban campuses such as New York University, through which you drive as an extension of the urban street grid, UCLA allows only service vehicles to breach the peripheral loop road, thus firmly demarcating the boundary between town and gown and creating an auspicious pedestrian environment.

The north, central and south precincts of campus each have a distinct character. Upon central campus, the Romanesque and 1950s transitional buildings are arranged in geometric rigidity. With its formal patterns and defined open spaces, it is a Beaux-Arts tour-de-force. North and south campuses reacted against its order and coherence. Circulation is organized by free-form garden paths that entreat relaxed perambulation, and building style is based upon individual design rather than stylistic uniformity. South campus is overwhelmingly the most densely developed campus precinct, and the least successful. Its indistinct planning ideology is represented in its sprawling distribution of buildings and scarcity of open spaces, which create a feeling of engulfment amid a maze of functional yet homogenous brick buildings. The campus's chief shortcoming is that UCLA's main entrance is through south campus. Insensitive post-war planning resulted in a mediocre medical complex, yet it is this that forms UCLA's face to the outside world. Landscaping has ameliorated the situation, with the addition of the 1990s gateway, screens of eucalyptus trees, and low brick walls that form a continuing southern boundary.[112]

In broad terms, UCLA's hard and soft landscaping has consistently melded the different generations of campus architecture. Niches of handsome open space throughout campus are visible, accessible and well-used. The most iconic is Dickson Plaza, surrounded by

2.77 Janss Steps, UCLA
Photo: Chris Welch/Gardiner & Theobald

the Romanesque buildings that dominate the campus core. For the past two decades, UCLA has preceded over a reversal of the philosophy that each building should be the creative statement of the individual planner, which took hold of the campus in the 1960s. Planning, architecture, and landscaping have sought the cultivation of a consistent, integrated environment, respectful but not imitative of the brick, tile and limestone colouring and forms of Royce Hall and Powell Library. The result has been a strengthening of the elements that make UCLA a special and memorable place.

2.78 Plan, University of Cambridge

University of Cambridge
Cambridge, UK

After 800 years of opulent architectural patronage and fervent institutional continuity, the University of Cambridge is one of the world's most attractive university environments. Lining the city's labyrinth of cobbled streets, its buildings and the open spaces that they enclose are theatres of memory, testimony to the illustrious history of the institution and its colleges. Its environment has grown serendipitously, rather than to any pre-formed growth plan, but this study will highlight the most distinguishing episodes in its formation.

Despite their reciprocity, the physical fabric of the colleges and the university itself has developed along markedly different lines, the university proving much more tardy in distinguishing its presence within the city. For many years after its foundation in 1209 the institution had no premises of its own. Private lodgings provided rooms for lectures while ceremonies and meetings were held in Great St Mary's parish church. Hostels soon provided accommodation for scholars, and colleges gradually appeared alongside them. The first college, Peterhouse, was established in 1284, and in the following century it was followed in quick succession by a flurry of other foundations. Benefiting from generous endowments and owning their own property, the colleges supplanted the hostels and little material evidence of them remains. Peterhouse typified the development pattern of the early colleges. Initially residing within modest houses, in 1286 construction on a hall began. Expansion was slow, and the college evolved piecemeal as funds permitted. Early colleges like Peterhouse were unassuming in their appearance. It was not until the fifteenth century that a discernable 'collegiate' grouping emerged at Peterhouse, with buildings ranged around a court.[113]

The Cambridge colleges followed a distinctive format:

> Among these narrow, ugly and dirty streets, are tumbled in, as it were at random (for the whole place looks as if it had been dancing to Amphion's music, and he had left off in the middle of a very complicated figure) some of the most beautiful academical buildings in the world. However their style of architecture may vary, according to the period at which they were built or rebuilt, they agree in one essential feature: all the colleges are constructed in quadrangles or *courts*; and, as in the course of years the population of every college

2.79 Old Court, Queens' College, University of Cambridge
Photo: John Linwood

2.80 Gatehouse, Queens' College, University of Cambridge
Photo: Wayne Boucher

2.81 King's College, University of Cambridge
Photo: Andrew Holt/Photographer's Choice/Getty Images

except one [Downing], has outgrown the original quadrangle, new courts have been added… Sometimes the 'old court', or primitive part of the building presents a handsome front to the largest street near it; but frequently, as if to show its independence of, and contempt for, the town, it retires from the street altogether, showing the passer by only its ugliest wall, and smallest, shabbiest gate.[114]

The quadrangle was the basic planning unit. The quadrangular enclosure had defensive advantages, for incidents of town–gown violence were common, and was, furthermore, practical in terms of land use. Land was already scarce in medieval Cambridge. By building right up to their site boundaries, the colleges maximized building space. The scale and organizational pattern of New College, Oxford (founded 1379) was highly influential upon Cambridge's development. The concept of a college planned as a coherent whole was first realized in Cambridge at Queens' College in the 1440s. Its simple plan was structured around two courts, Old Court and the supplementary Cloister Court. Old Court, built 1448–1449 (Figure 2.79), featured a library and chapel on its north range, a hall on the west and a gatehouse on the east. Its scale is small, yet the intensity of its plan and speed of construction resulted in unity unprecedented in Cambridge. Building practices of contemporary domestic architecture seemingly had great impact upon its design. The red brick of its ranges imparts a domestic warmth. The prevalence of brick in medieval Cambridge reflected the county's abundant clay but lack of good building stone, resulting in a marked visual disparity with Oxford where limestone is plentiful. Queens' layout recalls fourteenth- and fifteenth-century manor houses, such as Haddon Hall or Herstmonceux Castle, which contained a sequence of rectangular courtyards, one of them bounded by a covered walk akin to Cloister Court. The gatehouse was another feature of manorial building. Following its appearance at New College the gatehouse became a common collegiate motif, yet in Cambridge it appropriated a far more pronounced, militant demeanour. At Queens', it presents a formidable façade to the street, formed of corner towers and intermediate turrets (Figure 2.80). It served not a defensive but a psychological purpose, for its authoritative posture suggested the growing self-assurance and status of the late-medieval colleges.[115]

As the colleges grew in number and importance in the fifteenth century, their physical fabric became increasingly impressive. Each new founder desired to surpass the last in the size, grandeur and comprehensiveness of his college. Epitomizing this were Henry VI's plans for King's College. Established in the 1440s, its foundation transformed the topography of medieval Cambridge. By the fourteenth century, building space within the town boundaries had been all but exhausted, forcing many founders to erect their colleges upon the east bank of the River Cam and creating the vista known today as the Backs. Henry VI had extravagant ambitions for his institution, and cleared a whole quarter of the medieval town on the east bank. This sweeping act engendered a process of transition whereby the town centre came increasingly under the mastery of academia. King's College was planned around an enormous court bounded to the north by a vast chapel. Since its foundation stone was laid in 1446, the chapel has given a false impression as to the nature of a college chapel (Figure 2.81). The richness of its Perpendicular Gothic architecture ornately decorated with a plethora of heraldry, its extensive programme of stained glass, and the renowned fan vault that roofs it are breathtaking. A chapel had not been a requisite in the plans of the earliest colleges, and most made use of parish churches.

Following King's, however, an independent chapel was considered an integral element of all new foundations. King's College Chapel represents the pinnacle of Lancastrian megalomania, but ultimately Henry's purse did not match his ambitions. Upon his overthrow in 1461, the skeleton of the chapel was the only visible expression of his visionary plan. Little additional construction took place until the eighteenth and nineteenth centuries.[116]

The royal connections of the late-medieval colleges, such as King's, Queens', Trinity and St John's, invested them with an éclat and importance which manifested itself in their physical appearance. The material presence of the university itself, however, was far less conspicuous. During the fourteenth century, the university began to accumulate property on a city centre site, today known as Senate House Hill where it erected a complex known as the 'Schools'. The first of these buildings housed the theology school on the ground floor and a chapel and senate house above. Completed in 1372, it is the oldest building in Oxbridge specifically intended for university use. The theology school formed the north side of the Schools Court, which gained a western range in the 1430s housing a law school and library, and an east side containing a courtroom and library in 1473. Thus by the early modern period, the University of Cambridge consisted of a tiny ancient core with the Schools at its centre, around which converged the colleges.[117]

In the mid-sixteenth century, the enclosed quadrangular format was challenged by the development of the three-sided court. After refounding Gonville Hall as Gonville and Caius College in 1557, Dr Caius added a new court largely identical to its medieval precursors barring one notable innovation. He forbid the enclosure of the south side 'lest for lack of free ventilation the air should become foul, the health of our college...impaired, and disease and death be thereby rendered more frequent'. The south perimeter was defined only by a wall with a gate. Such three-sided courtyards were fashionable for French chateaux of the time, and its adoption at Gonville and Caius revealed the declining influence of the medieval plan in favour of Renaissance ideals. The three-sided courtyard was imitated at Emmanuel and Sidney Sussex Colleges, founded in 1584 and 1596 respectively. Emmanuel had close connections with New England, especially Harvard, and possibly transmitted this layout to its earliest colonial colleges.[118]

Despite a significant drop in student numbers, from the 1660s the university and colleges embarked upon an apparently ceaseless building campaign. The most important individual presence in these years was Christopher Wren, who set Cambridge upon a new trajectory with the introduction of fully-fledged classicism. Pembroke College Chapel (1665) was the first building that he designed. It is a simple rectangle in shape, modest in scale, but distinguished by its street front. Based on a design of Sebastiano Serlio, it has a temple-like façade with four giant pilasters beneath a pediment. The chapel introduced the university to a definitive classical language, but it was at Trinity College that Cambridge experienced Wren in his maturity. Trinity College Library (designed 1676) demonstrates Wren's mastery of classicism in its rich yet unaffected design (Figure 1.8). Wren's follower, James Gibbs, was commissioned by the university to provide an appropriate setting for its ceremonial functions on land alongside the Schools Court. The first British architect trained abroad, Gibbs represented the height of fashion. For Senate House Hill he devised a three-sided court of dignified institutional edifices, but insufficient funds and internal politicking meant only one range, Senate House, was built (Figure 2.82). A single, large room for the conferring of degrees, Senate House (1730) is a dignified Portland stone building. It forms a unified, stately ensemble with the later Cockerell Library (1842) and the Schools range, refaced in the 1750s.

The vogue for classicism brought with it an aversion for Gothic, and in the seventeenth and eighteenth centuries several colleges refaced their medieval brick structures with stone. The stone fronts of Christ's and Pembroke Colleges, for example, hide their medieval origins beneath.

In the nineteenth century, the classical idiom continued to be considered the most becoming for university expansion. George Basevi and C. R. Cockerell's Fitzwilliam Museum, begun 1837, is a prodigious example of neo-classicism. Dominating its streetscape, the resplendent front entrance is elevated upon stone stairs where visitors enter through a giant Corinthian portico with sculptured pediment and coiffered ceiling. Gothic Revival, though, was favoured for the belated completion of King's Great Court. The south range and eastern screen designed by William Wilkins in 1823 are a neo-Gothic fantasy. The pinnacles, perpendicular windows, assortment

2.82 Senate House, University of Cambridge
Photo: ©iStockphoto.com/Graham Taylor

of insignia and turreted gatehouse of the screen recall features of the adjacent chapel. The south range fuses octagonal turrets, oriel windows and battlements in an original invention on the medieval theme. With these two buildings, Wilkins achieved the formidable task of completing the court, harmonious in scale and execution with the overwhelming chapel and the eighteenth-century Fellows' Building. Indeed so unified is the ensemble that Wilkins's work is frequently assumed to be contemporary with the chapel.

Wilkins's Gothicism at King's stood in stark contrast to the tenor of his other major Cambridge commission. He was appointed in 1805 to design the university's first new foundation in two centuries, Downing College, where he gave full vent to his fastidious zeal for Grecian architecture. Wilkins pioneered a new collegiate layout, whereby the closed quadrangle was superseded by individual pavilions surrounding three sides of a huge lawn (Figure 2.83). The sense of openness occasioned by the court's tremendous size and separate buildings was wholly new to Cambridge. Downing's finances proved inadequate for the task, though, and only the east and west ranges of Wilkins's plan were erected. Nevertheless, Wilkins's vision has exerted a powerful legacy upon the site. Twentieth-century development adhered to the broad lines of the original design, and guided by classicist architects, generally proved sympathetic to Wilkins's ideal.

Howell, Killick, Partridge and Amis's Senior Combination Room (1964) interpreted this ideal in modernist fashion; its temple-like form of stepped base and concrete pilasters structurally reworks Wilkins's neo-classicism. Quinlan Terry's restrained classical Howard Building (1989) and Maitland Robinson Library (1992) equally have made play with a Grecian vocabulary.[119]

Downing was the first Cambridge college to have been designed as a whole. However, with massive expansion in the mid-twentieth century came the creation of several new colleges whose grounds were conceived as a planned entity, including Churchill, New Hall and Fitzwilliam Colleges. The 1959 design competition for Churchill College attracted a blaze of publicity and entries from many of the most innovative British practitioners of the time. Sheppard, Robson & Partners' winning design fused collegiate orthodoxy with high architectural ambition. Its central feature was a large, loosely defined court bounded by communal buildings, surrounded by interlocking residential quadrangles. The openness of the plan and the raw, unpolished aesthetic of its dark brick and concrete buildings rooted the design in 1960s avant-gardism, yet the hierarchy of quads and importance placed upon the communal facilities reflects its institutional heritage and fidelity to the format of the medieval colleges long after the Middle Ages had passed.

2.83 Downing College, University of Cambridge
Photo: By kind permission of the Master and Fellows of Downing College Cambridge

The new colleges of the 1950s and 1960s reinvigorated the Cambridge tradition of commissioning work by leading contemporary architects. The trend was also engaged by the university itself. Stung by a critical indictment by architectural historian Nikolaus Pevsner that the lack of radical thought in twentieth-century development discredited its distinguished architectural history, in 1953 it made an enlightened move in commissioning Sir Hugh Casson to master plan a new arts campus. It was amongst the first modernist university plans adopted in Britain. The Sidgwick Site plan was organized around a series of informally linked courtyards loosely defined by low, long blocks – a modern imagining of medieval Cambridge. 'In campus planning,' Casson later expounded, 'the spaces between the buildings and relationships of one to another are more important than the buildings themselves.' Inter-building spaces, or 'outdoor rooms', allowed informal social encounters. Buildings were intended as a 'series of incidents' encountered on the journey through the site. Casson envisaged buildings in varied styles united by a controlling framework that allowed for different architects to bring different approaches to the buildings, set to be realized over a long time period. Staged growth was key to the plan. The courtyards, for example, permitted incremental growth while ensuring the site appeared complete and satisfying at each stage.[120]

Financial difficulties resulted in only the southern part of the site being developed initially, focused upon the Raised Faculty Building (1961). Delays marred construction, and the northern area of the site was subsequently completely modified. Casson's outdoor rooms were not defined as planned; most notably the history faculty was sited on the proposed water court. James Stirling's History Building (1968) was one of the most imaginative and controversial buildings of modern Cambridge (Figure 2.84). A glass-enclosed library formed a quadrant bounded by an L-shaped red-tile teaching block. While observers praised its monumentality, its greenhouse format led to complaints of uncomfortable working conditions. Norman Foster's Law Building (1995) has likewise promoted unfavourable user criticism. Angled to respond to Stirling's adjacent building, the Law Building utilized Foster's typical sleek steel and glass vocabulary. Casson planned for understated buildings linked by well-conceived outdoor spaces, yet Stirling and Foster introduced highly individualistic buildings to

2.84 History Faculty, University of Cambridge
Photo: Janet Hall/RIBA Library Photographs Collection

the site that made little attempt to engage with their surroundings and to define interstitial landscapes. With these landmark structures fighting for attention, the townscape ideal of the Sidgwick Site has been diminished. Confusing to navigate, the site has no clear gateways or vistas to lead between different faculties, whose front doors are rarely well identified. The rows of parked cars and minimal signage on the site's southern boundary made for a disparaging first impression. These problems formed the context for a new master plan, produced in 2000 by Allies and Morrison with the objective of unifying the site into a harmonious and accessible entity. Vehicular parking has been partially redressed by a new bus service and cycle routes, while its new buildings, such as the English Building (2004), espouse the low-key, human-scale design and linking outdoor spaces intended by Casson.[121]

Open space is increasingly becoming scarce in Cambridge, yet landscape is key to the essence of the university's environment. College gardens constitute a distinctive aspect of the landscape. Surrounded by ancient walls and buildings and glimpsed through grilles or doorways, they create an atmosphere of secret gardens. Cambridge's most iconic landscape is the Backs. The Backs is essentially the 'back gardens' of six river colleges spatially divided by ditches and avenues of trees. The space affords long axial vistas often dominated by the university's landmark structures, such as King's College Chapel, that have graced countless postcards and chocolate boxes and form some of the most marketable images of the university and city.

These vistas, buildings and landscapes have possessed a special and enduring hold upon generations of scholars and visitors. Its built environment evidences a connection with the august history and customs of the university, while also serving as a compendium of architectural practice and fashions of the last 800 years. It is the language of spatial organization that is, however, most important to Cambridge. Its structure of linked quadrangles surrounded by low ranges of buildings is interwoven with the urban fabric and yet presents an impenetrable façade to the town. The narrow passageways and hushed courts with their heavy gates and towers impart a distinct sense of place which in turn has created a campus saturated with meaningful experiences.

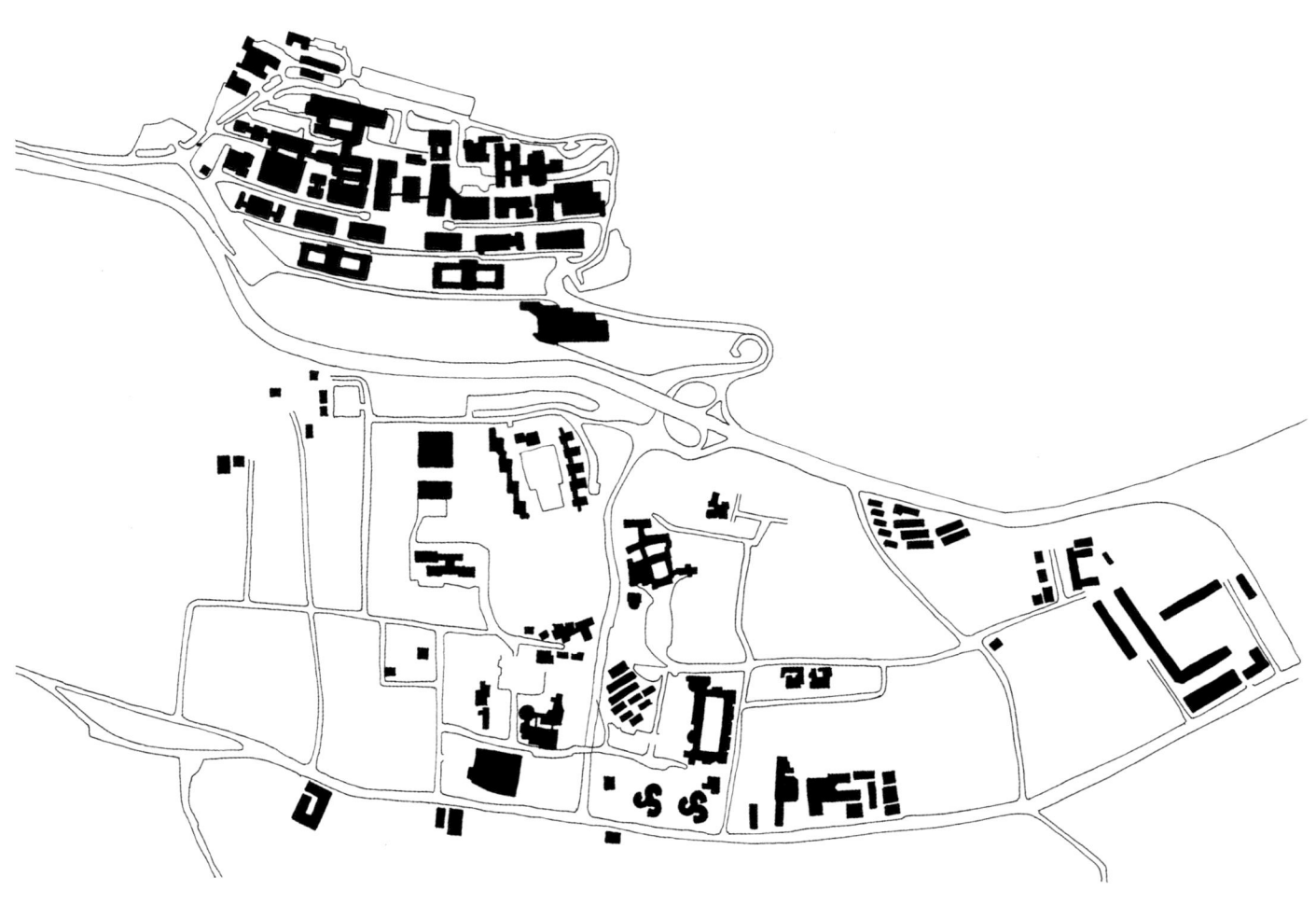

2.85 Plan, University of Cape Town

University of Cape Town
Cape Town, South Africa

South Africa's oldest university was founded in 1918 and a decade later it moved to its new permanent home at Groote Schuur, on land bequeathed to the nation by Cecil Rhodes, former Prime Minister of the Cape, as the site for a national university. Leading architects Herbert Baker and Edwin Lutyens were approached to design the new campus but, both being engrossed with the construction of the new Indian capital, New Delhi, the commission instead went to Baker's young protégé Joseph Solomon with Lutyens acting as adviser when in Cape Town.

The university's Committee quickly dispatched Solomon on a tour around the universities of Western Europe, Britain and North America to study the latest in university design. He was profoundly impressed by the University of Genoa's approach to the task of building on a steeply inclined ground, for this was a palpably pressing concern for the Cape Town site. The Groote Schuur estate is one of great natural beauty, set on the lower slopes of Devil's Peak, buttressing Table Mountain. Solomon was highly conscious of the grandeur of its location, likening it to the dramatic mountainsides of Ancient Greece. The magnificence of its views was a key influence upon his 1919 master plan.[122]

Solomon's plan was well-structured and clear. It was strongly informed by the Beaux-Arts campuses he had encountered in North America, but moreover embraced the original organization of the site. From 1657 until the nineteenth century, the land was the site of Rustenberg Farm. The farm was structured around a distinctive axial walk running east–west up the mountainside and aligned with the crest of Devil's Peak. A summer house was constructed circa 1760, terminating the walk. After Rhodes acquired the farm in 1883, the axial walk was planted with japonica shrubs, earning it the epithet Japonica Walk. The summer house and Japonica Walk formed the basic structuring elements of Solomon's plan. The summer house established the alignment of a powerful east–west axis stretching from the walk upwards to terminate in a commanding focal building, Jameson Hall, aligned on the peak of Table Mountain. A secondary

2.86 Upper Campus, University of Cape Town
Photo: © Eric Nathan/ Loop Images/Corbis

UNIVERSITY OF CAPE TOWN

2.87 Jameson Hall, University of Cape Town
Photo: Communication & Marketing Department, University of Cape Town

cross axis, lined with academic buildings and named University Avenue, bisected the main axis (Figure 2.86). The plan contrived a clear spatial framework that structured the land into a progression of three stepped terraces, connected by a grandiose series of steps. Jameson Plaza is the nucleus of the academic terrace, which is the highest plateau and below which step the residential terrace, then playing field terrace, giving views across the distant mountains. The intersection of the main axis with University Avenue created a plaza of great visual importance, dominated by the raised Jameson Hall to the west. Although built as a reduced version of Solomon's vision, Jameson Hall is the university's symbol building; it is where students process on graduation and the image utilized in promotional material (Figure 2.87). Flanking Jameson, the Jagger Library and student union defined the plaza. The quality of the space is exceptionally high and demonstrates Solomon's skill in using buildings to define public environments.[123]

Solomon envisaged a university of classical simplicity. The large, symmetrical buildings of his campus share a quiet dignity, united by their buff exteriors and red tile roofs. The Jameson Plaza ensemble bears witness to the pervasive influence of the University of Virginia. Echoes of its Rotunda are clearly traceable in Jameson Hall's placement as the focal point terminating a principal axis, as well as in its classical pedimented portico. From the Hall's elevated portico of Ionic columns extends a colonnade linking it with the library and student union. The grouping established the skylines, scales and finishes for buildings along University Avenue. The Jeffersonian influence on the academic terrace gave way to Oxbridge-influenced planning on the residential terrace. The ivy-clad Smuts (Figure 2.88) and Fuller Halls assumed quadrangular formats with inner courtyards surrounded by cloisters.

Depressed by delays and illness, Solomon committed suicide in 1920. Cyril Walgate, working with the practice Hawke and McKinley, assumed control. Under their governance, the project largely followed Solomon's scheme. However, it was Walgate's decision to curve University Avenue to meld with the contours of the mountainside, as it was to reduce the scale of Jameson Hall to lower costs. By the late 1950s, Solomon's revised scheme had been completed. The result realized his vision of grand, axial simplicity reflective of the institution's high ambitions. Yet this arcadia was soon injured by the repercussions of two extraneous occurrences: the insertion of a motorway bisecting the primary axis and the post-war baby boom. The former event cleaved Upper Campus from the Summer House and from what was to become Middle Campus, thus resulting in disjunction. The baby boom sent enrolment figures soaring, inciting a massive construction programme in the 1960s and 1970s. Much of the building occurred behind the academic terrace, where no development had been

2.88 Smuts Hall, University of Cape Town
Photo: Julian Elliott

intended, and outside of the architectural guidelines that had been enforced to unify the Upper Campus. In 1957, there was only one building above the line of Jameson Hall; two decades later a row of concrete structures existed there. The contemporary aesthetics and planning of the Chemical Engineering Building exemplified the disruptions in scale and character that the new buildings, designed for modern teaching methods, brought. Many of the new structures infringed the visual consistency which had distinguished Solomon's campus, lessening the dramatic impact of the site.[124]

In 1969 remedial measures were taken with the establishment of a planning unit to combat the degeneration of the quality of the campus. A scheme was duly prepared which opened up the Groote Schuur estate into Upper, Middle and Lower campuses within a single, interrelated environment. Construction on Upper Campus ceased and expansion was diverted to Middle Campus, south of the

2.89 Aerial view of Upper and Middle Campuses, University of Cape Town
Photo: Julian Elliott

motorway, where the faculties of education, law and commerce could be regrouped. The planning framework for the redesign of Middle Campus was produced in 1983, guided by Revel Fox, Julian Elliott and Neil Grobbelaar. The principles of the design were informed by Solomon's axial layout of Upper Campus. A diagonal axis was established from the summer house, the focal point of Solomon's design, which extended north-east to terminate at the Cricket Oval (Figure 2.89). Like Upper Campus, development was structured around a series of stepped terraces to manage the difficulties of building on a slope. Nevertheless, in other respects the Middle Campus Plan differed significantly from Solomon's. Upper Campus was informed by an urban planning model, in which a dense pattern of buildings was used to frame public spaces. Middle Campus adopted a more informal, suburban organization. Essentially, structures were conceived as independent entities surrounded by green space, each with its own parking and access, enabling the campus to be realized in phases with each stage resulting in a feeling of completeness. Development was planned to be lower than the tree canopy, preserving the vistas to and from the mountain. The Kramer Law Building (1984) (Figure 2.90) was one structure built along the new diagonal axis. Designed with recall to Renaissance villas in its open colonnades, its buff colouring and red tile roofs established visual correlation with Solomon's buildings.

However, its height and siting negatively impacted on the mountainside vistas that are so pivotal to the university's physical environment. The reduced density of the Middle Campus reduced the integration of the whole as compared to the Upper Campus. Nevertheless, a pedestrian network linking the buildings – most pronounced on the principal diagonal axis – partly redressed this. A sunken pedestrian tunnel provided access from Upper to Middle Campus.[125]

With the expansion of the university to Middle and Lower Campuses, travelling distances across campus inevitably increased. The sloping site means that the uphill walk to Upper Campus is, though by no means intolerable, rather taxing. The circulation system is, therefore, greatly augmented by the campus's efficient transport service, the Jammie Shuttle. Instituted in 2005, the buses service all areas of main campus and have proved remarkably successful. In 2008 the service was averaging 42,000 passenger trips per day, reducing vehicular presence on site.

A successful approach to circulation that featured in both Solomon's vision and the 1983 plan is the use of avenues of trees to frame and reinforce pedestrian routes. Most notably this exists in Japonica Walk, but its use extends to a lesser degree across Middle Campus. Maintaining the quality of the landscape was a priority of the Middle Campus plan. The estate has a historical wooded character which

2.90 Kramer Law Building, University of Cape Town
Photo: Communication & Marketing Department, University of Cape Town

has largely been preserved. Screens of trees, for instance, front the buildings of Middle Campus. In the 1980s, new japonicas were planted along Japonica Walk thus conserving the historic open space and reinforcing the campus's integrating east–west axis. The university has consistently responded to the landscape, most notably in its arrangement of terraces which step down the gradient of the mountainside and its exploitation of views. This affinity with the natural setting has proved a key placemaking device.

Upper Campus in particular successfully cultivates its sense of place. Jameson Hall immediately assumed this function. 'Stepsitting' on the steps of Jameson enjoys a long tradition, as photographs from the early 1930s of students gathered before it illustrate. With its well-defined hardscape court and views over Cape Town, Jameson Plaza is a paragon of spatial organization. Sitting at the intersection of the visual east–west axis and the operational north–south axis (University Avenue), the plaza is intensively used and valued. Placemarking is continued by the academic buildings surrounding it and Smuts and Fuller Halls below. Clad with Virginia creeper, they intentionally evoke the environments of Oxbridge and the Ivy League, thus building Cape Town into a tradition of the educational elite.

The University of Cape Town has created an eloquent and photogenic setting through diligent planning. While its first phase of development under Solomon adopted a Beaux-Arts plan urban in character, the second phase in the latter half of the twentieth century followed a much looser, informal approach. Yet both were informed by a strong spatial framework and a consistent architectural image of simple classicism, buff-coloured walls and red tile roofs. Above all, the campus has exhibited a near constant sensitivity to landscape. By employing an axial arrangement predicated upon Table Mountain and two of the site's historic features – an avenue of plants and a summer house – the campus's plan has capitalized on the splendour of its natural setting.

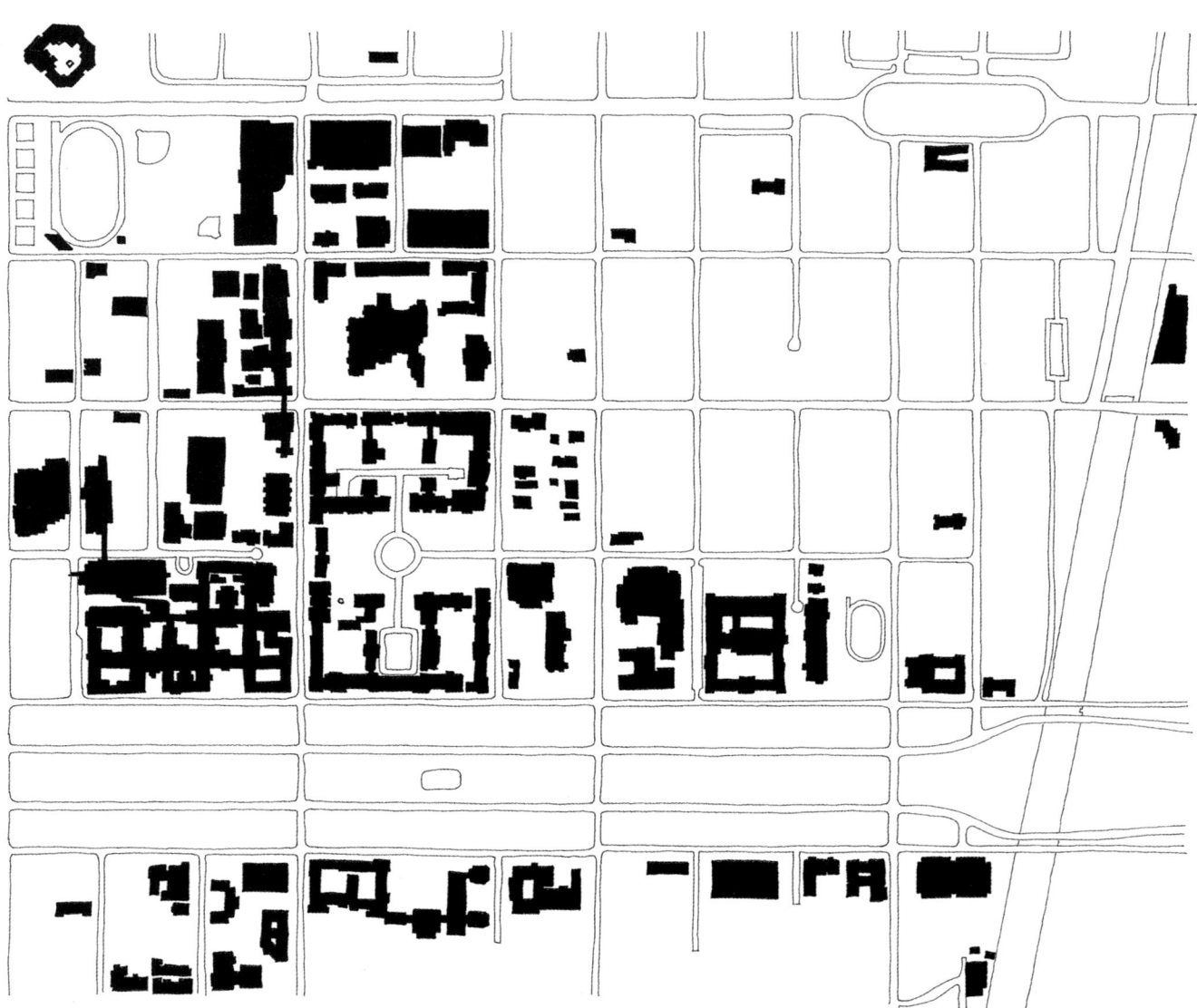

2.91 Plan, University of Chicago

University of Chicago
Chicago, USA

As the twentieth century approached, a new phenomenon crept over America's cities – the comprehensive, large-scale planning scheme. The cities of Cleveland, Chicago, San Francisco, Washington DC, Denver and Minneapolis were the subjects of major planning proposals. This tenor quickly swept too across the nation's campuses. Universities both old and new were transformed in the 1890s as institutions such as Columbia, New York, Berkeley, Washington, and Stanford embarked upon panoptic plans, radically and permanently altering the landscape of the American college.[126]

The University of Chicago, founded in 1890 by the American Baptist Education Society and oil magnate John D. Rockefeller, exemplified this current. The new university was sited upon a four-block site 11 kilometres south of downtown Chicago, which faced a long strip of parkland (Midway Plaisance) created for the 1893

2.92 Cobb Gate, University of Chicago
Photo: Special Collections Research Center, University of Chicago Library

UNIVERSITY OF CHICAGO

World's Exposition, then in its planning stages. The university was envisaged as a modern research university that merged an English-style undergraduate college with a German-style graduate research institute. Its complex programme necessitated a diverse array of teaching rooms, laboratories, dormitories, a library, and gymnasium. The diversity of its curriculum occasioned the need for heightened unity and systematized expansion within its physical environment to ensure that it fostered a collegiate coherence. The university's trustees thus determined that their new establishment needed a strong master plan and that within this plan, its buildings were 'to stand as the expression of a great University'.[127]

The man employed to incarnate this vision was Henry Ives Cobb. His 1893 plan structured the university around seven quadrangles, known as the Main Quadrangles, built onto four city blocks unbroken by through roads (Figure 1.34). Its layout reflected the urban setting of the university, where the city grid iron met the Chicago park system. In their rectilinearity, the courts echoed not the organic, ad hoc English medieval quadrangles, but the Chicago grid into which they have been inserted. Yet in framing a series of lawned chambers through which green spaces flow, the Chicago quadrangles provided a continuation of the parks that surround it.[128]

Cobb's plan physically embodied the pedagogic philosophy of the university. It contained residential quadrangles, a chapel, administration building, library, museums, laboratories, small teaching classrooms and relatively few large lecture theatres. While the women's dormitories formed the eastern façade of the Main Quadrangles, the men's residences formed the western. The first buildings to be erected, Goodspeed, Gates, Blake and Cobb Halls, created a long, fortress-like western boundary to the outside world. Initial building focused not on the centre but on the perimeters of the campus, immediately demarcating the university's enclave and stressing its aloofness from its mercantile setting. In so doing, the university began its life by establishing itself as a place apart. This persona of scholarly retreat was enforced by the choice of architecture.

Cobb first proposed that the architecture should employ Romanesque Revival style, but this was quickly dismissed for one that carried with it the most compelling connotations of learning – the Gothic. With its lofty connotations of permanence, truth and erudition, the Gothic appeared as the superior route to the creation of a distinct intellectual realm in the midst of industrial Chicago. On a limited budget, Cobb designed a repertoire of functional buildings enlivened by a simple scattering of medieval devices, such as pointed arches, oriel windows, pinnacles and turreted towers. Their simple, chaste elegance was to set the tone for the campus and foster unification in the face of the college's disconcerting complexity. Stylistically consistent, safe from the vagaries of individual donors, the Gothic Revival vocabulary prevailed within the Main Quadrangles, forging for the university a trenchant identity within only ten years of its founding.[129]

Cobb's scholastic wonderland is entered from the north, via Cobb Gate (1900) (Figure 2.92). The Indiana limestone gate is best known for the grotesques that perch along its steep gable and which have come to occupy an entrenched place within university myth. Its dragon-like predators have come to be mythicized as admissions officers; the nervous, rodent-like creatures are overwrought first-year students; while the imperious winged griffon atop its apex symbolizes a fourth-year student, glorying in his position at the pinnacle of the social hierarchy. Such unique gestures, embedded within student lore, create the illusive quality that anchors a place in the memory. Its steep red-tile canopy established a kinship with the pitched roofs of the buildings around Hull Court, directly inside the entryway. Hull Court (1897), the central northern quadrangle, is bounded by four buildings, the Zoology Building, Anatomy Building, Culver Hall and Erman (or Botany) Hall. Although similar in massings, the four edifices differed in their decorative detail to contrive the random asymmetry of medieval buildings risen over time.[130]

To the east of Hull Court is Hutchinson Court (1903), which was designed by the rising stars of the architectural world, the Boston firm of Shepley, Rutan and Coolidge, who replaced Cobb in 1901. Charles Coolidge, the lead architect of the project, followed Cobb's lead in many ways, adhering to the materials and general style of the earliest quadrangles. Nevertheless, Hutchinson Court espouses a different aesthetic to its neighbour, conditioned by the changing circumstances of the university. Rockefeller's endowments were becoming ever more generous, allowing Coolidge a financial laxity that Cobb did not benefit from. The court's buildings – Hutchinson Commons, Mitchell Tower, Reynolds Club and Mandel Hall – evidenced a new stylistic current, as Cobb's economic Gothic Revival was displaced by

2.93 Rockefeller Memorial Chapel
Photo: ©Michele Falzone/JAI/Corbis

ornamental Collegiate Gothic. The university took satisfaction that its buildings made specific reference to structures of the University of Oxford. Hutchinson Commons is modelled after the sixteenth-century Christ Church Hall, the Reynolds Club after St John's College, and Mitchell Tower after the bell tower of Magdalen College (1509). Coolidge did not merely reproduce the Oxonian models, though; rather he thoughtfully and imaginatively revised the medieval forms to respond to the demands of the individual project. Thus, the crocketed finials of Magdalen Tower were replaced on its Chicago counterpart with octagonal turrets to harmonize with the towers of Cobb's Ryerson Laboratories on the opposite side of the court. With its picturesque and stimulating enclosing ranges, the quadrangle is ranked amongst the best in the central complex.[131]

As vital to the character of the Main Quadrangles as their buildings is the landscape they enclose. The landscaping to this day largely follows a plan prepared by the Olmsted Brothers in 1902, which prescribed a formal, rectilinear layout. John C. Olmsted proposed a network of roadways and walkways to allow the movement of pedestrians, supplies and waste across campus laid out upon a simple geometric system with axial vistas at each end. Hutchinson Court was designed as a sunken grassed space, ringed by a drive and single row of trees and spanned by diagonal paths. Harper Court, the central south quadrangle, was structured around clearly defined walkways and drives that provided a logical sequence of access routes, while its planting evidenced a special concern not to block axial vistas or sunlight from buildings.[132]

Harper Court was the centrepiece of Coolidge's humanities and social sciences complex, designed around the impressive William Rainey Harper Memorial Library (1912). The vast, highly elaborate Collegiate Gothic structure formed the southern termination of the north axis of the Quadrangles composition. Its southern door, facing out towards the Midway, marked a change in the course of campus planning for, up to then, entrance to campus had been via the more defensive, reserved means of gates.

As development proceeded in the twentieth century, Cobb's design continued to hold sway. The East Campus to the east of the

2.94 Law School, University of Chicago
Photo: Special Collections Research Center, University of Chicago Library

Quadrangles arose largely in the 1920s, to be dominated by Bertram Goodhue's Rockefeller Memorial Chapel (1928) (Figure 2.93). Its 63-metre tall silhouette dominates the university's skyline. Goodhue was at the peak of his fame as America's foremost architect of Gothic Revivalist churches, but the Rockefeller Chapel was also markedly modern in style. Sleek, angular planes and simplified geometry were synthesized with a tableau of filled niches and intricate tracery. Seven decades on, the hybridized mode was employed on East Campus at Rafael Viñoly's Graduate School of Business (2004). Tubular steel arches carrying a spectacular vaulted glass ceiling referred to the campus's neo-Gothic heritage, while externally the building's strong horizontality and interlocking cubes clad in smooth limestone placed it firmly in a twenty-first-century context.[133]

The South Campus was largely the result of post-Second World War development, on land south of the Midway. In 1955 renowned Modernist, Eero Saarinen, was commissioned to produce a master plan. Saarinen was sorely dissatisfied at what he perceived as the disregard for integrating modernist design with earlier styles, especially on college campuses. At a time when revivalist architecture was reviled as impractical and unfashionable, his plan emphasized the importance of maintaining the architectural integrity of the Gothic core, and stipulated that contemporary design should not infiltrate into the Gothic superblock. In the second half of the twentieth century, though, the university simply did not have the funds to replicate the masterworks of Cobb and Coolidge, so in the 1950s and 1960s much-needed expansion largely assumed contemporary forms lining the Midway's southern edge. Regrettably, much of Saarinen's plan remained unrealized. What was completed, however, was his Laird Bell Law Quadrangle (1959) directly south of the Main Quadrangles on the opposite side of the Midway.[134]

Saarinen's Law School is a four building complex, dominated by a six-storey library and office building, massed around an open court with reflecting pool which separates it from the Midway (Figure 2.94). It is connected at the west to the Gothic Burton-Judson Dormitories (1931). The architect's chief concern was to contrive a façade which would sit graciously alongside the Gothic campus without resorting to literal eclecticism. Transposing the thin, glass-filled walls, pinnacled outline and soaring verticality of High Gothic cathedrals, the reinforced concrete library was enclosed by a pleated, black glass curtain, which created a serrated roofline accentuated by thin aluminium finials. 'By stressing a small, broken scale, a lively silhouette, and especially verticality in the library design,' Saarinen commented, 'we intended to make it a good neighbour with the neo-Gothic dormitories.'[135] Other development on the South Campus was often less successful. The capacious, horizontal expanse of the Midway is not a forgiving setting, and units can easily appear isolated and dwarfed. Rather than sustaining the principle of intimate, urban courtyard spaces, South Campus development proceeded along the conventional model of downtown streets circumscribed by buildings. The traditional Gothic language of the campus was, furthermore, displaced by a fervid modernism. Edward Durrell Stone's Graduate Residence (formerly the Centre of Continuing Education, 1962) exemplified this pattern. A large, rectangular building, it has little contextual relationship with its surroundings. The lack of a common stylistic and planning approach at the South Campus is at the expense of the unifying vision of fellowship that makes the Main Quadrangles and its adjoining areas so impressive.[136]

The planning and design approach of the campus became the subject of reawakened interest at the end of the 1990s. As the university reassessed the extent to which its values were expressed through its built environment, it commissioned planners Naramore, Bain, Brady and Johanson to produce the university's third master plan. The results are still being felt on campus. A key feature of the plan is the expansion and reorganization of the North and West Campus. New structures that have arisen as part of the plan include the Gordon Centre for Integrative Science (2005) and the Max Palevsky Residential Commons (2001). These buildings fulfil important functions in allying existing buildings to form new quadrangular spaces. The Palevsky Residential Commons, for instance, designed by Ricardo Legorreta, encloses a space bounded to the south by the university's main library, the vast Brutalist Regenstein Library (1970). Some of the new structures appropriate a modernist aesthetic, as the neon exterior of the Palevsky Residential Commons demonstrates, while others adopt a more traditional veneer. The limestone-clad Kovler Gymnasium with its carved figural sculpture and vertical fenestration adumbrates the Gothic Main Quadrangles.[137]

The landscape was not forgotten in the rejuvenated campus plan. Ellis Avenue, the axis running north to south that separates

2.95 University of Chicago
Photo: Special Collections Research Center, University of Chicago Library

the West Campus and Main Quadrangles, has been the subject of landscaping efforts to ensconce it as the new visual artery of the campus, bridging the science facilities to the west and the liberal arts to the east. A focus has been placed upon creating an inviting environment. The Midway Plaisance, although owned by the City of Chicago and managed by the Chicago Park District, is considered an integral part of the university's landscape and it forms a key aspect of the school's development plans. The organizations have co-operated with the school's efforts to maximize the parkland's use and render it more socially welcoming. The panel of parkland between the Main Quadrangles and the Law Quadrangle has been transformed since 2002 with an ice-skating rink and the North (2003) and South Winter Gardens (2009), which have enlivened and beautified the space for the benefit of university members and local residents.[138]

The Midway provides numerous recreational opportunities not ordinarily found in an urban university. Indeed, the university is privileged to have an archipelago of peaceful outdoor spaces within the sprawling, industrial metropolis. Still valid are the remarks made in 1906 by H. G. Wells, that the university's green spaces were 'a wonderful contrast to the dark congestion of the mercantile city of the north'. Within the Gothic core, nature flows from the surrounding park through the ordered geometry of Cobb's quadrangles creating a varied palette of outdoor chambers. Some courts are shaded, some are sunny, some enclosed and intimate, while others more expansive. Linking arches draw the pedestrian from court to court, through narrow passages that burst into outdoor expanses, in a subtly artful manipulation of space that makes the campus a pleasure to navigate (Figure 2.95). For instance, in Coolidge's Theology group (1926) in the south-west quadrangle, an enclosed, traceried cloister entices visitors through its passages until it unexpectedly reveals the dramatic and ornate façade of the Bond Chapel.

The captivating picturesqueness of the campus's neo-Gothic heart has been a crucial factor in creating an institutional identity. The spaces and the buildings that frame them play a crucial role in establishing a recognizable presence, or 'brand' image, that symbolizes the university as an entity. Vital in achieving this has been Cobb's planning and design legacy. He created the outline for an enclosed community structured around quadrangles of consistent scale and limited architectural vocabulary. The buildings that have come to populate them are demurely elegant evocations of the Gothic idiom, which have successfully brought to the university a sense of history and permanence. Despite being erected decades apart, its buildings largely work together within the greater impress of the university. From its earliest days, the campus strove to enfold all its various departments within a single image, and much of the campus's effect results from the depth to which its original vision was carried out. Although the South Campus has come under criticism for its sense of separation, the sense of collectiveness at the University of Chicago has been remarkably well preserved for an urban institution.

2.96 Plan, University of Colorado at Boulder

University of Colorado at Boulder
Boulder, USA

Upon its ordination as the home of the state university in 1872, the inhabitants of Boulder were spurred into raising $15,000 to construct the University of Colorado's first building, Old Main (1876) (Figure 2.97). Following the pattern established in colonial times, it was a large monostructure housing classrooms, library, laboratories, and accommodation for the president. From 1880 it was joined by other buildings – the President's residence (1880, now Koenig Alumni Centre), Cottage No 1 (1885), Woodbury Hall (1890) and Hale Science (1894). These early buildings lined public streets, orientated towards the community and valley. However, at the beginning of the twentieth century the outline of a quadrangle began to be traced behind them. With the construction of University Theatre (1903), Guggenheim Geography (1908), and the Macky Auditorium (1910–1922), the campus grew around a vast cruciform-shaped space that became Norlin Quadrangle and has remained at the heart of all subsequent campus plans. These eclectic buildings represent a

2.97 Old Main viewed from Norlin Quadrangle, University of Colorado at Boulder
Photo: Eli Nixon

2.98 University of Colorado at Boulder
Photo: Jason Holmberg

survey of historicism. Macky Auditorium espouses a Tudor-Gothic style, Guggenheim Geography is a Renaissance palazzo with neo-Classical portico, and the theatre is Romanesque.

In 1917 the decision to increase Boulder's student body motivated President Ferrand to engage an architectural practice to prepare a campus plan. The campus was in a state of disorganization. The loose formation of buildings prompted later university president George Norlin to observe that it resembled 'a third rate farm'. The university appointed Charles Klauder, one of the country's leading academic architects, to deliver a remedy. Through his work at Princeton and Wellesley, Klauder had become a prominent practitioner of Collegiate Gothic and Beaux-Arts planning. His 1919 plan for Colorado was, in essence, a Beaux-Arts system of symmetrically dispersed buildings along intersecting axes. The plan formalized the geometry of the existing buildings, connected these with new structures to enclose open spaces, and emphasized axial connections between them. The Hellems Building (1921) was the first to be completed by Klauder on campus, and its siting opposite to Macky established the basis for the cruciform shape of Norlin Quadrangle. The primary axis runs east–west along this cross, and the buildings that define its boundaries are orthogonally aligned. The strong visual connection between Macky and Hellems exemplifies the powerful axial vistas that Klauder established in this space and across campus.[139]

Hellems also established the stylistic tone for Klauder's buildings. The university was situated in the dry rugged environs of the Rocky Mountain Front Range against a breathtaking mountainous backdrop, which directly inspired Klauder's designs:

> There should be no scheme either of education or of architecture that is not firmly rooted in Mother Earth. Aspiration begins there. And the architectural conception should be guided by what is appropriate to mountains, to rugged knolls with rock outcroppings, to more amenable rural and suburban sites or to places amid unbroken horizons of the plains.[140]

In what has been ranked his most innovative stylistic experiment, Klauder devised a scheme for Colorado synchronized to the natural environment. Noting a similarity between the Tuscan and Colorado countryside, he drew upon the hillside villages and rural farmhouses that he had seen in Tuscany to devise a style later dubbed Tuscan vernacular. An imaginative combination of towers, gabled roofs, cloister-like arcades and Renaissance-inspired cartouches embellished his individual buildings that were united by a palette of shared

2.99 Cristol Chemistry viewed across Dalton Trumbo Fountain court, University of Colorado at Boulder
Photo: Jim Steinhart of TravelPhotoBase

materials. Robust sandstone walls, limestone trim, clay barrel-tile roofs of various hues and black wrought iron accents characterized the structures. Local quarries provided the sandstone, which was laid in long slices with the fractured face exposed, creating varied patterns of shadows and colouration ranging from light buff to red to brown (Figure 2.98).[141]

Sewall Hall (1934) is probably the finest example of the style. The warm sandstone building has Renaissance limestone flourishes and varying roof lines punctuated by dovecote chimneys, echoing the mountainous setting. Its H-shaped plan, which was adopted for most dormitories, formed intimate courtyards. Akin to the Tuscan communities he emulated, Klauder organized buildings around courtyards and quadrangles, the whole linked by walkways. Arched openings in the courtyards revealed vistas to the Rockies. To terminate the eastern axis of Norlin Quadrangle, Klauder designed a suitably monumental library (1939). A raised portico with rectangular tapered limestone columns formed Norlin Library's entrance façade. Conifers that grew naturally in the Boulder foothills were planted across campus and continue as a defining feature of the campus landscape today.

The strength of Klauder's vision was such that it continues to dominate the campus. Klauder's death in 1938 and the after effects of the Second World War, however, brought changes to the campus. Enrolment soared and demands on university facilities increased and altered. Under the direction of architects Trautwein & Howard, new buildings continued to conform to the Tuscan vernacular, albeit devoid of some of Klauder's *élan*. Their Wardenburg Health Centre (1959), Cristol Chemistry (1958) (Figure 2.99) and Cheyenne Arapaho Hall (1954) utilized a pared-down version of the sandstone and red-tile vocabulary. The residences Farrand and Libby Halls preserved Klauder's H-shaped plan. Campus growth in these years was rapid. Although Klauder's master plan had called for further building to occur along Broadway, campus's western boundary, development instead occurred to the south and east. The 1950s and 1960s saw an energetic land acquisition policy. The university added 284 acres to its plant with the procurement of East Campus, Research Park and Williams Village. Peripheral construction projects began to deviate from the prescribed Tuscan vernacular, such as the Litman Research Laboratory on East Campus, raising concerns over the approach to campus design.

In the early 1960s, Sasaki, Walker & Associates were charged to prepare a new master plan. Their 1963 plan adopted a flexible approach to Klauder's design principles that upheld his palette of materials, spatial framework and human scale, but permitted

UNIVERSITY OF COLORADO AT BOULDER

modernized concepts and forms. New structures were sited to create courtyards and important buildings continued to be used to anchor major axes. Sandstone and terracotta tile continued to superabound yet cost-effective concrete was in places employed for exterior walls and increasingly replaced limestone for door and window trim. The university ended its commitment to a single architectural practice, and numerous architects were hired to effect the Sasaki plan. The Engineering Centre (1965) was the first major building to realize the plan. Sited at the east of main campus, it anchors one end of a subsidiary east–west axis. Inspired by Klauder's design, it nevertheless was not a slavish imitation. Tile and sandstone were combined with vast concrete planes, while its mass was broken down into varying height towers, sloping roofs and projecting wings, both to relieve the building's enormous size and recapture Klauder's vernacular style expressive of its mountain setting. New residence halls, the Kittredge Complex, were built at the south-east corner of main campus from 1963–1964. The red tiled, sandstone dormitories form a loose quadrangle around a lake, while the irregular plans of the individual units create a series of forecourts. From the early 1960s to the mid-1970s, the building footprint on campus doubled. An internal planning office was established to ensure Klauder's architectural values were maintained, with positive results. Even modernist Harry Weese conformed to Klauder's concept. His Duane Physics Building (1971) was a huge L-shaped complex wrapped around a court with a varied silhouette punctuated by wings, towers and a range of sloping roof forms. Variegated barrel tiles, sandstone and white concrete trim characterize its exterior.

The Tuscan vernacular continued to guide more recent construction. Filling a prime space on Norlin Quadrangle, the Eaton Humanities Building (2000) has varied massing with rich sandstone walls, white trim and tile roofs. The 2006 Alliance for Technology, Learning and Society Building was likewise cloaked in this familiar vernacular, bar its corner tower whose glass elevations reveal its twenty-first-century genealogy. Recent building has utilized a basic formula that echoes many of Klauder's themes but without direct imitation. Current planning precepts stipulate that new additions should have a familial resemblance to their predecessors in terms of massing, materials, and human scale, while framing open space to create a variety of quadrangles, plazas and courts.[142]

Main Campus is approaching its development maximum, and the university is now looking at vacant land on East Campus and Williams Village to accommodate future growth. Non-academic functions are increasingly being transferred to these peripheral properties. Masonry walls and human scale visually link them to main campus, but more freedom is visible in the materials, style and costs of this construction.

The East Campus and Williams Village are disadvantaged, nevertheless, by a lack of the well-defined, landscaped outdoor spaces that enrich Main Campus. On the newer precincts, the vertical conifers of main campus, which provide much welcome visual relief in the stark winters, have been planted only occasionally. Its many outdoor 'rooms' are amongst Main Campus's chief assets. Peaceful spaces along Boulder Creek or Varsity Lake, for instance, contrast with the bustling courts of major buildings. Forecourts are an outstanding characteristic of Colorado. Dalton Trumbo Fountain Court exemplifies this pattern. Surrounded by seating, the fountain of Dalton Trumbo has been a focus of activity for 40 years. Hawthorne Court, south of Norlin Library, has a central lawn circumscribed by walkways which adroitly guide passing pedestrian traffic under a canopy of mature trees. The most striking space is the expansive Norlin Quadrangle. A tree-shaded haven, it is a symbolic space redolent of romance. With no western enclosure, it has an impressive vista towards the mountains.

Paved pathways traverse the quadrangle, providing functional pedestrian linkage between departments. Throughout Main Campus, pedestrians and cyclists are prioritized over vehicles. The number of streets crossing it has systematically been cut, and today only two city streets run through it. The result is a park-like atmosphere favourable for pedestrians and cyclists. Peculiarly and confusingly, though, there is no one main vehicular or pedestrian gateway, and the perimeter is punctuated by numerous access points.

The University of Colorado at Boulder is a valuable example of a campus that has continuously upheld a common design and planning code. Since 1919 the legacy of Charles Klauder has dominated its development, and the result is a highly unified and attractive environment. The vocabulary of native sandstone, clay barrel tile roofs, limestone trim and black wrought iron and commitment to human scale, varied open spaces and axial alignment established by

UNIVERSITY OF COLORADO AT BOULDER

2.100 University of Colorado at Boulder against the flatirons backdrop
Photo: Corey Denis

Klauder created a distinctive environment. Successive generations have sensitively reinterpreted these precepts to ensure the preservation of this identity. This consistency is testimony to Klauder's success in fulfilling the institution's desire for a signature image and creating a rapport with its setting. The campus environment is greatly enhanced by its spectacular mountain backdrop, and its design has striven to respond sensitively to it (Figure 2.100). Buildings appear to rise naturally from the topography, with their silhouettes frequently echoing the ragged outlines of the Front Range. Finally, the university has a long tradition of producing master plans and of executing them. The necessity of such long-term planning is well illustrated in the coherence of Colorado's campus.

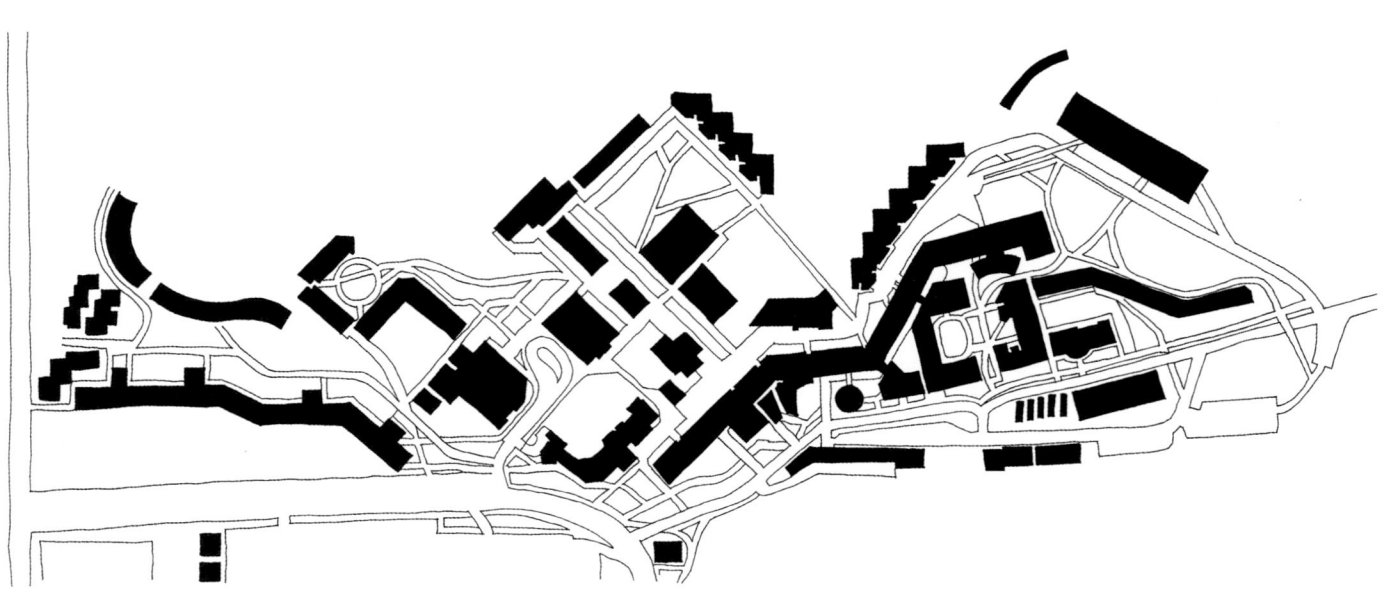

2.101 Plan, University of East Anglia

University of East Anglia
Norwich, UK

After Sussex and York, the University of East Anglia (UEA) was the third of the New Universities that transformed higher education in 1960s Britain. From the outset, it basked in a blaze of publicity, much of which was generated by its gregarious architect-planner, Denys Lasdun. Lasdun, appointed in 1962, was affiliated with a new generation of designers grouped under the banner 'New Brutalists'. They championed not only the use of swathes of raw concrete, but new thinking in planning that displayed a concern with spaces of movement in towns and housing estates. These 'social architecture' theories came to the fore in Lasdun's plans for UEA. His designs represent the first 'urban' scheme amongst the New Universities, creating a tight, dense development that was nothing short of radical. The enterprise was driven by a precocious spirit of experiment. Lasdun announced he had never done 'anything like it before', while his clients insisted 'Lasdun had no brief'. All previous models of university design were denounced, from the adventitious complexes

2.102 Aerial view, University of East Anglia
Photo: University of East Anglia

2.103 Ziggurats, University of East Anglia
Photo: University of East Anglia

of the Redbricks, to the parkland campus-type displayed at Sussex, and the collegiate examples of Oxbridge. A fresh understanding of university education was sought, which engendered a new total vision of architecture and landscape integrated as one.[143]

The essence of Lasdun's designs lay with the natural setting. Set in 165 (since expanded to 320) acres of rolling parkland, three kilometres from Norwich and edged by the River Yare, the impressive location moulded the form of Lasdun's designs. The buildings follow the contour of the site, stepping down with the rise and fall of the land, while key consideration was given to exploiting natural vistas. Allowing as much of the grounds as possible to remain open and viewable, the urban scheme grouped buildings in a dense cluster, structured in three distinct parts: the Teaching Wall, the Walkways and the Residences (Figure 2.102).

The Teaching Wall was planned as one continuous block, an idea inspired by the continuity of line that derived from following the site contour. One continuous structure, 460 metres long, it housed all the teaching and research activities. It demonstrates Lasdun's response to his client's demands that the campus would be a 'coherent entity at each stage of the growth so that early generations of students should not have the sense of living in a broken and unfinished development'. The Teaching Wall's format easily allowed for extension. Furthermore, it evinced the fusion of educational ideals and built environment. Unlike traditional institutions, UEA was not to be formed from a series of separate departments, but rather seven or eight 'Schools of Study' in which interdisciplinary boundaries were purposely blurred. The university sought to forge close physical relationships between subjects via architecture. The singular form of the Teaching Wall unifies the schools into one entity. Arts are placed in the eastern end, with sciences at the western end. Throughout, ceiling heights are kept constant at 3.25 metres, while the only identifying feature of each school is its main entrance off the walkway on the southern side.[144]

The walkways were equally informed by academic philosophies. The campus was envisaged as a compact unit that could be traversed within five minutes aided by connecting walkways, which would convey students across campus whilst removing them from vehicular traffic. A system of walkways on stilts, four to eight metres above ground level, stretch 300 metres along almost all the Lasdun structures, while 400 further metres of walkways course alongside, on top of, or lead through the buildings. The main entries to the schools and the library, which forms a separate block to the east, are located on these walkways. Not only did they unite distinct parts into one larger whole, but Lasdun saw the system as a means of creating an intimate university community, offering opportunities for informal and chance meetings. Like the Teaching Wall, their course is dependent on the topography of the parkland. The beginning of the walkway system is at the highest point of the campus, but as the ground sweeps down, the walkways are elevated off the ground proffering dramatic views across the surrounding countryside.

The walkways provide access from the Teaching Wall to the third principal feature of Lasdun's plan, the residences. Norfolk and Suffolk Terraces, otherwise known as the Ziggurats, are undoubtedly the most distinctive, and the most complicated, buildings of the UEA campus (Figure 2.103). A series of stepped blocks, the Ziggurats were staggered down the contours of the land, so, although some rise to eight storeys, they are embedded into their green surroundings to make them appear lower than they are truly are. Internal university reports of 1962 demonstrate that from the beginning, a new student housing solution was desired. Vice Chancellor, Frank Thistlethwaite, contrasted two traditional housing options, the collegiate form in which educational, social and cultural functions were grouped, and the unitary form, in which residential halls were merely somewhere to sleep. The founders sought 'an architectural form which would avoid the financial hazards of the collegiate arrangement and yet foster small and socially cohesive groups within an integrated community'. The architectural device of the Oxbridge staircase was suggested as the means to achieve this. Each staircase accesses 60 rooms in units of 12 study bedrooms clustered around a kitchen and common room, creating informal social groups within an integrated architectural whole.

The Ziggurats, like the Teaching Wall and walkways, employed reinforced, prefabricated concrete. Lasdun, inspired by Le Corbusier's later work, shared the preference of many post-Second World War designers for this medium, justifying its use at UEA by noting,

> The infinite variety of colour in the valley landscape makes the choice of external materials and colour of particular importance. Of all the suitable materials available today concrete in its natural grey state appears to enhance the colours of the landscape to greatest advantage.[145]

Economical considerations were no doubt another factor in its plentitude at Norwich. Yet amidst this preponderance of solid grey mass, Lasdun's plans were careful to interlace grassed areas throughout. The most conspicuous of these was the vast swathe of rough grass, termed the 'Harbour' by Lasdun, that bridged the two terraces of Ziggurats running down to the river below.

In 1969 Richard Einzig's and I. A. Niamath's photographs of the emerging campus appeared across the glossy pages of international architectural journals to critical acclaim. Yet behind the scenes, scepticism and squabbles spiralled, and in 1968 Lasdun was replaced by Bernard Feilden as consulting architect. Feilden, a local practitioner generally regarded as competent albeit conservative, largely respected his predecessor's plan and vocabulary of materials. By 1974, phase one of Lasdun's programme had been completed, including the Teaching Wall and Library, and Feilden set to work on the social centre. Whereas Lasdun had never envisaged a central, open meeting place, the new architect created a horse-shoe shape square, partially surrounded by communal facilities (Figure 2.104).[146]

The next major presence at UEA came with the arrival of Rick Mather in 1987. Foreseeing its expansion, UEA commissioned Mather to prepare a development plan for the campus. A reduction in funding checked the lavish building of the Lasdun era, yet the new structures erected under Mather by no means evidenced architectural stagnation. Mather's new buildings, while retaining the overall grey and white colours of Lasdun's campus, broke away from the concrete aesthetic. The School of Education and the Climatic Research Building (opened in 1984 and 1985) were white tile-clad structures built to the north of the Teaching Wall. This area had descended into a confusion of overflow parking, and the presence of these new structures ordered the void. The horse-shoe-shaped School of Education surrounded an open courtyard. Contrasting with Lasdun's highly regular, horizontal fenestration, Mather revels in irregularity, interspersing the box-like façade with capricious openings. Its block-like shape provided a foil to the small, circular Climatic Research Building. With a clean, sleek white exterior clad over a reinforced concrete frame, the Climatic Research Building acted as a self-contained gatehouse to the new schools of education. In both structures, interiors are simply faced with inexpensive blockwork with thin metal bridges and perforated steel floors.[147]

Development on the north side of the Teaching Wall continued with the erection of the Queen's Building (1992–1994) and the

UNIVERSITY OF EAST ANGLIA

2.104 The Square, University of East Anglia
Photo: University of East Anglia

Elizabeth Fry Building (1993–1995) by John Miller & Partners. Expanding the vocabulary of materials on campus, both have a stonefaced blockwork base with render and engineering brick bands above. The firm gave it the white, smooth façade that was its trademark, informed by the starkness of 1920s Modernism and a post-modernist geometrical patterning of circles and diagonals. The Queen's Building interacts with Mather's Education Building, by mirroring its courtyard shape creating an open court to the east enlivened by a partly free-standing drum containing the entrances. The Elizabeth Fry Building to its west was loudly applauded for its environmental credentials.

With student numbers soaring rapidly in the 1990s, attention was also turned to new residential buildings. Mather designed two new residences, Constable Terrace (1991–1993), at the western end of campus, and Nelson Court (1991–1993), at the east. Both display a deference to the 1960s campus in their elongated forms. Constable Terrace's double curve subtly echoes the 45 degree angles of Lasdun's meandering Teaching Wall; Nelson Court, in its angular length, responded to Waveney Terrace (since demolished). Nelson Court forms a three-sided courtyard open to the south with views across the lake and countryside.[148]

More recently constructed residences at the university, such as those designed by LSI Architects in 2004, continue the theme of continuously curving blocks. These residences constitute part of LSI Architects' master plan for the development of the eastern campus. A key element of this was the construction, completed in 2008, of the INTO building, a study centre for international students. Clad in white tiles, recalling the buildings of Mather, the five-storey building provides academic and residential accommodation curled around a courtyard, a product of LSI Architects' plans to create a new social piazza at this further end of campus.

The succeeding phases of the campus development from Lasdun to LSI Architects have, however, encountered negative reactions. By 1970, denunciation of the Seven New Universities was rife, and, despite their initial glorification, Lasdun's buildings came under censure. 'Lasdun's buildings…a dream, socially and educationally a nightmare' was the view expressed by one student. The vast expanses of exposed concrete met with mixed responses. General agreement found that Lasdun had overlooked the effects of rainfall, concurring that the material 'looks miserable when wet'. The anonymity of the Teaching Wall was found to be 'institutional'. Waveney Terrace, a residence erected to the east of the campus in the early 1970s under Feilden's

2.105 View across the Harbour, University of East Anglia
Photo: University of East Anglia

tenure, was judged to be prison-like, especially in contrast with the grandeur of the Ziggurats. Designed to an exceptionally tight budget, Waveney was Spartan; its breeze block interiors were left unpainted with only minimal furniture. It comes as little surprise that the block was demolished in 2006. On the whole, however, Norwich's students fared well with their residential accommodation: 'Students are on the whole satisfied [since] the rooms have been particularly well designed.' By the 1970s, 70 per cent of its students were housed in university accommodation, higher than Oxford or Cambridge. Such a proportion bodes well for a vibrant campus community.[149]

The continuous stages of the university's development have each wielded its impact upon the campus. Lasdun's, Feilden's, Mather's, Miller's, and LSI Architects' contributions to the campus function as individual elements of a whole, united by colours, forms and geometry. Its unique character is well defined, and its sense of place is strong. A vital aspect of this is the continuing appreciation of the site. Although changing educational needs and an expanding population have necessitated building on land that Lasdun sought to preserve, the university has retained what is its most distinguishing factor – its parkland scenery. Views across the Plain from Constable Terrace, from the Library to the lake, and across the Harbour from the Ziggurats make everyday campus life memorable (Figure 2.105). The buildings' often sensitive responses to the site's topography root them to this environment. Equally laudable is the spirit of adventure that invigorated its earliest days. Although 1960s Brutalist architecture has been a victim of changing aesthetic tastes, Lasdun's rich imagination and concentration on detail produced exciting visual results. Searching for new solutions to modern higher education is undoubtedly important in itself. The Teaching Wall and Ziggurats are evidence of the university's desire to fuse its innovatory academic philosophies with architectural plan, creating a university environment unique to the Norfolk plains.

2.106 Plan, University of Illinois at Chicago

University of Illinois at Chicago
Chicago, USA

Heralded as one of the most significant pieces of legislation ever produced by the Federal Government, the passing of the G. I. Bill in 1944 rocked the United States socially, economically and politically. A key element was the provision of college or vocational education for returning Second World War veterans, a previously unreachable ambition for the average American. Figures of college attendants rose from 160,000 pre-war, to nearly 500,000 in 1950, necessitating a momentous expansion of the higher education system. The total of research universities rose from 25 to 125. The foundation of the University of Illinois at Chicago (known as Chicago Circle until 1982) was one of the products of the bill. Planning for the new 'instant campus' began in the mid-1950s. In 1961, a central urban

2.107 Great Court, University of Illinois at Chicago
Photo: University of Illinois at Chicago Archives and Photo Services

2.108 Walkways, University of Illinois at Chicago
Photo: University of Illinois at Chicago Archives and Photo Services

location was obtained adjacent to the Loop, at the nexus of a traffic interchange. Comprising 106 acres, it was amongst the largest of the new urban campuses constructed at this time. Critically, the campus was, and remains, one of the most easily accessible locations in the city, ideal for the university's role as a commuter college.[150]

As architect, the university selected the renowned Walter Netsch, of the Chicago practice Skidmore Owings and Merrill. Having already earned acclaim for the campuses of the Naval Postgraduate School (1955) and the Air Force Academy in Colorado Springs (1959), Netsch was an experienced choice. His designs for the Chicago Circle campus led to it becoming the most famous of the new urban campuses of the 1960s. Netsch's designs evidenced the burning point in question then occupying the nation's college planners, that of the appropriation on American campuses of urban models. Reacting to the restricted plot and the philosophies of the new institution, he devised what he called a 'micro-environment' of the modern-day city. The result, when opened in 1965, was hailed by many as the paradigm for the American city campus.[151]

Netsch's master plan was a detailed mosaic of buildings of different heights, silhouettes and interrelationships (Figure 1.39). The centrepiece was an aberrant lecture theatre block containing 21 theatres, whose roof formed a rectangular plaza incorporating four open, stepped seating areas known as exedras and a large sunken amphitheatre, seating 10,000 (Figure 2.107). Around the lecture commons, Netsch planted a variety of larger buildings, including the Student Union, the library, laboratories, a 28-storey administration building, and smaller classroom blocks in an arrangement far more compact than the typical campus plan. As it was a commuter college, no residences were built. The design reflected the university's tight financial and time restrictions, and was also modelled to allow it to function practicably and aesthetically at its initial size while expanding quickly to its expected size. Predominantly though, its design was informed by two principles – circulation and communication.[152]

Uniquely, Netsch's plan called for the campus to be arranged by function rather than discipline. Rather than allocating each department a separate building, all departmental offices were located in the high-rise tower, the lecture rooms were in the central block, another building held the library, and others held laboratories and classrooms that could be assigned flexibly for any discipline. Based on the metaphor of a stone dropped in a pool of water, buildings were hierarchically grouped by function, with the most important – the lecture commons – in the centre, encircled by the classroom buildings, library and Student Union. The next ring included offices and laboratories, and furthest from the centre were the athletic fields. All activities requiring mass movement were located in low rise structures, with the other functions in high rise buildings, consequently pushing tall edifices to the campus boundary with its centre dominated by low rise buildings. Accordingly, the central structures were screened from the noisy traffic of the Loop. Primary function buildings were built first, followed by specific services in phased construction. This approach to organization permitted a great amount of flexibility, which enabled both a rapid construction pace and a terrific expansion rate. Moreover, this programme was conceived to foster interdisciplinary communication.[153]

To counteract the isolation often inherent to commuter schools, Netsch strove for a plan that would 'provide the meeting-in-the-corridor on a grand scale'. He forced the faculty to walk distances from classrooms to offices, while students were constantly brought together by the proximity of the lecture theatres in a central grouping. Many spaces for informal social contact were formed, the focal point of which was to be the rooftop of the lecture complex, the Great Court. Inspired by the classical agora, this symbolized the centre of learning. The four exedras provided seating on which students and teachers could converse and relax while the great open-air amphitheatre provided space for concerts and performances. 'What happens between classes', said the architect, 'came to be regarded as being as important as what happens in classes.'

Converging on the Great Court were the elevated walkways – Netsch's other renowned device (Figure 2.108). For the first three decades of its existence, the campus was navigated by an extensive system of pedestrian 'expressways'. Designed to provide quick, efficient transit across the site, these massive granite walkways raised upon precast concrete piers linked the peripheral car parks and rail station to all buildings on campus. Traversing the busy roads that bounded the site, they allowed pedestrians to avoid traffic for greater safety. The long walkway running from the northern boundary to the Great Court and the Science and Engineering South Building created a north–south axis, visually as well as functionally organizing the campus. The mesh of levels added visual interest, as did the openings which punctuated large sections of the walkways through which shrubs and trees could grow. The granite and concrete of the walkways illustrate two key materials which are found in repetition across the university. Selecting a robust, urban aesthetic, Netsch employed granite, concrete and brick for the structures. The Minnesota granite was chosen for its durability, while brick and concrete were easily available and could withstand dirt and damage. The concrete was treated with six different finishes while a variety of colours and sizes of bricks were employed.

Reinforced concrete was utilized for the skeleton of Chicago Circle's tallest structure, University Tower (Figure 2.109). The 28-storey administration building plied Chicago's epithet of the 'City of the Big Shoulders', for the building swells as it rises, expanding from 46 metres wide at floor eight, to 49 metres at floor 16, to 52 metres at floor 28 using a cantilever system. Vast columns at ground floor level support the colossal structure. Belonging to the first phase of campus construction, its soaring silhouette created a symbolic campus landmark. Also impressive in size is the Science and Engineering Laboratories, supported by massive concrete columns rotated by 45 degrees. A brick structure, Netsch used very large bricks to correspond with the complex's size and strength. He referred to it as a 'city underneath a roof'. Examples of classroom buildings include Lincoln, Douglas and Grant Halls, all connected by enclosed walkways. Grant has recently undergone renovation, reflecting the university's current green approach. The building now uses geothermal wells for efficient cooling and heating, while Netsch's narrow recessed windows have been replaced by a new façade of energy efficient glass.

From 1965, Netsch's design departed from the rectangular block-like forms of his earlier buildings, to embrace multi-angled, interlocking structures. The Architecture and Art Building, built in 1967, was the first such example of this experimental approach, known as Field Theory. Field Theory involved rotating simple squares into complex geometric patterns to create innovative but interrelated spaces that eschewed the 'boredom of the box'. The layout of the Architecture and Art Building was predicated upon overlapping squares around

2.109 University Tower, University of Illinois at Chicago
Photo: University of Illinois at Chicago Archives and Photo Services

a central space bordered by mezzanines. The floors are dispersed in uninterrupted succession, each one metre apart in distance from one another. Inspired by the DNA double helix, a helical path connects these interior spaces. The second Field Theory building, and the example Netsch regarded as his most sophisticated illustration of the approach, was the Behavioural Sciences Building (Figure 2.110). A four-storey concrete and brick building, it housed offices, classrooms and lecture rooms for several departments alongside a cafeteria. Again its complex geometry is based upon a rotated square. Circulation was clearly carefully thought through. A pedestrian bridge, connected to the central walkway system, led to its main entrance. Functions which necessitated the greatest movement of people, primarily the lecture theatres and cafeteria, were placed nearest this entrance, in the eastern half of the building. This area was designed with seats and gathering spaces to promote social interaction.[154]

During the last phase of construction, other architects were commissioned to design individual buildings, albeit outside Netsch's core. Harry Weese, for instance, was responsible for the Physical Education Building and the Education, Performing Arts and Social Work Building. Both are less ambitious in terms of architectural experiment, but retain Netsch's concrete and brick vocabulary.[155]

From the mid-1960s, the campus received extensive publicity. Praised in architectural journals for the power of its geometrical forms, the harmonious relationships between buildings, and its emphasis on promoting community, it was bestowed awards from the local division of the American Institute of Architects and the National Society of Interior Designers. Simultaneously however, numerous criticisms were levelled at the campus. The Field Theory buildings have suffered many detractors, who consider the structures impractical to work within, citing the physical separation of offices, classrooms and lecture halls, and the difficulty of navigating through them. Despite Netsch fitting channels into the raised walkways to carry away rainwater, water still dripped from them to form puddles on the ground floor paths below them. Comments often mentioned the campus's detachment from its community. Its layout, with low-rise buildings at its heart and buildings getting taller towards the campus edge, presented a self-contained, fortress-like façade to the surrounding neighbourhood. The distinctive walkway system was accused of diluting campus life by channelling pedestrians

2.110 Behavioural Sciences Building, University of Illinois at Chicago
Photo: University of Illinois at Chicago Archives and Photo Services

away from ground level, while their popularity was severely affected in winter because of build-up of snow or ice. Maintenance proved problematic. The concrete used for the stairways leading to the walkways deteriorated upon contact with the salt used to dissolve the snow, and the heating elements embedded in the concrete steps to melt the snow broke and were never replaced.[156]

In the mid-1990s, criticisms were addressed in a radical overhaul of the campus that aimed to render it a friendlier and more comfortable environment. The brick prison-like walls that enclosed the campus perimeter were in many cases substituted by iron fences, softening its façade to its local community. The most decisive of the modifications was the removal of Netsch's expressways and Great Court. Removing these signature elements of Netsch's design was a highly controversial decision that profoundly altered the spirit of Chicago Circle.

Another major digression from the 1960s campus vision has been the addition of student residences. Evidential of the move from a commuter-only institution to an increasingly residential one, the construction of dormitories began in the 1980s and has since continued. In 2000, the university commenced a south campus expansion over 80 acres, creating an area known as University Village. Including a College of Business Administration, a performing arts centre, and blocks of apartment-style residences with shops and restaurants on the ground floors, University Village was completed in 2008. Its objective was to increase its residential population to 25 per cent of full-time students, and to transform the campus into a 24-hour living and learning environment. With a welcoming atmosphere and a variety of recreational spots, time will tell as to whether the University Village fulfils its ambitions.

Despite the ravages enacted upon Netsch's vision, its importance in the history of campus design cannot be diminished. It thoroughly captured the spirit of the age both in its ambitious and assertive Brutalist architecture, and in showcasing many of the new ideas in planning. In its scale, complexity and emphasis on circulation, flexibility and communication, it translated the tenets of urban planning to campusdom creating a pioneering format in answer to the challenges of the new American city campus.

2.111 Plan, University of Oxford

University of Oxford
Oxford, UK

Notwithstanding its supreme contribution to human knowledge, Oxford could claim a place amongst the world's greatest universities simply on account of its built environment. Its attraction is born of the collective efforts of eight centuries of architectural patronage, attesting to the university's institutional vigour and perpetuity.

The university came into being from 1167 when the expulsion of foreigners from Paris led many scholars to settle in Oxford. Teaching was conducted in rented rooms, ceremonies took place in St Mary's church, and students boarded in private houses. During the thirteenth century, domestic properties began to be appropriated for academic halls where young scholars could live under the watch of Masters of Arts. Halls came and went and their domestic nature meant they left little imprint upon the university's physical setting. Simultaneously, the first endowed colleges made their appearance. These differed from the academic halls principally in that they were financed by wealthy prelates and statesmen, investing them with a financial and institutional independence that the halls lacked, not least ownership of their own buildings. With such advantages, colleges gradually supplanted the halls.

The colleges are Oxford's most distinctive component. They were responsible for the first impressive buildings that gave them from the outset a strong institutional identity. The earliest collegiate

2.112 Radcliffe Camera, University of Oxford
Photo: David Cowlard

structures belong to Merton College. Upon Merton's foundation in 1264, there was no established formula for the form an Oxford college should assume. The communal, celibate life of the community and its religious undercurrent, though, seems to have suggested the layout of a monastery as an apt template. From 1266 buildings were erected at Merton in piecemeal fashion around a rudimentary quadrangle, Front Quad, displaying a pattern common to contemporary bishops' palaces (Figures 1.5 and 1.6). A dining hall formed its south range, a Warden's house was on the north, and a chapel lay to the west. The chapel is Oxford's finest late-thirteenth-century structure. Intended to be a full-scale monastic church, the nave was never built resulting in its chancel and transepts forming a T-shape plan. The adoption of this unusual plan by subsequent colleges made this inadvertent feature into one of Oxford's many idiosyncrasies. Construction of Mob Quad to provide fellows' accommodation began in 1287, although its completion was delayed by almost a century. Built to the south of the chapel, it was Oxford's first four-sided court of equal-length sides. Pointed arched doorways leading directly from the quadrangle accessed staircases around which bedrooms were arranged on either side. This layout of accommodation was almost universally adopted by Oxford's colleges.[157]

The systematization of the physical environment of the Oxbridge college took an enormous leap with the building of New College, beginning in 1380. Founded by the powerful prelate and experienced architectural patron, William Wykeham, New College established the model for a carefully orchestrated layout on grand proportions, with the most important components, the hall and chapel, aligned. For the first time in Oxford, we can see a carefully orchestrated plan; nothing here is adventitious or incremental and buildings were designed as a harmonious unit. The plan centred upon a large courtyard entered via a tall gatehouse, displaying an exclusivity and prestige that was new to Oxford. The quadrangle was surrounded by ranges of chambers, with the library on the upper floor of the eastern range, and the chapel and hall placed side by side on the north range. The ideological importance of this latter range to collegiate life is conveyed through its elaborate Perpendicular Gothic architecture. To the west of the T-shape chapel, a disengaged cloister created a sheltered arcade. Upon completion, New College was the most splendid educational complex in the country. Its series of enclosed spaces provided settings for collegiate events, exercise and recreation. Unquestionably the ensemble had a decisive impact upon Oxford's future development.[158]

New College formalized a building programme that remained essentially consistent until the mid-sixteenth century. With the quadrangle as the basic planning component, masonry buildings were arranged around a sequence of courtyards and gardens enclaved within high brick walls. This moulded the city into a dense streetscape of fortress-like communities invisible behind tall buildings and walls. Behind these impenetrable façades, each college shared a basic recipe of gate tower with porter's lodge, members' rooms, dining hall, kitchen, common rooms, chapel and library. With Cardinal College (begun 1525) this formula reached its peak. It enlarged Wykeham's plan to an exceptional size and, though never completed in the form envisaged, it forms the nucleus of Oxford's largest medieval foundation, Christ Church.

The medieval fabric of the university exhibited remarkable cohesion. Overwhelmingly, the architectural vocabulary was that of Perpendicular Gothic. A microcosm of current English architecture, its buildings reflected the most fashionable architectural currents through the direct patronage of the highest echelons of court and church. Henry VI for, instance, co-founded All Souls; Exeter College was established by Walter Stapleton, Bishop of Exeter and treasurer; Richard Fox, founder of Corpus Christi, was Bishop of Winchester, king's secretary and keeper of the privy seal. Eminent patronage led to the selection of distinguished master masons, and construction was consistently of the highest obtainable quality.[159]

The rapid development of the colleges leading up to the Reformation was not matched by the university itself. Ceremonies, ecclesiastical trials and much day to day administration took place in the town church, St Mary the Virgin. It was not until the 1420s that construction began on the university's first permanent lecture hall, the Divinity School. The Divinity School was the first major building of the university, as distinct from the colleges, and is the jewel in the crown of medieval Oxford. Planned as a single-storey, single-room structure for the teaching of theology, the building was completed in the 1480s, with the erection of the extravagant stone vault. The Divinity School is an opulent piece of display, with rich carving and

2.113 Keble College, University of Oxford
Photo: Will Pryce/Thames & Hudson/Arcaid

large perpendicular windows. It has existed as one of Oxford's most iconic structures for over five centuries.

With the reformation, development within Oxford ground almost to a halt. The opening of the seventeenth century, however, brought with it a flurry of new building. The most conspicuous addition of these years was to the fabric of the university itself. Beginning in 1610, Thomas Bodley funded the building of a Schools Quadrangle attached to the east of the Divinity School. Arts End (1610–1612) was a two-storey structure built to house the growing library and designed to harmonize with the older Divinity School and Duke Humfrey Library. Its eastern elevation panelling closely echoed that of the Divinity School, while its main window replicated the seven-light window of the library that was demolished in its construction. In 1613 work commenced on a three-storey quadrangle extending Arts End. The Schools Quadrangle, as it was called, employed the same late-Gothic style as the earlier library extension, with the incongruous exception of the inner-face of the gate tower, which was adorned with a flamboyant classical frontispiece of the Orders – a palatial and seigneurial motif derived from France. To contemporaries, this mixture of Gothic and classical did not strike the discordant note that it does today; it reflects the deep-rooted traditionalism that informed much early-seventeenth-century building within the university and colleges. Classical detailing was found in prominent locations to impart specific messages, yet medieval forms and techniques continued to be used, simultaneously reflecting listless conservatism, a desire for visual conformity, and reverence for the past. The conscious cultivation of a consistent institutional image at Oxford was a powerful rationale even at this stage.[160]

Classicism was slow to settle at the university, but in the second half of the seventeenth century its panorama was transformed with a series of exceptional classical structures. A young don, Christopher Wren, emerged as a new brand of architect, one

2.114 St Catherine's College, University of Oxford
Photo: Stanley Hare/Alamy

versed in Renaissance design and scientific understanding. His first project in Oxford answered laments that the university lacked a formal setting for academic ceremonies, and in 1663 he began designs for a theatre patterned upon antique models (Figure 1.7). The Sheldonian Theatre had a D-shaped plan and superimposed orders that directly recalled the Theatre of Marcellus in Rome. Wren's first public building has prompted mixed responses. Architecturally it is rather a confused effort, and its limited site adjacent to the Schools Quadrangle meant its main façade is pushed close to the Divinity School where it cannot properly be seen. Yet its decisive break from Gothic and authoritative classicism set Oxford upon a new architectural trajectory which endured for the next 200 years. Wren's influence upon Oxford was decisive. He went on to design for Trinity and Christ Church Colleges, while his legacy was ministered by his followers, including Nicholas Hawksmoor and James Gibbs. With Hawksmoor's Clarendon Building (1715) and Gibb's Radcliffe Camera (1749) (Figure 2.112), a classical cluster grew up around the Gothic Schools and the university finally possessed a physical presence befitting its scholarly achievements.[161]

The stranglehold of classicism upon the university ceased in the mid-nineteenth century with the ascendancy of neo-Gothicism. This was the style chosen for the first college to be built on a new site for over two centuries, Keble (1868–1882) (Figure 2.113). Keble College's architect, William Butterfield, broke with Oxford tradition in his use of red brick with distinctive polychromatic patterns. Brick was such a provocative issue in Oxford that a secret society was formed whose membership depended upon removing a brick from Keble's walls in the hope that its buildings would eventually collapse. In its layout, Keble maintained the quadrangular plan with residences, chapel and hall enclosing a lawned court. However, for the first time, bedrooms were not set around staircases but along corridors in a more economical organization to encourage communal dining in hall befitting the simple scholastic life envisioned by the founders. Butterfield's design was a declaration of institutional change, and its materials and layout constructed a unique sense of place for a college intended to stand out within the historic centre of learning. Although this sentiment remains undiminished, the 1977 Hayward Quad did little to perpetuate it. The fortress-like buildings lining the site's south-west boundary exerted no attempt to harmonize with their Victorian neighbours.[162]

The twentieth century significantly changed Oxford's academic landscape. The century saw more construction that any of its predecessors, largely driven by the pace of scientific research. In the late nineteenth century a science area arose clustered around the University Museum (1860) to the north of the city centre, and it has proceeded to grow piecemeal ever since. University research has greatly benefited from grouping its science departments in a fairly confined space which encourages interdisciplinary research. In 1934 Southwell and Griffith produced a rationalization plan for the area which sub-divided it into medicine and biology, Museum subjects and chemistry. With few exceptions, new construction and extensions followed this plan. However, while the University Museum continues to present a commanding outward face, behind it to the east the science area appears more opportunistic than planned. The precinct grew in response to scientific progress in ad hoc fashion with structures growing upwards and outwards in varying styles. The site does not make the most efficient use of space and proves difficult to navigate. Traversing it has been described as trespassing into a back world of servicing and deliveries. These issues are currently being addressed in a long-range master planning effort.

The master plan emphasizes the university's custodian role of much of the city's built environment, and affirms that the redevelopment of the science area will enhance it. In responding to change in the twentieth century, Oxford succeeded in preserving the historic landscape and has moderated new development to attune to its heritage and traditions. A restrained blending of tradition and modernity was at work in the New Bodleian Library (1940), built to designs by Giles Gilbert Scott. Scott had already designed a new university library for Cambridge on a site distanced from the city centre. At Oxford, the new library was located, perhaps unadvisedly, next to the Schools Quadrangle site connected to the old library via an underground tunnel. Scott's design revealed the influence of European modernists such as Willem Marinus Dudok and Eric Mendelsohn in its horizontal windows, curved corners and stair tower for instance, but combined this with simplified classical motifs reflective of the surrounding buildings. Built of Bladon rubble, the building has a heavy quality that estranges it from modernism and creates a monumental effect in keeping with its Oxford context.[163]

University of Technology Petronas
Perak, Malaysia

The founding of the University of Technology Petronas in 1997 constituted a significant element in Malaysia's plan to become a developed nation by 2020. Fully funded by the oil giant Petronas, the institution was established with the clear objective of combining academic instruction with first-hand industrial experience to produce a new generation of technically qualified, well-rounded graduates capable of contributing to Malaysia's industrial development. The site chosen for this material enterprise was Bandar Seri Iskandar, a stunningly impressive landscape 33 kilometres north of Kuala Lumpur, identified as a key zone for regeneration. The new university borders a planned new town and administrative regional capital, and the institution was intended to act as a catalyst for future development in the locality. In the model of other new cities in Malaysia, for example Cyberjaya and Putrajaya, and universities in other parts of the globe, such as Stanford, Petronas was founded with the ambitious goal to encourage economic growth through establishing industry close to the stream of highly qualified graduates that the university would send forth. It was critical for the university to possess a physical

2.122 Aerial view, University of Technology Petronas
Photo: Nigel Young/Foster + Partners

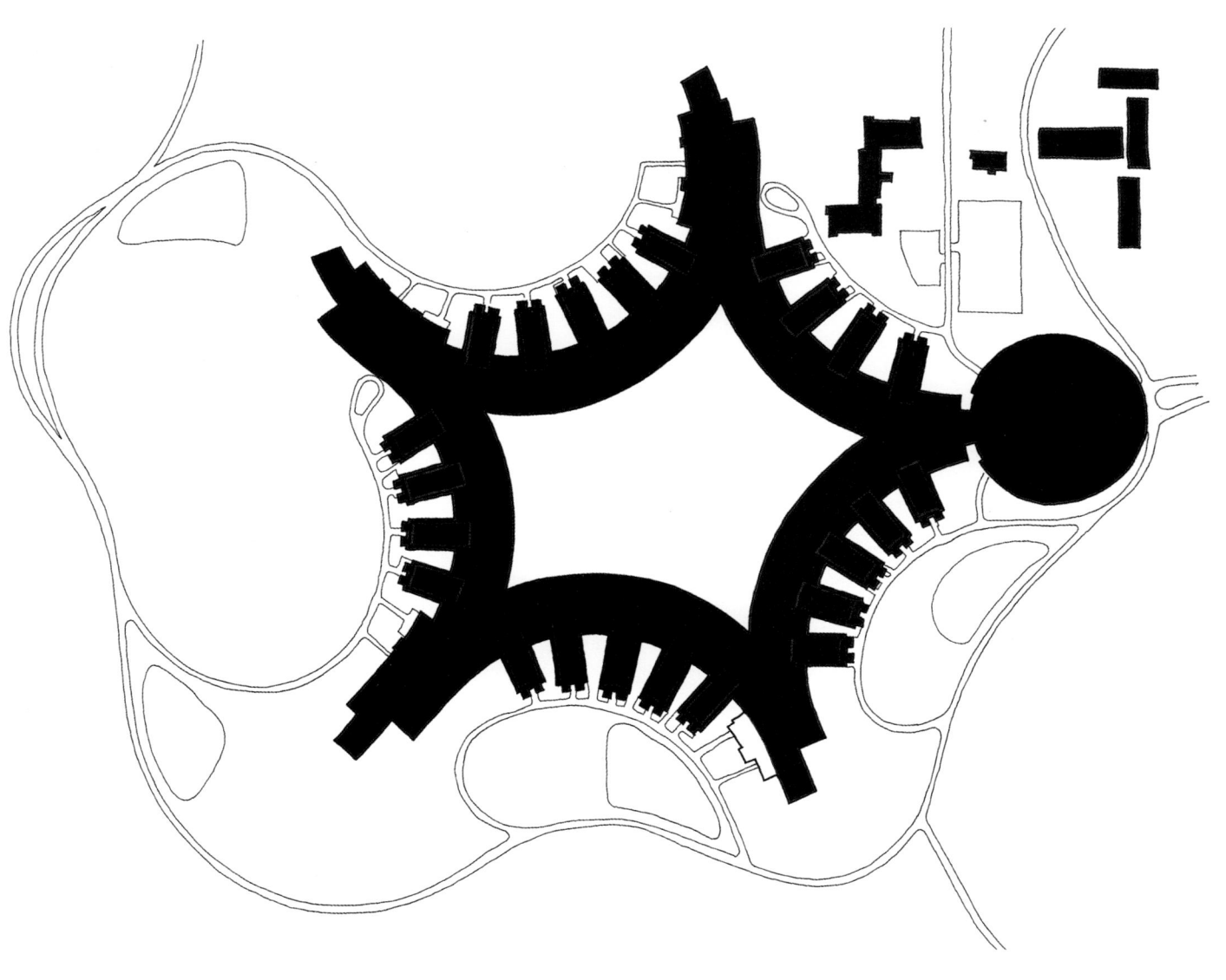

2.121 Plan, University of Technology Petronas

2.120 Locust Walk, University of Pennsylvania
Photo: Davi M. J. Barbosa

bond brickwork and south façade projecting bay, with contemporary design, in its continuous glass strip window. The vocabulary of red brick and light stone prescribed by Cope and Stewardson in the 1890s was once again favoured by the university's trustees and planners as a unifying device. The palette is exemplified by the new Gateway Building for the 1915 Dental Institute, begun in 1999 by architects Bohlin Cywinski Jackson. Echoing the material, scale and wall articulation of the older building, the new centre integrates perfectly into its setting yet its simplified forms appropriates it to the modern day and prevents it appearing a pastiche.[173]

By the millennium, Pennsylvania was endowed with a remarkably varied but unified campus that responded to the evolving needs of a leading institution. Yet outside the privileged world of red brick and limestone, the surrounding community had grievously deteriorated. Although over 50 per cent of America's higher education establishments are found in cities, it frequently comes to pass that their relationship with their urban environment is less than propitious. The University of Pennsylvania is a particularly acute example. As the university grew, it forced its way into surrounding neighbourhoods, depopulating them of local inhabitants and leading to rising crime figures. From the 1950s West Philadelphia coursed upon a downward spiral, reaching a climax in the late 1980s and early 1990s. Blighted by crime and devoid of facilities, students and staff avoided the area. Matters had escalated to such a degree that, under President Judith Rodin (1994–2004), the university embarked upon a tremendously ambitious project to reinvigorate its local community. Through its implementation, the University of Pennsylvania has become an instructive, albeit controversial,

model for building and rebuilding essential links with urban neighbours. By offering incentives to buy the neighbourhood's neglected historic houses and creating a new public school, the university determined to reconstruct a permanent local community. The institution relocated unsightly fast-food trucks from threatening city streets to newly-created designated fresh-air food plazas on campus. To the north of campus, it funded a retail and recreation complex, Sanson Common, completed in 1999. Featuring a cinema, retail outlets, and restaurants, the mixed-use development transformed the insalubrious area into a destination for the university and wider community. Empty streets are becoming animated by pedestrians and cafés pouring onto the pavements. The university has come under fire for wishing to turn Pennsylvania into a shopping centre, yet it achieved its objectives of improving public safety and quality of life adjacent to its campus.[174]

The campus itself certainly is not without flaws. It suffers from several lacklustre buildings. The Van Pelt Library (1962 by Harbeson, Hough, Livingston and Larson) despite occupying a prime location lining Blanche Levy Park, is uninspiring. Similarly, Meyerson Hall (1965–1968, by Stewart, Noble, Class and Partners) housing the architecture faculty, is a disappointing parody of Kahn's pattern of central communal spaces and peripheral 'servant' functions.[175] However, the campus is an enlightening example as to the merits of embracing a historic past through carefully orchestrated master plans to establish a unique sense of place. Finally, the enterprises of the Rodin era also suggest the university as a model for how urban universities can combat depressed local surroundings and embittered community relations.

Cret and Warren Laird in the university's first consummate master plan in the early twentieth century, and it remained the custom until the 1950s.[169]

During the Depression, Philadelphia's industry, upon which the university had depended for financial support, waned and consequently so too did Penn's building programmes. Construction again became a priority after the Second World War. Yielding to the architectural vogue, post-1945 campus building at Pennsylvania professed disaffection with locale and history. Many structures fell to the wrecking ball, including Richards's Hare Laboratories and Cope and Stewardson's Italianate Chemistry Laboratory, both replaced by disappointing substitutions. The university administration became impelled by a conviction that innovation was of higher value than visual harmony and it sought the services of a host of avant-garde designers. But within the architectural medley that ensued, emerged several noteworthy structures that fused modernism with contextual resonance. Many of these laid out the agenda of the budding so-called Philadelphia School, centred around Pennsylvania's new professor of design, Louis Kahn. The Alfred Newton Richards Medical Research Laboratory (1961) was Kahn's first world-renowned commission (Figure 2.119). It took the form of three brick and concrete towers, attempting a kinship with the neighbouring Collegiate Gothic Quad. Eero Saarinen's dormitory, Hill College House (1960), revelled in combining contemporary design with historical allusion. Using fiery red brick Saarinen designed a medieval fortress entered by a bridge and with a crowing iron cornice. Its exterior is dominated by a rhythmic pattern of horizontal and vertical slit windows.[170]

In 1957, central thoroughfare Locust Street was closed to vehicular traffic and repaved in brick and cobblestones to form a pedestrian spine, Locust Walk, now a tree-lined, heavily traversed axis (Figure 2.120). Yet generally, the expansion of the 1960s and 1970s left the landscape of central campus in a woeful condition. No attention was paid to the landscapes between the new buildings, and, consequently, they sat in isolation from one another. Patched asphalt and scarred lawns characterized the Pennsylvania campus in these years. This was remedied by Peter Shepheard, a landscape architect, who initiated a complete re-evaluation of the central campus with the aim of creating a fitting backdrop for the life of the university. The pinnacle of his landscape plan was the creation of Blanche Levy Park (1977) at the heart of the site, surrounded by College Hall, Furness's library, Logan Hall and others. Originally known as College Hall Green, the space was little more than a wasteland. Paths traversed the Green, but their thoughtless placing had resulted in numerous desire lines trampled across the grass. Working with the extant trees and surrounding buildings, Shepheard created an outdoor room that interlaced the key pedestrian routes to form a functional yet handsome and well-used area. The creation of this pastoral setting had a radical effect upon student enrolment. In the year after the completion of Blanche Levy Park, undergraduate applications soared by 250 per cent. Through the Landscape Development Plan, the campus obtained a unified appearance and atmosphere that undoubtedly contributed much to the enhancement of Pennsylvania's image. This result prompted the university community to reassess the historic campus as a whole, particularly its attitude to historic buildings.[171]

The dawning of the 1980s saw the birth of the historic preservation movement. Much of Pennsylvania's historic architecture was the subject of restoration, realigning the university's treasured place-making buildings with the needs of contemporary higher education. The University Library, for instance, was revitalized by a dramatic restoration by Venturi, Scott Brown and Associates (completed 1991). On the exterior, terracotta roof tiles, skylights, red bricks and sandstone base were restored and replaced. The firm was similarly responsible for the redesign of Wynn Commons (2000), one of the campus's great exterior spaces. Low walls around its boundary created places for sitting and gathering, while heraldry and inscriptions scattered the space, signalling a rich history. Lined by Collegiate Gothic and High Victorian structures, with shade-providing trees, the Commons now numbers amongst the campus's most memorable spaces, proudly proclaiming entry into the university's historic core.[172]

Venturi, Scott Brown and Associates have led the post-modern direction of Pennsylvania's construction since the 1980s. Formed to harmonize rather than to jar with the generations of earlier buildings, this new wave of design nevertheless embraces innovation in favour of vapid contextualism. Venturi's Vagelos Laboratories (1997) utilized the red brick and brownstone tones of Furness's adjacent library, while its varied interior functions are given full expression on the exterior by its fenestration. Lauder-Fisher Hall, built from 1988–1990 to plans by Davis and Brody, combines historicism, in its Flemish

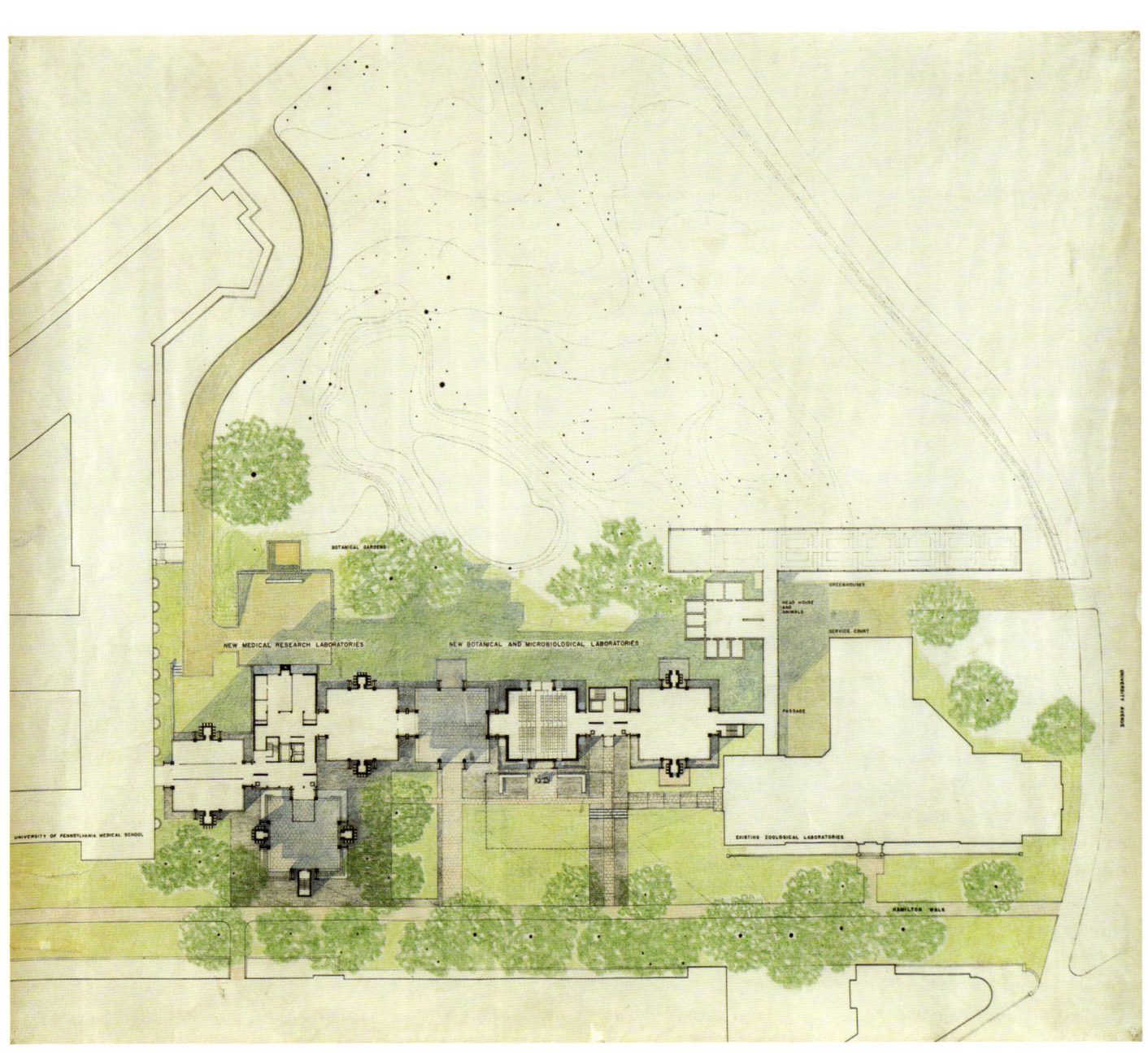

2.119 Kahn Louis I. (1901–1974): Alfred Newton Richards Medical Research Building and Biology Building, University of Pennsylvania. Second-to-last version: plan. Philadelphia, Pennsylvania, 1965. New York, Museum of Modern Art (MoMA), colour pencil on whiteprint, 32¾ x 36¾' (83.2 x 93.4 cm), gift of the architect SC9, 1966
Photo: ©2010. Digital image, The Museum of Modern Art, New York/Scala, Florence

2.118 The Quad, University of Pennsylvania
Photo: ©Ted Spiegel/CORBIS

and floored iron-framed stack, designed to be extended as book holdings grew, was only the second example in the country. Yet this functionality was clothed by a highly imaginative mantle of fiery red brick, expressive of its locality. Philadelphia's character had long been dominated by the preponderance of red brick; its first brickyard was founded as early as 1695. Constructed of brick, with accents of terracotta, Nova Scotia sandstone and Mediterranean-style roof tiles, the library exterior is unified by a blaze of red, drawing together its conflation of towers, dormers, dragons' heads and chimneys derived from Furness's idiosyncratic language. The building is characterized by vigour and sturdiness, set upon a thick rusticated base with a robust tower 90 metres tall, demarking the library's presence and status upon campus. The mass of the crenellated tower and the basilica-like projecting reading room conferred upon the site a neo-Gothic ecclesiastic tenor, reminiscent of Harvard's Memorial Hall built 15 years earlier. The University of Pennsylvania, the library proudly announced, was an equal match to any other in the country.[167]

Other buildings of the Pepper tenure include the Wilson Brothers' power plant, now destroyed, which shared with Furness's library an industrial quality in its red brick exterior and foundry-like appearance. The Wistar Institute of Anatomy (1894), built to designs by George and William Hewitt, is a celebration of the modern age, possessing an impressive iron staircase while its form signals its iron frame. Although this phase of construction made recall to historic design elements, its buildings embraced Philadelphia's native mores, forming a distinctive ensemble.

Under the subsequent provost, Charles Harrison (1894–1910), the campus was rebranded once more. Much of Pennsylvania's present appearance is the result of Harrison's vision of romantic historicism, which led to the appointment of Cope and Stewardson as college architects. Becoming increasingly renowned for their Collegiate Gothic designs, the pair embarked upon a campus transformation that aligned the university with the national current of historically-based campus design. This new direction reflected not only Philadelphia's deep 'Anglomania', as observed by British architect and designer C. R. Ashbee in 1900, but also the cachet attached to the nostalgia of the English colleges.[168]

In the 1890s Cope and Stewardson prepared a plan for south campus to provide the campus with residential accommodation. The master plan featured the type of linear construction the pair had pioneered at Bryn Mawr, in which a picturesque screen of buildings defined the site's boundary and created a series of enclosed courts. The arrangement cloistered the university from the hostile influences of the city and utilized the scarce commodity of building land to the maximum. The awkward triangular shape of south campus resulted in a progression of interlinked, irregular sized and shaped courtyards. Its informality and asymmetry represented the antithesis to the Beaux-Arts planning then becoming fashionable on American campuses. Directly inspired by the red brick and white limestone palette of St John's College, Cambridge, Cope and Stewardson's residential complex (1894–1912) has come to symbolize undergraduate experience at the university. A stately neo-Tudor tower marks its entrance, which leads through an archway into the Upper Quad (Figure 2.118). Its Collegiate Gothic architectural vocabulary is extended into a series of quadrangles, creating a vibrant silhouette of dormers, towers, chimneys, archways, oriel windows and sculpted bosses. Under Cope and Stewardson's influence, brick and limestone buildings, in styles based upon English sixteenth- and seventeenth-century architecture, dominated construction on campus until the 1930s. Furthermore, their linear, space-enclosing organization was preserved by Paul

University of Pennsylvania
Philadelphia, USA

The University of Pennsylvania is one of the five Ivy League campuses inhabiting an urban environment, condensed within a site of two by three blocks in West Philadelphia. Since moving to this site in 1872, the university has faced the growing infringement of the city's commerce and traffic and the need to expand itself with more and bigger facilities. Yet in spite of these demands, the university possesses a well-preserved core of historic buildings that transports the visitor back 100 or more years to its initial construction in the late nineteenth and early twentieth centuries.

Pennsylvania moved from its confined position in the city centre to the Philadelphia suburbs under Provost Charles Stillé (1868–1880), obliging the construction of a new complex of academic buildings which constitute the hub of today's university. Under Stillé, the university buildings sported a distinctive aesthetic, characterized by green serpentine stone, neo-Gothic style, and economy. The first structure, College Hall (1873), was designed by Thomas Webb Richards. It was a many-towered, many-spired Gothic hybrid conceit in brilliant green serpentine stone, with yellow sandstone and purple brownstone trim accented with red pointing and blue roof slates. Carved ornamentation, finials, and towers suggested the architecture of the celebrated English colleges, yet its tempered interiors reflected the financial restraint of the Stillé administration. Richards's Logan Hall (now Cohen Hall, 1874), Robert Hare Laboratory (1878, now demolished) and the Hospital building (1874) shared this aesthetic. No master plan survives but the Victorian buildings surrounded lawned space in a manner that foretasted the later enclosed quadrangles and composition of buildings that would come to define the university's approach to planning.[165]

William Pepper (1881–1894) succeeded Stillé as provost, and with the regime change came a new approach to campus construction. Pepper belonged to the new professional elite of Philadelphia and supplemented the university's curriculum with business, engineering, dentistry and science courses, which required additional buildings. He turned to the bevy of architects that had transformed the prospering industrial city in the previous decade, architects such as the Wilson Brothers, Collins and Autenrieth, and George and William Hewitt. The city's architecture was unmistakably different from other American cities, shaped by its culture of engineering and manufacture in comparison with the financial, commercial and academic centres of New York, Boston and others. By many, buildings were thought

2.117 Fisher Fine Arts Library, University of Pennsylvania
Photo: Jonathan Adams

of as machines. Pepper and the university trustees, coming as they did from the industrial culture, ascribed to this thinking, and in the Pepper years, the college's new buildings increasingly bore kinship with the structures of Philadelphia.[166]

Frank Furness became the principal architect of the university. His masterpiece was the University Library (now the Fisher Fine Arts Library, 1890) (Figure 2.117). Furness's plan was a functional paradigm designed to redress the failings of nineteenth-century libraries, creating 'a modern factory of learning'. The glass-roofed

2.116 Plan, University of Pennsylvania

2.115 Said Business School, University of Oxford
Photo: Said Business School, University of Oxford

UNIVERSITY OF OXFORD

The university enlarged rapidly in the post-war era. The student body increased from 4,000 in the early 1920s to 9,500 by 1965. Yet modernism was slow to take hold and Oxford's architectural patronage remained characterized by conservatism until well after the Second World War. Oxford's first and principal contribution to modernism was the new college, St Catherine's (1964), designed by Danish architect Arne Jacobsen (Figure 2.114). Built on the periphery of the city centre amongst the water meadows of the Cherwell, Jacobsen was not burdened by the contextual restraints of a central site and St Catherine's is a college of refreshing architectural freedom. It was designed to rework the traditions of an Oxford college within a modern context, resulting in an environment both practical and attractive. At its heart is a rectangular quadrangle lined with dining hall, library and bedrooms in a staircase arrangement, but this was not an enclosed quad in the traditional manner. Jacobsen planted the majority of buildings upon a rectangular plinth, upon which each major function is housed in a separate block. Distinct from the appearance of natural accretion traditional to Oxford colleges, St Catherine's is unremittingly symmetrical in its organisation and rectilinear in its lines. The horizontal skyline is relieved only by a bell tower. The strict geometry was softened, though, by sensitive landscaping. Hedge-lined walks and low walls provided a sense of enclosure. The garden was integral to the design. It is a series of rooms delineated by yew hedges, brick walls and walkways that provide a wealth of tranquil spots for individual contemplation and facilitate navigation. New building on the site retains the strong imprint of Jacobsen. In 1992 Stephen Hodder completed a new master plan, which added a quadrangle north of Jacobsen's work. Modestly deferential to the original design, the new quadrangle extended Jacobsen's emphatic geometry. The blocks' upper storeys overhang meticulously planned cloisters and covered walkways. Hodder's buildings integrate well with their predecessors. The two generations share a sympathy with Oxford's historic fabric not through revivalism, but rather through the application of superior detailing and workmanship. These are both displayed to a rare quality at St Catherine's, and together with the yellow brick that characterizes its buildings, act as a unifying force upon the campus.[164]

Hodder's work at St Catherine's demonstrates the capabilities of recent building in Oxford given a perspicacious patron and ample budget. The most prevailing trend of Oxford's recent development is its extreme stylistic diversity. Staunch modernism was in play at Chamberlin, Powell and Bon's residence block at St Peter's college (1989), while trite conservatism informed an extension to Harris Manchester College in the early 1990s. The design for the Said Business School (2001, Sir Jeremy Dixon and Edward Jones) is an eclectic fusion of three millennia of construction (Figure 2.115). It combines a modern retelling of the classical amphitheatre and medieval cloisters and its stepped glass spire is another addition to Oxford's 'dreaming spires' skyline. This spire announces the beginning of the scholastic realm from the west. In an area away from the university's historic core next to the railway station, the building acts as a gateway to the city and university. Although distanced from the hub of academia, its sense of place is distinctively that of twenty-first-century Oxford. While the Business School had no near neighbours to contextualize with, the Rothermere American Institute (2003, Kohn, Pedersen, Fox) was sited to create a new green quad, with Mansfield College defining its south and eastern boundaries. Although modernist in style, the new structure defers to its neo-Gothic neighbour through its linearity and scale. Its plinth, sides and rear are clad in the same Bath stone as Mansfield College Library.

The fabric of Oxford constitutes one of the most charismatic of university environments. The environment reflects the institution's many idiosyncrasies born of its ancient history, which serves to create an unmistakable sense of place. While in Paris and elsewhere the collegiate system waned, in Oxford it thrived and wielded a critical impact upon the physical development of the university that distinguishes it and Cambridge from the majority of higher education establishments. Oxford first acquired its distinctive physical framework with the development of the medieval colleges, and over the course of its eight-century history this schema has been enriched with seventeenth- and eighteenth-century classicism and post-Second World War modernism. Uniting much of its fabric has been the consistent application of local building materials. The academic hub radiates with the warm, honey-coloured limestone serving as a metaphor of institutional presence. While its retrospective outlook can be perceived as a weakness, the University of Oxford's buildings, landscape and setting perpetuate one of campusdom's most powerful institutional and emotional identities.

2.123 University of Technology Petronas
Photo: Nigel Young/Foster + Partners

setting that presented an image compatible with these visionary aspirations.[176]

The 1,000-acre plot selected for the campus is characterized by lush, undulating terrain. Approximately two thirds is covered by steep hills and forests, while the rest is a plain scattered with man-made lakes formed from flooded disused tin mines. It was this, relatively flat portion of land that was selected as the location for Petronas's new complex of buildings. Some earlier campus buildings existed on the site, but the project effectively presented the opportunity for a 'whole cloth' design, which offered the scope to address the whole from the outset. The integration of communal spaces with areas of linkages and teaching accommodation, within a scheme that enabled for future expansion and invested the new institution with a strong identity, was planned for to provide a comprehensive yet lucid complex for the foundling university.[177]

In 1998 the architectural firm Foster & Partners, assisted by Kuala Lumpur-based practice GDP Architects, began work on the university's master plan. Delivered in 2002, the master plan provided for entrance buildings, academic buildings, ancillary banking, retail, recreational and religious facilities, plus housing for all students and lecturers, within an inventive design shaped by a series of innovative features. These features are its built configuration, sensitivity to climate, defined social and circulation zones, and integration with the natural setting.

Completed in 2004, the core academic buildings are set out upon a radial plan to form five 'crescents' that surround a central landscaped park (Figure 2.122). The arrangement recalls a tropical translation of the age-old quadrangle format. Nestled at the intersections of the crescents, support facilities are housed within node buildings, containing lecture theatres, shops, and cafes. The complex is united by an all-encompassing canopy supported by tall, slender columns that updates the traditional motif of an umbrella providing cover from the excesses of the sun and rain. New student residences were sited to the north of this star-shaped core. The sweeping curves of the expansive canopy form not only an eye-catching design feature, but moreover demonstrate the project's sensitivity to the equatorial climate of the local region. Known for its hot and humid weather, the Malay Peninsula frequently experiences bouts of intense sunshine and heavy rain. The crescent roof shelters the pedestrian pathways that link the main junctures, thus offering protection from both these elements and facilitating movement around the campus in all weather conditions (Figure 2.123). Its open structure, furthermore, permits for refreshing cross-ventilating breezes. The canopy, and the decked walkway below that echoes it, physically define the circulation routes and the social spaces. The crescent walkways merge at a plaza, the Chancellor Complex. This drum-shaped building spans 150 metres in diameter and 21 metres in height, and forms Petronas's signature building (Figure 2.124). Divided into two halves, one half houses the library, its stacks of books visible through its soaring glass and steel wall, while the other half houses an auditorium. Between these spaces is a public forum, open to the sides yet under the cover of the vast roof (Figure 2.125). Alive with students and faculty passing through or chatting informally, this is the social hub of the university. As the termination of the ceremonial entrance road to the university, the Chancellor Complex immediately establishes upon visitors an impression of impressive, technologically-advanced architecture housing a vibrant student body.[178]

No less impressive is the relationship of the built fabric with the natural environment. The buildings and landscape sit together in harmony, as the topography of the site has been attentively heeded by the master plan. Development has followed the contours of the ground, for the star-shaped structure is wrapped around the bases of the knolls that scatter the site and encloses jungle-like parkland, natural to the terrain. The paths that wind across the site adhere to the curves of the land. The steel columns that carry the overhanging roof are thin so that views from the building across the landscape are not impeded, and creating the illusion from a distance of the canopy floating amongst the natural canopy of trees. The red tint of the local earth has been mimicked in the finish of the building at numerous junctures while covered spaces are paved in hues that echo the earth tones of the landscape, strengthening the marriage of outdoors and in, of man-made and natural, which infuses the design at Petronas. The main structures are fabricated from reinforced concrete covered by the great aluminium canopy and with glass-panel elevations, yet the design espouses an aliveness to the potential of local materials. Locally-sourced ceramic tiles are used to clad exteriors, creating a variety of iridescent surfaces. The interior of the Chancellor Complex is lined with silk panels, made from a traditional technique in which

2.124 Chancellor Complex, University of Technology Petronas
Photo: Nigel Young/Foster + Partners

gold and silver thread is incorporated within a rich, woven design. This responsiveness to setting and location effectively anchors the complex to its site.[179]

Two other concerns, of vital importance to modern development, strongly shaped the university's master plan: sustainability and provision for growth. The long-term growth of the university was predicted from the outset, in terms of student enrolment and added academic programmes, but the design also had to cater for immediate mutability. As the specifications for the university and its curriculum were being refined simultaneously with the design process, Foster & Partners produced a pragmatic scheme of versatile buildings that would adjust to house more specific functional requirements as these became known. The radial organization of the complex, moreover, establishes a clear, rational framework for the future expansion of the university. The five axes of the star-shape can be extended as necessary into the surrounding land. Ground to the south-east of the site has been specifically delineated as a land bank for future development. Given that much of the Petronas property was once occupied by tin mines, the university's location on previously excavated land permits growth without further encroachment into the Malay Peninsula's forests, revealing a concern for sustainability.[180]

In many aspects of its design, the campus has adopted a holistic attitude to sustainability. Energy-minimizing features include the canopy that shades both pedestrians and buildings; open passages between building blocks to permit cooling airflow; opaque glass to minimize solar glare; and water collected from the roof reused for irrigation. The campus demonstrates a commitment to reducing vehicular traffic with its extensive and efficient pedestrian and bicycle circulation system that fosters walking as the leading method of movement across site. Despite the size of Petronas's plot, the campus has been developed upon the traditional module of the distance that students can walk in the ten-minute break between lectures (800 metres). Academic, recreational and residential facilities are in

2.125 Chancellor Complex, University of Technology Petronas
Photo: Nigel Young/Foster + Partners

accessible proximity to one another, with scenic, meandering paths connecting the different precincts. Car parking is limited to the campus boundary. Such a focus on pedestrian movement, of course, is also advantageous to creating a social and dynamic campus.[181]

The holistic approach of the campus plan as a whole has resulted in the successful cultivation of an institutional identity and sense of place, an objective of key importance to new colleges like Petronas. The pedestrian-friendly campus is one component of this identity, together with its unified design and its strong regional links. Planned and executed as a whole cloth campus, Petronas enjoys the benefit of a harmonious built environment. The device of a sweeping canopy with functional blocks underneath unites the academic components of the university, yet their radial organisation gives each department a distinct integrity. The classroom buildings are generally restricted to three- or four-storeys for uniformity, although some four to six-storey buildings are subtly huddled into the hillside. Only the Telecommunications Tower and Library Clock Tower exceed the height limits, and these stand as landmarks of the campus against the regional skyline. Landscape is also a vital element of place-making at Petronas. The built environment enjoys a sympathetic, enhancing relationship with its naturally dramatic surroundings. Open space has been roughly split into three categories: forested areas untrammelled by development; naturalistic landscape that has been touched by construction or is set aside to be so in the future; and landscaped parks, such as the central court, arrival court and entry drive. A buffer of forests surrounds the campus, thus defining the university's territory.

The scale of the project has proffered Foster & Partners the rare opportunity to design a 'whole-cloth' campus for the twenty-first century. Illustrating such values of sustainability, circulation, and place-making, the design explores the most au courant themes of the field and it is a matter of time to uncover whether these have translated into a physical environment that will fulfil the objectives of the young institution.

2.126 Plan, University of Virginia

University of Virginia
Charlottesville, USA

It is the physical form of this place that is its truly sublime aspect – the perfection of the proportions, the exquisite way the campus sits poised between civilization and wilderness. The University of Virginia is, in the end, an essay about balance. It is open, yet enclosed; rhythmic, yet serene; a model village, yet a set of discrete buildings. And it is at once an homage to Western civilization, and a celebration of all that is new and profoundly American.

(P. Goldberger[182])

Designed by America's third president, Thomas Jefferson, in the early nineteenth century, the intensity of the vision and accomplishment of the Lawn at the University of Virginia numbers amongst the most awe-inspiring of architectural experiences. The only university in the United States to be designated an UNESCO World Heritage Site, the lawn – its central heart – was voted in 1976 by the American Institute of Architects as the 'proudest achievement in American architecture' (Figure 1.16).

The university was a product of the Age of Enlightenment, an era which aspired to replace theocracy and oligarchy with self-governance, democracy and reason. Upholding the country's newly-gained democratic constitution, Jefferson contended, could only be achieved through an educated populace and thus, far in advance of his contemporaries, he envisaged the state taking upon itself this responsibility and in 1817 construction began on a state university in Charlottesville, Virginia.[183]

2.127 Pavilion X, University of Virginia
Photo: Dan Addison/UVA Public Affairs

UNIVERSITY OF VIRGINIA

An experienced architect in his own right,[184] Jefferson managed every aspect of the fledgling university's development, from selecting the location to planning its layout, designing its buildings and devising the curriculum; moulding each of these elements to reflect his own distinct, innovatory social and pedagogic vision. He termed his campus the 'Academical Village', expressing an intimacy of scale contrived to foster intellectual exchange between professors and students. Its layout and architectural expression was formed around this educational ambition. It is this link between design and pedagogic ideology that marks Jefferson's campus as such an innovation in the history of the American university.

Jefferson's design sprung fundamentally from his vision of the ideal education. Upon being asked for advice about plans for a lower school in central Virginia in 1805, Jefferson counselled,

> The greatest danger will be [the college authorities'] over-building themselves, by attempting a large house in the beginning, sufficient to contain the whole institution. Large houses are always ugly, inconvenient, exposed to the accident of fire, and bad cases of infection. A plain small house for the school and lodging of each professor is best. These connected by covered ways out of which the rooms of the students should open would be best. These may be built only as they shall be wanting. In fact a university should not be a house but a village.[185]

Later, in 1810 Jefferson cautioned the trustees of the new East Tennessee College,

> I consider the common plan, followed in this country but not in others, of making one large and expensive building, as unfortunately erroneous. It is infinitely better to erect a small and separate lodge for each separate professorship, with only a hall below for his class, and two chambers above for himself; joining these lodges by barracks for a certain portion of the students, opening into a covered way to give a dry communication between all the schools. The whole of these arranged around an open square of grass and trees, would make it, what it should be in fact, an academical village...

Every professor would be the police officer of the students adjacent to his own lodge...These separate buildings, too, might be erected successively and occasionally, as the number of professorships and students should be increased, or the funds become competent...Much observation and reflection on these institutions have long convinced me that the large and crowded buildings in which youths are pent up, are equally unfriendly to health, to study, to manners, morals and order.[186]

These ideas constitute the essential form that Jefferson's University of Virginia was to take: a large open space lined with houses serving as professors' residences and classrooms from which covered arcades open on to student rooms (Figure 1.15). It was a scheme which, Jefferson promoted, could be erected in stages as the school grew in numbers and budget.

Building commenced at the university in 1817, and the university was ready to open eight years later. A simple plan, the composition featured a wide, tree-lined avenue open to the south end and flanked on the longitudinal sides to the east and west with ten pavilions, each housing a separate department and its professor's residential quarters. From these extend colonnades leading to students' apartments. Behind the pavilions, gardens were planted enclosed by serpentine walls, and beyond these, ranges were added to the east and west housing dormitories and dining halls. The highlight of the composition, though, was the domed rotunda at the northern end of the rectangle. The most expensive building, it was not completed until 1826 and served as the library. This impressive structure formed the functional and symbolic apex of the Lawn, and indeed it stands today as the intellectual heart and lustrous emblem of the university. For the first time in American collegiate tradition, the library constituted the institution's heart. Jefferson was clearly proclaiming the new institution's dedication to expanding the nation's knowledge through research. To Jefferson, the university's built environment was an expression of its aspirations and motivations, and he consciously turned to the most superior architectural models in order to express them, notably the vocabulary of the antique transcribed through the work of Andrea Palladio in the sixteenth century. Pavilion I (1819–1822) has a Doric order based upon the Baths of Diocletian in Rome,

2.128 Cabell Hall, University of Virginia
Photo: Jane Haley/UVA public affairs

while Pavilion II's (1819–1822) Ionic columns were modelled upon those at the Fortuna Virilis, Rome. The Rotunda was a quarter-size imitation of the Pantheon, one of Jefferson's favourite buildings. Jefferson's designs also betray the influence of the neo-classical architecture he saw whilst in France from 1784 to 1789. The Château de Marly (1679), which he visited in 1786, is a possible source for the University of Virginia. The complex featured a U-shaped garden lined by six pavilions with the principal building at its high end. Terraces and pergolas linked the buildings. Informed by superior models of architecture, Jefferson intended that the buildings would serve to educate and cultivate in matters of taste forthcoming generations of architects and patrons.[187]

Jefferson's deployment of a wide array of architectural sources provided for an arrangement that achieved variety within unity. Each pavilion is slightly different in form and decoration (Figure 2.127). Yet in its shared precedents and consistency of materials, the Lawn accomplishes a totality that distinguishes it as a community. The core building materials of the Lawn are red brick and wood, painted white. White wooden balconies encircle the open space, visually grouping the ensemble of brick structures to form a unified entity. The light wood trim of the buildings acts as a counterpoint to the substantial permanence of the brick, creating a marriage that enables a sense of human-scale and refined proportions that contributes to the transcendental experience of the Lawn.

The green itself, nearly 60 metres wide by 600 metres in length, was conceived as the focus of college life, a space for intellectual exchange, campus gossip and recreation. The conductivity of landscape to academic study was fundamental to Jefferson's vision.

When doors were opened to the first students in 1825, the University of Virginia was a staunch compendium of Jefferson's visionary and scholastic philosophies. The complex of dormitories and pavilions, rather than one large building, fostered a mentoring relationship between lecturers and pupils that was directly expressive of Jefferson's own university days. Whilst attending the College of William and Mary from 1760–1762, he experienced the traditional American college format in which all students and faculty lived, ate and studied under one large roof. In this environment, life was characterized by food fights and drunkenness, with one professor routinely piloting drunken raids in the local town with his young charges. Jefferson found his most satisfying university moments through close exchange with teachers, a relationship he pursued when acting as a teacher himself to young law students.[188] The layout of the University of Virginia is a rational expression of this collegial ideal. In focusing on the total experience of place as a key element in the scholastic endeavour, Jefferson's design revolutionized campus planning. He introduced to the discipline the symbolic capacity of design to embody and champion social ideologies. The lesson of the powerful relationship between architecture and ideology has been one that the university has endeavoured to uphold through its trajectory of development ever since.[189]

Jefferson died in 1826, only a year after the university opened, and the institution quickly encountered challenges that its founder could never have predicted. Notable amongst these was the significant burgeoning of enrolment figures beginning in the 1840s. The student body rose from 128 in 1842 to 645 in 1856, necessitating more housing and teaching rooms. Campus development in the mid-nineteenth century marked a distinct shift from Jeffersonian classicism to the eclectic historicism and picturesque styles then in vogue nationally. Meandering paths were installed at the periphery of the Lawn, contrasting with the original orthogonal layout. A new infirmary (now Varsity Hall, 1857) violated Jefferson's formal geometrical grid, being laid out to correspond to the natural topography of the land and fronting north-east. Brooks Hall, constructed 1876–1877 to designs by John Thomas, introduced the French Second Empire style to the neo-classical campus, while the Chapel was built in a Gothic Revival idiom (completed 1890). Erected to the north of the Rotunda, Brooks Hall and the Chapel marked the first northward expansion of the grounds.

In 1895, tragedy struck as the Rotunda was engulfed in flames. Its restoration was a priority, and New York Beaux-Arts architectural practice McKim, Mead and White was engaged. Their appointment marked a new phase in the history of the campus. As the twentieth century was dawning, Jeffersonion architecture was experiencing a revival. Confronted with mass immigration, race riots and Communism, American architects looked to the classically-derived architecture of the colonial era and the early republic to create a distinctive national architecture. Jefferson's architecture came to the fore. His ideas accorded with those of the ascendant Beaux-Arts Movement, with

2.129 Darden School of Business Administration, University of Virginia
Photo: Jack Looney

its emphasis on classical styles and rational, coherent planning. This style was espoused by Stanford White in his work at the University of Virginia in the 1890s. In restoring the Rotunda, White added a shallow portico with six columns to its north side with a flight of stairs to the street below, changing the building's orientation northwards away from the Lawn. He constructed a fireproof domed roof, and removed the upper floor of the interior to create a grand vaulted space with great Corinthian columns. Matching wings were added to the Rotunda's northern face, connected to the original south arcades by arched passageways that enclosed small courtyards. The restored structure presents a façade faultlessly Jeffersonian. White was also responsible for a contentious new grouping of buildings at the south end of the Lawn that provoked controversy by closing the original view to the mountains. Built on the axis of the Rotunda, Cabell Hall (classroom building) was the largest of White's three new structures (Figure 2.128). It was flanked by Cocke Hall (Engineering) and Rouss Hall (Physics). White was highly attuned to the relationship of these new edifices with the revered Lawn, and the three buildings fit well into the Academical Village. The acute descent of the terrain to the south allowed him to slot the new buildings into the slope and erect what appear from the Lawn to be one-storey buildings whereas they are in fact two to three storeys. The Jeffersonian-style architecture he employed for them was regarded as so successful that it remained the approach for subsequent construction until the 1950s.

The 1950s witnessed the beginning of an important phase in the University of Virginia's development. Enrolment soared and to accommodate its growth, the university turned to two models: the satellite and the infill. Beginning in the 1950s and accelerated in the 1960s, the university developed a separate satellite precinct known as the North Grounds. Including the Copeley residences, the Law School and later the Darden Business School, the precinct followed a suburban model of planning. Accordingly, the complex shows a much greater orientation to vehicular traffic. While the car has little impact on the pedestrian central campus, the tremendous ubiquity of vehicular transport on the North Grounds is illustrated by the suburban atmosphere and large areas devoted to parking, a trend visible on satellite campuses at large. The physical distance between the North Grounds and other university precincts has engendered concerns of isolation and lack of community. Its suburban model presents challenges of community interaction, of a visual core, and of connecting pedestrian and vehicular routes, that are not encountered within the Academical Village. The post-war years also saw efforts to mitigate the negative effects of geographic sprawl through building on infill sites. A student centre, Newcomb Hall (1958), was constructed to the west of the Lawn. A large building, it was pushed into the

2.130 Aerial view of central campus, University of Virginia
Photo: Dan Addison/UVA Public Affairs

slope of the ground in order that it did not challenge the scale of surrounding buildings. New Cabell Hall (early 1950s) containing classrooms and offices, was similarly built into sloping terrain at the south end of the Lawn. The two buildings countered the campus's centrifugal growth by directing student activity to the Lawn, thus ensuring it continued to function as the communal heart of the university as Jefferson intended.

Development in the later twentieth and early twenty-first centuries has responded to the challenges of maintaining a relationship between the centre and the outlying precincts, and of safeguarding the totality of the buildings and landscape of the campus's inner sanctum. The university directed much of their development efforts to creating a middle route between the satellite and infill models. Small residential colleges were planned. Brown College (1986) and Hereford College (1990–1992), for example, were envisioned as a solution to the personal isolation and anonymity accompanied by the university's centrifugal mushrooming. Housing dining facilities, informal classes and faculty residences, these colleges allowed for the type of enhanced student-faculty interaction espoused by Jefferson. They were conceived as new Academical Villages embedded within an ever growing, ever more complex university. The original model of the Academical Village has increasingly gained in importance in terms of the institution's planning, with its 'mixed-use' precepts being re-envisioned for contemporary life.

From the post-war years onwards, the university's architects and planners have also faced stylistic challenges. In light of the canonical status of Jefferson's architectural masterpiece, succeeding generations have been trapped between trying to marry new work with the iconic Lawn structures or creating buildings of their own time. Modernism influenced a spate of new buildings in the mid-twentieth century. Gilmer Hall (designed 1962) was the University of Virginia's first excursion into modern architecture. It was to be the nucleus of a new science area. Away from Jefferson's long shadow, the North Grounds was executed in a spirit of greater architectural freedom. University Hall (1965) was the centrepiece of the North Grounds' athletic complex. Its vast scale and distinctive scalloped dome signalled a disregard for the past that set the mood for the precinct's development until the construction of the Darden School of Business Administration (1992–1996) by Robert A. M. Stern (Figure 2.129). Its architecture makes obvious reference to the nineteenth-century university through its materials (red bricks and white trim) massing and detailing (black shutters, white wooden balconies, covered arcades). Nonetheless, in its planning the Darden School exhibits considerable digressions from the Academical Village. Its large scale of buildings compared to the Lawn reflects the possibilities of modern building materials and techniques. While the Academical Village was envisioned as a self-contained micro-community, the Darden School is not residential so is populated only during working hours by users dependent on the car for access to it. The practice of establishing an aesthetic continuity between new development and the founder's vision, though, is now an engrained principle at the university. Robertson Hall was built in 2005–2007 as an extension to Stanford White's Rouss Hall at the south end of the Lawn. While its decidedly twenty-first-century interiors cater for high-tech study, its exterior blends seamlessly with Rouss Hall and in turn with the iconic Jeffersonian architecture around it. Space for the new structure was carved out of the significantly sloping ground to the rear of Rouss Hall so as not to disturb the present distribution of the sacrosanct Lawn. The revival of the planning principles of the Academical Village and Jeffersonian architectural idiom points to the strengths of the original vision; it continues to serve as the basis of the University of Virginia's success as a campus.[190]

Almost all the campus appears visibly touched by Jefferson's legacy. Most prominent of all is the continuity of the vocabulary of building materials instituted by Jefferson – red brick and white trim – timeless materials that evoke central Virginia (Figure 2.130). The brick expresses a quality of permanence which Jefferson wanted to invest into his university, while also embracing Virginia's traditional red clay production and tying the university enduringly to its specific locale. The white painted wood, used for the balcony rails and classical details, is resonant of the setting, for it was sourced from regional forests. The campus's shared tradition of materials creates an encompassing aesthetic commonality that unites its disparate precincts and enforces the history and continuity of the institution.

To Jefferson as important as the buildings, the landscaping of the campus is a compelling device. Pivotal to the enduring influence of Jefferson's vision is the strength of the Lawn as an experiential space. Despite the dispersal of campus facilities the Lawn remains the emotional and social heart of campus, the scene of students sunbathing, studying or playing Frisbee. Its lasting resonance is evinced by the fierce competition amongst students to live in its dormitory rooms, despite a long, cold trek to the bathrooms in the basement. The Lawn has a magnetism that is hard to compete with. Extending from this greensward, the outdoor experience fluidly leads from space to space, from grass to arcaded walkway, from pavilion to garden. The density of buildings against open space in Jefferson's plan was kept low in comparison with contemporary universities. The green spaces of the central grounds – the Lawn, the libraries' quadrangle, and the pavilion gardens – are timeless, memorable fundamentals of the University of Virginia experience. Such potential is not capitalized upon, however, in some of the more ill-defined areas of the campus's landscape. The North Grounds, for example, would profit from the development of central green space which invites activity in the same vein as the Lawn.

The University of Virginia was a new paradigm for the structuring, organization and planning of an institution of higher education. It pioneered the concept that the built environment was an influential component of the educational experience. To Jefferson, the values it embodied were of such importance that, amongst all the accomplishments of his remarkable life, it was one of only three deeds that he chose to be remembered for on his gravestone: 'Author of the Declaration of American Independence, of the Statute of Virginia for religious freedom and Father of the University of Virginia'. Its appeal has proved engrossing and enduring. Within an age of the 'mass-university' where the notion of individual, enlightened teaching is becoming increasingly transcendental, Jefferson's vision of the model community of scholars nurtured through physical surroundings continues to capture the imagination.

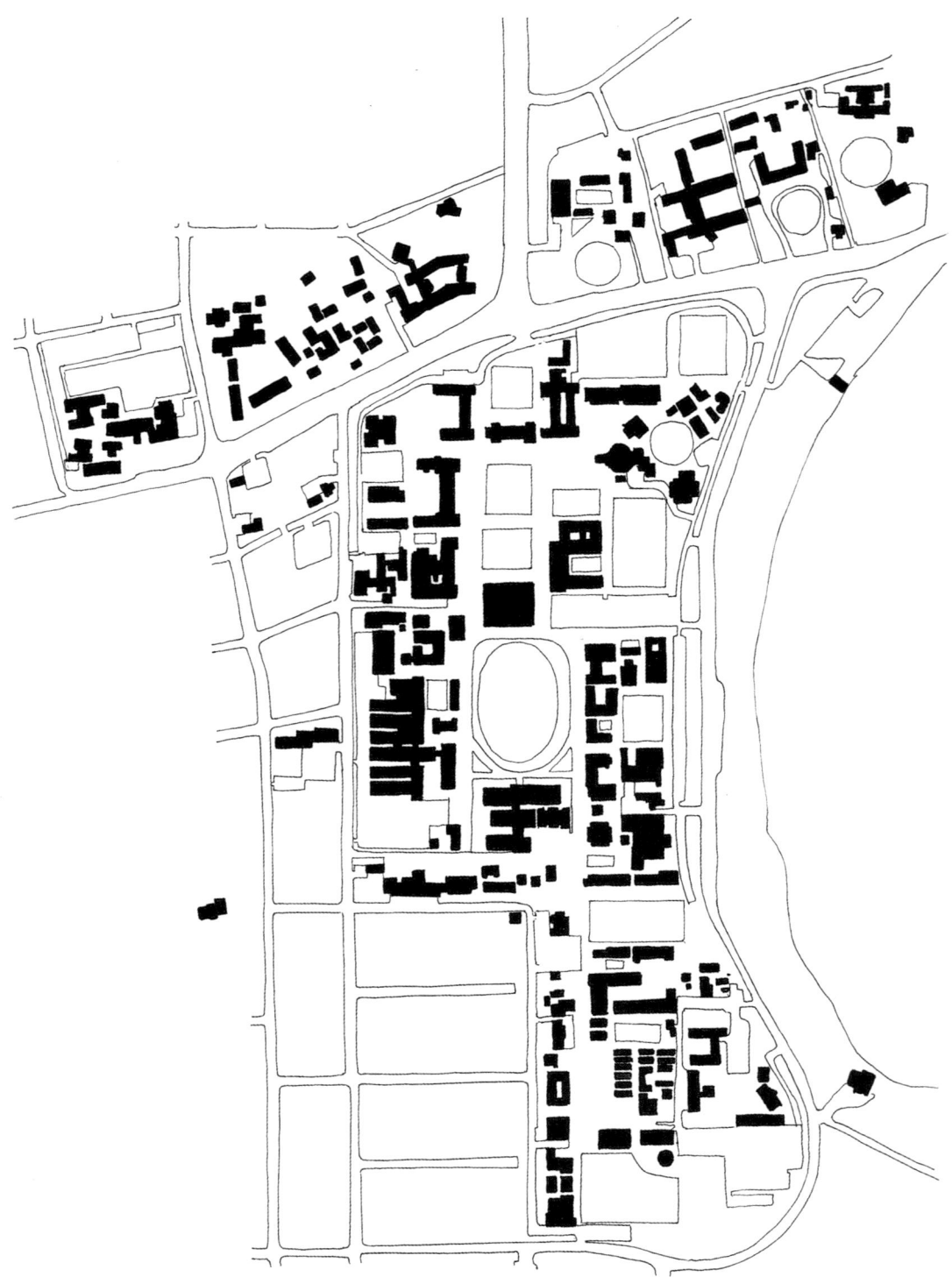

2.131 Plan, University of Western Australia

University of Western Australia
Perth, Australia

The University of Western Australia (UWA) was created in 1911 as the State's first university. The wooden and iron huts erected on a temporary site in central Perth that acted as its first classrooms have long since been replaced, and its campus is today considered by many as one of Australia's most idyllic (Figure 2.132).

In 1914, the Government offered to the fledgling university a 104-acre tract of land five kilometres from Perth's centre in an impressive natural setting bounded by the Matilda Bay waterfront and the King's Park bushland reserve. In emulation of the widely-broadcast precedents of the Hearst competition for the design of Berkeley's campus and the 1911 competition for the new capital, Canberra, UWA launched an international contest for the plan of its site. Harold Desbrowe-Annear's winning design was based on a system of radiating axes fanning out from the highest point of the site, at the north-western corner. Five residential colleges were sited on the north side of the Perth Fremantle Road that traversed the campus. The First World War and the death of the founding chancellor, John Winthrop Hackett, stalled the realization of Desbrowe-Annear's plan, yet some elements of his plan are visible in today's campus. His siting of the residential colleges has remained, as has the location of the main sports oval (James Oval) and the north-east axis which determined the alignment of Somerville Auditorium and the Music Building.[191]

In 1926, a sizeable bequest stimulated the university once more into action, and the ground was laid for an extensive development

2.132 Aerial view, University of Western Australia

2.133 Winthrop Hall, University of Western Australia
Photo: Ray Scott

of the campus. Renowned for his role in the design of the University of Sydney, Leslie Wilkinson was engaged as Consultant Architect. His 1927 plan established the fundamentals of the modern campus. The plan re-orientated the campus from Desbrowe-Annear's diagonal axis, to the north–south alignment that dominates today. Along this spine, he established the campus's three major open spaces – a Court of Honour (Whitfeld Court), a Great Court, and a tree-encircled practice oval, James Oval – which form the heart of the institution today. Buildings were tightly grouped to the west of this axis, which in later years impeded expansion.[192]

With a campus plan in place, in 1927 the university initiated a design competition for the ceremonial, administration and student buildings that were to frame Whitfeld Court. Rodney H. Alsop and Conrad H. Sayce were awarded first place, and when completed in 1932 the ensemble was quickly established as the university's 'signature' buildings (Figure 2.133). Not only does the lofty clock tower of the centrepiece building, Winthrop Hall, rise above the tree canopy as a symbol of the university's presence, but it moreover symbolizes Western Australia as a whole. Alsop and Sayce were keenly attuned to the personality of the region and its Mediterranean-like climate suggested Italy and Greece as natural sources for its architecture. Sicilian and early Christian buildings informed the design of Winthrop Hall's upper colonnade, especially its carved capitals; its tower recalls the campaniles of the Italian Renaissance; and Venetian-style mosaics insets and Byzantine winged beasts embellish the exterior. The immediate context was meanwhile evoked in the great beams of Winthrop's great hall which carried indigenous aboriginal motifs. The rich texture and warm hues of the Hackett Memorial Buildings' sandstone, limestone and cordova tiles established a design standard and theme that was to dominate the architectural character of the campus (Figure 2.134). These colours and textures immediately became a guiding prescript for subsequent development, beginning with the Physics and Chemistry Building (now Geography and Geology) to the west of the Great Court, designed by Baxter, Cox and Summerhayes and completed in 1935.[193]

Post-war planning at UWA has predominantly organized new buildings in quadrangular layouts along and in extension of the north-south spine. In the immediate post-war years, attention was focused upon rapidly expanding the campus's facilities to meet with a rapidly expanding student population. In 1953, Gordon Stephenson, Professor of Civic Design at the University of Liverpool, was retained as a consultant to the university to guide this growth. His 1954–1955 plan prescribed the construction of dispersed structures around the central north–south axis, resulting in a rational, flexible

2.134 Winthrop Hall, University of Western Australia
Photo: Ray Scott

yet attractive composition of buildings and open spaces. Faculties were grouped into cognate clusters, such as the Engineering group to the west of James Oval and the Biological Sciences zone half-way down the campus. He presided over a considerable construction effort, including the Arts building (Marshall Clifton, 1963), the Economics and Commerce Building (Marshall Clifton, 1966), and the Law School (R. J. Ferguson, 1967). A new main library, the Reid Library (1964), was inserted into a central position between the Great Court and James Oval. The principles of Stephenson's plan were retained when Arthur Bunbury succeeded him in the newly-created post of University Architect in 1966, and who in turn was succeeded in 1985 by R. J. Ferguson and Associates as consultant architect.[194]

Development also progressed on the stretch of campus lying north of the Perth-Fremantle highway, occupied by the university's five residential colleges. These colleges largely assumed a loosely quadrangular layout. In its red brick, Tudor-esque buildings following the pattern of the Oxbridge colleges, St George's College made a notable departure from the Mediterranean idiom of the Hackett Buildings constructed at the same time. Yet the other colleges, built at various times over the course of the university's development, have largely deferred to the architectural and landscape qualities of the main campus.

The main campus is, for the most part, remarkable for its visual unity (Figure 2.135). In terms of architectural design, the Whitfeld Court buildings inaugurated a distinctive, yet practicable design trajectory that set the standard for the campus's evolution. They introduced the repertoire of pitched terracotta roofs, limestone walls, buff-coloured local stone, colonnades, and porches and a palette of warm hues that has come to define the university's built environment. Bar a few exceptions, later additions to campus have respected this lexicon, achieving a totality of design. The notable anomaly of the 1960s Engineering buildings sully this harmony. Built at a time when the vivid mosaics of Brasilia were in vogue, the buildings are flat-roofed and adorned inside and out with bold tile designs, which establishes an individual aesthetic at odds with the integrity of the rest of campus. The 1961–1965 Chemistry and 1961 Physics buildings espoused a minimalist style whose clay brick walls and flat concrete roofs contrasted with the texture of the limestone walls and pitched roofs of the original buildings. Chiefly, though, construction has been submissive to Winthrop Hall's buff colouring and burnt-orange tiles. The elongated mass of the Reid Library, for instance, was tempered by its limestone-coloured concrete exterior and clay tile roof. While possessing individual identities, the buildings accorded with the earlier structures and enhanced the architectural character of the site.[195]

2.135 Aerial view with Winthrop Hall in the foreground, University of Western Australia

Fault could be found in the sober restraint of the buildings, homogenized by consistent roof heights and terracotta tiles, but so doing would be to misunderstand the psyche of the campus. The campus is informed by a vision of architecture and landscape conceived as an entity, working in harmony to create a subtly beautiful environment. The buildings are deliberately planned not to monopolize attention in the naturally stunning setting. The landscape is, in fact, UWA's defining asset. The university's gardens were instituted into the National Estate in 1980, while in 1986 the campus received the Western Australian Civic Design Award for excellence in civic design. From the campus's foundation, landscape has been valued at least equal to architecture, rather than as a subordinate element. Hackett's recognition that the creation of a campus was predicated as much upon landscaping as building, resulted in an immediate landscaping campaign. In 1926, Henry Campbell set to work on a planting programme. He set out features of Wilkinson's 1927 plan such as James and Riley Ovals, defined the north-east axis with palm trees, and installed blocks of exotic geometric planting around the Hackett Memorial Buildings. Following encouragement in 1927 from William Somerville, a member of the university's Senate, a 'cathedral of trees' used as an open-air theatre was planted alongside the north-east axis with arboreal walls of Norfolk Island pines and regional peppermint trees. Trees dominate at UWA. Many of the campus's smaller buildings are camouflaged by its dense tree canopy, while the conservation of existing trees has long been an important factor in the planning of new buildings.[196]

The series of open spaces defined in Wilkinson's 1927 plan have continued to govern the development of the landscape system. Whitfeld Court, as befitting its role as the entrance to the grounds, is a suitably grand space with a formal and symmetrical landscape character. The less orderly yet large-in-scale Great Court is used for informal activities, while the vast expanses of James and Riley Ovals, used as playing fields, are the lungs of campus. Under Stephenson's tenure, peaceful courtyards between buildings were introduced onto campus, such as the small, secluded space between the Biochemistry and Anatomy departments and the shaded Prescott Court lined by the Physiology and Agriculture buildings.[197]

Another characteristic of Stephenson as planner was his concern for circulation within the landscape setting. He installed a network of promenades and covered walkways, which has been gradually extended as the campus grows to create a comprehensive, serviceable pedestrian system. The group surrounding Oak Lawn comprised of Law, Economics and Commerce, Social Sciences and the Student Guild is connected by sheltered pathways which visually connect the individual buildings of varying ages. Circulation could be improved, however, by addressing the inadequacy of the connection between the main campus and the residential colleges, separated by a busy thoroughfare. The precincts are linked by two underpasses, completed in 1966 and 1970, but their siting is inconvenient for access to and from the most easterly colleges, St Thomas More and St George's, and the university's circulation system would benefit greatly from another underpass. Stephenson's other legacies included the exclusion of cars from the campus's inner green spaces and the relegation of car parks to the campus edge, which greatly enhance the campus's 'walkability' and tranquillity.[198]

The university's parkland campus is additionally a leading tool in cultivating relations with the surrounding community. The grounds form a natural extension of the neighbouring landscape system comprising King's Park and the Matilda Bay reserve. The local community makes full use of these precincts for recreation, including the university grounds which operate an 'open campus' policy.[199] The campus's original relationship with Matilda Bay has, however, diminished as development has proceeded. The screen of buildings that has been erected along the eastern boundary of the campus means that views of the site's previously pervading winning attribute can now only be caught in intermittent glimpses. Especially along the river foreshore, the landscape is detrimentally affected by the accumulation of parked cars. Such drawbacks, though, cannot easily be avoided at a burgeoning institution in a city possessing distinctly inadequate public transport.[200]

Despite reduced connection with Matilda Bay, the campus grounds are a rich botanical collage, integral to the image of the university. UWA's persona is not defined by individual buildings, but by the aggregate of landscape and the organic placement of architecture within it. The significance placed upon the collective campus landscape that was first emphasized by Desbrowe-Annear and Wilkinson remains paramount in the university's physical development today. The result is an unaffectedly compelling campus, dominated by its natural environment and vistas of the campanile tower of Winthrop rising imperiously above the trees.

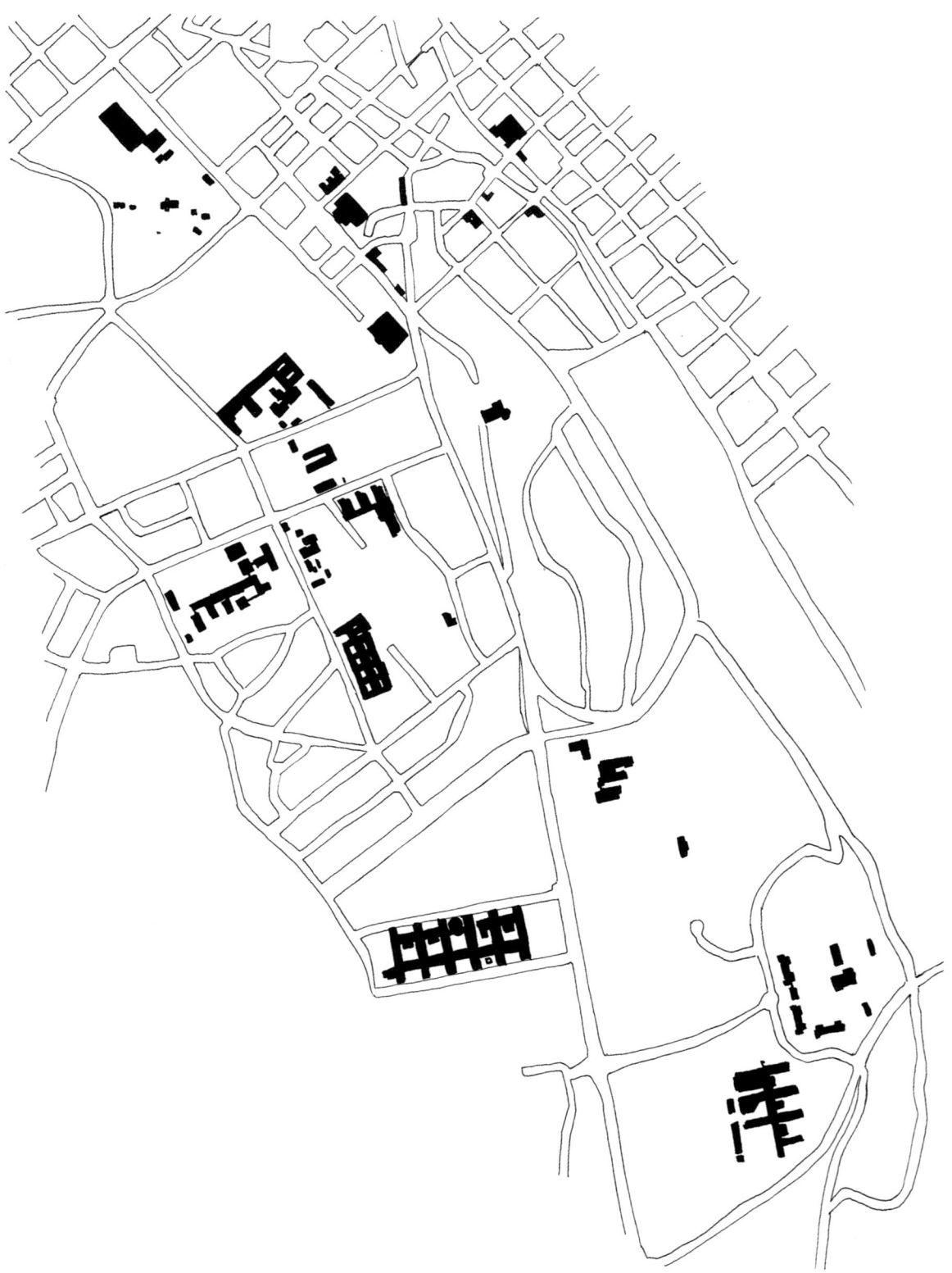

2.136 Plan, Uppsala University

Uppsala University
Uppsala, Sweden

The late Middle Ages was a boom time for Sweden. Foreign trade prospered, towns and the bourgeoisie flourished and the nobility and the Church enjoyed increased prosperity. Together with the building of impressive castles, monasteries and churches, the outgrowth of this golden age was the founding of Sweden's first seat of higher learning in 1477. Championed by the Archbishop of Uppsala, the university was established in Uppsala in the stone-built houses that surrounded the cathedral in the town centre, marking the beginning of the university's integral relationship with the city centre environment. Although the university has expanded centrifugally in its 500-year history, it remains intrinsic to the life of the city, and this is its chief quality and asset.

At the heart of historic Uppsala is the university's oldest surviving building, the Gustavianum (Figure 2.137). Built immediately adjacent to the cathedral, it was a product of a substantial expansion of the institution in the seventeenth century. In a conscious attempt to revive the university after its decline during the Reformation, King Gustav II Adolph bestowed a generous donation that afforded the construction of bigger and grander accommodation than hitherto possessed by the university. Begun in the 1620s to designs by Casper Panten, the simple, rectangular building is crowed by a huge cupola capped with a sundial that creates a distinctive silhouette in the cityscape. Its large, dignified form reflected Gustav II's ambitions to aggrandize the university's person in complement with the growing power of the Swedish state. The extraordinary anatomic theatre under the dome of the cupola was added in the 1660s by the brilliant professor Olaf Rudbeck. The sciences flourished at the university, particularly in the eighteenth century, when the university erected numerous laboratories around the town centre, such as the Laboratorium Chemicum (1753).

The nineteenth century yielded another surge of physical growth. The century saw the erection of the university library and Main Building, which alongside the Gustavianum, constitute the principal landmarks of the university. The library, christened the Carolina Redivivia, was allotted a prominent position, high atop a ridge that terminated one of the city's principal streets (Figure 2.138). Begun in 1819 it was not opened until 1834. Of palatial proportions and Renaissance in style, it was designed by Carl Fredrik Sundvall. Sympathetic additions have been designed by Axel Anderberg in

2.137 Gustavianum, Uppsala University
Photo: Tommy Westberg

2.138 Carolina Redivivia, Uppsala University
Photo: Pereric Öberg

the 1910s and 1930s and Peter Celsing (1952–71), reflecting the continual growth inherent to any research library. Contemporaneous with the Carolina Redivivia's construction, a park was created behind it, known as the English Park because of its informal plan filled with mature trees. By the 1870s the university had become again short of space, in particular for ceremonial purposes. Thus parliament funding was secured for a spectacular new Main Building, and from 1879 to 1887 it rose to designs by Herman Teodor Holmgren (Figure 2.139). Standing today largely as it did when completed, Holmgren's red brick building is a masterful evocation of a Renaissance palace, elegant and magisterial on an elevated site neighbouring the cathedral and Gustavianum. The great neo-classical entrance hall, with its grand double staircase and trio of coiffered domes, has been ranked one of Sweden's most exquisite spatial experiences. The building was intimately interwoven with the identity of the university, expressive of an agenda of heroism and self-glorification. In a pamphlet written to stimulate donations to the building fund, the university's rector eulogized that the Main Building was a matter of national pride, necessary to establish Uppsala on an equal footing with the many European universities that had recently embarked upon building campaigns. The Main Building, Carolina Redivivia and Gustavianum remain as vital as physical symbols of the university in the present day as they did when first constructed.[201]

In the early years of the twentieth century, the tangible image of the university was further consolidated by the gradual accretion of a science precinct upon the western portion of the English Park. Chemistry and physics buildings, erected in 1904 and 1908 respectively, joined a chemistry institute (1858) already on the site. Further science buildings in various architectural modes and materials were added to the complex from the 1930s up until 1970 when the Teknikum, housing engineering facilities, was completed, furnishing the university with a densely-built science quarter close to the city centre.[202]

The visible organization of Uppsala University's sciences was again transformed in the aftermath of the Second World War. Following government directives for the expansion of higher education in the 1950s, student numbers at Uppsala rocketed from approximately 4,000 in 1945 to over 20,000 circa 1970 resulting in extreme overcrowding. The higher-education boom was a Europe-wide phenomenon and across the continent it gave rise to a trend for satellite science campuses. At Uppsala, a prominent biological sciences complex rose in the 1960s, positioned apart from the city centre yet conveniently closer than comparable examples at other European institutions. The BMC, as the centre is known, is Scandinavia's largest university building. Set in green surroundings bounded by woodland and disused artillery fields, it was built in stages to designs by Stockholm modernist architect Paul Hedqvist between 1964 and 1984, during

2.139 Main Building, Uppsala University
Photo: Tommy Westberg

which time biological sciences relocated here from the English Park. Its modular plan facilitated this staged construction. Despite the 20 year duration of its construction, it utilizes the same materials and building style throughout.

Towards the close of the twentieth century, the sciences expanded to the university's most southerly site upon a vacated military garrison, Polacksbacken, creating another satellite sub-campus two and a half kilometres from Uppsala's centre. Between 1986 and 1991, the garrison's impressive red brick buildings dating 1908–1913 were renovated to house the information technology department (Figure 2.140). Few conspicuous changes were made to the existing structures, although several raised glass walkways were inserted between buildings to aid movement in the inhospitable Swedish winters. The large interiors and high ceilings of these buildings rendered them practicable for teaching purposes, while their age and stately bearing meant they possessed a desirable cultural cachet. The leafy courtyard at the complex's centre and the parkland that surrounds it furthermore gave the precinct an aesthetic appeal often lacking on European science campuses. The city of Uppsala has a tradition of preserving informal green parkland at its core, and it is a legacy that the university has embraced. Leafy preserves, such as that on the Polacksbacken, are found around the sub-campuses. In 1996 the Polacksbacken site became home to the Ångström Laboratory. A vast laboratory complex set in undulating green grounds complete with volleyball courts, it has proven popular with inhabitants. Its 250 metre spine, stretching the length of the building is devoted to social and library functions, generating a 'meeting in the corridor' atmosphere. In architectural terms, the laboratory makes no attempt to contextualize with the neighbouring barracks; rather it is perceived as a landmark building for the cutting-edge research of the institution.

The completion of the Ångström Laboratory in 2000 was a manifestation of an epochal period of transition undergone by the university in the 1990s, which stemmed from a major reform in the management of public buildings and property in 1993. Swedish state-run universities have been prohibited since 1830 from owning buildings or real estate. Prior to 1993, the National Board of Public Buildings managed all higher-education premises, leasing it to individual universities. The acquisition of new university premises was controlled by the National Board via a very slow procedure criticized for its rigidity and inefficiency. This changed in 1993 with the reorganization of the National Board, one consequence of which was the formation of the state-owned company Akademiska Hus to own and manage higher-education buildings. Its foundation simplified the procurement of new property and was the impetus for a heady phase of development at Uppsala University. In 1995 a new master plan for the entire university was prepared, initiating

UPPSALA UNIVERSITY

2.140 Information Technology Centre, Uppsala University
Photo: Pereric Öberg

several new projects which transformed the physical environment of the university. Between 1997 and 2004, the master plan affected 250,000m² of its 425,000m² footprint.

Under the master plan, the function of the English Park was changed from a science to a humanities campus. Physics and chemistry were relocated from the English Park's outdated facilities to the Ångström Laboratory. The vacated buildings were occupied by the humanities, a move that allowed all the constituent institutes to be gathered on one site for the first time and thus encouraged inter-disciplinary co-operation. Interiors were renovated and adapted but the only significant addition to the English Park campus accompanying its change of function was a new glass entrance building (2004) on an infill site bridging two older units. The premises previously occupied by some humanities faculties to the north of the English Park was in turn reassigned to Economics and renamed the Ekonomikum. The large complex, which had been built in 1975 to designs by Swedish modernist Peter Celsing, was enhanced by the addition of a glass roof spanning the once-open courtyard creating a new library. The master plan likewise converted the Gustavianum from a teaching space to a museum.

The evolutionary biology sub-campus, a short distance south of the English Park, also featured in the plan. From 1917, when a Zoology building was erected, the site expanded periodically with building campaigns in the 1930s, 1950s and 1960s. The master plan outlined an entrance building for the complex, facing inwards upon a grassed, leafy courtyard that encouraged a new internal orientation for the whole site. Completed in 1999, the building's design evinced a sensitive response to the context of its older neighbours. Its white façade corresponds with the adjacent Zoology Building, its scale complements the 1950s and 1960s buildings lining the courtyard, and similarities in their façades create a dialogue between the entrance wing and the Pathology Museum (1930) opposite. Elevated, enclosed glass walkways provide further visual connections between the new building and two flanking buildings.

With the exception of the Gustavianum, the initiatives implemented by the master plan were controlled by Akademiska Hus. Seventy-three per cent of all the university's space is leased from Akademiska Hus and the two bodies have a symbiotic working relationship. The arrangement is viewed in a predominantly favourable light. With Akademiska Hus responsible for maintenance issues, the university appreciates that it is free from any maintenance backlog. Furthermore, when the institution outgrows a building it can relocate to another with much less hindrance than had the university owned it. However, the system of renting space from Akademiska Hus and other private landlords, whose objective is ultimately to make a profit, does arguably have implications on the image and coherence of the university's built environment at large. The buildings of Uppsala University do not aspire to architectonic uniformity. The most pronounced example of this is the English Park, where a melange of building materials and architectural styles from the mid-nineteenth to the early twenty-first centuries sit side by side. The buildings resulting from the university's expansion in the second half of the twentieth century do not employ analogous architectural or planning themes; neither do they show interest in statement architecture. In fact, development of the past five decades has been very modest and, arguably, prosaic. It has been concerned purely with function. Undoubtedly fitness for purpose is of prime importance, but a sense of place is vital in establishing the university as something with which to identify. Perhaps the lack of concern for this at Uppsala is a by-product of its rental system, in which new premises must be marketable should the university move out.

Nonetheless, the university is not devoid of an institutional identity. Its built environment is deliberately representative of the institutional motto, 'a tradition of constant renewal since 1477'. The essence of this is a fusion of tradition and history with innovatory research. The clearest manifestation of this conscious identification with its prestigious heritage was the resolution to retain and adapt the buildings of the English Park in the 1990s, demonstrating an awareness of the importance of historical association. In the 1990s the university also embarked upon a signage campaign, identifying each building with external signs with a consistent format. The aim was to construct a brand image to foster a sense of institutional belonging amongst its staff and students.

Fundamentally, the image of the university revolves around the Main Building, Carolina Redivivia and Gustavianum, and the green informal parkland that edifies the different university precincts. These three structures are amongst the most important landmarks of Uppsala itself, and so the identity of the university is intrinsically bound to that of the city and visa versa. That the university has sustained its unrivalled cultural presence within the city despite its continued centrifugal expansion towards the periphery is testimony to the strength of the identity that it has succeeded in forging.

2.141 Plan, De Uithof, Utrecht University

Utrecht University
Utrecht, Netherlands

Founded as an academic degree granting institution in 1636, Utrecht University has enjoyed a lengthy relationship with its host city. Like many continental universities, its historic buildings in the urban centre are much beloved and admired in Utrecht's architectural panorama. The most celebrated of its scattered inner-city premises is University Hall. Ingrained with history, the building physically manifests the spirit of the university's illustrious past. Although it dates back to the fifteenth century, its façade is a product of the nineteenth-century building boom amongst European universities. Built in a Dutch Renaissance style from 1891–1894, it is an elegant red brick structure with an L-shape plan and lively silhouette of dormer windows, chimneys and a lantern tower that functions to give the university a public façade of prestige and venerability. Yet progressively since the 1960s, the university has expanded beyond its central historic campus so that now only the law and humanities faculties are taught there. It has breached the inner-city perimeters to form two new campuses, the University College Utrecht just outside this perimeter, and De Uithof, further to the east.

The acquisition of De Uithof campus in 1958 was typical of the planning ideology of continental universities in post-war years. Restricted by city-centre facilities, often cramped and aged, many institutions relocated their science faculties to satellite campuses. Bland architecture, ad hoc planning and atmospheres of isolation and lifelessness, especially out of working hours, has frequently characterized these environments up to the present day. Initially De Uithof suffered from these failings. Its setting within park-like scenery of rivers and fields was, for many years, the only aspect of the campus that was greeted positively. However, it stands as a thought-provoking instance of a campus that has transformed itself through astute master planning and cutting-edge architecture into a vibrant, award-winning learning environment.

The construction history of De Uithof can be divided into three distinct chapters. The first chapter, extending from the early 1960s to the mid-1970s, saw the erection of Brutalist concrete giants scattered across the campus, beginning with the Marinus Ruppert Building (1963) by Sjoerd Wouda. The earliest development took place on the peripheral corners, thus creating a very low-density site. With the second phase of development, the spaces in between were filled in piecemeal fashion to respond to the needs of the moment.

2.142 University Library, Utrecht University
Photo: Jan Bitter

UTRECHT UNIVERSITY

2.144 Smarties, Utrecht University
Photo: AkzoNobel

2.143 The Bishops, Utrecht University
Photo: J. P. Fiering

This phase lasted until the end of the 1980s. Buildings assumed a variety of architectural mantles. The Martinus Langeveld Building (Martinus Langeveldgebouw), also by Wouda (1980) belonged to this phase. Formed of two conjoined square courts, it is a plain, red brick structure. With views over the countryside, the high-rise Went Building (Wentgebouw) has a façade strongly reminiscent of a punchcard. Designed by Teun Koolhaas, it was built 1971–1974. The phase is characterized by a sense of uncertainty and heedlessness, with no clear plan or vision for the university. The outcome was a distinct lack of coherence. Positioned far apart, the departments were isolated from one another and the campus was overshadowed by an atmosphere of fragmentation and remoteness, compounded by its separation from the city by a six-lane motorway. No one wanted to work or study there and, with no residences, no one had the opportunity to live there.[203]

The third period of De Uithof's development was inaugurated in 1988, when the architectural firm OMA and architect Art Zaaijer were commissioned to devise a master plan to reverse this gloomy state of affairs. The master plan aimed to transform the area from a desolate commuter campus to a community much more akin to the Anglo-American model. Amongst its chief objectives was to remedy the alienation between departments. 'The Uithof', Zaaijer advised, 'had to be cured from its addiction to space.' The master plan proposed a concentration of buildings of varying functions, to encourage social interaction. It prescribed a dense Kasbah-like layout. Within a compact layout, new construction was keenly attuned to location and relationships with neighbouring buildings. Since the programme has been instituted, the campus has begun to evolve into an architectonic environment of the most impressive standard.

Strengthened by commerce and motivated by an atmosphere of innovation, the Netherlands currently possesses one of the most vibrant and creative architectural scenes in the world. Since its rejuvenation began in the 1990s, De Uithof has exploited this culture and now stands as a showcase of ambitious modern architecture:

Utrecht University is not the only university having developed an impressive building programme, but other universities pale compared to what has been achieved at De Uithof by Dutch

architects of name and fame since the 1990s. Incidentally, the fact that only Dutch architects have been involved is remarkable in these days of increasing internationalisation.[204]

The Faculty for Economics and Management (1995) by the firm Mecanoo was the first in this parade ground of contemporary architecture. The large structure is arranged around three courtyards, each different in form and theme. One is called the Zen garden, composed of rocks and gravel enclosed by façades clad in wooden panels; the middle courtyard is a bamboo garden with a galvanized steel, first-floor walkway; surrounded by galvanized steel elevations, the third is a water garden with walls of glass and metal louvers. Through their diversity of materials and spaciousness, these gardens imbue the structure with an atmosphere of well-being and a range of visual experiences. The rest of the design exhibits similar variety. Diverse room plans, materials, and interchange between staircases and sloping ramps invest each area with its own identity. Each room has a view over the garden courts or across the natural polder landscape to the south.[205]

To its north-east is located the arresting Educatorium (1997). A central facility shared by the university, it contains two large lecture halls and examination rooms, a 1,000-seat canteen and a restaurant, and is conceived as a focus for social interaction for the staff and students spread over the site. Designed by the renowned Rem Koolhaas of OMA, it is a geometry-defying creation. The building has a multiple folded continuous concrete floor surface that rises from the ground floor through the building, curving back upon itself to create a projecting curve at the west end that then turns into a roof. This curious folding plane is the main organizing element in the design. Lecture theatres are located in the wedge shape above, while the cafeteria is located below the fold. A more traditional two-storey cube houses the examination rooms. Within, Koolhaas experiments with the spatial and circulation experience. Passing through thresholds without noticing them, the visitor imperceptibly glides from one level to another. Staircases are only present when the vertical distance to be covered so demands. Floors and internal walls are either transparent or illuminated, creating a shimmering, reflective interior.[206]

While Koolhaas displays the workings of his building through a transparent skin, Willem Jan Neutelings' Minnaert Building is a blunt, opaque box. Completed in 2002, the building provides shared facilities for the faculties of physics and astronomy, earth sciences, mathematics, and information studies, and is connected to their respective departmental buildings by elevated walkways. Three-storeys tall, the rectangular structure is clad in red-brown cement. Sprayed onto mesh that sporadically juts over steel tubes, the cement forms a pleated, leathery façade. Internally, the building is arranged around a central hall. The architects have yoked all the unprescribed space (for example, for circulation and services) that would typically be given over to tunnels of soulless corridors and voids, into a single cavernous space at the heart of the building. A common room, transit area and meeting spot, the hall is the nucleus of the building from which access is provided to almost all areas of the building. Half the space is occupied by a pool of water, into which rain water is conducted through funnels from the sloping roof above. Not only an aesthetic feature, this functions as an innovative energy management system that cools the building. Laboratories on the ground floor look out across landscaped gardens, and the triple height refectory at the east end gives access to a second floor roof terrace.[207]

The revitalization of De Uithof into a vibrant academic hub was acknowledged in 2004 with the relocation of the University Library from the historic city centre to a prominent central site at De Uithof, designed by Wiel Arets (Figure 2.142). A solid, shimmering mass, it is clothed in glass and black concrete imprinted with a pattern of bamboo. The relatively modest, tenebrous entrance produces a theatrical contrast to the space one finds within: a vast empty chamber, which at certain points spans the height, breadth or length of the structure.

A pivotal factor in the transformation of the campus was the decision to site student housing there. From 1998, a series of accommodation buildings, informed by the same values of innovation and imagination as their academic neighbours, began to appear. Temporary accommodation was provided at La Capanna, a complex of colourful containers. Permanent accommodation came in the form of the Cambridgelaan, designed by Rudy Uytenhaak; The Bishops, two graceful towers designed by Köther-Salman Architects (2007) (Figure 2.143); and Smarties (2008) by Marlies Rohmer (Figure 2.144). With student housing, a local bar was needed. This came in 2003 with the Basket Bar, a unique combination of a bar with a basketball

2.145 Basket Bar, Utrecht University
Photo: Luuk Kramer/NL Architects

court on its roof and a glass skylight as its focal point, designed by NL-Architects (Figure 2.145).

The development of De Uithof is not yet complete, yet its rejuvenation stands as an illuminating example of how to engineer a vibrant, visually exciting academic community from a previously isolated satellite campus. Today, De Uithof teems with life. The programme of densification and mixed-use espoused by OMA's masterplan has been a key factor in redressing its atmosphere of separation. Buildings are placed in close proximity and communal spaces are treated with importance, establishing the prerequisites for exchange and contact that facilitate a community ethos. The introduction of student housing greatly contributed to the mixed-use strategy, for now the campus stays alive after the end of the working day. In terms of architectural styles, there is no visual unity, but a sense of totality is achieved through the physical connection shared by the buildings. Walkways exist between many, such as the Minnaert Building and the Buys Ballot Laboratory, or the H. R. Kruyt Building and the Centrum Building, while many also abut one another. Aspects of the campus have attracted criticism, however. Koolhaas's Educatorium, for example, has been denounced as a labyrinth, valuing form over function. The lack of seating or ledges to encourage casual meeting is neglectful, while the industrial glass and concrete do not serve for a comfortable, warm environment.

The story of Utrecht's Uithof campus illustrates both the potential dangers of satellite campuses if their development is not guided by prior planning and the ameliorating effect that master planning can have. It advertises the lessons of mixed-use planning and dense layouts and suggests the vibrancy that can come with progressive, high-quality architecture. While the University Hall retains symbolic capital that serves to give the university a presence as a historic learning institution, the day to day activities of the university are increasingly being focused upon this site. Through its show ground of architectural experiments, De Uithof is earning Utrecht University an enviable reputation for innovation and forward-thinking.

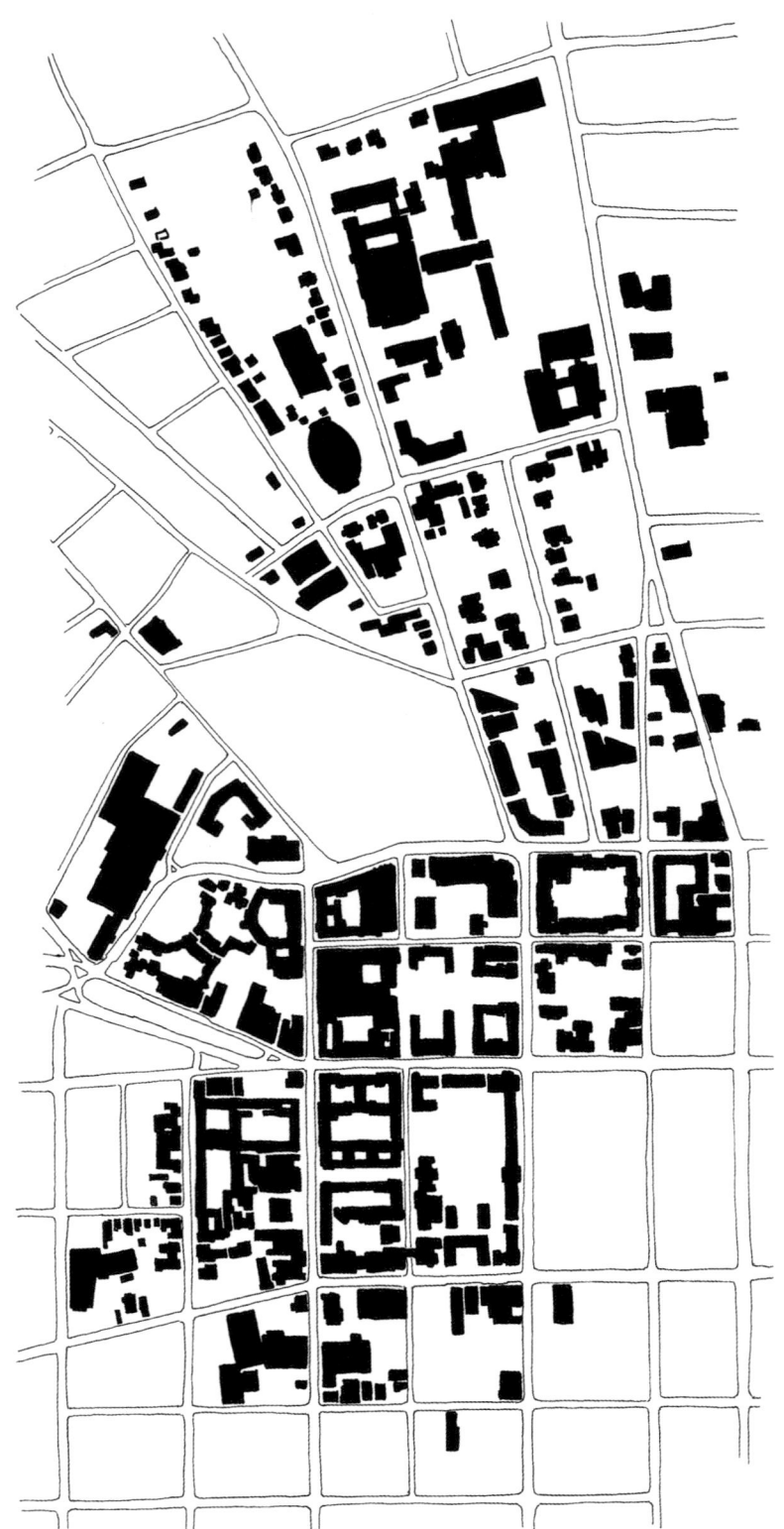

2.146 Plan, Yale University

Yale University
New Haven, USA

Yale University is, in many respects, a campus of two faces. On the one hand, it has been innately woven into its host city, New Haven, since it settled there in 1717. On the other, it has come to be characterized by an internalized world of enclosed courts and hidden gardens. Yale's complex persona reflects its complex planning history which has been in turn informed by the changing directions of its institutional self-identity and ambitions, and its relationship with New Haven.

New Haven was the first geometrically planned city in the colonies. Founded in 1638, it was laid out upon a grid plan of nine square blocks with the central square left as a 16-acre open green. In 1717, 16 years after its founding, Yale moved permanently to New Haven and its first building (constructed in the same year, razed 1775–1782) was built in conformity with the city's gridiron layout. Sited alongside the central green, the elongated rectangular building formed an imposing presence outwards to the town. Early Yale College adhered

2.147 Connecticut Hall, Yale University
Photo: Michael Marsland/Yale University

2.148 Harkness Quadrangle, Yale University
Photo: Michael Marsland/Yale University

to this pattern, setting its earliest buildings facing the Green in a linear arrangement that was unparalleled at earlier colonial campuses. The dormitory Connecticut Hall (1753) is the single remaining relic of this configuration (Figure 2.147). It is a modest yet genteel red brick building, typical of colonial university architecture.

By 1792, the institution's built environment consisted of two other buildings aside from Connecticut Hall: a chapel and a one-storey dining hall. Dissatisfied that the dormitory housed only half its student population, in 1792 the college's governing body took counsel from John Trumbull to plan the formal creation of a campus. Trumbull proposed a series of structures lining the broadside of the Green that faced out toward the city and underlined New Haven's geometric organization. New Haven Green was itself being remodelled as a grand city focal point, and Trumbull's design responded to this. His vision was bold and innovative. It comprised a progression of five buildings: the existing chapel and Connecticut Hall, a projected dormitory to the south, and another dormitory building and academic building to the north. In order to harmonize the old with the new, the shape of the new academic building echoed that of the chapel while the architecture of the dormitories emulated that of Connecticut Hall. Trumbull was keen to champion both the visual and pragmatic underpinnings of his plan: '[It] would admit of being pursued gradually, and whether partially or compleatly executed, would be in all its stages handsome.' Importantly, this marks the earliest documented concern in the United States that a campus should be aesthetically pleasing at each construction stage. Over a decade-long period, Trumbull's plan was executed. The sequence of five buildings formed the categorical image of Yale's campus, and was known as Yale Row or Old Brick Row (Figure 1.14). In creating an ambit along New Haven's chief urban axis, Old Brick Row gave the college an assertive and integral place at the heart of the community.[208]

The Row format enjoyed considerable currency at many schools in the early nineteenth century, including Dartmouth, Brown, Amherst, Colby and Bowdoin and directed Yale's expansion until the mid-nineteenth century. Yet later in the century, its popularity waned, being considered outmoded and prosaic as campus planning patterns became ever more complex and insular. In the mid-nineteenth century, Yale embarked upon a new phase of expansion that radically altered its physical character. Its orientation was turned away from the Green and the urban fabric of New Haven, and Yale withdrew behind screens of Gothic buildings. The fact that New Haven was moving away from its genteel colonial past towards an increasing industrialization seems no coincidence. This distinctive era in Yale's growth was begun by its new library, Dwight Hall (1842–1846) at the rear of the college's grounds. Designed by Henry Austin in a spare Gothic Revival idiom, it marked a distinct break from the hefty, unstylized buildings of Old Brick Row, and inverted the focus of the school inward to its library. In 1860, Old Brick Row (bar Connecticut Hall) was demolished and replaced gradually with a wall of five- to six-storey dormitories. With the construction of Farnham (1869), Durfee (1870) and Lawrance Halls (1885) and Battell Chapel (1876) to designs by architect Russell Sturgis, and Vanderbilt (1894) and Phelps Halls (1924) to designs by Charles Haight around a large internal court, Yale had effectively become an enclosed city within a city. Its campus – now known as Old Campus – became a tangible symbol of institutionalized learning and the school's increasing sense of superiority and self-interest. The space became a vessel of 'Yale myth' as the university increasingly became an 'arcadian never-never land', a recondite world shrouded in mystique divorced from everyday life.[209]

Old Campus remained the psychological heart of the campus, but by the early twentieth century Yale had expanded dramatically. A distinct science district, named Science Hill, had grown up in the nineteenth century stretching north of the core. But the growth had occurred without any overarching plan, leading to a rather incoherent sprawl of structures. By the 1910s this unbridled growth was recognized as a deterrent to increasing endowments and an obstacle to fostering community. To recover its sense of community, from 1919 until the Second World War Yale undertook a process of momentous reinvention. It was born of a context of widespread uneasiness that American collegiate life was becoming increasingly depersonalized as the organizational and physical fabric of these institutions mushroomed. Across America, the ancient models of Oxford and Cambridge, with their clubby intimacy and fellowship, were commonly perceived as the remedy to their problems, and the planning and architectural traditions of the English colleges wielded a growing influence upon many schools. Chief amongst these was the enclosed quadrangle format, championed as an ideal setting for the nurturing of an intellectual community. The quadrangle, with its monastic connotations, suited the new temper of introspection and exclusivity that prevailed at the country's leading schools.

2.149 Law School, Yale University
Photo: Michael Marsland/Yale University

This formula was imported to Yale by the prodigious influence of architect James Gamble Rogers. No other architect shaped the Yale that exists today more decisively than Rogers. His 1924 plan transformed Yale into an Oxbridge-inspired composition of inward-looking courtyards and secret landscapes, human-scaled and comfortable yet lyrical and engaging. The most successful of these spaces is the Harkness Quadrangle (1917–1921) (Figure 2.148). In plan, it appropriates the Oxbridge model of a cloistered realm accessible only through turreted gateways. Built on the west side of Old Campus, Rogers designed a complex of six differently-sized courts, dominated by a lordly tower. The arrangement exemplified Rogers's talents for site-specific modulation and tight compositions. The result is a sophisticated visual tapestry. Beginning in the large central court, the eye is drawn through a rich pattern of openings into the peripheral courtyards, each bounded by ranges enchanting in their multiplicity. Buildings differ in height, size and surface treatment, brought together by a rhythmic array of towers, turrets and gables. Rogers concerned himself little with the historical accuracy of his medieval architecture; it was the irregularities and idiosyncrasies of centuries of Oxbridge that inspired him. The Quadrangle was made more enclosed to the north and west, the sides which came into contact with the town. To flood the Quadrangle with as much sunlight as possible, building heights were pitched lower to the south than the north. The seemingly rambling, ad hoc progression of spaces and vistas of Harkness Quadrangle belies its careful contrivance. At the heart of the complex, the Harkness Tower rises proudly upward, functioning as a symbolic marker of the new, expanded university, its silhouette visible and bells audible across campus. Rogers's compositional ingenuity is supplemented by his capacity for historicism. The names of each courtyard were drawn from Yale's past, its locations before it settled in New Haven and early Yale institutions, such as Calliope and Brothers-in-Unity. Above each archway or door is an inscription exhorting the principles of the Yale community. The message is one of Yale's dense and powerful past, and its ideals and aspirations for the future. Above all, the Harkness Quadrangle powerfully demonstrates two qualities that Rogers brought to the campus: the art of composition and spatial experience, and the symbolic potential of the built environment as a bearer of meaning.[210]

Rogers designed several more important facilities at Yale. The Law School (1927–1931) was modelled on the London Inns of Court (Figure 2.149). Seemingly an adventitious composition that has organically grown over time, the Law School is rich with the same kind of historical resonance as Memorial Quadrangle. The Gothic Revival idiom was also embraced by other practitioners working at Yale at this time. Architect John Russell Pope was responsible for the Payne Whitney Gymnasium, built 1926–1932. An enormous, austere building at the western fringe of the campus, it takes the form of a robust tower flanked by two massive wings. It is 155 metres long and rising to 60 metres, it dominates the streetscape, and provides a bulwark presence to the north-western boundary of the university enforced by the architecture's martial overtones. The summit of the tower is crenellated, while its stocky, stepped towers expend a defensive air. The entrance is marked by a cathedral-like portal at the base of the tower adorned with sculpture celebrating Yale's sporting achievements.[211]

By the end of the 1920s, Yale was set firmly on a medievalizing course toward an ambiance of collegiate intimacy and venerable heritage. This was heightened in the 1930s by the inauguration of the residential college system, beginning with the transformation of the Harkness Quadrangle into two undergraduate colleges, Saybrook and Branford by the addition of dining halls, common rooms and libraries. The first seven colleges opened in 1933, a mixture of old and new construction. Each college was given its own identity, shaped by variations in style, size and planning, yet they were unified by a set of common features. Chief amongst these was the organizing principle of the courtyard. The dining hall was to be the focus of the central courtyard and a tower was to be sited over or near the main entrance. To the outside world, the colleges presented a façade of closed walls. Davenport College, designed by Rogers in 1931, makes for a particularly interesting example. Its interior court is Georgian in style, but its eastern exterior façade is Gothic. Its stone-mullioned bay windows with leaded casements and gabled roofline ensure an affiliation and continuation with Saybrook and Branford Colleges opposite. With the flourishing of the colleges, Yale was firmly cast in a historicizing mode, both in terms of its architecture and in its configuration of a medieval walled town sequestered from the surrounding city.[212]

The years following the Second World War, however, saw dramatic changes. Yale's new president, A. Whitney Griswold (1950–1963) shook off Yale's historical mantle by commissioning renowned architects to pioneer campus growth. The process began with Louis Kahn's art gallery (1953). On a commercial street at the southern termination of the campus, the simple, four-storey building introduced an angular, modernist glass and concrete aesthetic to Yale. The ground floor is given over to retail outlets, reflecting a rapport with its urban context that Yale had previously turned its back to. Modernism became a growing presence on campus, as works by eminent practitioners filled vacant plots. Gordon Bunshaft designed the Beinecke Rare Book Library, Paul Rudolph was responsible for the Art and Architecture Building, and Philip Johnson designed the Kline Science Centre. Each of these architects was given a free hand to respond to the project as they best saw fit, unrestrained by matters of stylistic coherence. 'Buildings, like people, ought to be different from another,' rationalized Griswold. The Beinecke Library (1961) signalled a break with traditional planning. It sits isolated like an island upon a huge granite plaza, its beauty intended to be appreciated from a distance, departing from Yale's tradition of buildings lining the streets.[213]

2.150 Ingalls Hockey Rink, Yale University
Photo: Michael Marsland/Yale University

The biggest modernist presence on campus was that of Eero Saarinen. His first work for the university was the Ingalls Hockey Rink, completed in 1958 (Figure 2.150). Built to the north of the historic campus, its avant-garde design must have caused a storm in its residential setting. Its exhilarating, curving roof is suspended on cables hung from a 100-metre reinforced concrete parabolic arch. Saarinen's second commission for Yale was two new colleges, Ezra Stiles and Morse Colleges. University commissions carried a particular resonance for Saarinen. To him, the college campus was the last stronghold of community spirit in an increasingly self-serving world and nurturing the fellowship and citizenship that was cultivated within Yale's older colleges was a priority in his designs for Morse and Stiles Colleges (Figure 1.43). Sited on the north-western edge of the central campus, the colleges are formed of irregular, interlocking spaces bounded by low-rise polygonal buildings interspersed with two high-rise towers. In sight of several of Yale's neo-Gothic buildings, the design translates the spaces, forms and textures of Gothic Revival into a modern idiom: vertical strip windows, rough stone walls, craggy silhouette and punctuating towers. Narrow pathways offered changing vistas through the colleges and into Old Yale, while the assymetrical room plans illustrated Saarinen's hope they would be 'as individual as possible, as random as those in an old inn'. The art of spatial experience that Rogers perfected earlier in the century was recalled in modernist form.[214]

Yale survived the experimental mood of the 1950s and 1960s better than many American campuses. In fact, it is one of the great repositories of modern architecture. The buildings are popular features of the campus landscape, and do not sit uneasily with the historicizing buildings of Rogers, Pope and others. Despite having undergone remarkable growth, variety and change in its physical environment, the university is united and consistent in its physical character. This consistency largely results from the fact that Yale's planning approach has been conditioned by two factors: the recurring form of the quadrangle and its interaction with its host city. Since the Old Campus was created in the mid-nineteenth century, enclosed quadrangles have formed the mainstay of Yale's planning strategy and created a distinctive spatial experience which has come to characterize the university. Many of its buildings surround and draw life from the courtyards almost invisible to the street. One of the chief delights for the pedestrian at Yale is catching glimpses of these green courts channelled through stone arches and doorways (Figure 2.151). The courtyard of Old Campus remains its spiritual centre. Entering Old Campus from New Haven Green via Phelps Gate (1896) is an evocative experience. The tunnel-like archway draws movement from New Haven's public realm into Yale's private, semi-sacred atmosphere. The university has espoused a long commitment to its exterior spaces. Beginning in the 1920s, noted landscape architect Beatrix Ferrand worked at Yale, designing and refining its outdoor spaces, such as Memorial Quadrangle. The courts of Memorial Quadrangle, the Law School, Sterling Library, Graduate School and colleges nurture a tranquillity and intimacy of scale that renders Yale with an easy, magnetic charm. They proffer spaces for individual reflection and ritual, thus nourishing an emotional attachment which is the basis for the school's dedicated and committed alumni base.

Yale's spatial organization has also been shaped by its relationship with its urban surroundings. Yale's construction has adhered to New Haven's historic gridded layout; its buildings lined the city's streets. The college's unusually long and narrow plan – over three kilometres long by one kilometre wide – means that no point on campus is ever more than one block distanced from the campus edge. However, Yale's initial openness and interaction with New Haven was replaced in the mid-nineteenth and early twentieth centuries by an attitude of aloofness as the school retreated into a private world of enclosed courtyards reflective of its growing institutionalism and distaste for New Haven's industrial character. In the post-war era, Yale again effected a connection with the city through Kahn's Art Gallery with its public façade incorporating a ground floor of retail units. This dual personality has resulted in a campus integrated into its urban context yet simultaneously psychologically distinct from it.

Yale's physical environment is also bound together by the consistency of the quality of its construction. Branford and Saybrook Colleges, for instance, radiate with the quality of materials and workmanship. The materials were carefully selected and worked to create a rich surface texture. At Branford and Saybrook, Rogers arranged stone in untooled, irregular chunks; in places he inserted sand blasted bricks to inject enriching colour and texture. This attention to detail inspired Eero Saarinen 40 years later, at Morse and Stiles Colleges. Faced with smaller budgets than Rogers, Saarinen sought an inventive way to replicate the sumptuous colours and textures of Rogers's stone by placing rough pieces of granite in moulds, into which concrete grout was poured in at high pressure.

Such attention to detail is, however, lacking in other areas of campus. Ease of movement is hindered by the system of signage around campus to guide pedestrians and identify buildings. Outside the core, some of the campus's open tracts have been neglected. The Ingalls Rink, for example, is ringed by an expanse of asphalt and parked cars, a somewhat less than satisfactory backdrop for one of Yale's great modern landmarks. Primarily, though, Yale takes its role as custodian of its valuable setting seriously. After a period of 'deferred maintenance' in the 1970s and 1980s, during which a miasma of neglect diffused over the campus, since 1993 the university has spent more than $4 billion on construction and renovation. The Sterling Memorial Library has undergone extensive restoration, the pinnacle of which is the new Irving S. Gilmore Music Library (1998), which has transformed an open-air courtyard into a magnificent, contemporary vaulted reading room. Twenty metres above the ground, Gothic-inspired arched trusses raise the gently curving roof creating a spacious, light place for study. Applauded both by students and architecture connoisseurs, it has become one of the most popular locations to study on campus.[215]

Over its three centuries, Yale has constantly rebuilt itself. Its original linear organization – Old Brick Row – was a distinctive planning solution for colonial academia that betokened the university's consentient attitude to New Haven. Its attempts to replicate the collegiate intimacy and institutional identity of Oxbridge caused this to be superseded by a planning agenda of cloistered courtyards and interlinked buildings. Its consistent planning approaches have united a stylistically varied campus and given it a definite identity. Yale is at once of, and yet divorced from the public sphere, imparting to its members a precious quality of specialness and privilege that ensures a strong alumni identification of inestimable value.

2.151 Yale University
Photo: Michael Marsland/Yale University

CHAPTER THREE
Designing the Twenty-First-Century Campus

The series of case studies that constituted the preceding chapter demonstrate how universities have striven to create educational environments responsive to their individual objectives and circumstances. Since the founding of the first university over 900 years ago, the university campus has born some of the most challenging and innovative examples of architecture and planning. Yet why does an institution that is ostensibly dedicated to enlightening and enriching those that pass through its doors, demonstrate such concern over its physical appearance? Academic reputation is undoubtedly the primary objective for any higher education organization, and high-quality education continues as the prerequisite in attracting the best calibre students and faculty. However, this alone is no longer enough. All but the most exclusive universities are facing increasing competition for scholars and staff, and an aesthetically pleasing and emotionally compelling campus is one way to tip the balance.

At a lucky few universities, this type of environment has been created organically, serendipitously over time. The narrow, winding passages and secret gardens lying in wait behind arched gateways of the University of Cambridge exemplifies this scenario. But, predominantly, its accomplishment is the result of a thoughtfully-conceived, well-adopted and properly-monitored campus plan that has shaped its design.

A campus plan is a comprehensive plan for physical growth, predicated upon a needs assessment responsive to the university's vision, academic strategy, history and culture. The plan outlines and explains the function, scale, siting, and cost of new development and the improvement of existing facilities to produce an academic setting that is both functional and special. In essence, a campus plan functions to:

- **Communicate institutional values and missions**. All too frequently, planning decisions do not reflect the institutional vision. University leaders do not recognize how physical changes (creating additional parking or a new building for instance) can enforce or counteract their institution's values and mission.
- **Create a sense of place**. Attractive, welcoming spaces enhance the ways in which people experience a campus. Both memory and sense of place invoke the same part of the brain – the hippocampus – revealing the importance of the physical environment in creating meaningful experiences. Creating memorable spaces on campus where people can interact provides occupants with a feeling of institutional belonging.

  Memorable places also act to immediately identify institutions. Uniquely attractive spaces, such as the University of Virginia's Lawn, or significant buildings or constellations of buildings, such as the Gilbert Scott Building at the University of Glasgow (Figure 3.1) or the Hackett Buildings at the University of Western Australia, have come to symbolize the university as a whole. Such recognizable places establish a campus brand, tying the idea and reputation of the university to its physical image. The campus ranks amongst the university's most effective marketing tools. It can brand the university, establishing the identity and recognition that many institutions covet to help them stand out in an intensely competitive market. Especially in the United States and United Kingdom, in-person campus visits are increasingly important. In 2002 the front page of *The Boston Globe* reported that 'a study…presented at a national conference of college admissions counsellors ranked the campus visit first among 15 "influential information sources" considered by college applicants.'[1]
- **Facilitate social and organizational change**. As well as shaping memory and identity, physical change is a powerful catalyst for change along other avenues. A new science quarter, for instance, with shared facilities between faculties may encourage further interdisciplinary communication, galvanizing cutting-edge research and course programmes. The design of buildings and spaces can have real effects upon learning patterns and community ethos. Nevertheless, it is crucial to remember that when planning decisions are made on an individual, departmental basis rather than on an institutional-wide basis, their effects will not necessarily promote the greater aims and values of the university as a whole. Decisions made in isolation from the long-term and bigger picture tend only to provide stopgap solutions.

3.1 Gilbert Scott Building, University of Glasgow
Photo: University of Glasgow

Campus planning is a complex procedure. A master plan ties together all campus systems to create a strategy for approaching the physical, social, intellectual and sustainability challenges with which the university must contend in the twenty-first century. In general terms, three fundamental physical form-giving components tend to constitute the basis of any plan:

- Landscape
- Buildings
- Circulation

These components overlap, coincide and work together to support the core mission and values of the university.

LANDSCAPE

The campus landscape should be viewed in terms of a sequence of encountered experiences, a visual progression of connected landscapes met with on the journey through campus. Frequently, little heed has been given to ensure that this experiential sequence is one of fluidity and lucidity and the role of landscape within the campus whole is diminished.

A well-ordered landscape shapes and strengthens the campus plan, reinforces circulation routes, roots the university to its locality, and expresses its individual character and values. The landscape of Rice University epitomizes this. The 1910 General Plan used trees and hedgerows planted in *allées* to direct vistas and movement. They played a far greater role than buildings in establishing rhythm, sequence and directionality upon the vast, empty Texan plain.

As at Rice, landscaping should be used to define the hierarchy and layout of pedestrian and vehicular circulation. This can be achieved by the consistent planting of trees that give structure, pedestrian pathways that are pleasant to traverse, and coherent way-finding signage.

The landscape should also respond to its location by reflecting the natural environment of the region and its climate. Planting native vegetation is one way of achieving this. At Stanford, for instance, Frederick Law Olmsted planted Californian species of oak and poppies at home in the Palo Alto setting. In so doing he enhanced the campus's identity through a sense of belonging to a specific place or region. The cacti at Arizona State University and the peppermint trees at the University of Western Australia both exemplify how regional plants can enforce a sense of place. To reflect the climate, exterior spaces can be screened and shaped to promote user comfort. Again at Stanford, arched walkways were an integral design feature planned to offer protection from the intense Californian sun and have become a visual emblem of the university. Landscapes thus designed can be intuitional markers of identity. Beatrix Farrand's creation at Princeton of a coherent landscape policy, which advocated native species planted in response to existing building lines or potential construction sites, set in place a landscape heritage that has nourished the campus's pride of place.

BUILDINGS

Open spaces and the buildings that frame them work in tandem to determine the identity and quality of a campus. When planning new structures, the dictum that 'every campus is the sum of its parts' is an important one. All buildings must function collectively on campus to create a lucid, connected whole. The task lies in designing buildings that strengthen the master plan, perform their individual functions, respond to their context and accord to the overarching campus image.

Each university environment should aim towards establishing an individual character, and this can be realized through architecture in terms of materials, style, scale and so forth. The University of Colorado at Boulder well illustrates a campus that has consistently applied a defined set of building principles to create a distinctive identity. Its architect, Charles Klauder, inaugurated a series of design guidelines that established a repertoire of scales, massing, forms and materials. This framework has allowed succeeding architects the scope for experimentation whilst preserving Colorado's distinct identity. Similarly Peking University has utilized a framework of quadrangular planning and traditional Chinese architectural motifs. Harvard Yard too has consistently built to coherent principles, resulting in one of the most resonant spaces in the university realm. Although its constituent buildings exhibit a variety of architectural styles, because they utilize common materials (predominantly red brick), a coherent scale and are planned around quadrangles, they appear unified. The University of Oxford is an example of an institution hundreds of years old whose setting vividly narrates the changing architectural tastes of the centuries. Yet because of its extensive use of limestone, consistent scale and quadrangular organization, it's environment is exceptionally harmonious.

Guidelines for a homogenous and harmonious architecture can be a key factor in creating a sense of place upon campus. However, it does not follow that all buildings need be identical; creating a coherent and consistent architectural image does not necessitate reproducing existing structures. Of greater importance is achieving a masterly synthesis of scale, materials, colours, textures and landscapes. Architectural features such as rooflines and fenestration can often provide distinctive visual identities, for example. The challenge is to tread the line between unity and triteness. As Oxford and Harvard Yard demonstrate, changing architectural fashions can be blended harmoniously without becoming an unsightly hodgepodge provided that buildings are planned with skill and originality. Each building on campus should assert its individuality within the entity, but simultaneously, when looked at in context, should be seen as contributing to the identity of the university as a whole.

Some campus buildings from their outset have been intended as landmarks. Indeed, signature buildings have played a key role in university design for many centuries. These structures can physically encapsulate the university's missions and identity, particularly when sited in a conspicuous location or fulfilling a conspicuous function, such as a library. Successful examples bestow the campus with an architectural statement that confirms the institution's academic prestige and forward-thinking.

Commanding locations, such as the termination or intersection of axes, may invite the construction of a unique building. The Low Library at Columbia University exemplifies this. It not only served a central role as the library but moreover was sited as the climax of the campus's Beaux-Arts axial plan. It has since become an icon of the institution. A location at the entryway of campus also often justifies a landmark. Acting as gateways between the public and scholastic realms, structures in these locations can symbolize the public face of the university to its neighbourhood and visitors. Frank Gehry's Stata Center at MIT has this role.

As the Stata Centre demonstrates, universities are increasingly looking to distinguish themselves by commissioning landmark structures from internationally-renowned architects. Typically awe-inspiring and striking, the design of these buildings and their headline-generating potential can mesmerize trustees and donors alike into delivering funds that would not be as forthcoming for a less colourful commission. Nevertheless, landmark buildings do carry risks:

- **Campus harmony:** A campus of notable architecture is undoubtedly something to aspire to, but if each building was conceived to be different then each would lose their significance and the environment would descend into stylistic chaos. The campus's visual integrity would be sacrificed.
- **Longevity:** Will the 'starchitecture' that some universities are commissioning today as publicity or branding devices have long-term appeal? Many of the individualistic modernist structures of the post-war years, then considered heroic representations of the modern age, are now considered outmoded and obsolete. The iconic architecture of this age is open to the same fate.
- **Cost:** Iconic architecture typically runs to higher-than-average costs and often exceeds budgets.

Universities have long stood at the forefront of cutting-edge architecture. King's College Chapel, Cambridge, or Frank Lloyd Wright's Florida Southern College both symbolize how successful iconic design and star architects can be in a campus environment. Certainly, universities should continue to push the boundaries of architectural innovation in pursuit of design excellence but this experimentation should always take place within the framework of the overall master plan and complement the identity of the institution as a whole.

Key factors to consider when planning buildings:

- Produce an index of basic characteristics within core campus buildings.

- Systematize these characteristics into design guidelines outlining general terms such as scale, materials, colours, textures and so forth.
- Use these guidelines as criteria for assessing building proposals.
- Consider the landscape when designing buildings.

CIRCULATION

The term circulation encompasses all the elements involved in the movement of people, goods and services across campus, and the movement and storage of cars. Essentially, therefore, campus circulation can be divided into three systems: service vehicles, car movement and parking, and pedestrians. These three systems should be logically structured by the master plan.

Circulation issues addressed within the master plan should include:

- The degree to which foot and bicycle circulation is advocated and how much vehicular transport is permitted.
- How close vehicles can come to core buildings and spaces.
- Creating a campus with a sense of safety.

Many universities prioritize vehicular circulation, often to the detriment of the campus as a whole. The well-planned environment should, in contrast, give precedence to the pedestrian through the provision of spacious footpaths linking lecture theatres, libraries and recreational facilities, and consigning vehicular roads to peripheral campus areas. Prioritizing pedestrian movement does have the effect of restricting the size of the campus, but vibrant pedestrian activity is what lends a sense of life and community to an institution. Circulation ways should connect campus destinations hierarchically, so that the largest volumes of pedestrian activity are routed along chief desire lines, heightening potential for social interaction and the perceived sense of security through mass pedestrian activity.

Storing cars is an almost ubiquitous problem upon university campuses. Although offering staff and students parking spaces close to every destination is a desirable amenity, its realization fractures the campus. It requires buildings to be constructed at large distances apart, reducing a campus's 'walkability' and diminishing the sense of safety and community. University planners must be equally aware, however, of the repercussions of surrounding the campus with a necklace of parking. Its presence may damage the image of the campus as well as create a hostile barrier to surrounding neighbourhoods to the cost of community relations. The ideal master plan should provide a carefully conceived circulation and parking system in combination with mixed-use planning to moderate the demand for car parking.

GOOD PRACTICE

A well-designed estate, lucidly organized with attractive buildings and connecting landscapes is a valuable tool. This statement is widely acknowledged amongst university leaders, yet it is not widely acted upon. The ameliorating potential of physical change upon a campus is habitually restricted because of the attitude of university leaders, often falling into three categories:

- **Don't know:** those who are unaware of the importance of the physical fabric of the campus.
- **Don't care:** those who may be aware of the significance of a campus of quality, but regard the physical environment as divorced from the practicalities of university leadership and are apathetic to high-quality design and pursuing a campus planning strategy.
- **Don't understand:** those who appreciate the relevance of campus planning and aspire to best practice, but through misguidance adopt planning strategies that fail to improve the campus and can, in fact, impair it.

Successfully developing and executing a master plan is, undoubtedly, no easy feat. Achieving excellence in design necessitates high standards, hard discussions, an adherence to principles and a refusal to compromise long-term goals for short-term convenience.

How should the practicalities of developing and executing a campus plan be approached? To advocate a single method would be ill-advised and naive. Each institution should be moulded by a plan reflective of its own circumstances. Yet, certain steps for producing an effective master plan can be universally applied to all universities:

1. **Commitment:** Adhering to the prescriptions of a master plan is demanding, and bears fruit only over the long term. From the outset, participating parties must recognize the extent of the commitment involved in devising and implementing a master plan and ensure that the structures are in place to allow its realization over a prolonged period.
2. **Institutional strategy:** A master plan should be a tool to implement strategy; it should not be considered *the* strategy. Oftentimes, master plans are prepared out of context of the larger vision of the university. The defining element in planning for a new campus, enlargement or re-organization, should always be the strategic missions and values of the institution. The university's mission statement and academic plan affirms its objectives and projections for components such as courses, services, facilities, class size, fiscal resources and so on. These prescriptions influence the form the master plan will take.
3. **Leadership:** The formation of the leadership group – that is the group responsible for the synthesis and implementation of the master plan – is critical to its success. The enthusiasm for and familiarity with planning for physical change of university administrators, trustees, architects, and consultants can vary, and thus the selection of the leadership is an important early task. The group has several responsibilities:
    - To maintain a consistent membership. The planning effort should be directed by a small group of senior officers and non-executive officers of the institution ensuring sufficient authority for the group's decisions to hold sway. Its membership should remain constant so that the driving ethos of the project is not diluted.
    - To maintain a commitment to meeting the strategic objectives of the university in the long-term. The group decides whether an individual scheme accords within the master plan. Its leadership should ensure that the university's overreaching objectives do not become subservient to any single building project or to the whims of any single president or donor.
    - To ensure that funds are judiciously allocated to component projects and that each project spends these funds wisely to support the entire vision of the master plan. When seeking to deliver site-wide infrastructure development (green and hard landscaping, outdoor furnishings, etc.), the leadership should take note that coupling together infrastructure costs with individual building projects can lead to a disjointed environment.
    - To contract professional services, beginning with a master planner to prepare the master plan.
4. **Master plan:** The two principal form-giving components of a campus are the site and the institutional strategy. A master plan is vital in coordinating the many and, sometimes, conflicting uses of the site and specifications of the strategy, and coalescing these into a long-range planning tool. Their long-term function is crucial. More prescriptive plans, such as that devised for Columbia University by McKim, Mead and White, can prosper if scheduled to be executed as set-pieces in a limited time-span, but it is more pragmatic to adopt a longer-reaching scope. Master plans can be undermined if they are too rigid; the result of this can be that a plan has to be amended in its early stages, causing its validity to be questioned. Rather, plans should accommodate changing attitudes, styles and technology. Nevertheless, a fine line must be trod between efficacious long-range forecasting and diluted, indeterminate planning.
5. **Master planner:** This is often known as the campus or university architect, and may be internal or external to the institution. The purpose of the master planner is to reconcile the institutional mission statement with the physical environment, and guide its development. Generally speaking, the role is best filled by an appointment external to the university because it lends to the master planner a detachment that is conducive to fulfilling their purpose. For example,

a master planner should temper the clamouring influence of individual faculties or architects whose interests lay in ensuring the completion of their particular building project and not in the interests of the wider plan.

The selection of the master planner is a delicate decision. The task requires sound judgement and diplomacy. A successful appointment, though, engaged for a term of, say, five years, is amongst the most important ingredients for realizing a master plan.

In the early decades of the twentieth century, both Princeton and Yale were transformed by the dynamic visions of master planners, respectively Ralph Adams Cram and James Gamble Rogers. Cram and Rogers changed the characters of the two pre-existing campuses into a neo-Gothic realm of cloistered quadrangles, in response to the universities' new sense of elitism and introversion. The impact of the two master plans was prodigious, and at each university cultivated a sense of place that continues to define the institutions to the present day.

6. **Monitor and review:** The master-planning process should be reviewed periodically to ensure its objectives are being met, and to allow for new information or changing circumstances to be factored into the plan. Monitoring ensures that those responsible for the plan's implementation are held to account for its progress, either annually or biannually. If a course of monitoring and review are followed, then the master plan will continue to thrive long after its formation and the quality and efficiency of the university estate will flourish.

The demanding nature of a master plan may run counter to the daily pressures faced by university administrators, yet the long-term and measured direction of a master plan is the most efficient and effectual route to an aesthetic campus that will serve the institution for years to come.

Notes

PREFACE

1   C. Klauder and H. Wise, *College Architecture in America*, Scribner & Sons, New York and London, 1929, p. 1.

CHAPTER ONE
UNIVERSITY PLANNING AND ARCHITECTURE 1088–2010: A CHRONOLOGY

1   This discussion features only those institutions recognized in the strict sense of the word as a university, as an institution of higher education and research which issues academic degrees. In view of this definition, the classification of many of the oldest learning institutions as de facto ancient universities in continuous operation can be contentious. Unlike the European universities, non-western institutions of higher learning were not autonomous corporations of scholars and were never known to issue degrees to their graduates and therefore do not meet what many hold to be the technical definition of university. However, there were important centres of learning that can be compared to the European universities, such as Nalanda in India and Nanjing University in China.

2   R. Rait, *Life in the Medieval University*, Cambridge: Cambridge University Press, 1912, p. 7; F. Rhodes, *The Creation of the Future: The Role of the American University*, Ithaca and London: Cornell University Press, 2001, p. 2.

3   S. Ferruolo, '*Parisius-Paradisus*: the city, its schools, and the origins of the University of Paris', in T. Bender (ed.), *The University and the City: From Medieval Origins to the Present*, New York and Oxford: Oxford University Press, 1988, p. 23.

4   A. Gieysztor, 'Management and Resources', in W. Rüegg (ed.), *A History of the University in Europe: Universities in the Middle Ages*, vol. I, Cambridge: Cambridge University Press, 2003, pp. 136–8; P. Grendler, *The Universities of the Italian Renaissance*, Baltimore and London: Johns Hopkins University Press, 2002, p. 18.

5   L. Cremin, *American Education: The Colonial Experience 1607–1783*, New York: Harper & Row, 1970, p. 198; Grendler, op. cit., p. 172.

6   G. Tyack, 'The architecture of the University and the Colleges', in J. Prest (ed.), *The Illustrated History of Oxford University*, Oxford and New York: Oxford University Press, 1993, p. 86; P. Turner, *Campus: An American Planning Tradition*, Cambridge, Mass., and London: Architectural History Foundation, 1995, p. 9; C. Andrews, *Oxford Scene*, Oxford: Chris Andrews Publications, 2000, p. 7.

7   Tyack, 1993, op. cit., pp. 87–8.

8   Turner, op. cit., p. 10.

9   He is referred to as a conqueror of Gothic by Corbet Owen in his *Carmen Pindaricum in Theatrum Sheldonianum in solennibus magnifici operis Encaeniis recitatum Julii die 9 anno 1669*.

10   P. Rudolph, *The American College and University: A History*, Georgia: University of Georgia Press, 1990, pp. 5–6; V. Green, *A History of Oxford University*, London: Batsford, 1974, p. 49.

11   Quoted in Turner, op. cit., p. 23.

12   Ibid., pp. 24–7; T. Gaines, *The Campus as a Work of Art*, New York: Praeger, 1991, p. 19.

13   Turner, op. cit., pp. 21, 37.

14   M. Perry Chapman, *American Places: In Search of the Twenty-First Century Campus*, Connecticut: Praeger, 2006, p. 6; B. Edwards, *University Architecture*, London and New York: Spon Press, 2000, p. 15.

15   Chapman, op. cit., p. 12; Turner, op. cit., p. 101.

16   C. Thwing, *American Colleges: Their Students and Work*, New York: G. P. Putnam's Sons, 1878, p. 48; D. Schulyer, 'Frederick Law Olmsted and the origins of modern campus design', *Planning for Higher Education*, vol. 25, Winter 1996–1997, 2.

17   Chapman, op. cit., pp. 18–19; Turner, op. cit., pp. 163–7.

18   M. Montalvo, *Havana: History and Architecture of a Romantic City*, New York: Monacelli, 2000, p. 256; Turner, op. cit., pp. 196–202; Chapman, op. cit., pp. 19–20.

19   P. Gerbod, 'Resources and management', in W. Rüegg (ed.), *A History of the University in Europe: Universities in the Nineteenth and Early Twentieth Centuries (1800–1945)*, vol. III, Cambridge: Cambridge University Press, 2004, pp. 102–3.

20   Quoted in M. Klinge, 'Teachers', in Rüegg (ed.), 2004, op. cit., p. 160.

NOTES

21 Marburg and Freiburg Universities did adopt a neo-Gothic style, but this was unusual for mainland Europe.
22 For further information see: C. Cunningham and P. Waterhouse, *Alfred Waterhouse 1830–1905: Biography of a Practice*, Oxford: Oxford University Press, 1992.
23 G. Zhaoye (ed.), *World Architecture 1900–2000: A Critical Mosaic, Vol 9: East Asia*, Vienna and New York: Springer-Verlag, 2000, p. 51; Turner, op. cit., pp. 114–16.
24 Quoted in D. Kenney et al., *Mission and Place: Strengthening Learning and Community through Campus Design*, Westport: Greenwood Press, 2005, p. 195.
25 Quoted in Turner, op. cit., p. 117.
26 A. Duke, *Importing Oxbridge. English Residential Colleges and American Universities*, New Haven and London: Yale University Press, 1996, p. 52.
27 Thomas Gaines has suggested that the first appearance of Collegiate Gothic was at Trinity College in Hartford, Connecticut in 1878. English architect William Burges designed Seabury and Jarvis Halls in this style, reminiscent of St John's College, Cambridge. Bryn Mawr's buildings were, however, most probably far more influential. Gaines, op. cit., p. 86.
28 Turner, op. cit., pp. 223–7.
29 Turner, op. cit., pp. 241–4.
30 R. Adams Cram, 'Princeton architecture', *The American Architect*, 21 July 1909, 24.
31 S. Muthesius, *The Postwar University: Utopianist Campus and College*, New Haven and London: Yale University Press, 2000, p. 3; Turner, op. cit., pp. 249–50; D. Doordan, *Twentieth-Century Architecture*, London: Lawrence King, 2001, p. 181.
32 Chapman, op. cit., p. 41; Doordan, op. cit., p. 36; K. Frampton, *Modern Architecture: A Critical History*, London: Thames and Hudson, 1997, p. 248.
33 Turner, op. cit., p. 251.
34 Doordan, op. cit., p. 183.
35 Chapman, op. cit., p. 42.
36 Turner, op. cit., p. 262.
37 W. Mitchell, *Imagining MIT: Designing a Campus for the Twenty-First Century*, Cambridge, Mass.: MIT Press, 2007, pp. 29–33, 121.
38 Quoted in Muthesius, op. cit., p. 49.
39 Muthesius, op. cit., p. 53; Gaines, op. cit., p. 63.
40 T. Birks, *Building the New Universities*, Newton Abbot: David and Charles, 1972, p. 9; Muthesius, op. cit., p. 95.
41 Muthesius, op. cit., pp. 114, 142–5.
42 Ibid., p. 222.
43 Ibid., pp. 227, 230–1.
44 Quoted in J. Barnett, 'The new collegiate architecture at Yale', *Architectural Record*, April 1962, vol. 131, 129.
45 Turner, op. cit., p. 97.
46 Turner, p. 297.
47 R. Rhinehart, *Princeton University: The Campus Guide*, New York: Princeton Architectural Press, 1999, pp. 110–11.
48 Chapman, op. cit., p. 49.
49 See J. Merrick, 'Empty vessels: eye-con architecture', *Independent*, 15 October 2008; M. Weaver, 'The truth about those iconic buildings: the roofs leak, they're dingy and too hot', *Guardian*, 14 October 2006.
50 M. Pearce, *University Builders*, Chichester: Academy Press, 2001, p. 15.

CHAPTER TWO
CASE STUDIES

1 T. Faber, *A History of Danish Architecture*, Copenhagen: Det Danske Selskab, 1978, pp. 188–9.
2 O. Lind, *ArkitekturFortaellinger – om Aarhus Universitets bygninger*, Aarhus: Arhus Universitets Forskningsfond, 2003, p. 171.
3 W. Wang (ed.), *World Architecture 1900–2000: A Critical Mosaic, Vol 3: Northern Europe, Central Europe, Western Europe*, Vienna: Springer-Verlag, 2000, p. 115.
4 Lind, op. cit., p. 154.
5 P. Skriver, 'The University of Aarhus: a long-term project', *Casabella*, no. 584, 1991, 63.
6 P. Lykke, *A Pictorial History of the University of Aarhus*, Aarhus: Aarhus Universitetsforlag, 2001, p. 98.
7 A. Dolkart, *Morningside Heights: A History of Its Architecture and*

Development, New York: Columbia University Press, 1998, pp. 121–30; L. Roth, *McKim, Mead and White Architects*, London: Harper & Row, 1984, pp. 190–5; J. Robson, *A Guide to Columbia University*, New York: Columbia University Press, 1937, p. 35; F. Passanti, 'The Design of Columbia in the 1890s, McKim and his Client', *Journal of Society of Architectural Historians*, May 1977, vol. 36, 78–80.

8   Passanti, op. cit., p. 74; Roth, op. cit., p. 191; Dolkart, op. cit., pp. 123, 140.

9   Dolkart, op. cit., pp. 164–70 and 198; M. Susi, *Columbia University and Morningside Heights*, San Francisco: Arcadia Publishing, 2007, p. 41.

10 Quoted in Stern et al., *New York 1960: Architecture and Urbanism between the Second World War and the Bicentennial*, New York: Monacelli Press, 1995, p. 739.

11 Ibid., pp. 750, 879–80; Dolkart, op. cit., pp. 200, 337.

12 Dolkart, op. cit., p. 160.

13 Muthesius, op. cit., pp. 205–07; K. Kiem, *The Free University Berlin (1967–1973): Campus Design, Team X Ideals and Tectonic Invention*, Weimar: VDG, 2008, p. 22.

14 Kiem, op. cit., p. 26.

15 Feld et al., *Free University Berlin*, London: Architectural Association, 1999, p. 97; Kiem, op. cit., p. 52.

16 Kiem, op. cit., pp. 52, 144; H. Hertzberger, *Lessons for Students in Architecture*, Rotterdam: 010 Publishers, 2005, pp. 116–17; Feld et al., op. cit., p. 25.

17 Muthesius, op. cit., pp. 220–1.

18 Kiem, op. cit., pp. 14, 98; C. Brensing, 'The Free University still embodies the social and architectural dynamic of the 1960s', *The Architects' Journal*, 15 September 2005, vol. 222, no. 9, 34.

19 Brensing, op. cit., p. 36; Kiem, op. cit. pp. 54, 162; D. Neuman, (ed.), *Building Type Basics for College and University Facilities*, Hoboken, NJ: Wiley, 2003, p. 61.

20 Brensing, op. cit., pp. 36–7; Neuman, op. cit., pp. 61–3.

21 Turner, op. cit., pp. 23–7; B. Bunting, *Harvard: An Architectural History*, Cambridge, Mass. and London: Belknap Harvard, 1985, pp. 5–6.

22 Rudolph, op. cit., p. 24; Turner, op. cit., p. 28; Bunting, op. cit., p. 23

23 H. Morrison, *Early American Architecture: From the First Colonial Settlements to the National Period*, New York: Dover Publications, 1987, p. 466.

24 Bunting, op. cit., pp. 39–42.

25 Ibid., p. 124.

26 Ibid., p. 189.

27 Ibid., pp. 235–41.

28 Quoted in ibid., p. vi.

29 *Sovietkoye Iskusstvo*, 28 February 1947. Quoted in A. Tarkhanov and S. Kavtaradze, *Stalinist Architecture*, London: Laurence King, 1992, pp. 120–32.

30 A. Ikonnikov, *Russian Architecture of the Soviet Period*, Moscow: Raduga Publishers, 1988, p. 234; Tarkanov, op. cit., p. 120; Doordan, op. cit., p. 186; W. Brumfield, *Landmarks of Russian Architecture: A Photographic Survey*, Amsterdam: Gordon and Breach, 1997, p. 230.

31 Ikonnikov, op. cit., p. 234.

32 V. Anisimov, *Architectural Guide to Moscow*, Rotterdam: 010 Publishers, 1993, p. 98.

33 C. Jencks, *The Iconic Building: The Power of Enigma*, London: Frances Lincoln, 2005, p. 91.

34 Tarkanov, op. cit., p. 136.

35 J. Cody, *Building in China: Henry K. Murphy's 'Adaptive Architecture' 1914–1935*, Hong Kong: The Chinese University Press, 2001, p. 158.

36 Quoted in D. Edwards, *Yenching University*, New York: United Board for Christian Higher Education in Asia, 1959, p. 223.

37 Edwards, 1959, op. cit., pp. 216–20.

38 H. Murphy, 'Revised programme of requirements of the new group of buildings for Peking University', 24 December 1919, p. 5.

39 J. Stuart, *Fifty Years in China: The Memoirs of John Leighton Stuart: Missionary and Ambassador*, New York: Random House, 1954, p. 56.

40 J. L. Cohen and J. A. Cohen, *China Today and Her Ancient Treasures*, New York: Abrams, 1980, p. 239; Cody, op. cit., p. 121.

41 T. D. Webb (ed.), *Building Libraries for the 21st Century: The Shape of Information*, Jefferson, NC: McFarland & Company, 2000, pp. 54–7.

NOTES

42 Edwards, 1959, op. cit., p. 216.
43 Rhinehart, op. cit., pp. 2–7; Turner, op. cit., pp. 47–50; R. Gambee, *Princeton*, New York and London: Norton, 1998, p. 156.
44 Rhinehart, op. cit., pp. 9–12.
45 Ibid., pp. 18, 23–37.
46 Letter from Wilson to his wife, 26 July 1899. Quoted in Turner, op. cit., p. 227.
47 R. Adams Cram, 'Princeton Architecture', *The American Architect*, 21 July 1909, 24.
48 Ibid., p. 25.
49 Rhinehart, op. cit., pp. 42–3.
50 Ibid., pp. 69–71.
51 Ibid., pp. 101–2, 109–11; C. Leigh, 'Must the minimum be the maximum?', *Princeton Alumni Weekly*, 19 May 1999. Accessed online: http://paw.princeton.edu/issues/2009/05/13/sections/search-and-archives/search.xml (accessed 5 June 2009)
52 D. Egbert, 'The architecture and the setting,' in C. Osgood et al. *The Modern Princeton*, Princeton: Princeton University Press, 1947, p. 47.
53 Quoted in D. Kenney et al., op. cit., p. 145.
54 D. McGuire (ed.), *Beatrix Jones Farrand (1872–1959): Fifty Years of American Landscape Architecture*, Washington DC: Dumbarton Oaks Research Library and Collection, 1982, pp. 59–63.
55 See U. Kultermann, 'Education and Arab identity. Kamal El Kafrawi: University of Qatar, Doha', *Architectura*, 1996, vol. 26, 84–88, for more information.
56 El Kafrawi, *Design Philosophy*, 1992. Accessed online: www.archnet.org/library/files/one-file.jsp?file_id=708 (accessed 8 January 2010).
57 Kultermann, 1996, op. cit., p. 85; El Kafrawi, op. cit.
58 Kultermann, 1996, op. cit., p. 86; El Kafrawi, op. cit.
59 Ibid.
60 Ibid.
61 El Kafrawi, op. cit.
62 Ibid.
63 A. Salama, 'When good design intentions do not meet users' expectations: exploring Qatar University campus, outdoor spaces', *International Journal of Architectural Research*, 2008, vol. 2, issue 2, 71.
64 Quoted in S. Fox, *Rice University: Campus Guide*, New York: Princeton Architectural Press, 2001, p. 9.
65 Ibid., p. 26.
66 R. Adams Cram, *My Life in Architecture*, Boston: Little Brown & Co, 1936, pp. 124, 126.
67 J. Henry, *Architecture in Texas 1895–1945*, Austin: University of Texas Press, 1993, p. 153; E. Anthony, *The Architecture of Ralph Adams Cram and His Office*, New York and London: W.W. Norton & Co., 2007, p. 162; R. Muccigrosso, *American Gothic: The Mind and Art of Ralph Adams Cram*, Washington: University Press of America, 1980, p. 87; Fox, op. cit., pp. 1–2.
68 Henry, op. cit., p. 155; Fox, op. cit., p. 126.
69 Fox, op. cit., pp. 14–15, 24.
70 Fox, Ibid., pp. 109–13.
71 R. Maxwell et al., *James Stirling Michael Wilford And Associates: Buildings and Projects 1975–1992*, London: Thames & Hudson, 1994, p. 77; D. Sudjic, *Norman Foster Richard Rogers James Stirling: New Directions in British Architecture*, London: Thames & Hudson, 1986, p. 141; Fox, op. cit., p. 18.
72 Fox, op. cit., pp. 109, 116–20.
73 Muthesius, op. cit., p. 192.
74 Quoted in H. Johnston, *Radical Campus: Making Simon Fraser University*, Vancouver: Douglas & McIntyre, 2005, p. 43.
75 R. Ingersoll (ed.), *World Architecture 1900–2000: A Critical Mosaic, Vol 1: Canada and the United States*, Vienna: Springer, 2001, p. 159; Johnston, op. cit., pp. 48–9.
76 Johnston, op. cit., pp. 50–2.
77 A. Erickson, *Canadian Architect*, February 1966, no. 2, p. 41. Quoted in N. Olsberg and R. Castro, *Arthur Erickson: Critical Works*, Seattle: University of Washington Press, 2006, p. 116.
78 Johnston, op. cit., p. 54; Olsberg and Castro, op. cit., pp. 71, 115.
79 Johnston, op. cit., pp. 54–5, 59, 337.
80 A. Stout, 'New towns from gowns: urban form and placemaking at college campuses', unpublished MA thesis, MIT, 2008, pp. 103–5.
81 Quoted in Johnston, op. cit., p. 52.
82 P. Turner et al., *The Founders and the Architects: The Design of*

82 *Stanford University*, Stanford: Dept. of Art, Stanford University, 1976, pp. 12, 59–60, 83; R. Joncas et al., *Stanford University*, New York: Princeton Architectural Press, 2006, pp. 4, 24; J. Todd, *Frederick Law Olmsted*, Boston: Twayne, 1982, p. 139; Gaines, op. cit., p. 126.
83 Turner et al., 1976, p. 11; C. Beveridge and P. Rocheleau, *Frederick Law Olmsted. Designing the American Landscape*, New York: Universe, 1998, p. 111; Todd, op. cit., pp. 137–8; Chapman, op. cit., p. 21; Gaines, op. cit., pp. 122–6.
84 Joncas et al., pp. 5, 35; Turner et al., 1976, pp. 48–54.
85 Joncas et al., pp. 56–61.
86 Ibid., pp. 6, 104–5, 117.
87 Ibid., p. 165.
88 Edwards, 2000, op. cit., p. 26.
89 Quoted in 'Temasek's work-and-play design', *Straits Times*, 28 November 1991.
90 M. Pearce, *University Builders*, Chichester: Academy Press, 2001, p. 201.
91 Edwards, 2000, op. cit., pp. 26–7.
92 P. Davey, 'Building utopia – James Stirling, Michael Wilford and Associates' design of the Temasek Polytechnic in Singapore', *The Architectural Review*, June 1996, vol. CXCIX, no. 1192, 54.
93 Quoted in 'Temasek's work-and-play design', *Straits Times*, 28 November, 1991.
94 McParland, E., 'Trinity College, Dublin – I', *Country Life*, 6 May 1976, 1168; McParland, E., 'Trinity College, Dublin – II', *Country Life*, 13 May 1976, 1244–5; J. Luce, *Trinity College, Dublin: The First 400 Years*, Dublin: Trinity College Dublin Press, 1992, p. 41; Maxwell, C., *A History of Trinity College, Dublin, 1591–1892*, Dublin: Trinity College University Press, 1946, p. 171.
95 W. Macneile Dixon, *Trinity College, Dublin*, London: F. E. Robinson & Co, 1902, p. 212; Luce, op. cit., pp. 72–3.
96 Luce, op. cit., pp. 99–100; McParland, III, op. cit., 1311–13.
97 Trinity College, Dublin, *Development Control Plan*, 2004, p. 5; Luce, op. cit., pp. 156–66, 218; C. Casey, *Dublin: The City within the Grand and Royal Canals and the Circular Road with the Pheonix Park*, New Haven: Yale University Press, 2005, p. 407.
98 Trinity College, Dublin, *Development Control Plan*, p. 7.
99 R. Lowe, *A Western Acropolis of Learning: The University of California in 1897*, Berkeley: Center for Studies in Higher Education and Institute of Governmental Studies, 1996, p. 1.
100 Ibid., p. 27.
101 S. Cerny, *Berkeley Landmarks*, Berkeley: Berkeley Architectural Heritage Association, 2001, p. 139; Lowe, op. cit., p. 25.
102 Cerny, op. cit., pp. 132–3; Lowe, op. cit., p. 41; Chapman, op. cit., p. 29.
103 L. Partridge, *John Galen Howard and the Berkeley Campus: Beaux-Arts Architecture in the 'Athens of the West'*, Berkeley: Berkeley Architectural Heritage, 1978, p. 19.
104 Ibid., pp. 25–6; S. Woodbridge, *John Galen Howard and the University of California*, Berkeley: University of California Press, 2002, pp. 98–103; Cerny, op. cit., p. 146.
105 Woodbridge, op. cit., p. 110; Cerny, op. cit., p. 146.
106 Partridge, op. cit., pp. 30–1; Cerny, op. cit., p. 152; Woodbridge, op. cit., p. 139.
107 Cerny, op. cit., p. 134.
108 R. Nystrom, 'UCLA, an interpretation considering architecture and site', unpublished PhD thesis, UCLA, 1968, pp. 54, 65; D. Gebhard and R. Winter, *An Architectural Guidebook to Los Angeles*, Layton: Gibbs Smith, 2003, p. 144.
109 Nystrom, op. cit., pp. 74–93.
110 Ibid., pp. 151–3, 156.
111 UCLA, *Long Range Development Plan 2002*, 2003, p. 15.
112 Nystrom, op. cit., pp. 188–90.
113 D. Leader (ed.), *A History of the University of Cambridge* (gen. ed. C. Brooke), vol I, Cambridge: Cambridge University Press, 1994, p. 61.
114 Charles Astor Bristed, *Five Years in an English University*, New York: G. P. Putnam & Sons, 1873, p. 13.
115 Leader, op. cit., p. 64; T. Rawle, *Cambridge Architecture*, London: Trefoil Books, 1985, p. 11; D. Watkin, *A History of Western Architecture*, London: Laurence King Publishing, 2005, p. 184.
116 Rawle, op. cit., pp. 21–3.
117 Leader, op. cit., pp. 223–4.

NOTES

118 Ibid., p. 64; Turner, op. cit., p. 12.
119 C. Sicca, *Committed to Classicism: The Building of Downing College Cambridge,* Cambridge: Downing College, 1987, pp. 96–101.
120 D. Chablo, 'University architecture in Britain, 1950–1975', unpublished PhD thesis, University of Oxford, 1987, pp. 32–3.
121 N. Taylor and P. Booth, *Cambridge New Architecture*, London: Leonard Hill Books, 1970, p. 177.
122 J. Elliott, 'Universitas: a study of spatial development of Western universities, exploring their emergence as distinctive space, building and planning types', unpublished PhD thesis, University of Cape Town, 2004, pp. E3–4.
123 Edwards, 2000. op. cit., p. 21; Elliott, 2004, op. cit, pp. E3–5.
124 Elliott, 2004, op. cit., pp. E5–6.
125 J. Elliott, 'What may happen to UCT at Groote Schuur', in A. Lennox-Short and D. Welsh, *UCT at 150: Reflections*, Cape Town: Rowman and Littlefield, 1979, p. 45; Elliott, 2004, op. cit., p. 134.
126 J. Block, *The Uses of Gothic: Planning and Building the Campus of the University of Chicago 1892–1932*, Chicago: University of Chicago Library, 1983, pp. x–xi.
127 Letter from C. L. Hutchinson to President William Rainey Harper, 2 March 1891. President's Papers, University of Chicago Archives.
128 M. Sorkin, *Other Plans: University of Chicago Studies, 1998–2000*, New York: Princeton Architectural Press, 2002, pp. 10–12.
129 Block, op. cit., p. xiii; Pridmore, p. 18.
130 J. Pridmore, *University of Chicago, the Campus Guide*, New York: Princeton Architectural Press, 2006, pp. 19–23.
131 Ibid., pp. 26–8; R. Dober, *Campus Design*, New York: John Wiley & Sons, 1992, p. 79; Block, op. cit., p. 67.
132 Block, op. cit., pp. 192–9.
133 Pridmore, pp. 73–5.
134 Dober, 1992, op. cit., p. 79; Pridmore, op. cit., p. 102.
135 A. Temko, *Eero Saarinen,* London and New York: G. Braziller, 1962, p. 30; *Architectural Record,* November 1960, p. 132; J. Merkel, *Eero Saarinen*, London: Phaidon, 2005, pp. 141–2.
136 Pridmore, op. cit., p. 98; F. Schulze and K. Harrington, *Chicago's Famous Buildings*, Chicago: University of Chicago Press, 2003, pp. 247–8.
137 Schulze, op. cit., pp. 248–50.
138 Ibid.
139 Chapman, op. cit., p. 22.
140 Klauder and Wise, op. cit., p. 18.
141 Gaines, op. cit., p. 131; F. Halsband, 'Charles Klauder's brilliant invisible hand', *Chronicle of Higher Education*, 2 March 2005, vol. 51, Issue 29, B24.
142 *Design Guidelines,* University of Colorado at Boulder, 2007, p. 16.
143 Muthesius, op. cit., p. 138–42.
144 P. Dormer and S. Muthesius, *Concrete and Open Skies: Architecture at the University of East Anglia 1962–2000*, London: Unicorn, 2001, p. 78; W. Curtis, *Denys Lasdun. Architecture, City, Landscape*, London: Phaidon, 1994, p. 88.
145 Lasdun, Development Plan, December 1962. Quoted in M. Sanderson, *The History of the University of East Anglia, Norwich*, London: Hambledon Continuum, 2002, p. 153.
146 Muthesius, op. cit., p. 149.
147 Dormer and Muthesius, op. cit., pp. 22–3.
148 Ibid., p. 14.
149 Muthesius, op.cit., p. 181; Sanderson, op. cit., p. 165.
150 A. Drexler and A. Menges, *Architecture of Skidmore, Owings and Merrill, 1963–1973*, London: Architectural Press, 1974, p. 224.
151 Turner, op. cit., p. 274.
152 Chapman, op. cit., p. 45; Muthesius, op. cit., pp. 196–9.
153 Drexler, op. cit., p. 224; Turner, op. cit., p. 274; Muthesius, op. cit., pp. 196–9.
154 Drexler, op. cit., p. 232.
155 W. Jones, 'Some fields are in the city'. Available online: www.chilit.org/JonesW1.htm (accessed 30 November 2009).
156 Ibid.; W. Netsch, *Walter A. Netsch FAIA: A Critical Appreciation and Sourcebook*, Evanston: Northwestern University Press, 2008, p. 39.
157 Tyack, 1993, op. cit., pp. 86–8.
158 Tyack, 1993, op. cit., pp. 87–9; J. Harvey, 'Architecture in Oxford 1350–1500', in J. Catto and R. Evans (eds), *The History of the*

NOTES

     University of Oxford: Late Medieval Oxford, vol. II, Oxford, 1992, pp. 755–62.
159 Harvey, op. cit., pp. 747, 768.
160 Tyack, 1993, op. cit., pp. 93–6; J. Newman, 'The architectural setting', in N. Tyacke (ed.), *The History of the University of Oxford: Seventeenth Century Oxford*, vol. IV, Oxford: Oxford University Press, 1997, pp. 150–3.
161 Newman, op. cit., pp. 174–6.
162 Dober, 1992, op. cit., pp. 137, 140–1.
163 D. Kay, 'Architecture', in B. Harrison (ed.), *The History of the University of Oxford: The Twentieth Century*, vol. VIII, Oxford: Oxford University Press, 1994, p. 505.
164 Chablo, op. cit., p. 81; Kay, op. cit., pp. 513–14.
165 D. Brownlee and G. Thomas, *Building America's First University*, Philadelphia: University of Pennsylvania Press, 2000, pp. 53–7, 158.
166 Ibid., pp. 61–5.
167 E. Bosley, *University of Pennsylvania Library: Frank Furness*, London: Phaidon, 1996, pp. 4–20; Brownlee and Thomas, p. 160.
168 Brownlee and Thomas, pp. 13, 74–90; G. Thomas, *The Campus Guide: University of Pennsylvania*, New York: Princeton Architectural Press, 2002, pp. 15–16.
169 Brownlee and Thomas, op. cit., pp. 93–5, 235–6.
170 Thomas, op. cit., p. 87; Brownlee and Thomas, pp. 205, 239–40.
171 West Philadelphia Landscape Project. Available online: http://web.mit.edu/wplp/plan/blp.htm (accessed 1 December 2009).
172 Thomas, op. cit., pp. 23, 29; P. Goldberger, 'In Philadelphia, a Victorian extravaganza lives', *New York Times*, 2 June 1991, 232.
173 Brownlee and Thomas, op. cit., pp. 134–5, 185–6, 195, 208, 314; Thomas, op. cit., pp. 64, 77.
174 J. Rodin, *The University & Urban Revival: Out of the Ivory Tower and into the Streets*, Philadelphia: University of Pennsylvania Press, 2007, pp. 3–4, 114–19; Thomas, op. cit., pp. 25, 127.
175 Brownlee and Thomas, op. cit., pp. 163–5.
176 H. Kara, *Aga Khan 2007 Award Cycle, On Site Review Report: Petronas University of Technology*, 2007, pp. 2–6; Universiti Teknologi PETRONAS: University Profile. Available online: www.utp.edu.my/theUniversity/ (accessed 12 January 2010).
177 Neuman, op. cit., p. 49; Aga Khan Foundation, *Intervention Architecture: Building for Change*, London: I.B. Tauris & Co., 2007, p. 70.
178 Kara, op. cit., pp. 2–6; Aga Khan Foundation, op. cit., p. 68; Neuman, op. cit., p. 49.
179 Kara, op. cit., p. 9; Aga Khan Foundation, op. cit., pp. 68–70.
180 Neuman, op. cit., p. 49; Aga Khan Foundation, op. cit., p. 70.
181 Kara, op. cit., pp. 7, 10, 14.
182 P. Goldberger, 'Perfect space: University of Virginia', *Travel and Leisure*, vol. 19, September 1989, 128–9.
183 R. Wilson (ed.), *Thomas Jefferson's Academical Village: The Creation of an Architectural Masterpiece*, Charlottesville: University of Virginia Press, 1993, pp. 4–5.
184 Jefferson designed numerous houses including Farmington (1816), the George Diers House (1802) and his own residence Monticello (1769–1809), as well as the Virginia State Capitol (1785–1792).
185 Letter of 5 January 1805, to L. W. Tazewell, in the Jefferson Papers of the University of Virginia.
186 Letter of 6 May 1810, to Hugh L. White et al., 'Trustees of the Lottery of East Tennessee College'. Quoted in Turner, op. cit., p. 79.
187 Turner, op. cit., p. 83; W. O'Neal, *Jefferson's Buildings at the University of Virginia: The Rotunda*, Charlottesville: University of Virginia Press, 1960, pp. 1–3; M. Brawne, *University of Virginia the Lawn: Thomas Jefferson (Architecture in Detail)*, London: Phaidon, 1994, p. 15.
188 Turner, op. cit., p. 83.
189 Wilson, op. cit., p. 23.
190 Wilson, op. cit., pp. 132–3; K. Stein, 'Business school connects to distant past', *Architectural Record*, July 1996, 74.
191 R. Ferguson, *Crawley Campus: The Planning and Architecture of the University of Western Australia*, Nedlands: University of Western Australia Press, 1993, pp. 8–10; C. Vernon, 'Landscape (+) architecture at UWA', *Architecture Australia*, 2001, vol. 90, 4, 2001, 42.

NOTES

192 UWA, *Campus Plan 2000*, 2000, p. 17.
193 Ferguson, op. cit., 46; Vernon, op. cit., 44.
194 UWA, *Campus Plan 2000*, p. 19.
195 Ferguson, op. cit., 96–7.
196 Ibid., p. 52; Vernon, op. cit., 44.
197 R. Woldendorp, *The University of Western Australia: Its Grounds and Buildings*, Perth: University of Western Australia, 1981, p. 13; Ferguson, op. cit., 53–4.
198 Woldendorp, op. cit., pp. 9, 13.
199 UWA *Campus Plan 2000*, p. 43.
200 G. Seddon and G. Lilleyman, *A Landscape for Learning: A History of the Grounds of the University of Western Australia*, Perth, 2006, pp. 174–6.
201 S. Lindroth, *A History of Uppsala University 1477–1977*, Uppsala: Almqvist & Wiksell International, 1976, p. 204.
202 Ibid., p. 217.
203 A. Zaaijer, 'Utrecht campus developments: one university, two campuses', in K. Hoeger and K. Christiaanse, *Campus and the City*, Zurich: GTA Verlag, 2007, p. 59.
204 H. Ibelings, 'Architecture at De Uithof'. Accessed online: www.uu.nl/EN/utrechtuniversity/culturearchitecture/Documents/De%20Uithof%20ENG.pdf (accessed 30 January 2010).
205 B. Lootsma, *Superdutch: New Architecture in the Netherlands*, London: Princeton Architectural Press, 2000, pp. 105–7.
206 C. van Cleef, 'Campus landscape', *Architectural Review*, March 1999, 50; Lootsma, op. cit., pp. 177–9.
207 Cleef, op. cit, 52; Lootsma, op. cit., p. 147.
208 Turner, op. cit., pp. 38–41; E. Brown, *New Haven: A Guide to Architecture and Urban Design*, New Haven and London: Yale University Press, 1976, p. 120–1; P. Pinnell, *Yale University: The Campus Guide*, New York: Princeton Architectural Press, 1999, p. 12.
209 A. Betsky, *James Gamble Rogers and the Architecture of Pragmatism*, New York: Architectural History Foundation, 1994, p. 104; Brown, op. cit., pp. 121–2; Pinnell, op. cit., pp. 12–13.
210 Pinnell, op. cit., pp. 60–1; Betsky, op. cit., pp. 111–12.
211 S. McLeod Bedford, *John Russell Pope: Architect of Empire*, New York: Rizzoli, 1998, pp. 165–6.
212 Pinnell, op. cit., pp. 66–70; Betsky, op. cit., p. 144.
213 Brown, op. cit., p. 130; Pinnell, op. cit., p. 112; Turner, op. cit., p. 262.
214 E. Pelkonen and D. Albrecht (eds), *Eero Saarinen: Shaping the Future*, New Haven and London: Finnish Cultural Institute, 2006, p. 212; Merkel, op. cit., pp. 143–5; Temko, pp. 27, 118.
215 P. Needham, 'The architecture of Richard Levin', *Yale Daily News*, 16 April 2009. Available online: www.yaledailynews.com/articles/view/28789 (accessed 22 May 2009).

CHAPTER THREE
DESIGNING THE TWENTY-FIRST CENTURY CAMPUS

1 J. Russell, 'On campus visits, bid for high marks', *The Boston Globe*, 7 September 2002, vol. 262, 1.

Bibliography

Aga Khan Foundation, *Intervention Architecture: Building for Change*, London: I.B. Tauris & Co., 2007.

Andersson, S. and Høyer, S., *C. Th. Sørensen: Landscape Modernist*, Copenhagen: Danish Architectural Press, 2001.

Andrews, C., *Oxford Scene*, Oxford: Chris Andrews Publications, 2000.

Anisimov, V., *Architectural Guide to Moscow*, Rotterdam: 010 Publishers, 1993.

Anthony, E., *The Architecture of Ralph Adams Cram and His Office*, New York and London: W.W. Norton & Co., 2007.

Architectural Record, 'Law School Center, University of Chicago', November 1960, vol. 128, no. 5, 132–5.

Ayers, A., *The Architecture of Paris*, Stuttgart and London: Edition Axel Menges, 2004.

Barnett, J., 'The new collegiate architecture at Yale', *Architectural Record*, April 1962, vol. 131, 125–32.

Bendall, S., Brooke, C. and Collinson, P., *A History of Emmanuel College, Cambridge*, Woodbridge: The Boydell Press, 1999.

Bergdoll, B., *European Architecture 1750–1890*, Oxford: Oxford University Press, 2000.

Betsky, A., *James Gamble Rogers and the Architecture of Pragmatism*, New York: Architectural History Foundation, 1994.

Beveridge, C. and Rocheleau, P., *Frederick Law Olmsted: Designing the American Landscape*, New York: Universe, 1998.

Birks, T., *Building the New Universities*, Newton Abbot: David and Charles, 1972.

Blaik, O., 'Campuses in cities: places between engagement and retreat', *Chronicle of Higher Education* 25, 23 February 2007, vol. 53, 25.

Blaser, W., *Mies van der Rohe: IIT Campus Illinois Institute of Technology, Chicago*, Basel: Birkhäuser, 2002.

Block, J., *The Uses of Gothic: Planning and Building the Campus of the University of Chicago 1892–1932*, Chicago: University of Chicago Library, 1983.

Bosley, E., *University of Pennsylvania Library: Frank Furness*, London: Phaidon, 1996.

Brawne, M., *University of Virginia the Lawn: Thomas Jefferson (Architecture in Detail)*, London: Phaidon, 1994.

Brensing, C., 'The Free University still embodies the social and architectural dynamic of the 1960s', *The Architects' Journal*, 15 September 2005, vol. 222. no. 9, 33–47.

Brockliss, L., 'Gown and town: the university and the city in Europe, 1200–2000', *Minerva 2*, vol. 38, 2000, 147–70.

Brown, E., *New Haven: A Guide to Architecture and Urban Design*, New Haven and London: Yale University Press, 1976.

Brownlee, D. and Thomas, G., *Building America's First University*, Philadelphia: University of Pennsylvania Press, 2000.

Brumfield, W., *A History of Russian Architecture*, Cambridge: Cambridge University Press, 1993.

Brumfield, W., *Landmarks of Russian Architecture: A Photographic Survey*, Amsterdam: Gordon and Breach, 1997.

Bunting, B., *Harvard: An Architectural History*, Cambridge, Mass. and London: Belknap Harvard, 1985.

Casey, C., *Dublin: The City within the Grand and Royal Canals and the Circular Road with the Pheonix Park*, New Haven: Yale University Press, 2005.

Casson, H., *Hugh Casson's Cambridge*, London: Phaidon, 1992.

Cerny, S., *Berkeley Landmarks*, Berkeley: Berkeley Architectural Heritage Association, 2001.

Chablo, D., 'University architecture in Britain, 1950–1975', unpublished PhD thesis, University of Oxford, 1987.

Chapman, M. Perry, *American Places: In Search of the Twenty-First Century Campus*, Connecticut: Praeger, 2006.

Cleef, C. van, 'Campus landscape,' *Architectural Review*, March 1999, 50–3.

Cobban, A., *The Medieval English Universities: Oxford and Cambridge to c.1500*, Berkeley and Los Angeles: University of California Press, 1988.

Cody, J., *Building in China: Henry K. Murphy's 'Adaptive Architecture' 1914–1935*, Hong Kong: The Chinese University Press, 2001.

Cohen, J. L. and Cohen, J. A., *China Today and Her Ancient Treasures*, New York: Abrams, 1980.

Cohen, J., *Mies van der Rohe*, London: E & F.N. Spon, 1996.

Cram, R. Adams, 'Princeton architecture', *The American Architect*, 21 July 1909, 21–30.

Cram, R. Adams, *My Life in Architecture*, Boston: Little Brown & Co, 1936.

BIBLIOGRAPHY

Cremin, L., *American Education: The Colonial Experience 1607–1783*, New York: Harper & Row, 1970.

Croft, C. 'The Møllers' tale', *Building Design*, 23 April 2004, 22.

Cunningham, C. and Waterhouse, P., *Alfred Waterhouse 1830–1905: Biography of a Practice*, Oxford: Oxford University Press, 1992.

Curtis, W., *Denys Lasdun: Architecture, City, Landscape*, London: Phaidon, 1994.

Davey, P., 'Building utopia – James Stirling, Michael Wilford and Associates' design of the Temasek Polytechnic in Singapore', *The Architectural Review*, June 1996, vol. CXCIX, no. 1192, 48–62.

Dixon, W. Macneile, *Trinity College, Dublin*, London: F. E. Robinson & Co, 1902.

Dober, R., *Campus Planning*, New York: Reinhold, 1963.

Dober, R., *Campus Design*, New York: John Wiley & Sons, 1992.

Dolkart, A., *Morningside Heights: A History of its Architecture and Development*, New York: Columbia University Press, 1998.

Doordan, D., *Twentieth-Century Architecture*, London: Laurence King, 2001.

Dormer, P. and Muthesius, S., *Concrete and Open Skies: Architecture at the University of East Anglia 1962–2000*, London: Unicorn, 2001.

Drexler, A. and Menges, A., *Architecture of Skidmore, Owings and Merrill, 1963–1973*, London: Architectural Press, 1974.

Duke, A., *Importing Oxbridge. English Residential Colleges and American Universities*, New Haven and London: Yale University Press, 1996.

Edwards, B., *University Architecture*, London and New York: Spon Press, 2000.

Edwards, D., *Yenching University*, New York: United Board for Christian Higher Education in Asia, 1959.

Elliott, J., 'What may happen to UCT at Groote Schuur', in A. Lennox-Short and D. Welsh, *UCT at 150: Reflections*, Cape Town: Rowman and Littlefield, 1979, 42–7.

Elliott, J., 'Universitas: a study of spatial development of Western universities, exploring their emergence as distinctive space, building and planning types', unpublished PhD thesis, University of Cape Town, 2004.

Faber, T., *A History of Danish Architecture*, Copenhagen: Det Danske Selskab, 1978.

Feld, G., Mostafavi, M., Schiedhelm, M., Smithson, P., Tzonix, A., Lefaivre L. and Wagner, G., *Free University Berlin*, London: Architectural Association, 1999.

Ferguson, R., *Crawley Campus: The Planning and Architecture of the University of Western Australia*, Nedlands: University of Western Australia Press, 1993.

Ferruolo, S., '*Parisius-Paradisus*: the city, its schools, and the origins of the University of Paris', in T. Bender (ed.), *The University and the City: From Medieval Origins to the Present*, New York and Oxford: Oxford University Press, 1988, 22–43.

Fox, S., *Rice University: Campus Guide*, New York: Princeton Architectural Press, 2001.

Frampton, K., *Modern Architecture: A Critical History*, London: Thames and Hudson, 1997.

Gaines, T., *The Campus as a Work of Art*, New York: Praeger, 1991.

Gambee, R., *Princeton*, New York and London: Norton, 1998.

Gebhard, D. and Winter, R., *An Architectural Guidebook to Los Angeles*, Layton: Gibbs Smith, 2003.

Gerbod, P., 'Resources and management', in W. Rüegg (ed.), *A History of the University in Europe: Universities in the Nineteenth and Early Twentieth Centuries (1800–1945)*, vol. III, Cambridge: Cambridge University Press, 2004, 101–21.

Gieysztor, A., 'Management and resources', in W. Rüegg (ed.), *A History of the University in Europe: Universities in the Middle Ages*, vol. I, Cambridge: Cambridge University Press, 2003, 108–43.

Goldberger, P., 'Perfect space: University of Virginia', *Travel and Leisure*, September 1989, vol. 19, 128–9.

Goldberger, P., 'In Philadelphia, a Victorian extravaganza lives', *New York Times*, 2 June 1991, 232.

Green, V., *A History of Oxford University*, London: Batsford, 1974.

Grendler, P., *The Universities of the Italian Renaissance*, Baltimore and London: John Hopkins University Press, 2002.

Halsband, F., 'Charles Klauder's brilliant invisible hand', *Chronicle of Higher Education*, 25 March 2005, vol. 51, Issue 29, B24–5.

Hamlin, A., 'The educational influence of collegiate architecture', *Architectural Forum*, December 1925, vol. 43, 321–6.

Harte, N. and North, J., *The World of University College London 1828–1978*, Portsmouth: University College, 1978.

Harvey, J. 'Architecture in Oxford 1350–1500', in J. Catto and R. Evans (eds), *The History of the University of Oxford: Late Medieval Oxford*, vol. II, Oxford, 1992, 747–68.

Heinemann, T. (ed.), *The University Building in Uppsala 1887–1987* Uppsala: Uppsala University Press, 1987.

Henry, J., *Architecture in Texas 1895–1945*, Austin: University of Texas Press, 1993.

Ikonnikov, A., *Russian Architecture of the Soviet Period*, Moscow: Raduga Publishers, 1988.

Ingersoll, R. (ed.), *World Architecture 1900–2000: A Critical Mosaic, Vol. 1: Canada and the United States*, Vienna: Springer, 2001.

Jencks, C., *The Language of Post-Modern Architecture*, London: Academy Editions, 1984.

Jencks, C., *The Iconic Building: The Power of Enigma*, London: Frances Lincoln, 2005.

Johannisson, K., *A Life of Learning: Uppsala University During Five Centuries*, Uppsala: Uppsala University Press, 1989.

Johnston, H., *Radical Campus: Making Simon Fraser University*, Vancouver: Douglas & McIntyre, 2005.

Joncas, R., Neuman, D. and Turner, P., *Stanford University*, New York: Princeton Architectural Press, 2006.

Jones, W., 'Some fields are in the city'. Available online www.chilit.org/JonesW1.htm (accessed 30 November 2009).

Kay, D., 'Architecture', in B. Harrison (ed.), *The History of the University of Oxford: The Twentieth Century*, vol. VIII, Oxford: Oxford University Press, 1994, 499–518.

Kenney, D., Dumont, R. and Kenney, G., *Mission and Place: Strengthening Learning and Community through Campus Design*, Westport: Greenwood Press, 2005.

Kersting, A., and Ashdown, J., *The Buildings of Oxford*, London: Holmes & Meier, 1980.

Kiem, K., *The Free University Berlin (1967–1973): Campus Design, Team X ideals and tectonic invention*, Weimar: VDG, 2008.

Klauder, C. and Wise, H., *College Architecture in America*, New York and London: Charles Scribner's Sons, 1929.

Klinge, M., 'Teachers', in W. Rüegg (ed.), *A History of the University in Europe: Universities in the Nineteenth and Early Twentieth Centuries (1800–1945)*, vol. III, Cambridge: Cambridge University Press, 2004, 123–61.

Kultermann, U., 'Education and Arab identity. Kamal El Kafrawi: University of Qatar, Doha', *Architectura*, vol. 26, 1996, 84–8.

Kultermann, U. (ed.), *World Architecture 1900–2000: A Critical Mosaic, Vol. 6: Central and Southern Africa*, Vienna: Springer, 2000.

Leader, D. (ed.), *A History of the University of Cambridge* (general editor C. Brooke), vol. I, Cambridge: Cambridge University Press, 1994.

Leigh, C., 'Must the minimum be the maximum?', *Princeton Alumni Weekly*, 19 May 1999. Online http://paw.princeton.edu/issues/2009/05/13/sections/search-and-archives/search.xml (accessed 5 June 2009).

Levi, J., 'Expanding the University of Chicago', in J. Rork and L. Robbins (eds), *Casebook on Campus Planning and Institutional Development: Ten Institutions*, Washington DC: U.S. Department of Health, Education, and Welfare, 1962, pp. 107–27.

Lind, O., *ArkitekturFortaellinger – om Aarhus Universitets bygninger*, Aarhus: Arhus Universitets Forskningsfond, 2003.

Lindroth, S., *A History of Uppsala University 1477–1977*, Uppsala: Almqvist & Wiksell International, 1976.

Long, P., and Thomas, J. (eds), *Basil Spence Architect*, Edinburgh: National Galleries of Scotland, 2008.

Lootsma, B., *Superdutch: New Architecture in the Netherlands*, London: Princeton Architectural Press, 2000.

Lowe, D., 'Now they're deconstructing the Columbia campus', *City Journal 7*, Autumn 1997, 84–97.

Lowe, R., *A Western Acropolis of Learning: The University of California in 1897*, Berkeley: Center for Studies in Higher Education and Institute of Governmental Studies, 1996.

Luce, J., *Trinity College, Dublin: The First 400 Years*, Dublin: Trinity College Dublin Press, 1992.

Lykke, P., *A Pictorial History of the University of Aarhus*, Aarhus: Aarhus Universitetsforlag, 2001.

McConica, J. (ed.), *The History of the University of Oxford: The Collegiate University*, vol. III, Oxford: Oxford University Press, 1986.

McGuire, D. (ed.), *Beatrix Jones Farrand (1872–1959): Fifty Years of*

BIBLIOGRAPHY

American Landscape Architecture, Washington DC: Dumbarton Oaks Research Library and Collection, 1982.

McLeod Bedford, S., *John Russell Pope: Architect of Empire*, New York: Rizzoli, 1998.

McParland, E., 'Trinity College, Dublin – I', *Country Life*, 6 May 1976, 1166–9.

McParland, E., 'Trinity College, Dublin – II', *Country Life*, 13 May 1976, 1242–5.

McParland, E., 'Trinity College, Dublin – III', *Country Life*, 20 May 1976, 1310–3.

Marcuse, P. and Potter, C., 'Columbia University's heights: an ivory tower and its communities', in D. Perry and W. Wiewel, *The University as Urban Developer: Case Studies and Analysis*, New York: M.E. Sharpe, 2005, 45–64.

Maxwell, C., *A History of Trinity College, Dublin, 1591–1892*, Dublin: Trinity College University Press, 1946.

Maxwell, R., Muirhead, T. and Wilford, M., *James Stirling Michael Wilford and Associates: Buildings and Projects 1975–1992*, London: Thames & Hudson, 1994.

Merkel, J., *Eero Saarinen*, London: Phaidon, 2005.

Mitchell, W., *Imagining MIT: Designing a Campus for the Twenty-First Century*, Cambridge, Mass.: MIT Press, 2007.

Møller, C. F., *Aarhus Universitets Bygninger*, Aarhus: Aarhus Universitetsforlag, 1978.

Montalvo, M., *Havana: History and Architecture of a Romantic City*, New York: Monacelli, 2000.

Mordaunt Crook, J., 'The architectural image', in F. M. L. Thompson, *The University of London and the World of Learning 1836–1986*, London and Ronceverte: Hambledon Press, 1990, pp. 1–33.

Morgan, V. (ed.), *A History of the University of Cambridge*, vol. II, (general editor C. Brooke), Cambridge: Cambridge University Press, 2004.

Morrison, H., *Early American Architecture: From the First Colonial Settlements to the National Period*, New York: Dover Publications, 1987.

Muccigrosso, R., *American Gothic: The Mind and Art of Ralph Adams Cram*, Washington: University Press of America, 1980.

Munitz, B., 'Place and history matter on all campuses', *Chronicle of Higher Education*, 22 October 2004, vol. 51, Issue 9, B15.

Muthesius, S., *The Postwar University: Utopianist Campus and College*, New Haven and London: Yale University Press, 2000.

Netsch, W., *Walter A. Netsch FAIA: A Critical Appreciation and Sourcebook*, Evanston: Northwestern University Press, 2008.

Neuman, D. (ed.), *Building Type Basics for College and University Facilities*, Hoboken, NJ: Wiley, 2003.

Newman, J., 'The architectural setting', in N. Tyacke (ed.), *The History of the University of Oxford: Seventeenth Century Oxford*, vol. IV, Oxford: Oxford University Press, 1997, 135–77.

Nystrom, R., 'UCLA, an interpretation considering architecture and site', unpublished PhD thesis, UCLA, 1968.

O'Neal, W., *Jefferson's Buildings at the University of Virginia: The Rotunda*, Charlottesville: University of Virginia Press, 1960.

Olsberg, N. and Castro, R., *Arthur Erickson: Critical Works*, Seattle: University of Washington Press, 2006.

Olsen, D., *The City as a Work of Art: London, Paris, Vienna*, New Haven and London: Yale University Press, 1986.

Partridge, L., *John Galen Howard and the Berkeley Campus: Beaux-Arts Architecture in the 'Athens of the West'*, Berkeley: Berkeley Architectural Heritage, 1978.

Passanti, F., 'The design of Columbia in the 1890s, McKim and his client', *Journal of Society of Architectural Historians*, May 1977, vol. 36, 69–84.

Pearce, M., *University Builders*, Chichester: Academy Press, 2001.

Pelkonen, E. and Albrecht, D. (eds), *Eero Saarinen: Shaping the Future*, New Haven and London: Finnish Cultural Institute, 2006.

Pinnell, P., *Yale University: The Campus Guide*, New York: Princeton Architectural Press, 1999.

Pridmore, J., *University of Chicago: The Campus Guide*, New York: Princeton Architectural Press, 2006.

Rait, R., *Life in the Medieval University*, Cambridge: Cambridge University Press, 1912.

Ramsay, C., *William Wilkins and the Building of University College, London*, unpublished PhD thesis, UCL, 1984.

Rawle, T., *Cambridge Architecture*, London: Trefoil Books, 1985.

Rhinehart, R., *Princeton University: The Campus Guide*, New York: Princeton Architectural Press, 1999.

Rhodes, F., *The Creation of the Future: The Role of the American University*, Ithaca and London: Cornell University Press, 2001.

Robson, J., *A Guide to Columbia University*, New York: Columbia University Press, 1937.

Rodin, J., *The University and Urban Revival: Out of the Ivory Tower and into the Streets*, Philadelphia: University of Pennsylvania Press, 2007.

Roth, L., *McKim, Mead and White Architects*, London: Harper & Row, 1984.

Rudolph, P., *The American College and University: A History*, Georgia: University of Georgia Press, 1990.

Salama, A., 'When good design intentions do not meet users' expectations: exploring Qatar University campus, outdoor spaces', *International Journal of Architectural Research*, 2008, vol. 2, issue 2, 57–77.

Sanderson, M. *The History of the University of East Anglia, Norwich*, London: Hambledon Continuum, 2002.

Sanz, N., *The Heritage of European Universities*, Strasbourg: Council of Europe, 2006.

Schorske, C., *Fin-de-Siècle Vienna, Politics and Culture*, London: George Weidenfeld & Nicolson, 1979.

Schulze, F. and Harrington, K., *Chicago's Famous Buildings*, Chicago: University of Chicago Press, 2003.

Schulze, F., *Illinois Institute of Technology*, New York: Princeton Architectural Press, 2005.

Schuyler, D., 'Frederick Law Olmsted and the origins of modern campus design', *Planning for Higher Education*, Winter 1996–1997, vol. 25, 1–10.

Seddon, G. and Lilleyman, G., *A Landscape for Learning: A History of the Grounds of the University of Western Australia*, Perth: University of Western Australia Press, 2006.

Sicca, C., *Committed to Classicism: The Building of Downing College Cambridge*, Cambridge: Downing College, 1987.

Skriver, P., 'The University of Aarhus: a long-term project', *Casabella*, 1991, no. 584, 46–63.

Sorkin, M., *Other Plans: University of Chicago Studies, 1998–2000*, New York: Princeton Architectural Press, 2002.

Spaeth, D., *Mies Van Der Rohe*, New York: Rizzoli, 1985.

Spence, D., 'Building a new university', in D. Daiches (ed.), *The Idea of a New University: An Experiment in Sussex*, London: MIT Press, 1970, 201–15.

Stein, K., 'Business school connects to distant past', *Architectural Record*, July 1996, 72–9.

Stern, R., Fishman, D., and Tilove, J., *New York 1960: Architecture and Urbanism between the Second World War and the Bicentennial*, New York: Monacelli Press, 1995.

Stout, A., 'New towns from gowns: urban form and placemaking at college campuses', unpublished MA thesis, MIT, 2008.

Stuart, J., *Fifty Years in China: The Memoirs of John Leighton Stuart: Missionary and Ambassador*, New York: Random House, 1954.

Sudjic, D., *Norman Foster Richard Rogers James Stirling: New Directions in British Architecture*, London: Thames & Hudson, 1986.

Summerfield, C. and Devine, M., *International Dictionary of University Histories*, Chicago: Fitzroy Dearborn, 1998.

Susi, M., *Columbia University and Morningside Heights*, San Francisco: Arcadia Publishing, 2007.

Tarkhanov, A. and Kavtaradze, S., *Stalinist Architecture*, London: Laurence King, 1992.

Taylor, N. and Booth, P., *Cambridge New Architecture*, London: Leonard Hill Books, 1970.

Temko, A., *Eero Saarinen*, London and New York: G. Braziller, 1962.

Thomas, G., *The Campus Guide: University of Pennsylvania*, New York: Princeton Architectural Press, 2002.

Thwing, C., *American Colleges: Their Students and Work*, New York: G. P. Putnam's Sons, 1878.

Todd, J., *Frederick Law Olmsted*, Boston: Twayne, 1982.

Turner, P., *Campus: An American Planning Tradition*, Cambridge, Mass., and London: Architectural History Foundation, 1995.

Turner, P., Vetrocq, M. and Weitze, K., *The Founders and the Architects: The Design of Stanford University*, Stanford: Dept. of Art, Stanford University, 1976.

Tyack, G., 'The architecture of the University and the Colleges', in J. Prest (ed.), *The Illustrated History of Oxford University*, Oxford and New York: Oxford University Press, 1993, 84–122.

Tyack, G., *Oxford: An Architectural Guide*, Oxford: Oxford University Press, 1998.

Vernon, C., 'Landscape (+) architecture at UWA', *Architecture Australia*, vol. 90, 4, 2001, 42–5.

Waldheim, C., Rüedi, K. and Ray, K., *Chicago Architecture*, Chicago: University of Chicago Press, 2001.

Walker, E., *The South African College and the University of Cape Town 1829–1929*, Cape Town: University of Cape Town, 1929.

Wang, W. (ed.), *World Architecture 1900–2000: A Critical Mosaic, Vol. 3: Northern Europe, Central Europe, Western Europe*, Vienna: Springer-Verlag, 2000.

Watkin, D., *A History of Western Architecture*, London: Laurence King Publishing, 2005.

Watkin, D., *Radical Classicism: The Architecture of Quinlan Terry*, New York: Rizzoli, 2006.

Webb, M., *Architecture in Britain Today*, Middlesex: Country Life Books, 1969.

Webb, T. D. (ed.), *Building Libraries for the 21st Century: The Shape of Information*, Jefferson, NC: McFarland & Company, 2000.

Webber, H., 'The University of Chicago and its neighbours', in D. Perry and W. Wiewel, *The University as Urban Developer: Case Studies and Analysis*, New York: M.E. Sharpe, 2005, 65–79.

Willis, R., *The Architectural History of the University of Cambridge and of the Colleges of Cambridge and Eton*, vol. I, Cambridge: Cambridge University Press, 1886.

Wilson, R. (ed.), *Thomas Jefferson's Academical Village: The Creation of an Architectural Masterpiece*, Charlottesville: University of Virginia Press, 1993.

Wilson, R. and Butler, S., *University of Virginia: Campus Guide*, New York: Princeton Architectural Press, 1999.

Woldendorp, R., *The University of Western Australia: Its Grounds and Buildings*, Perth: University of Western Australia, 1981.

Woodbridge, S., *John Galen Howard and the University of California*, Berkeley: University of California Press, 2002.

Woodman, F., *The Architectural History of King's College Chapel and Its Place in the Development of Late Gothic Architecture in England and France*, Oxford: Routledge, 1986.

Zaaijer, A., 'Utrecht campus developments: one university, two campuses', in K. Hoeger and K. Christiaanse, *Campus and the City*, Zurich: GTA Verlag, 2007, 59–76.

Zhaoye, G. (ed.), *World Architecture 1900–2000: A Critical Mosaic, Vol. 9: East Asia*, Vienna and New York: Springer-Verlag, 2000.

Index

Page numbers in italic denote an illustration/table; page numbers in bold denote a major section devoted to an entry

Aalto, Alvar 26
Aarhus University 40, **41–5**, *41*, *42*, *43*, *44*, *45*
Aberdeen, University of *see* University of Aberdeen
Abrosimov, Pavel 69
academical village 11, 28, 202, 206, 207
Adelaide, University of *see* University of Adelaide
agricultural colleges: Iowa Agricultural College *see* Iowa State University; Kansas State Agricultural College 14; Massachusetts Agricultural College 13; Michigan Agricultural College 14
Ahrends, Burton and Koralek 125
Akademiska Hus 217
Allies and Morrison 147
Allison, David 135, 136, 137
Alsop, Rodney H. 210
American Baptist Education Society 155
American colleges/universities: and Beaux-Arts movement 14–16; and Collegiate Gothic 23–4; colonial 1, 8–13, *8*, *9*, 23, 36; and Frederick Law Olmsted 13–14; and Gothic Revival 20–3; and modernism 25–6, 31, 82, 111; and picturesque nature 13–14; and postmodernism 32–3, 82, 97, 192; post-war development 25–9, 175; *see also* individual names
Anderberg, Axel 215
Antioch College 9
Arets, Wiel 224

Arizona State University 35, *35*, 237
Ashbee, C.R. 190
Austin, Henry 21, 229

Baker, Herbert 149
Bakewell and Brown 111
Balliol College *see* University of Oxford
Basevi, George 144
Bauhaus School 42
Baxter, Cox and Summerhayes 210
Beaux-Arts planning 14–16, 20, 26, 36, 47, 49, 74, 75, 93, 128, 131, 135, 139, 149, 164, 190, 204–5
Becket, Welton 137
Beijing Institute of Architectural Design 75
Bénard, Emile 128
Berkeley, University of California at *see* University of California at Berkeley
Berlin, Free University *see* Free University Berlin
Bethany College 22
Black Mountain College 25, *26*
Bo-Sung Special University 20
Bodley, Thomas 183
Bohlin Cywinski Jackson 193
Bologna, University of *see* University of Bologna
Brander, Georg Morris Cohen 17
British universities: medieval 4–5, 7; New Universities 29–30, 169; Redbrick 19–20, 29; *see also* individual names
Brown Jr, Arthur 133
Brutalism 104, 124, 133, 159, 169–171, 173, 179
Bryn Mawr College *22*, 23, 190
buildings: master plan component 237–9
Bulfinch, Charles 62

Bunbury, Arthur 211
Bunshaft, Gordon 26, 230
Burgh, Thomas 121
Butterfield, William 184

Caius, Dr 144
Cambridge, University of *see* University of Cambridge
Campbell, Henry 213
campus: origin of term 80
Candilis Josic Woods 54
Cape Town, University of *see* University of Cape Town
car parks *see* parking
Carnegie Mellon University 33
Casson, Sir Hugh 146
Celsing, Peter 216, 219
Chambers, William 122
Chicago Circle *see* University of Illinois at Chicago
Chicago, University of *see* University of Chicago
Christ Church *see* University of Oxford
Churchill College *see* University of Cambridge
circulation: and American colleges 27–8; Free University Berlin 55, 57; and landscaping 237; master plan component 239; Qatar University 88, 91; Stanford University 113; University of California at Los Angeles 139; University of Cape Town 152–3; University of Colorado at Boulder 166; University of Illinois at Chicago 177–8; University of Technology Petronas 197–8; University of Western Australia 213; walkways 27, 28, 170–1, *176*, 177–9, 225

INDEX

City Beautiful movement 14, 108, 128
classicism 7–8, 121–2, 144, 183–4
climate: influence of on campus design 88, 91, 93, 94, 102, 109, 119, 197, 237
Cobb, Harry 138
Cobb, Henry Ives 156, 157, 161
Cockerell, C.R. 144
College of California 13, *13*, 127–8
College of William and Mary 9, *9*
Collegiate Gothic 23–4, 81–2, 83, 157, 190
Collins and Autenrieth 189
colonial colleges: American 1, 8–13, *9*, 23, 36
Colorado, University of *see* University of Colorado at Boulder
Columbia University 14, *15*, 46, **47–51**, *47*, *48*, *49*, *50*, 238, 240
community: fostering of community in post-war campuses 28–31; *see also* Free University Berlin; University of East Anglia; University of Illinois at Chicago
Coolidge, Charles 62, 108, 109, 156–7, 161
Cope and Stewardson 23, 81, 190, 193
Copenhagen, University of *see* University of Copenhagen
Cornell University 23
Cram, Ralph Adams 23, 24, 81–2, 93, 94, 97, 99, 241
Cret, Paul 192

Darley, Frederick 122
Dartmouth College 9, 10, *10*, 80, 228
Day & Klauder 82
Delaware, University of *see* University of Delaware 14

Dennis, Michael 33
Desbrowe-Annear, Harold 209, 213
Dickson, Edward 136
Downing, Andrew 80
Downing College *see* University of Cambridge
Duban, Felix 19
Dudok, Willem Marinus 184

East Anglia, University of *see* University of East Anglia (UEA)
École des Beaux-Arts 17, 19
El Kafrawi, Kamal 87–8, 91
Eliot, Charles 62
Elliott, Julian 152
Emmanuel College *see* University of Cambridge
Emory University 14, 16
energy efficiency: Stanford University 112; University of Illinois at Chicago 117; University of Technology Petronas 198; Utrecht University 224
Engel, Johann Carl Ludwig 17
Erickson, Arthur 102–4
Essex, University of *see* University of Essex
European universities (nineteenth century) 16–20

Farquharson, David 128
Farrand, Beatrix 85, 232, 237
Feilden, Bernard 171, 172
Ferstel, Heinrich von 19
Fisker, Kay 42
Florida Southern College 25, *26*, 33, 238
Foster & Partners (Norman Foster) 35, 57, 113, 146, 197–9
Fox, Revel 152

Free University Berlin 35, *52*, **53–7**, *53*, *54*, *55*, *56*
Furness, Frank 189–90

Gallaudet College 14
GDP Architects 197
Gehry, Frank 7, 33, 35, 238
Genoa, University of *see* University of Genoa 149
German universities: post-war higher education 30–1, 53 *see also* Free University Berlin
Ghent University 17
G.I. Bill (1944) 24, 175
Gibbs, James 8, 144, 184
Giliardi, Domenico 71
Glasgow, University of *see* University of Glasgow
Goodhue, Bertram 159
Gothic 5, 7, 142, 182–3 *see also* Collegiate Gothic; Gothic Revival
Gothic Revival 20–4, 36, 62, 122, 144–5, 156, 159, 184, 189–90, 204, 228–30
Grafton Architects 125
Graves, Michael 99
Graz, University of *see* University of Graz
Greek Revival 17, 80, 145
Griswold, A. Whitney 26, 32, 230
Grobbelaar, Neil 152
Gropius, Walter 26, 65, 111
Guggenheim Museum (Bilbao) 33

Hackett, John Winthrop 209
Haight, Charles 229
Hamilton, Charles 104
Hammond, Beeby & Babka 99
Harrison and Abramavitz 50
Harrison, Charles 190

Harvard University 9, 20–2, *21*, 26, *58*, **59–65**, *59*, *61*, *63*, *64*
Havana, University of *see* University of Havana
Hawksmoor, Nicholas 8, 184
Hearst, Phoebe Apperson 128
Hedqvist, Paul 216–17
Helsinki, University of *see* University of Helsinki
Henry, Joseph 80
Hentrich Petschnigg and Partner 31
Hewitt, George and William 189, 190
historic preservation movement 192
historicism 24, 32, 164, 192–3, 204
Hodder, Stephen 186
Hodgetts and Fung Design Associates 138
Holl, Steven 35
Holmgren, Herman Teodor 216
Hornbostel, Henry 16
Howard, John Galen 128, 131
Humboldt University 17, 53
Hunter, Paul Robinson 137

iconic architecture and starchitects 33–5, 37
Illinois Institute of Technology 25, *25*, 26
Imperial College London 35
Indian Institute of Technology Kanpur 28
International Style 25, 65, 133
Iowa State University 14, *14*
Italian universities 1–3, 4, 16–17

Jacobsen, Arne 186
Jacobsen, Theodore 121
Jefferson, Thomas 10, 11, 13, 14, 36, 201, 202, 204, 207
Jencks, Charles 69
John Miller and Partners 172

Johns Hopkins University 16, *16*
Johnson, Philip 26, 105, 230
Jordan, David Starr 107

Kahn, Louis 26, 192, 230
Kanvinde, Achyut 28
Kazakov, Matvei 71
Keble College *see* University of Oxford
Kelham, George W. 133, 135
Kenitzer, Henry 128
Kent, University of *see* University of Kent
Kerr, Clark 28, 137
Khryakov, Alexander 69
King's College *see* University of Cambridge
Klauder, Charles vi, 23, 82, 164–7, 237
Koolhaas, Rem 35, 224, 225
Koolhaas, Teun 222
Koralek, Paul George 124
Köther-Salman Architects 224

Laird, Warren 192
Lancaster University 29
landscaping: Columbia University 51; master plan component 237; Peking University 77; Princeton University 85, 237; Stanford University 113; Temasek Polytechnic 117, 119; University of California at Berkeley 133; University of California at Los Angeles 138; University of Cambridge 147; University of Chicago 157, 161; University of Pennsylvania 192; University of Technology Petronas 197; University of Virginia 207; University of Western Australia 213; Yale University 232

Lanyon, Charles 122
Lasdun, Denys 30, 169–173
Latrobe, Benjamin Henry 80
Le Corbusier 25, 26, 55, 111, 171
leadership: and implementation of master plan 240
Legorreta, Ricardo 159
Letarouilly, Paul 19
lighting: and Qatar University 89
Liverpool, University of *see* University of Liverpool
Los Angeles, University of California at *see* University of California at Los Angeles (UCLA)
Lovett, Edgar Odell 83
Low, Seth 47
Lowe, Roy 127
Lowell, Abbot Lawrence 22, 62
LSI Architects 172
Lund University 17, *18*
Lutyens, Edwin 149
Lyndon, Maynard 138

McCosh, James 80
McKim, Charles 14, 47, 48, 51, 62
McKim, Mead and White 48–9, 204, 240
McShane, Frank 133
Manchester, University of *see* University of Manchester
Maryland, University of *see* University of Maryland
Mashrabiya 89
Massachusetts Agricultural College 13
Massachusetts Institute of Technology (MIT) 26–7, 33, *33*, *34*, 35, 238
Massey, Geoffrey 102
master plan 237; and buildings 237–9; and circulation 239; factors for successful development of 239–41;

and landscape 237; post-war rejection of 26–7, 37
Mather, Rick 171
Mecanoo 224
medieval universities 1–6
Meier, Richard 138
Melbourne, University of *see* University of Melbourne
Mendelsohn, Eric 184
Merton College *see* University of Oxford
Mies van der Rohe, Ludwig 25–6, 37, 111
MIT *see* Massachusetts Institute of Technology
Mitchell, William 27
Mitchell/Giurgola Associates 50
modernism 25–6, 29–30, 31, 37, 65, 82, 111, 133, 146, 159, 186, 192, 206, 230–1
Møller, C. F. 42–4
Moore, Charles W. 29, 33
Moore, Harvin C. 94
Moscow State University 66, **67–71**, *67, 68, 70, 71*
Müller, Gustav 53
Murphy, Henry Killam 16, 74–5

N L Architects 225
Nakagin Capsule Tower Tokyo 57
National Board of Public Buildings (Sweden) 217
nature: and nineteenth-century American colleges 13–14, 20, 80; *see also* landscaping
neo-classicism 10–11, 14, 17, 48–50, 80, 109, 128–133, 144, 145, 204, 216
Netsch, Walter 27, 176–8; Field Theory 177–8
Neutelings, Willem Jan 224
New College *see* University of Oxforrd

New Universities (Britain) 29–30, 169
New York University 139
Norlin, George 164

Ohio University 9, *10*
Olmsted Brothers (John C. Olmsted) 51, 157
Olmsted, Frederick Law 13–14, 36, 80, 108–9, 127–8, 237
OMA 222, 224, 225
Orléans, University of *see* University of Orléans
Orpen, Richard Caulfield 125
Outram, John 99
Owens, John 20
Oxford, University of *see* University of Oxford

Packard, David 112
Padua, University of *see* University of Padua
Palladio, Andrea 9, 202
Panten, Casper 215
Paris, University of *see* University of Paris
parking 138, 147, 177, 199, 213, 232, 239
Peabody and Stern 62
Pei Cobb Freed & Partners 35
Pei, I. M. 26, 138
Peking University 72, **73–7**, *73, 75, 76, 77*, 237
Pelli, César 97, 138
Pembroke College *see* University of Cambridge
Pennsylvania, University of *see* University of Pennsylvania
Pepper, William 189
Pevsner, Nikolaus 146
Philadelphia School 192

Pittsburgh, University of *see* University of Pittsburgh
Pope, John Russell 230
Porphyrios, Demetri 83
postmodernism 32–3, 82, 97, 192
Potter, William A. 80
Prentice & Chan, Ohlhausen 75
Princeton University 9, *9, 10*, 22–4, *32, 33, 78,* **79–85**, *79, 81, 83, 84,* 237, 241

Qatar University 86, **87–91**, *87, 88, 89, 90*
quadrangular planning 5, 8, 23–4, 36, 60, 74, 80, 82, 93, 94, 108, 112, 121, 141–2, 144, 145, 156, 165, 182, 184, 190, 197, 210, 229–32, 238
Queens' College *see* University of Cambridge

R.J. Ferguson and Associates 211
Redbrick universities 19–20, *19, 20,* 29
Rhodes, Cecil 149
Ricardo Bofill and Taller de Arquitectura 97
Rice University 14, *92,* **93–9**, *93, 95, 96, 98*
Richards, Thomas Webb 189, 192
Richardson, H. H. 62
Rochester, University of *see* University of Rochester
Rockefeller, John D. 155, 156
Rodin, Judith 193
Rogers, James Gamble 23, 49–50, 229, 230, 232, 241
Rohmer, Marlies 224
Romanesque 80, 109, 135–7
Rudbeck, Olaf 215
Rudnev, Lev 69

Rudolph, Paul 26, 230
Ruhr University Bochum *30*, 31

Saarinen, Eero 7, 26, 27, 31–2, 33, 159, 192, 231, 232
St Andrews, University of *see* University of St Andrews
St Catherine's College, Oxford *see* University of Oxford
Salamanca, University of *see* University of Salamanca
San Carlos, University of *see* University of San Carlos
Santa Cruz, University of California *see* University of California, Santa Cruz
Sasaki Associates 97
Sasaki, Walker & Associates 165
satellite campuses 30, 51, 205, 216, 221
Sayce, Conrad H. 210
scholastic guilds 1
Schuyler, Montgomery 65
Scott, Giles Gilbert 184
Scott Tallon Walker 125
Semper, Gottfried 17
Sert, Josep Luis 26, 65
Shapiro, Harold 85
Shepley, Rutan and Coolidge 62, 156
Sheppard, Robson & Partners 145
Shrum, Gordon 102
Siena, University of *see* University of Siena
Simon Fraser University *100*, **101–5**, *101*, *102*, *103*, *105*
Skidmore Owings and Merrill 176
Smith College 14
Sobotka, Franz Heinrich 53
Solomon, Joseph 149–50, 152, 153
Somerville, William 213
Sørensen, C.Th. 42–3

Southern Methodist University 14
Spence, Basil 30
Spencer, Eldridge T. 111
'spine/linear' planning 30, 102, 104, 116, 170
Stanford, Jane 107, 109
Stanford, Leland 107, 108–9
Stanford University 14, 32, 35, *106*, **107–13**, *107*, *108*, *109*, *110*, *112*, 237
Staub & Rather 94
Steadman, Charles 80
Stegmann, Povl 42
Stephens, Suzanne 50
Stephenson, Gordon 210–11, 213
Stern, Robert A.M. 206
Stillé, Charles 189
Stirling, James 97, 115, 119, 146
Stone, Edward Durrell 159
Stuart, John Leighton 74
Sturgis, Russell 229
Sundvall, Carl Fredrik 215
Sussex, University of *see* University of Sussex
sustainability: and University of Technology Petronas 198–9; *see also* energy efficiency
Swarthmore College 9
Swiss Federal Institution of Technology 17
Sydney, University of *see* University of Sydney

Temasek Polytechnic *114*, **115–19**, *115*, *116*, *117*, *118*
Temko, Allen 133
The Architects Collaborative 25 *see also* Gropius, Walter
Thistlethwaite, Frank 30, 171

Thomas, John 204
Thomas Phifer and Partners 99
three-sided courtyard 60, 144, 172
Thwing, Charles 13
Toronto, University of *see* University of Toronto
Trautwein & Howard 165
Trinity College, Cambridge *see* University of Cambridge
Trinity College, Dublin 120, **121–5**, *121*, *122*, *123*, *124*
Trumbull, John 228
Tschumi, Bernard 50
Tsinghua University 11
Turnbull, William 29
Turner, Paul 9, 25

UCLA *see* University of California at Los Angeles
UEA *see* University of East Anglia
universities: acquiring of property and academic quarters 2–4; and cities 2, 4; migrations 2; oldest 2; post-war higher education 24–32; scholastic guilds as forerunners of 1
University of Aberdeen 5
University of Adelaide 20, *21*
University of Bologna 1, *1*, 2, 3
University of California at Berkeley 13, *13*, 14, *126*, **127–33**, *127*, *129*, *130*, *132*, 209
University of California at Los Angeles (UCLA) *134*, **135–9**, *135*, *136*, *137*, *139*
University of California, Santa Cruz 28–9, *28*
University of Cambridge 2, 7–8, 29, 35, *140*, **141–7**, *145*, *147*, 184, 186; Churchill College 145; Downing

INDEX

College 17, 145, *146*; Emmanuel College 5, 7, 60, 144; King's College 20, 21, 142–5, *143*, 238; landscaping 147; Pembroke College 7, 144; Queens' College *141*, 142, *142*; St John's College, 190; Trinity College 7, *7*, 144
University of Cape Town 148, **149–53**, *149*, *150*, *151*, *152*, *153*
University of Chicago 23, **155–61**, *155*, *157*, *158*, *160*
University College London 17, *19*, 29
University of Colorado at Boulder 9, *162*, **163–7**, *163*, *164*, *165*, *167*, 237
University of Copenhagen 41–2
University of Delaware 14
University of East Anglia (UEA) 29, 30, 31, *168*, **169–73**, *169*, *170*, *172*, *173*
University of Essex 29
University of Genoa 149
University of Glasgow 5, 235, *236*
University of Graz 17, *18*
University of Havana 14, 16, *16*
University of Helsinki 17
University of Illinois at Chicago (Chicago Circle) 27–8, *27*, 54–5, *174*, **175–9**, *175*, *176*, *178*, *179*
University of Kent 29
University of Liverpool *19*, 20
University of Manchester 20, *20*
University of Maryland 14, *16*
University of Melbourne 20
University of Orléans 2
University of Oxford 1, 2, 4–5, *4*, *5*, *6*, *7*, 24, 29, 33, *36–7*, 157, *180*, **181–7**, *181*, *187*, 238; Balliol College 5; Christ Church *182*; Keble College *183*, 184; Merton College *4*, 5, *5*, 7, *182*; New College 142, *182*; St Catherine's College *185*, 186; University College 5
University of Padua 2, *3*
University of Paris 1, 2, 4, 16, 17, 181
University of Pennsylvania 23, *188*, **189–93**, *189*, *190*, *191*, *193*
University of Pittsburgh 23
University of Rochester 14
University of St Andrews 5
University of Salamanca 2, *2*
University of San Carlos 3, *3*
University of Siena 2
University of Southern California 14
University of the Sunshine Coast 35
University of Sussex 29, *29*, 30
University of Sydney 20, *20*
University of Technology Petronas 35, *194*, **195–9**, *195*, *196*, *198*, *199*
University of Toronto 20, 35
University of Vermont 14
University of Vienna 16, 19
University of Virginia (UVA) 10–11, *12*, 14, 200, **201–7**, *201*, *203*, *205*, *206*, 235
University of Warwick 29
University of Western Australia (UWA) *208*, **209–13**, *209*, *210*, *211*, *212*, 237
University of York 29
Uppsala University 17, *214*, **215–19**, *215*, *216*, *217*, *218*
Utrecht University 35, *220*, **221–5**, *221*, *222*, *223*, *225*
UVA *see* University of Virginia
UWA *see* University of Western Australia
Uytenhaak, Rudy 224

Vassar College 9
ventilation 89, 91, 94, 119
Venturi, Robert 33
Venturi, Scott Brown and Associates 33, 82–3, 192
Vermont, University of *see* University of Vermont
Vienna, University of *see* University of Vienna
Viñoly, Rafael 138, 159
Virginia, University of *see* University of Virginia
Voorhees, Walter, Smith & Smith 50

Walgate, Cyril 150
Walter and Wilson 22
Ware and Van Brunt 62
Warnecke, John Carl 111
Warwick, University of *see* University of Warwick
Washington University in St Louis 14, 32
Waterhouse, Alfred 20
Weese, Harry 166, 178
Wellesley College 23
Wells, H. G. 161
West, Andrew 23
Western Australia, University of *see* University of Western Australia (UWA)
White, Klatt & Porcher 97
White, Stanford 205
'whole cloth' campus design 28, 29, 31, 37; *see also* Qatar University; Simon Fraser University; University of Technology Petronas
Wilford, Michael 115, 119
Wilkins, William 17, 144–5
Wilkinson, Leslie 210, 213
Williams College, Museum of Art *32*, 33
Wilson Brothers 189, 190
Wilson, Woodrow 22, 81, 83

Woo, Kyu Sung 65
Woods, Shadrach 54–5, 57
World's Columbian Exposition in Chicago
 (1893) 14, 108, 128, 156
Wouda, Sjoerd 221, 222
Wren, Christopher 7–8, 144, 183–4
Wright, Frank Lloyd 25, 33, 238
Wright, Myles 124
Wyatt, James 8
Wykeham, William 182

Yale University 9–10, *9*, *11*, 21, 23, 24,
 24, 26, 31–2, *31*, *226*, **227–33**, *227*,
 228, *229*, *231*, *233*, 241
Yamasaki, Minoru 26, 82
Yenching University 16, 73–4
York, University of *see* University of York
YuanMing Yuan 77

Zaaijer, Art 222
Zhaoye, Guan 75